THE ANIMATION BOOK

THE ANIMATION BOOK

a complete guide to animated filmmaking— from flip-books to sound cartoons

KIT LAYBOURNE

PREFACE BY GEORGE GRIFFIN
INTRODUCTION BY DEREK LAMB

CROWN PUBLISHERS, INC.   NEW YORK

To My Father

Library of Congress Cataloging in Publication Data

Laybourne, Kit.
  The animation book.

  Bibliography: p.
  Includes index.
  1. Animation (Cinematography)   I. Title.
TR897.5.L39   1979   778.5'347   79-12774
ISBN: 0-517-53389-8 (cloth)
        0-517-52946-7 (paper)

10 9 8 7 6 5 4

Contents

Acknowledgments

For their help in providing stills from animated films in their outstanding collections, I wish to acknowledge the assistance of the following individuals and the production/distribution companies they represent: Alan Stanley at Dolphin Productions; Prescott Wright at Film Wright; Leo Dratfield and Vivian Bender at Films Incorporated; Sue Boland at Hubley Studios; Nancy Peck at Learning Corporation of America; Mary Healy at Phoenix Films; Brant Sloan at Pyramid Films; and Freude at Serious Business Company. Michelle Bischoff at the National Film Board of Canada was particularly generous and resourceful.

Many independent animators have extended themselves by locating original art materials and other animation paraphernalia for this volume. A warm thank you to Yvonne Andersen, Warren Bass, Preston Blair, John Canemaker, Al Jarnow, Ken Knowlton, Caroline Leaf, Eli Noyes, Janet Pearlman, Kathy Rose, Peter Rose, Maureen Selwood, and Lynn Smith. Artwork for the cover of this volume was adapted from George Griffin's *Viewmaster.*

In the course of preparing this book, I've received special assistance in a variety of ways from many people. For locating various graphic materials I am indebted to Elfreda Fischinger (Fischinger Studios), Leo Gobin (Bobbs-Merrill Company, Inc.), L. Bruce Holman (The Animation Center), Wendy Keys (New York Film Festival), Anita Mozley (Stanford University Art Museum), Russell Neale (Hastings House Publishers), and Jeffrey Pollock (Eastman Kodak Company). For their willingness to pool information in compiling a comprehensive set of resource listings, I want to thank again Jane Kearns and Diana Elsas of the American Film Institute. Each of these friends has given valued encouragement and support: Michael Curran, Jon Dunn, Lou Giansante, Anne Kendall, Mickey Lemle, and Karen Tilbor.

Finally, I want to express my deep gratitude to four who have been most important in my own study of animation and in the genesis of this book: Jim Anneshansley, a designer of animation equipment with the Oxberry Corporation; Jake Goldberg, my editor at Crown Publishers, Inc.; George Griffin, one of the most widely respected of the new generation of independent animators; and Derek Lamb, an animator with a special gift for directing and encouraging the growth of other animators.

George Griffin, standing beside a 35mm animation stand in his New York City studio.

Preface

A new method of making animated films has surfaced in the last decade and with it a new generation of artists who use the medium primarily for self-expression. The new animators assume direct responsibility for nearly every aspect of the filmmaking process: concept, drawing, shooting, even camera stand construction. This reclamation of creative authority contrasts sharply with the impersonal assembly-line production system of the studio cartoon industry and returns animation to its original experimental impulse as embodied in the work of Winsor McCay, Emile Cohl, Hans Richter, and Oskar Fischinger.

The new animation reflects a union of design (the style of a single frame) and movement (the relationship among a series of frames). These functions were strictly divorced in studio cartoon production: designers made pictorial decisions; animators made timing decisions. The new animators do both, often simultaneously, thereby expanding the notion of drawing from a mere prefatory activity to a completely dynamic process—drawing in time. An excellent example is the spontaneous frame by frame manipulation of materials like clay, sand, seeds, and string. The list is endless.

Even the more traditional technique of sequence drawing has undergone modifications to fit individual artists' needs. There has been a rediscovery of paper with its incredible variety of texture, color, and translucence, and media appropriate to paper such as watercolor, pastels, charcoal, and dyes. Variation in the scale of drawing, from the film frame itself to the standard 9 x 12 field creates variations in the value of line, shape, and detail. The actual process of drawing may reflect a concern for visual continuity, discontinuity, or a blending of both to affect transformation. A sequence may maintain consistency by careful cross-reference to beginning, ending, and intermediate phases. Or it may proceed "straight ahead" in a voyage of discovery rather than deliberate construction. And, finally, when a sequence is recorded on film, further decisions will affect framing, pacing, and color.

The new animation has grown from both a pictorial, cartoon tradition and a formal, abstract tradition. And though uniquely suited for drawing inspiration from these sources, it can delve as well into the more marginal areas of comic, naïve, decorative, "primitive," and children's art. Thus, what distinguishes the new animation is not a specific style but an experimental attitude toward technique and an irreverent eclecticism of form.

Kit Laybourne's encyclopedic introduction to the variety of procedures used by the new animators provides a significant advance over previous industry-oriented texts. His message is directed toward the experienced independent filmmaker and those, with little or no film experience, who aren't afraid to plunge in and take risks. The book describes the tools, techniques, materials, and prevailing costs with a simplicity clearly aimed at demystifying processes long obscured by professional jargon and a conservative guild mentality. (I can recall an opinion, oft-repeated in cartoon studios, that it would take at least ten years of drawing experience to become a competent animator.)

My only quarrel with Laybourne's work focuses on his inclusion of real time cinematography (as "kinestasis") and his exclusion of optical printing and rephotography, a burgeoning form of synthetic filmic collage. These objections stem from my theoretical bias against "animation" which doesn't move and a suspicion that optical restructuring, an elaboration and refinement of tricks used by Melies, and until recently typed as "special effects," has become yet another method of drawing in time.

Nevertheless, *The Animation Book* provides a most accurate and exciting mapping of the independent animation terrain. Laybourne's primary concern is the experimental method, which demands a personalization of technique and a rejection of formularized professionalism. As a guide, *The Animation Book* will be most valuable for its ability to catapult an artist into regions as yet uncharted.

—GEORGE GRIFFIN
New York City, 1978

Derek Lamb, at left, with animator Yossi Abolafia at the National Film Board of Canada.

A frame enlargement from Derek Lamb's *The Great Toy Robbery. Courtesy National Film Board of Canada.*

Introduction

In recent years, there has been widespread interest in all forms of the animated film. Students of animation constantly impress me with their knowledge about its history. Intimate details of Betty Boop's private life, Porky Pig's hat size, or Tex Avery's favorite breakfast cereal are everyday conversation. But, more importantly, more people are making their own films.

With the easy availability of inexpensive movie equipment, especially 8mm, animation workshops began to flourish in schools and colleges during the mid-sixties. People who previously would never have been exposed to animation were suddenly making films. By necessity, they had to be inexpensive to produce. Consequently, any and all inanimate material that could be made to move on the movie screen was used. Modeling clay, sand, flip pads, paper cutouts, and drawing directly on film were just a few of the dozens of ways filmmakers began to make cartoons.

In the mind of the general public, animated film is invariably associated with Disney, the Flintstones, and other similar cartoons. Since Winsor McCay drew the first animated cartoon, "Gertie the Dinosaur," in 1909, the animation industry has very much followed traditional characterizations and the humor of the newspaper comic strip. This has always made good business sense to producers as the public never seems to tire of that comic formula. Also, by systematizing studio production and using the cell technique, complete prediction and control of the end result is possible.

The studio system is still very much alive and will continue to flourish. Quite frankly, for those of you who have the necessary drawing skills it is the surest way for an animator to make a living in this zany business. But there are dozens of other exciting ways to make animated films. The major international film festivals now consistently showcase and honor innovative approaches to the medium. Film distributors have found out that there is a ready audience for any film that is a good one. Here at the National Film Board of Canada, in the tradition set down by Norman McLaren, animators are encouraged to work in a wide range of styles and techniques that best fit the subject matter.

This book, by Kit Laybourne, supports this point of view and generously details a wide number of approaches that will be of great interest to anybody concerned with making animated films. In breaking down more than twenty individual techniques, the book introduces just about every item of hardware or software that you'd ever need—from inexpensive and simple super 8mm filmmaking gear to the most sophisticated and expensive pieces of 16mm equipment. The volume is well illustrated with graphics from recent works by individual film artists who conceive and execute almost every phase of their production. The most significant quality of *The Animation Book* is its eclectic spirit and inclusive scope. Every reader should find a technique, sample, project, or tool that stimulates his or her interest. And that is precisely where one ought to begin.

That's all folks, and good animating!

—DEREK LAMB
Executive Producer
English Animation
National Film Board of Canada

A frame from Ryan Larkin's *Walking. Courtesy of the National Film Board of Canada*

How to Use This Book

An animation renaissance is under way. A new generation of young animators has found new voice in a medium that just a few years ago seemed near exhaustion. Full-length animated feature films are in production again. Animated graphics are changing the look of television. And everywhere, it seems, new films are presenting new techniques and opening new vistas for yet another generation of animators.

Museums, schools, and the media are spearheading this revived awareness and appreciation. There is a growing demand for animation tools and for information about animation techniques. Colleges, high schools, and even elementary schools are setting up new courses and study units in animated filmmaking. Animation festivals are drawing large audiences, and increasing numbers of books have been published dealing with the history and criticism of the animated film. Most significant of all, a vital and broad range of people, many of whom might be called "amateurs," have begun creating their own animated movies.

In a way, this book does more than merely provide an introduction to the world of animation—it tries to coax you into becoming an independent animator. Throughout the text you'll be given problems to think about and take on. Sometimes you will be asked to grab a pencil and work right within these pages. Sometimes you'll be studying images that have been reproduced from many of the most exciting recent works by independent animators. At the volume's end there's a chapter that contains items you are encouraged to detach from this binding and then use when you make your own animated movies.

It is appropriate that this book ask you to actually do animated filmmaking. The vitality, the very existence, of the contemporary animation scene has as its foundation the notion that *animation can be done with simplified techniques and inexpensive tools that permit the individual to make films where personal expression is a primary goal.* As author, I certainly share this fundamental viewpoint.

The remainder of this introduction tells you how you might use this book. First, there is an outline of the major divisions within the text. Second, there are comments about a few signposts that have been used to help you find your way among various chapters. Finally, I'd like to offer some advice on how you might get yourself ready to experience animation.

The Animation Book is divided into four parts. It begins with an *Orientation.* The purpose here is to give you a warm-up. You'll find activities in drawing, generating ideas, and playing with various animation toys and principles. Part One also provides a quick introduction and preview of the equipment you will be using when you produce your own films. Actual production itself is what happens in Part Two. Here you will find more than twenty distinct categories of animated filmmaking. Each is unique. Each is discussed thoroughly. Each teaches something about the categories that follow it. Throughout the chapters on technique you'll find plenty of examples, illustrations, and projects. Part Two also contains information about basic production problems that are common to all the different techniques: working with sound, storyboarding, and production planning. Part Three: *Tools* is a catalogue. It describes and gives rough costs for all the equipment you will need to make your own animated films. This section of the book indexes both hardware and software, and you'll probably want to consult these chapters even as you are reading earlier ones. Finally, we have *Resources.* This section carries annotated listings of many places where you can get additional help, from books to films to festivals to professional associations. The last chapter contains visual aids that you can detach and use in your own filmmaking.

Within these four parts, the various chapters attempt to break down the overall material into manageable pieces and to facilitate quick cross-referencing. I hope that the extensive use of cross-references will increase your tendency to browse through these pages and to use the book in a circular, self-programmed way. Information, after all, is useful only when it's needed. It is important that the volume accommodate your own individual needs, interests, and questions precisely when and where they arise. Please be encouraged to move through these pages freely, even impulsively.

Style is the ultimate achievement. I don't think there can be a more difficult or a more rewarding goal than developing one's own unique vision through an art form like animation. As you begin the process of exploring animation and of working with this book, I'd like to suggest that you try out at least a few of the following strategies.

Start from Strength. The best place to begin is where your interest is strongest. Read along until you come to a project that you find yourself eager to try. And then do it. When you feel finished, move on. Don't allow yourself to agonize when you want to skip or quit a particular project. It is important at the beginning to build up a momentum. It's also good to create a string of successes as you get your commitment centered and your confidence strengthened.

Build a "Studio." Claim a space that can become the symbolic home for your work as an animator. There is no need to be fancy. When I started my own work I allocated a single drawer to the new enterprise. It was a modest studio, to be sure. But it gave me an important "psychological space" in which to develop new skills. In addition to commandeering a physical place, I urge you to commit a specific amount of energy, time, and expense to your exploration of animated filmmaking. Everything you invest will be returned to you through increased productivity, efficiency, and pleasure.

Develop a Project Mentality. Let's say you decide to be an oil painter. No one, even yourself, would expect you to produce a masterpiece on your first canvas. Animated filmmaking is every bit as difficult to master as oil painting. So give yourself a break. Just as an oil painter begins with a sketch pad and a series of experiments, allow yourself the psychic freedom to develop your competencies at a reasonable pace. This book suggests different "projects." Try as many of them as you can. They have been carefully formulated to let you experience various processes and techniques. But as you do them, try not to be overly self-critical. Don't judge yourself by first efforts. Remind yourself that it is not the product of your animation that counts but the process of your learning. At least in the beginning that's true.

A sample reel is the filmmaker's equivalent to the artist's sketch pad. Save your exercises and experiments, however primitive and inadequate you may think they are. It is easy to splice everything you shoot onto one reel, since you'll most likely be doing all your filming with the same equipment. From time to time screen this sample reel for your friends (the applause won't damage your ego). And screen it often for your own study, analysis, and evaluation. You will learn more from your own mistakes than you'll learn from any other source—these pages included.

Keep an Animator's Diary. I strongly recommend that you consistently keep track of what you are learning and how you are feeling. I can't overemphasize the importance of devising some system that allows you to monitor and record what you experience. Any system will do. An easy one is to designate a special book, or section of a book, as a place where you can maintain a running record of your projects. The things you ought to keep track of include questions, frustrations, evaluations of projects, ideas for new films, personal goals, technical data, planning notes, expenses, words of encouragement and counsel that you've collected from favorite books, and so on.

Loose Time. Gauging your abilities as an independent animator ought to be a very long-term goal. But as you go along, periodically make informal and tentative assessments of your skills. This book tries to identify most of the individual skills that comprise the art and craft of animated filmmaking. There are many different things to master, and no one—no one—has ever been able to do them all. Walt Disney didn't. None of the independent animators mentioned in this book would say that they have total facility in all the skills it takes to produce a finished film. I certainly don't have them. You won't either.

And it's not important that you do. What can be important, however, is that you are able to make an assessment of areas where you are strong and areas where your skills are less developed. This is important because it can help you guide your own development. You must be able to gauge your own skills, interest, goals, and talents if you are to realize the ultimate goal of finding your own style.

THE
ANIMATION
BOOK

PART ONE:
FUNDAMENTALS

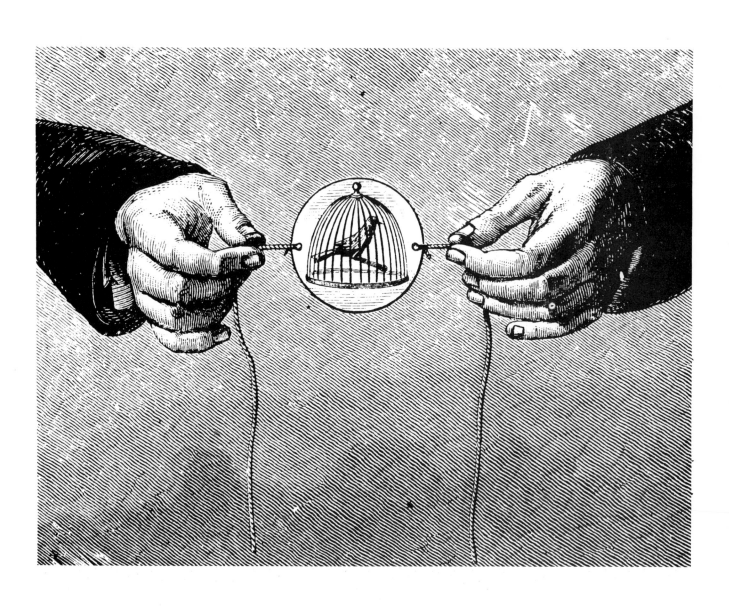

The goal of this book is to help you discover your own unique style as an independent animator. That's a lofty objective but an achievable one. It requires work. It requires experimentation. In the long run, finding a style means understanding a lot about yourself as well as about the thing you've set out to accomplish. This makes it worth doing well. And it makes it fun.

Animation requires a few innate skills and talents. Without these you might as well close the book right now. As it turns out, however, the essential skills are *not* the ones you'd expect.

An animator must be fascinated with the way things move. He or she must be a keen observer of the world. An animator must be something of an actor. The ability to give a cartoon figure character depends on the ability to feel a character within oneself. If a film is to work, what happens must happen with purpose. Actions must be motivated. So every animator has to be an actor, even if it's just a closet actor.

Like designers, fine artists, and inventors, animators need to enjoy the process of identifying a problem and then working out its solution. Sloppy thinking and lazy execution guarantee failure. An animator has got to know how to think.

Finally, everyone who has ever done it will agree that the art of animation requires liberal measures of patience, precision, perseverence, and pride. Please note, however, that these are not innate skills as much as they are personality traits, or elements of one's character.

It's all in the head. If you want to animate, if you've always been fascinated by cartoons and cameras and the process of filmmaking, if you like making things move, then you've got all the requisite talents. Don't just take my word for it. Make up your own mind about what it takes by exploring the notions and the problems that follow.

1
Basic Skills

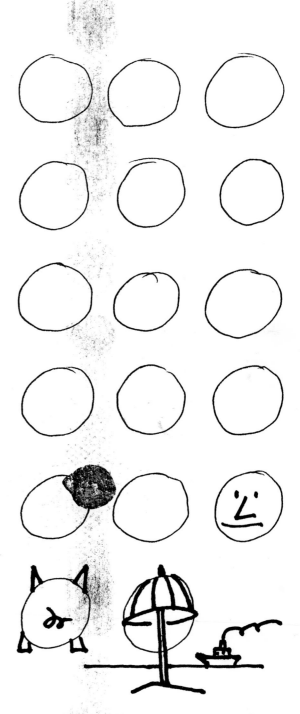

The biggest single misconception about animation is that you need to be an artist to do it, that you need to know how to draw. To disprove this, just skim through the pages of this book and you'll find frame enlargements from many films that don't have a single drawn line in them. You can be a prizewinning animator and never touch a pencil or paintbrush.

For some people, the ability to express themselves in visual terms, in images, has been blocked. Most usually this is expressed as, "but I can't draw." It's an all too familiar phrase. It's also a self-defeating phrase, for it shuts down an individual's innate impulse to draw. Worse, a fear of drawing separates a person from that special kind of thinking that involves making marks—a kind of thinking that is commonly acknowledged as among the most creative known to man. I'm referring to visual thinking—a form of problem solving and communication that is quite different from verbal thinking, the mental process most valued within formal education.

Visual Thinking

Whether or not you feel that your artistic impulse has atrophied or even that it has never existed, the exercises that follow are intended to pump new energy and awareness into your use of eye and hand and imagination. As their subtitles will tell you, the following six exercises each ask you to perform a specific mental process—but to do it entirely through images, not words. In tackling these problems I hope you will notice that what you are actually doing is not "drawing" per se, but rather a form of thinking, which takes place through the dialogue between hand and eye, between pencil and paper. In visual thinking it is the *process* of working graphically that counts, rather than the product of that thinking. In fact, it's very important not to confuse drawing to extend one's thinking (what you'll be doing in Figures 1.1 to 1.6) with drawing to communicate a well-formed idea (to be discussed later). As you'll experience, visual thinking also has to do with the working out of ideas, with idea generation.

Drawing and Art

So much for calisthenics. I do hope you plunged right into the preceding activities. If not, I recommend you do so now. They'll warm up your eye and limber up your fingers. And by doing them you'll show yourself how visual thinking—like thinking through words, writing, or other symbolic code systems—is a skill that one acquires, a skill that requires constant practice if you want to stay in peak form.

As we move into some discussion of real drawing technique, it may be important to step back for a moment and note that the most

1.1   IMPROVISE: Add a quick line or two to each of the circles as fast as you can so that they become different things. If you can get through this set in two minutes, try twenty more.

3

distinctive thing about our species is that we are symbol makers. Just as each human being is born with the impulse to speak, so each of us is also wired to create images. While it is true, of course, that some people are endowed with unique gifts or abilities for verbal or for graphic expression, it is also true that a facility in any expressive mode is something that must be developed. In other words, you can learn to draw. Artistic ability is not some mystical God-given gift. As with any type of expression, there are some skills that must be acquired through practice and by studying the basic principles and conventions of each form.

I grant that even the greatest self-discipline and tireless instruction won't equip you to sketch like Michelangelo or Leonardo, but a few exercises and tips can definitely improve the look and the impact of your drawings. Just as important, self-instruction may also give you more self-confidence.

Creative Cliches. A basic trick in drawing is to select and use just those details most often associated with what you are drawing. A simple box, for example, is immediately recognized as a house if it has a chimney belching smoke. But with a rounded rectangle drawn on one of its sides, the box becomes a television set. Similarly, suppose you want a character to look old. What cliches convey old age? A cane? A stooped walk? What else? White hair and old-fashioned spectacles? Symbols or attributes of old age are, by definition, all cliches, but used effectively in drawings they can communicate quickly, directly, and clearly. As you try the problem in Figure 1.6, keep in mind that the special art of caricature depends entirely on the artist's ability to determine which details make a particular individual recognizable.

Deep Structure. Probably the best way to make a quantum jump in your drawing abilities is to look past or beneath the visual detail of any image to those basic geometric forms that constitute its structure. Because simple geometric shapes are easy to create, they become ideal building blocks in the act of drawing. Figure 1.7 features some examples taken from Preston Blair's book *Drawing Animated Cartoons.* What holds for Pluto can easily be integrated into your own character design and drawing.

After you study the "deep structure" of the examples, try to construct your own character using just circles. Note that circles are the easiest of all shapes to draw because they don't change shape when viewed from different angles.

Exaggeration. A similar drawing strategy urges you to stress a particular visual quality by varying its size or shape beyond that of normal reality—way, way beyond. Throughout this volume you'll find virtuoso examples of exaggeration, but nowhere will it be more clear than in Figure 1.8. You'll spot exaggeration in both figures and backgrounds. Exaggeration is one of the central forces that build tension within animated filmmaking, and as a result, just about everything becomes exaggerated: line, shape, timing, movement, story, character—the works.

"Less Is More." What the architect Mies van der Rohe said about buildings is true also about drawing for animation. Simplify. Cut out all nonessential detail. Simplify still more. As you watch animated films on television or as you study the individual frames reproduced in these

1.2 EXPLORE: What objects can you find inside these scribbles? Use a marker to add details and emphasize form. When you've worked a while with this one, explore your own random scribbling.

1.3 SIMPLIFY: What simple geometric shapes can you find within these images? Use a pencil or marker to outline basic structures within each picture. Take a sheet of tracing paper and continue the exercise elsewhere in this book.

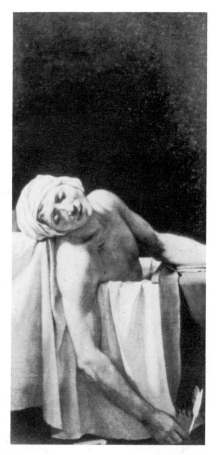

1.4 RECYCLE: With just a few quick pencil strokes, try to copy each of these items in corresponding frames on the opposite page. It is important to work very fast in this exercise. When you've finished, study the visual style of the resulting sketches. How would you characterize the kind of markings you've made (light, exact, cluttered, bold, loose, free, strong, delicate)?

pages, note how much is left out. See how simple and lean the drawings are, how uncluttered and unfussy, the graphic techniques. Figure 1.10 gives you a chance to practice the skill of eliminating unnecessary detail.

Graphic Styling. Just as there is more than one way of seeking knowledge and skinning a cat, so there is more than one way of representing the same thing in graphic terms. As an animator, you will prefer some drawing styles and you will dislike others. Some graphic modes will be beyond your reach and you'll have no feeling for others. Be that as it may, you should consciously explore new approaches. You should try to extend your repertoire for creating images. In fact, much of your eventual success and satisfaction will come from being able to exercise different options in selecting a graphic idiom. Try Figure 1.9.

Line and Body Languages. The quality of a line—its thickness, its precision, its tension, its relationship to other lines—all these elements should be examined, evaluated, and controlled in your drawing. Here is a sampling of "rules" that cartoonists and animators often employ: heavier lines attract our attention; angular lines suggest a feeling of tension; smooth and free lines create a peaceful, happy feeling. As with lines, so with bodies. A closed figure is "tight" or "angry." An open gesture or position is "friendly" or "relaxed." Frame enlargements throughout the book will suggest the range of lines that can be used and their various impacts.

Framing and Composition. Animation, like most graphic art forms, takes place within a frame. The changing composition within this rectangle is a factor continually affecting the impact of one's drawing. The most important tip about good composition is this: Avoid the center. It is a *dead* center. Positioning something in the middle of the frame creates a feeling of total stasis. Similarly, stay away from an even division of the frame or a composition that is too balanced. Sometimes, of course, you'll *want* your images to be centered and stable. As a way of exercising your sense of composition, I recommend the use of a set of "L" shaped pieces of cardboard to experiment with different framing possibilities. Which arrangements in Figure 1.12 do you find most dynamic? Which most static?

Importance of Background. Man is a pattern-seeking animal. We all search for meaning in all things. Context (background and surroundings) can be used to relay much information about the "subject" of a drawing. Almost any frame from a good animated film will make this clear and this book is filled with them. While it's true that backgrounds should be simple and never detract the viewer's attention from the main component of the drawing, be cagey in the selection of objects and details you place in the background in order to convey a strong feeling of place and atmosphere.

Color Psychology. Try in your drawing to exploit those standard conventions and cultural assumptions that your audience will share with you. For example, warm colors (reds and oranges) are perceived as active and they tend to come forward in a drawing or painting (at least in our culture they do). Cool colors, on the other hand, tend to recede into the background and are perceived as inactive. Everyone knows that a red face is angry, a blue face sad, and a green face sick. Incorporate such shorthand symbols into your drawing and coloring. But don't neglect to consider colors that do *not* conform to our cultural expectations. The best animated films use color as an equally powerful graphic element to line, shape, and even movement itself. The use of color is very, very important.

Depth Cues. Here's a quick but by no means complete list of visual cues that will create an impression of spatial depth within a drawing: heavier lines come forward and stand out; foot placement indicates the ground; place the horizon line high in the frame; use more detail in the foreground; employ perspective lines to indicate the relationship of the subject to the background; place shadows underneath people. Figure 1.13 provides a simple drawing that incorporates all of these cues. Can you find each of them?

Art in Movement

Animation is art in movement. More, it is the art of movement. In an animated film, drawings are not static as they must be in these pages. In film, the drawings come alive, and it is the quality of that life that matters, not the quality of a particular image or frame of film. Whether it is a drawing or a lump of clay or a puppet or a collage or whatever, the animator places life and meaning into his or her material by making it move.

The sheer movement of the animated film is something that simultaneously exists on many levels and speaks in many ways. Movement conveys story, character, and theme. It creates tension through the development of expectation and its release, through the arousal of curiosity and its resolution. Movement creates a structure for the passage of time. It is also intimately related to music, dialogue, and other elements of the audio portion of the film. Movement is the essential magic of motion picture technology. Why else did the first people to see them spontaneously label the experience "movies?" Movement is the beginning and the end.

By making a few drawings of your own, you'll best be able to appreciate and assimilate the fact that how something moves is more important than what it looks like. In Figure 1.11 you'll see some primitive drawings. Fill in the gaps between the implied sequence of five images and you'll get an idea of how movement fits into the picture, of how movement at once dominates and celebrates the image being animated.

If you've tried the problems so far, I'm hoping you'll have *experienced* the following truths: that *visual thinking is different from other kinds of thinking,* that *drawing skills are acquired as well as given,* and that *animation is art in movement.*

These truisms form a security blanket. You should never again feel terror when asked to pick up a pencil. But don't worry if you're still not quite convinced that you, a clutsy drawer, can still create magnificent and powerful animated films. Against a lifetime of being told that "art" is based on the ability to draw with representational precision, these few pages of encouragement and exercise can only begin to make you comfortable with whatever abilities you possess and can develop further. But keep at it. Here are four commonsense strategies that can help you solidify and extend your acquisition of greater drawing skills:

Planned Doodling. For a week or two carry around with you a cheap pad of paper and a pencil. Whenever you can, make doodles. It doesn't matter what you draw. It matters only that you draw. So do as much as you can and don't worry about saving the sketches. There will be time enough for that.

Sketch File. Find an old box, envelope, drawer, or file folder. Every time you make a drawing that interests you in some way, slip it into the file. Note that a drawing doesn't have to please you. It should just be interesting to you in some way. And don't worry about using the file. Just keep it.

Self-inventory. Systematically study how you go about drawing. Keep track of the way you seem to prefer working. Here are some questions you can ask yourself: Do you like to work with large or small formats? Which drawing implements do you prefer? Do you draw quickly or slowly? Do you like to try copying what others have drawn? Do you like to draw people or objects? What kinds? I encourage you to think up other questions and generally search for patterns among your attitudes, preferences, beliefs, and of course, your artwork itself.

Favorite Things. Don't waste time trying to draw things that don't interest you. Work only with stuff that is exciting to you. Take notes (literally) of what you are drawn to. Then draw it. Such a "passion list" can be immensely helpful in locating themes, characters, settings, effects, and other elements you can incorporate into later productions.

1.5   RESPOND: Give your hand and your imagination free reign in responding to each of these images. Turn them into stories. Give them details. Make them into visual jokes. Whatever comes to mind is fine. You can add new items or modify those you find. If you can, sketch in a number of responses to each stimulus.

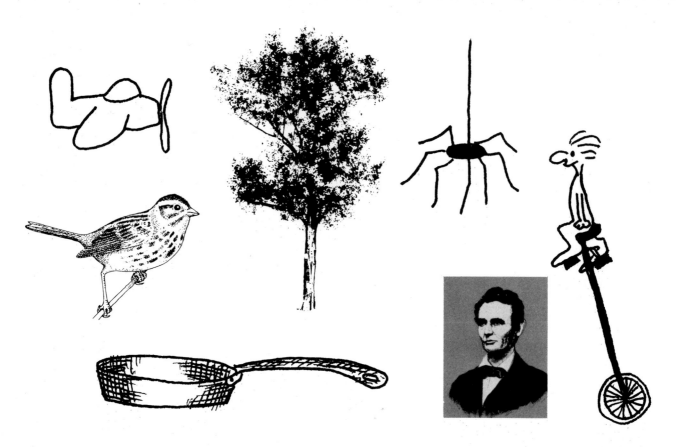

Getting Ideas

Is the creative process really a mystery? Many would say so. They view inspiration as a divine gift; invention as a form of genius; insight as something you luck onto; and original thinking in general as a mystical experience. Creativity, most people would agree, is something you are born with. Either you've got it or you don't.

Dr. Abraham Maslow, a pioneer in the field of humanistic psychology, has spent much of his life studying how creative individuals manage to function as they do. According to Maslow, primary creativity "is very probably a heritage of every human being and is found in all healthy children." So how come there's so little real creativity surrounding us? Thomas Edison has offered this quantification of the creative process he so regularly seemed to experience: "Invention," he said, "is 1 percent inspiration and 99 percent perspiration." This entire volume is based upon the axiom that everyone is creative and that with hard work and encouragement, everyone can come up with good ideas.

Insight and creativity happen when one is playing around. This doesn't mean goofing off, however. Getting ideas requires a delicate and determined playfulness—one that encompasses a variety of approaches, demands all the discipline you can manage, and usually ends up requiring plenty of sheer faith.

Because visual design is so essential to animation, it is likely that if

1.6 VISUAL CLICHÉS: Add whatever details you wish to transform the same basic body form into these different characters: a pirate, a hippy, an old woman, a creature from outer space, a monster. A few extra outlines are provided so you can try different solutions and create new characters.

1.7   DEEP STRUCTURE: A valuable approach to drawing cartoon characters is to begin with circular and rounded forms. Circles are easy to draw and they remain the same shape. These examples were created by one of the masters of character animation, and are reproduced from *Animation—How to Draw Animated Cartoons* by Preston Blair, published by Walter Foster. This modest book is extremely useful for analyzing animated drawings. Mr. Blair provides a step-by-step approach to designing and drawing cartoons.

you're already interested in animation, you will already have a built-in mechanism for finding new ideas. It is your own taste for graphics combined with your own abilities in drawing and image making that will lead you in idea hunting. You'll probably get a lot of help in tracking down good ideas from a set of latent tendencies most animators have toward being gag writers, mimes, shrinks, junk collectors, long-distance swimmers, jewelers, magicians, and all-around nonconformists. Here is a baker's dozen of strategies that can help you locate and stockpile good ideas.

Idea Book. Purchase a large format (at least 11 by 14 inches) spiral-bound sketchbook with large, white sheets of quality drawing paper. This book will become a home for your ideas. Use it freely. Jot down anything that strikes you as even remotely relevant as a film or part of a film you might one day make. Plunk into your book images or quotations or recollections of any kind.

The large size of the pages is important because it will promote a comparison of different ideas and visual elements. The absence of ruled lines forces you to write out ideas in unfamiliar ways. The wire binding allows you to lay the book flat for drawing. This kind of book also encourages the addition of odd materials—clippings, postcards, doodles, collages, and so on.

Weird Combinations. Search for comparisons and analogies in all things. You might carry around with you each day some sort of provocative idea and try to combine it with experiences and observations you make as your day proceeds. Pick just one object for, say, five minutes and see how, if, why, and with what effect it does or does not combine with any other object or environment or whatever. How does a toothbrush relate to the morning newspaper? What is a toothache like?

Dream Diary. Maslow says that creativeness emerges from our unconscious. "In our dreams," he writes, "we can be . . . more clever, and wittier, and bolder and more original . . . with the lid taken off, with the controls taken off, the repressions and defenses taken off, we find generally more creativeness than appears to the naked eye."

Write down your dreams just after you've awakened. You will find that your own unconscious communication system is a terrific source of good ideas. With practice you'll have no trouble remembering dreams in rich and fruitful detail. Try it. You'll like it. And it works.

Recycling Ideas. There isn't a new idea under the sun. Sometime before—someplace—someone must have come up with every possible combination of ideas. But this fact should only serve as an encouragement for copying ideas, borrowing them, refining them, making them your own. Go about this purposefully. When you come across an idea that is really attractive to you, jot it down. As you later work over these ideas you will select further and invariably infuse and alter what you like in your own way. The process of editing and transforming makes a found idea your idea—to the limited extent that any idea can ever belong to anyone.

You might even begin with this book. Draw a big arrow to notions or images or techniques that catch your interest. Better, write them on the inside of the covers where other ideas can join them. Better still, put them into your idea book.

Brainstorming. Here is a creative problem-solving technique that requires a group of people. The object of brainstorming is for the group to come up with as many alternative solutions to a problem as they can. Quantity is valued but quality is not judged. To brainstorm well, everyone participating must spontaneously call out every idea that enters into their heads. Allow no self-censorship. You don't say to yourself or to others, "Gee, I'm not sure if this is off-the-wall but . . ." Instead, you immediately spit out the idea. You free-associate.

Brainstorming works on the theory that the spontaneous generation of ideas will produce novel and valuable solutions and that a group will come up with a larger number of better ideas than will the same number of people working individually. The first part of a brainstorming session is given over to generating ideas. This is usually given a time limit—perhaps five minutes. Then there is a second part in which the ideas are evaluated. This can be a creative step too. Ideas can combine in interesting ways; discussion can lead to refinements or new directions that the shout-out speed of the first part of the session does not encourage.

The Back Burner. Sometimes the best way to solve a problem is to forget it. The mind's subconscious will keep working at a problem even after the conscious portion of the mind has gone on to other concerns. This incubation period is essential to creativity and it is the major reason why working under too tight a deadline will be unproductive if original thinking is required. So as a conscious strategy, allow yourself time for ideas to simmer and perk on the back burners of your mind.

Mixing Media. As media theorist Marshall McLuhan has pointed out, a tremendous release of raw energy occurs when information that is packaged in one medium is translated into another medium. A good place to look for ideas is within the other arts. This process of cross-fertilization has been long valued and used by artists of all forms: dance, theater, writing, mime, music, sculpture, painting, and so on.

Film—The Composite Medium. All films, including animated films, are made up of other expressive forms. Film, in fact, is an all-encompassing medium that combines the performing arts and the plastic arts, that unites the world of science and technology with the world of arts and letters.

Just one ingredient of a film's composite form can fire your imagination for the rest. For example, "sound" is made up of music, dialogue, narration, and sound effects. Any one of these can provide the source of a new idea on which to base your own film. Each element of a film is important. And all parts work together, even as they are bound together physically on the celluloid surface and bound together in the intellects and emotions of those who perceive them.

Materials. For animators, one of the richest sources of ideas comes from the material of animation itself. This will become evident as you study and try your hand at the twenty-odd animation techniques discussed in this book. You will discover, for example, that the character of sand being moved across a sheet of white Plexiglas will produce its own ideas. And so it will be as you animate other objects, as you work in clay, draw on registered paper sheets, combine collage imagery, or design a cutout character. In animation, every material must be used differently. Every material has its unique characteristics and potentials and these must be exploited fully by the film artist.

Hanging Tough. When nothing else seems to work, try brute

↑ A CONTOUR DRAWING OF MY HAND. TRY YOURS HERE. ↘

1.8 ANALYZE: In what is called contour drawing, you move your eyes very slowly along the edges or contours of an object. Working in unison with the movement of the eye, draw a line on the paper—slowly, evenly, carefully. This means you *cannot* look at the drawing as it develops. Remember to keep eye and hand perfectly synchronous. Try to imagine that the point of your pencil is actually touching the edge that your eye is slowly moving across. Note that the completed image should exhibit detail but that it won't necessarily look like the original object.

1.9 DRAWING STYLES: This jumbo project deserves as much time as you can afford to give it. The payoff will be commensurate with your investment. You are to make a number of different drawings of the same still life. The goal here is to explore different ways of seeing and different forms of graphic expression. The goal is *not* to create a series of masterpieces. Select a combination of objects that are interesting enough so that you'll be able to work with them for a while. Try each of the variations listed below. Use a separate sheet of paper for each and don't attempt more than one or two at a single sitting.

1. Draw the still life in exactly 60 seconds.

2. Choose a different point of view and draw it for 5 full minutes.

3. Change viewpoint again and draw the still life for 15 minutes.

4. Render the still life by ripping (not cutting) its basic shapes from a sheet of colored construction paper and then mounting it with glue onto a clean sheet of paper.

5. Study the still life from at least six different positions. From each simplify the still life into its basic geometric forms as you did in Figure 1.3.

6. Draw the shadows of the still life—but don't draw anything else.

7. Draw the tiniest possible image that still allows you to make out the still life. Keep trying until you draw one so small that you can't make out the still life.

8. Do a complete contour drawing of your still life—refer to Figure 1.4 for information on contour drawing.

9. Draw a huge enlargement of one detail from the still life.

8. Do a complete contour drawing of your still life—refer to Figure 1.4 for information on contour drawing.

9. Draw a huge enlargement of one detail from the still life.

10. Instead of drawing the still life, draw everything that surrounds it—its negative space.

11. Make a pointillist version of the still life by means of a series of tiny dots from a magic marker.

12. Try making a high contrast rendering of the still life. Eliminate all gray tones and emphasize zones that are either black or white; use no single lines and no intermediate shadings.

13. Make a full-color version using colored pencils or watercolors.

14. Render the still life through a glued assemblage of found objects such as pipe cleaners, paper clips, rubber bands, matches, string, and the like.

15. Do a version with "heightened color"—whatever that means to you.

16. Find a rubber stamp. Create the still life by building up a density and basic form with the stamp's pattern.

17. Sitting in one position, try to draw the still life as it would be seen from different angles, including directly above and below it.

18. Do a bas-relief version by building up layers of masking tape.

19. Use an implement with a rounded point to create an embossed image of the still life by pressing the point into a sheet of paper.

20. As a final version of the still life, find a way to portray it on a sheet of paper without using any standard art materials.

3

9

4

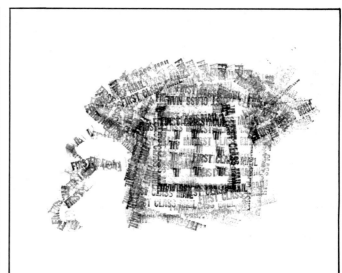

16

6

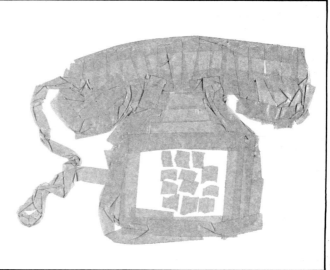

18

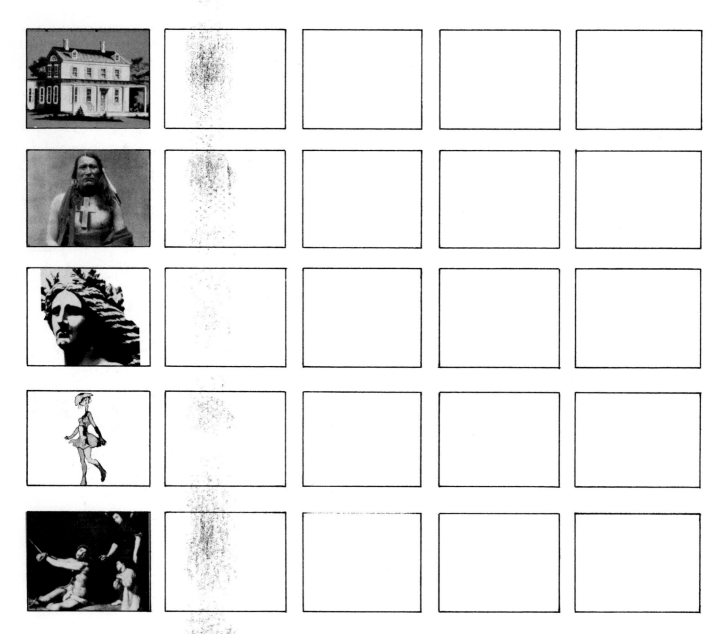

1.10 ELIMINATING DETAIL: Explore how far you can simplify a drawing and still have it remain recognizable. Take the objects in the first frame and progressively eliminate detail until it becomes impossible to distinguish it as the original object.

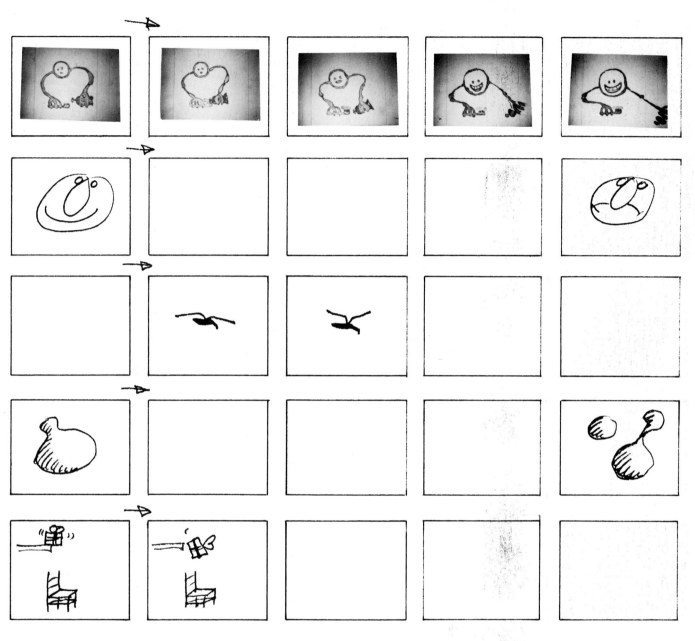

1.11 MAKING IT MOVE: Create the drawings that will complete the implied sequence. You'll see that figuring out how something ought to move requires both a sharp eye and an active imagination. Sometimes it also helps to literally act it out. If you have trouble, actually pantomime the movement, even if it means being a bird or a blob. When you've completed these, try some additional variations. For example, in the last set of drawings you might try to vary the nature of the falling box. Make it light, heavy, bouncy, gooey, or brittle. What else can you do to the chair? How or what is on the chair? And what is in the box? (The example is from Ryan Larkin's *Street Musique*.)

1.12 FRAMING: In animation the filmmaker has tremendous control over the composition of the motion picture frame. As this example shows, the way that the edges of the frame compose (or cut off) the subject—how the subject is *framed*—provides a significant aesthetic variable. If you cut two L-shaped pieces of cardboard, these can be used to practice different framing possibilities. Use the L or something similar to frame off part of the picture in a way that creates a new composition. Remember that the frame of a movie usually comes with a height to width ratio of 3 to 4.

force. Muscle your way to a good idea. Let inspiration come out of perspiration. The very discipline of work—of spending time at it even when it feels unproductive—will often yield a sudden breakthrough. If you spend twenty minutes every day, seven days a week, working in your idea book, then I promise that the discipline of doing this alone will get you through. Something worth pursuing will emerge. And eventually, a pursuit of one kind or another will get you somewhere.

You must trust yourself. All great artists have counted on such faith to get them through the "dry spells." Virtue is its own reward. Keep working.

Summary

The basic requirements for animation include, first, an interest in working with ideas through images. If there is a distinctive kind of "logic" in animation, it centers on the mental processes of visual thinking. Among the most common functions of visual problem solving

1.13 SUGGESTING DEPTH: This very simple drawing incorporates a number of the conventions commonly used to convey the dimension of depth.

are the abilities to improvise, explore, simplify, analyze, recycle, and respond.

In practical terms, animation often requires drawing. But what serves as an acceptable graphic style in animation is not the same as that which is generally accepted among other visual arts. The difference is in movement—the way drawings or other images move is what matters most and the skills of creating motion are quite different from traditional drawing skills. Still, drawing itself can be learned. And so can the art of placing images into movement.

Life's experience and our thinking about it constitute the substance of all the arts. A basic skill for animation thus becomes the ability to find something worth making a movie about. Getting ideas worth communicating is always the bottom line. Creativity and imagination are elements inherent in all of us, and the kinds of ideas best suited for animation can be encouraged through various disciplined forms of playfulness.

So much, then, for basic skills. Now let's move into technique. Some simple toys will get us there.

2
Cameraless Animation

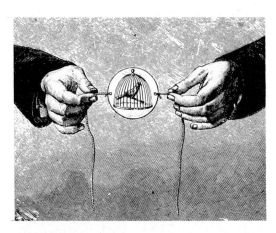

2.1 A THAUMATROPE: This 1826 French engraving shows how to spin a thaumatrope and it also suggests the device's effect. In this case, one side of the disc bears the image of a bird and the other side carries that of an empty cage. The superimposed image is created, of course, only when the device is being spun between fingertips. *Courtesy Stanford University Art Museum.*

The ancestors of animated films were a series of nineteenth-century mechanical toys that created the illusion of movement. None of these gadgets had any direct application within the worlds of commerce and science. Their existence was based solely on their ability to delight. They were toys in the real and best sense.

Over a hundred-year period, inventor after inventor further refined these optical devices. Along the way, machines combined with the emerging technology of photography to create yet another entertainment, the movies. Mechanical toys were wedded to celluloid and gave birth to cartoons.

It is both interesting and instructive to retrace the genealogy of animation and to study some of those crazy gadgets that led to contemporary animation techniques. If you try your hand at making some of these machines, not only will your appreciation of them be enhanced, but you'll pick up some valuable information and experience concerning the perceptual and mechanical foundations of animation, the techniques of designing pictures that move, and the process of spontaneous invention itself. As a bonus, you'll be creating materials that can be used later in making real cartoons.

The Thaumatrope

Animation prehistory begins with a simple device named the thaumatrope. This optical toy was in wide circulation in the early nineteenth century, and it may have been known far earlier than that.

The toy is simplicity itself: a disc that is attached to two pieces of string. When the disc is twirled by the operator's hands, images placed on either side of the disc are perceived together as a single image (Figure 2.1). Twirling the disc superimposes images upon each other by means of a perceptual phenomenon known as the *persistence of vision.* Our eyes hold on to images for a split second longer than they are actually projected, so that a series of quick flashes is perceived as one continuous picture.

Using a piece of heavy cardboard and some string, you can recreate the bird-and-cage effect or try out something more personal.

Project: Plastic Surgery. Locate a black-and-white photograph of yourself, not more than a couple of inches in length and width, in which your head is fairly large within the frame. Center your image and then cut this out and mount it on a piece of round cardboard. Punch two small holes at the opposite edges of the disc and attach a string to each. Design a number of alternative images to be attached to the reverse side of your thaumatrope: a beard, a scar, a hat, a mask, a missing tooth, or whatever else you'd like to superimpose on your own face. Try different effects using colors. See what happens when you place the photograph of a movie star on the opposite side. Twirl up a storm.

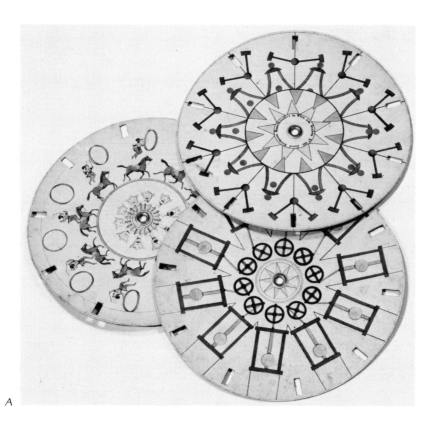

A

B

2.2 DISCS FOR PLATEAU'S PHENAKISTOSCOPE:
A simple wooden handle was used to hold these discs as the viewer spun the wheel while facing a mirror and sighting through the slits in the disc's surface. Plateau's fascination with mechanical movement is apparent in that moving machines provide the "content" within two of his discs *(A)*. The old etching *(B)* shows a variation of the phenakistoscope. To operate this device correctly, the viewer positions an eye close to the surface with slits. As the disc is spun, the animated movement is perceived by sighting through the series of slits to the series of drawings beyond. *Courtesy Stanford University Art Museum.*

The Phenakistoscope

In 1832 a Frenchman named Joseph Plateau invented the first machine that really created the illusion of sustained movement. His invention, the phenakistoscope, is a spinning wheel that bears a series of drawn images and viewing gates that frame the viewer's vision of the drawings (Figure 2.2).

Project: Mirror Movies. In Figure 2.3 you'll find a one-quarter-size pattern for creating your own phenakistoscope. Reproduce a full-size version, 8 inches in diameter, and attach it to a backing surface. After cutting viewing slits at the indicated places, draw something in the twelve frames outlined on the surface of the stylus. Note that you can actually try two different movements on a single sheet of paper by using the outside zone for one set of drawings and the inside zone for another set.

The last four suggestions cited in Figure 2.3 involve *cycles.* The figures all end with a position that is similar to (and leads into) the starting position. This creates a pattern that can be repeated endlessly. As you study your own phenakistoscope in a mirror, these cycles should continue smoothly just as long as you keep spinning the paper disc.

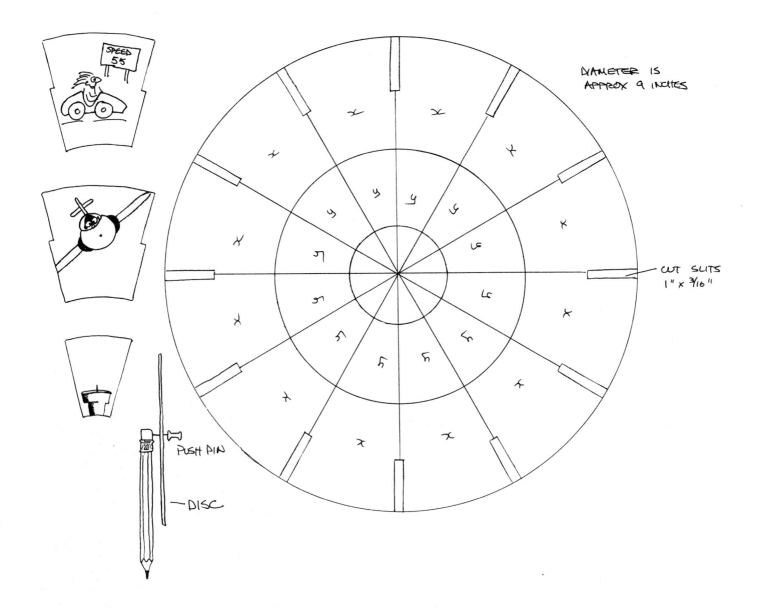

2.3   PHENAKISTOSCOPE STYLUS: This particular configuration of twelve wedges seems to work well, but you are encouraged to experiment with other formats. Use the sections marked "x" for one set of drawings and the sections marked "y" for the second set. Beside the stylus (which has been reduced in scale) are three possible drawings you might want to try: a sports car that zooms through the frame; an airplane that flies directly at you; and an exotic plant that you can make grow. The finished phenakistoscope (cut from cardboard or another heavy paper stock) can be mounted onto a pencil by securing its center to the pencil's eraser with a pushpin. Go to the mirror and watch the drawings come alive and move at various speeds.

The Zoetrope and Praxinoscope

It wasn't long before a new generation of inventors refined and extended Mr. Plateau's device. Among the most ingenious of the new toys were the zoetrope and the praxinoscope. Both machines provided more convenient projection devices for their drawings. Both extended the number of drawings that could be used—and hence the duration of the movement itself.

The zoetrope is a revolving drum that has slits in the sides, spaced equally. By looking through these slits as the drum is spun, the viewer is able to catch glimpses of a series of drawings that have been created on a strip of paper and then placed inside the drum (Figure 2.4). The larger the drum's diameter, the longer the "movie," and, of course, the same drum could present different strips of drawings. Incidentally, the machine's name means "wheel of life." It was so titled by Pierre Devignes in the year 1860, although earlier versions of the same basic device had been developed in England by William Horner around 1834.

A modern record player can substitute for the spinning mechanism of the early zoetropes. Figure 2.5 introduces schematics for making your own shutter device (slitted circles) and your own artwork (strips of paper). After creating your set of component parts, place the paper strips inside the drum and put the combined circular contraption on top of a phonograph. Set the machine's speed at 33$\frac{1}{3}$ rpm, position

A

2.4 A ZOETROPE: The photograph of early motion equipment *(A)* shows the circular metal drum and wooden base of a zoetrope. To the left of the zoetrope is a traumatrope disc and behind that a device that was cranked rapidly to animate a series of drawings on cards. The long strip in the foreground is the artwork that is placed inside the zoetrope's drum. Photograph *B* shows four nineteenth-century British zoetrope strips. *A, courtesy Museum of Modern Art/Film Stills Archives; B, courtesy Stanford University Art Museum.*

B

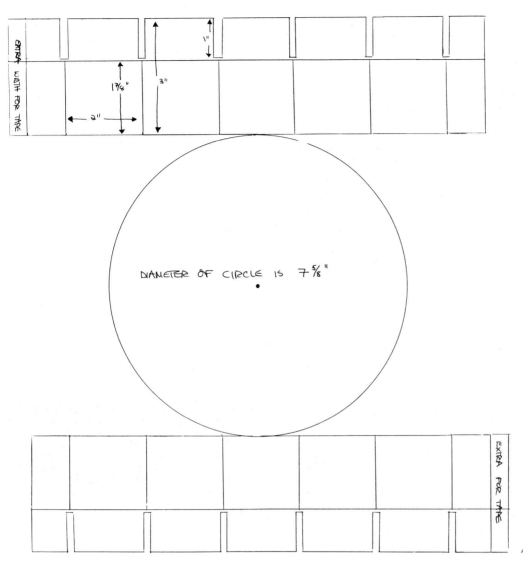

EXTRA WIDTH FOR TAPE

1"

3"

1⅞"

2"

DIAMETER OF CIRCLE IS 7⅝"

EXTRA FOR TAPE

A

2.5 ZOETROPE STYLUS: Drawing *A* shows in reduced scale one way of cutting a zoetrope drum from a single sheet of cardboard or heavy paper. Separate strips with twelve panels can then be cut from regular paper, drawn onto, and placed inside the drum. Drawings *B* and *C* suggest how the drum is assembled after it is cut out (the sides of the drum can be taped together) and how it is mounted on a phonograph's turntable.

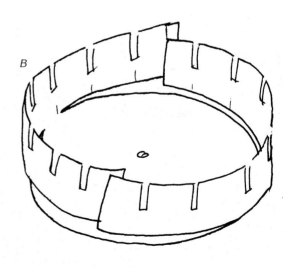

B

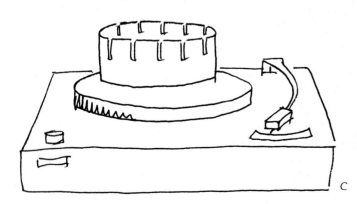

C

your eyes so that they look through the revolving slits, and turn on the record player. You'll discover that you have replaced music with a visual melody of your own design.

The praxinoscope represents a refinement on the zoetrope. The slits are replaced by a set of mirrors that spin in the center of the drum. You can try to make your own version of the prism device by using a shiny plastic material, which is available in art stores. The finished mirror structure is placed over the spindle of a record player. When the machine is turned on, the outside band of images is animated as one looks into the revolving mirrors. The same drawings you have made for the zoetrope can be modified for use in a model praxinoscope.

The inventor of the praxinoscope was Emile Reynaud, and in 1892 he opened the world's first movie theater in Paris. Reynaud's Theater Optique projected a "movie" that was made of individual drawings on a long piece of paper. The show lasted just a few minutes. In many ways, Reynaud's invention parallels the modern film projector.

2.6 REYNAUD'S PRAXINOSCOPE THEATER: By the turn of the century, this relatively sophisticated device was being commercially distributed in Europe and North America. Emil Reynaud combined his invention with a magic lantern to create his famous *Theater Optique.* Located in Paris and operating between 1892 and 1900, the Theater Optique entertained sizable audiences by projecting an extended series of animated drawings that had been made on long strips of translucent paper. *Courtesy Stanford University Art Museum.*

2.7   PREVIEWING A FLIP-BOOK: A finished flip-book with many pages is being flipped by its creator, George Griffin. This way of holding and fanning the pages will work with almost any kind of flip-book.

Flip-books

Remember those animated drawings you did as a kid on the dog-eared edges of a textbook? By flipping through the pages, you could make the characters or the design move. Sometimes you could buy a small flip-book at the local novelty store, or you'd discover one already created in a comic book, or get one as a Cracker Jack prize.

Flip-books also invite comparison with the technique of cel animation, one of the most sophisticated of all animation techniques. Each page in the flip-book corresponds to an individual piece of artwork that, along with all the other drawings, makes up a movie when it's filmed by an animation camera. The binding of the pad or flip-book acts as a *registration* system—a way of keeping things precisely sequenced and lined up. The act of thumbing through the pages of the flip-book is the act performed first by the camera and then by the projector.

The quickest and easiest way to make your own flip-book is to purchase a small, unruled pad of white paper. A convenient size is 5 by 7 inches, although smaller 3- by 5-inch books also work. You'll find these pads in any good stationery store. With one of these pads and a pencil, you're ready to start.

The first drawing is made on the last page of the pad. When the next page is permitted to fall forward and cover the page you've just drawn, you will be able to see through the new sheet well enough to make out the preceding drawing. You may now redraw or trace the first drawing, but not exactly. In order to create movement, you must alter each successive drawing in some minor way. These minute changes accumulate or build up to produce the illusion of movement.

The process of completing a drawing, covering it with a new sheet, redrawing, recovering, and so forth is continued until you work your way to the first page of the pad. To see the results of your labor, hold the book in one hand so that you can flip through the pages, back to front, with the other hand.

Standard index cards provide a superior alternative to the bound pages of a small note pad. The drawing technique is similar. With index cards a registration system is achieved by lining up the cards as you draw, one on top of the other. Index cards are thicker than regular paper. This makes them flip more efficiently, but it also makes them more difficult to see through as you draw one image on top of the preceding one. To remedy this you may want to make yourself a *light table*. This consists, very simply, of a piece of transparent or translucent glass or Plexiglas on which you draw, with a bright light projecting upward from beneath this surface, making it easy to see through a number of index cards or pages of regular paper. Chapter 17 provides more information on making or purchasing a light table.

Index cards provide greater flexibility than note pads. For one thing, you can easily throw away a particular drawing without weakening the binding. Similarly, you can insert one or more cards should you determine that you need more drawings to smooth out a particular movement. Most important, index cards allow you to reorder the sequence of a finished flip-book. This means that you can rearrange a finished flip-book so that it is viewed from front to back. Between showings a strong rubber band will easily hold the cards together.

With either pads or index cards, you have some options on just where to draw whatever it is you want to put on the paper. Figure 2.8 shows two common placement systems. Technically and aesthetically, there seems to be very little difference between the two. However, if you think you may eventually want to film one of your flip-books, you should work in an area with a length-to-height ratio of 4 to 3. This is the standard ratio for most movie screens.

Project: Circle Boogie. Using either a pad or index cards, try to solve the following problem. Your first drawing is to be a circle, roughly 1½ inches in diameter. In the following twelve pages, transform the circle into another object—for example, the circle could evolve into a set of lips. And in the following twelve sheets, try to get back to the original circle. But as you do this, follow a different route from the one you took in the first twelve drawings. You might, for example, have the lips blow out a bubble-gum bubble that grows until it hides the lips and becomes the same size as the original circle.

If you follow these directions, you will have a movement in twenty-four drawings, from a circle to something else to a circle again. Now repeat this process a second time, going to a different shape or object before returning on sheet 48 to the original circle. When you flip the completed book, you should see a movie that, while it lasts just a few seconds, creates a clear visual "beat." Do other variations within this basic structure and add these to your flip-book. Vary the amounts of movement between drawings and the degree of complexity of the transformations. Add color. Try having a number of things happening at once.

Sneak Preview. Save these first flip-books. Later, with an animation camera, you will be able to turn them into films. Instead of appearing as cramped drawings on small pages that are flipped with

A

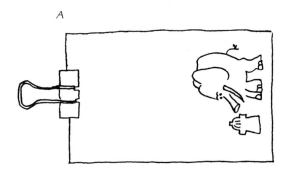

B

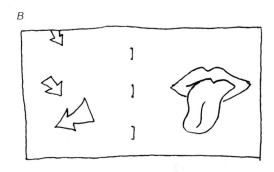

2.8 TWO FLIP-BOOK FORMATS: The scale and dimensions here are highly arbitrary. Flip-book A uses a #20 (small) binder clip to hold its pages firmly. One's hand can perform the same function. Flip-book B is stapled in the center. This arrangement creates two drawable, flippable surfaces on the same set of stapled pages. Select a paper stock and a size of drawing that will suit your preferences and resources.

unavoidably irregular speed, these flip-books can be produced into real movies, huge in scope, gracious in form, unfettered in presentation.

When you return to the Circle Boogie project, you'll be able to produce quite a successful movie. By cycling your drawing (position 1 to 12 to 1; then position 13 to 24 to 13; and so on), you will be able to double the length of the film and produce, with just the first fifty or so drawings, a visual rhythm that has 200 individual frames, lasts 8 seconds, and has a driving beat all its own. Since flip-books are one of the cheapest and simplest of animation techniques, they are ideally suited for learning those drawing techniques and styles that most effectively create movement. The size and cost of a flip-book are both small. So buy a book, carry one with you and work at your drawing in spare moments. It's like carrying around a movie in your pocket. *Your* movie.

2.9   FLIP-BOOK AS FILM AND PUBLICATION: These drawings represent part of the actual layout prepared by independent animator George Griffin for formal publication of one of his flip-books.

Cameraless Films

You can make your own animated films without a camera and without photographically developing the film itself. This is the technique of cameraless animation often called "scratch and doodle" filmmaking. It's a good place to begin your exploration of animation. It is cheap and fast. Few tools are required and you can see the results of your work immediately.

But there are more important reasons why cameraless animation is the best place to start working with actual film. First, the technique allows you to get to know the size and characteristics of the celluloid strips that comprise the physical material known as film. Second, drawing on film gives you a good area for experimentation with the perceptual phenomena that allow the movies to "move." Finally, cameraless animation is relatively simple. You don't need any previous experience or knowledge to create your very first World Premiere.

A friendly warning: Although cameraless animation is direct and simple, the technique is deceptively difficult to master. If you want to fashion a film that really works, you will need to do a lot of experimentation and try a number of different ways of working.

Clear leader is the term given to a strip of celluloid film that has no photographic image on it. Lay the clear leader out on a flat surface, draw directly on it and, presto, you've made an animated film. Most often, 16mm film is used for cameraless animation. It is easily available, inexpensive, and the surface is wide enough to permit control.

Sixteen millimeter clear leader comes with either one or two sets of sprocket holes running along its outside edges. These are termed *single-perforated* and *double-perforated* clear leader respectively. The single-perforated type is recommended because it makes it easier to determine on which side of the film to work. If you draw on the "wrong" side, your image will be projected in reverse.

There are two important facts that you need to know before attempting your first film. The first has to do with *projection speed*. At normal sound projection speed, 16mm film is projected at a rate of *24 frames per second* (fps). The standard projection speed for super 8mm film is *18 frames per second*. In the discussions that follow, I'll be talking about 16mm leader and the normal 24-fps speed.

Frame lines are another important concept. You will need to know where a single image or frame is placed on a strip of clear 16mm leader. The frame lines that mark off the area of the film that is actually projected are to be found crossing the width of the film opposite each sprocket hole.

Among the drawing materials that work well for marking on the acetate surface are *felt-tipped pens*. Make sure your markers adhere to the acetate base of 16mm clear leader. Many of those that promise to write on "anything" don't. *Grease pencils* work too. Because they are not completely translucent, grease-pencil colors are muted when projected. There are some kinds of *paints* that will work well on acetate. But you will have to do a test or two to determine how these paints hold up. On drying, some paints crack and flake off the film. This can clog the gate of the film projector and necessitate careful cleaning after every use. There are also special *inks* that can be applied to the leader with either brush or pen. Chapter 19 has a list of materials.

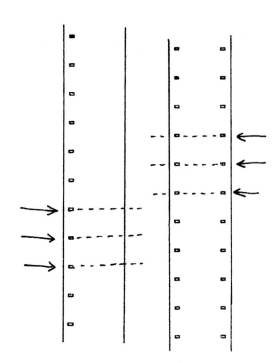

2.10   FRAME LINES: The frame lines are indicated by the arrows and dotted lines. They go straight across the film. Sometimes you may be working with leader that has only one set of sprocket holes. Location of the frame remains the same.

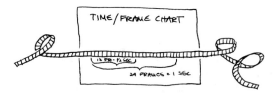

2.11   TIME/FRAME CHART: A sheet of white paper or any flat surface can be used to make a chart that indicates what number of frames will equal what duration of time when the leader is projected at the standard sound speed of 24 frames per second. You may, of course, modify the chart to indicate those time intervals that you'll be using frequently in your movie. Remember that a recurring visual "beat" will make almost any film more exciting to watch. Leave a few feet of blank film at the head of your strip. This is required in threading the projector.

Persistence of Vision

One of the first things you will need to know as an animator is, quite simply, what the human eye is capable of seeing. Quite obviously, everything in animation depends upon the viewer's recognition of an image and his ability to follow its movement.

The moving pictures of film don't actually move. All you have to do is look at a piece of film and you'll be reminded that, in fact, the medium is made up of a series of still images. It is the human eye and brain that make movies move. More accurately, the illusion of movement on film is created by a physiological phenomenon called the *persistence of vision,* as mentioned earlier. When a single image is flashed at the eye, the brain retains that image longer than it is actually registered on the retina. So when a series of images is flashed in rapid order, as a movie projector does, and when the images themselves are only slightly changed, one to the next, the effect is that of continuous motion. This very remarkable illusion is the perceptual foundation of film and television.

Project: Charting Visual Thresholds. How little can the eye actually see? If 24 individual images are projected during 1 second of film, can the eye see just one of these? Do different people have different perceptual thresholds? Can the viewer's eye be trained to see with new perceptual sensitivity?

You can conduct some experiments to answer such questions. Holding a length of clear leader against a white sheet of paper, create a time/frame stylus like that shown in Figure 2.11.

Here are some problems to figure out. Can the eye see one frame

2.12   WORK ON 16MM LEADER: *From left to right,* the samples show: two abstract ways of drawing on clear leader without reference to frame lines; an abstract technique that uses a stamp cut into a pencil eraser; an abstract treatment in which the entire surface is colored and then decorated; a carefully registered sequence in which a star grows larger and smaller; a representational narrative (a speedboat pulling a water skier); a registered series of abstract graphic forms that are scratched from black leader; two more examples of black leader with abstract patterns scratched onto the emulsion; and, finally, a piece of clear leader with the word "end."

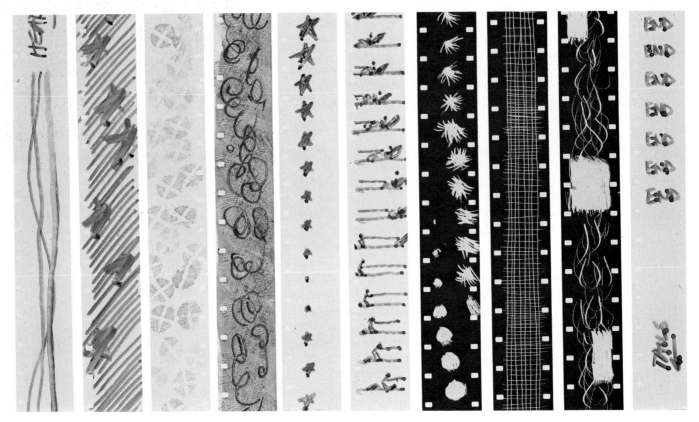

of color against a clear (white when projected) background? Also try filling in 2, 3, 4, 5, and 6 adjacent frames. How does color or hue affect what one sees? Can you make out 3 frames of green, for example, in the middle of a 2-foot length of film that is colored blue? What happens when primary colors are alternated rapidly (2 frames of red, 2 frames of green, 2 of red, 2 of green, and so on) for a total of 10 seconds or 240 frames?

Lay out a number of such experiments on a piece of 16mm clear leader. Separate each experiment by at least 3 or 4 seconds of clear film. Two feet of 16mm film contain 80 frames and will project for just over 3 seconds. Screen the results of your investigations and show these to different individuals to try to determine what the perceptual threshold of the average film viewer is. What you discover will be used in every animated film you make.

Frameless Style

A distinctive kind of cameraless animation is achieved by marking on the film's surface *without* reference to the individual frames that comprise a length of film. Markers, paints, or other media are applied to the clear leader in broad patterns that cross frame-line boundaries at will. The results are striking, unlike anything that a camera can record. And they are impossible to describe in words. Mixtures of color, movement, and shape bounce off the movie screen with psychedelic effect. This is not to say, however, that the frameless style of drawing on the leader always achieves a pleasing and provocative viewing experience. Quite the contrary. As an animator you will have to purposefully create a changing set of carefully fashioned markings if you want to come up with a film that is interesting to watch. A series of tests is the only way you can identify styles or effects that work for you; take the best of these and integrate them into a unified expression. The following project can help you to begin your explorations.

Project: Frameless Explorations. Measure out a 25-foot length of 16mm clear leader. Lay it out on your worktable so that the sprocket holes (if there is only one set) are on your left-hand side. At the top of the film write the word "head" and add your name. Measure off 4 feet (48 inches) of film and make a mark. You will begin working from this mark toward the end of the film. The remaining 18 feet of 16mm film equal 30 seconds of running time (projected at the sound speed of 24 fps). On the first 9 feet of film, try three specific effects for a length of 3 feet each. These will each last 5 seconds on the screen. Mix up your selection of designs so that you have some that are "random" and some that are "patterned," that is, ones that repeat themselves often within the 3-foot length of film (Figure 2.12).

On the last 9 feet of film, try to mix the patterns together and add new ones. In fashioning this 15-second sequence, pay particular attention to the transitions between various markings and, within the last 4 or 5 feet, try superimposing some or all of your designs. In this way, the end of your film will be the densest part and you will be able to see just how much the eye can assimilate. You should leave the final 2 or 3 feet blank and label the very end of your film with the word "tails" and your name.

Include in your experimentation the study of what effects are

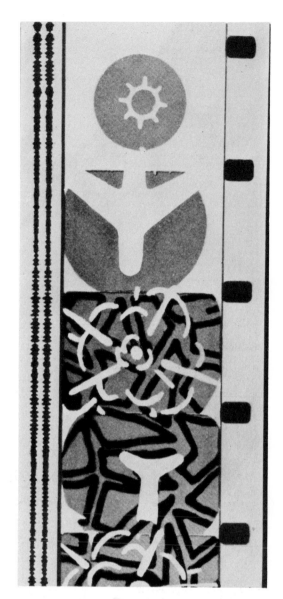

2.13 DRAWN-ON-PLUS-SOME: This photograph shows 4½ frames from *Uncle Sugar's Flying Circus*, a 2½-minute film produced without a camera by independent filmmaker Warren Bass. In addition to drawing with markers directly on clear leader, the techniques employed include hole punches, transfer-type printing black and white images onto color film stock using color filters, alternating black and clear frames, and punching images out of a 35mm slide and taping them with Mylar into holes punched in the 16mm leader. *Courtesy Warren Bass.*

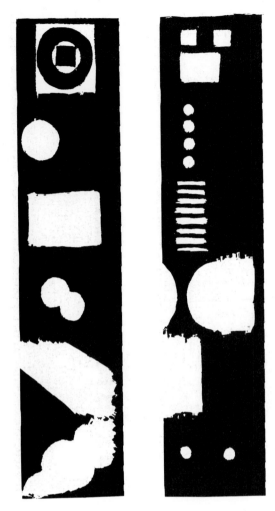

2.14 WORK ON BLACK LEADER: Four film clips from Pierre Herbert's *Op Hop* suggests the strong shapes and sharp edges that can be explored through scraping off the emulsion on black leader. This film was done in 35mm format, allowing the artist a larger working surface and therefore greater control. *Courtesy National Film Board of Canada.*

produced by different sorts of drawing and coloring styles and by various drawing materials. Experiment with different printing techniques—for example, the use of a sponge and ink, or an eraser used as a stamp, or your fingertips as printing tools. When you've completed some experiments on your own, I recommend that you see some cameraless films by Norman McLaren and other animators (see Chapter 21).

Frame-by-Frame Style

The second general style of marking on clear leader is centered upon using the frame lines. By modifying the shapes or the positions of images that are repeated on subsequent frames, the illusion of motion is created when the film is projected. Some samples are provided in Figure 2.12.

An important point to remember when you are drawing in this manner is that the individual frames are very small. Your working surface is much smaller than the smallest postage stamp. Its actual dimensions are six sixteenths of an inch wide and five sixteenths of an inch high. Remember these four elements as you try to create a recognizable image and then repeat it, with slight variations, frame after frame:

Simplicity. Reduce whatever it is you are drawing to its absolute minimum of detail.

Tools. If you're working representationally you will need drawing implements with fine points. A pen that leaves ink drops, for instance, is useless. A good magnifying glass can help control your marking tool.

Motor Skills. To a large extent, success in working representationally depends upon your own personal abilities as a draftsman. Physical control must be very exact.

Registration. In order to have the drawings appear to move consistently and somewhat smoothly, it is important to devise a system that gives you the ability to place each individual drawing in just the right place on each frame.

Registration Devices

This last item may very well be the most important. Fortunately, you can create a device that will help you achieve some measure of accuracy in placing one drawing in the proper relationship to the drawings preceding and following it. The need for registration is basic to all kinds of animation. Different techniques require different ways of registering the positions of camera and object. For cameraless animation, there are a variety of registration systems that can be used.

Graph Paper. Place your clear leader on a piece of graph paper and use the existing grid lines to help match specific places on one frame with those on the following frame. The sprocket holes are used to establish standard reference points to the graph paper beneath the film.

Discarded Film. Place the clear leader on top of a piece of discarded 16mm film that has been photographically exposed and developed in the normal way—that is, it is "used" film. Line up the sprocket holes as you begin working. You'll discover that the "old" image gives adequate reference between one of your doodles and those preceding and following it.

Hand-Drawn Registration Chart. Before you start working, place a short length of 16mm clear leader on a piece of white paper. With a pencil or pen, trace the outline of the film's edges and sprocket holes. Remove the leader. Draw a series of horizontal lines to show the frame lines crossing the film's surface at each sprocket hole. Draw one or two vertical lines down the length of the film tracing parallel to both edges of film. Finally, you can make two diagonal lines that intersect each frame. The result of all this measuring should be a series of frames that are exactly like each other. You place your leader over this chart as you draw, successively moving the film up onto the chart as the work continues.

Photographically Reproduced Registration Chart. The most accurate way of concocting a registration system is to actually use a 16mm camera to film a grid that has been drawn on paper. You can use such a piece of exposed film as something to put your leader directly over (as with the discarded film technique above). You can make a contact print of the piece of film on a sheet of photographic paper, or you can have a piece of 16mm film reproduced by offset printing or by xerography. Note that some copying systems change the actual size of what they duplicate. Even the smallest reduction or enlargement of the photographed grid will render the resulting registration chart absolutely useless.

In the last chapter you will find a full-scale registration guide that you can detach from these pages and use in your own cameraless animation.

Project: Frame-by-Frame Explorations. Make the following group of 3-second movies. Separate each with 2 seconds of clear leader. (1) Draw a dot in the middle of the frame that gets larger and larger (it will appear to come toward you when projected). (2) Draw a star that gets progressively smaller and also moves across the screen. (3) Draw a dot that divides into two dots and a vertical line that stays in the same place throughout the 72 frames. (4) Print your first name, or another short word, so that it does not move for the full 3 seconds. (5) Draw a simple face that changes expression during the mini-movie.

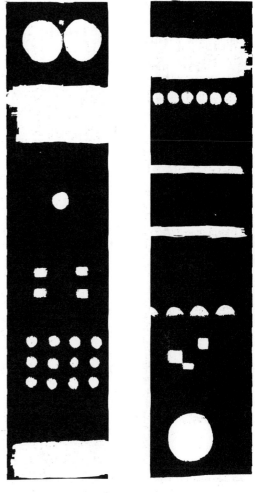

2.14

Scratching on Black Leader

Using the same general techniques and knowing the same basic facts, you can create a different kind of cameraless animation by using *black leader* instead of clear leader. Black leader (often called camera leader or opaque leader) is readily available from film laboratories or equipment sales/rental outlets.

It is easy to get a sharp, clean, thin line by scraping off the black emulsion (Figure 2.14). The resulting white lines (when projected) can be easily colored with felt-tipped pens and many people find that the results are the most pleasing form of cameraless film. In "scratch" films, the screen is black except for the images that have been etched onto the surface of the leader. The problem, of course, is that it's far more difficult to get accurate registration with black leader than with clear leader.

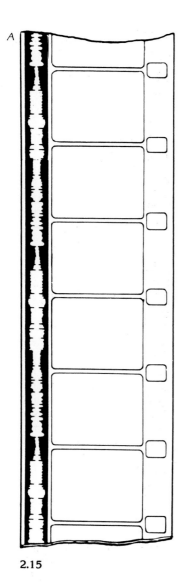

2.15

Scissors, straight pins, or any other sharp, pointed object is good for scraping off the emulsion. The first time you try this technique, be sure to test both sides of the leader to determine which has the emulsion coating. Otherwise you can scrape and scratch all day without producing any clear space through which the projector's light will pass. The most effective tool for scratching on black leader is a *silk-screen line cutter,* a sharp metal loop attached to the stem of a paintbrush.

Project: Visual Rhythms and Off-Beats. Make a 15-second scratch film that orchestrates the selection and development of images so that there will be a visual "beat" every second when the movie is projected. You will be creating a pulse out of line, color, form or other graphic elements.

At the same time, explore the relative movement of two design elements. For example, you could have a horizontal line moving "up" in the frame while some shape swings back and forth across the frame. Try to have these different elements move in different tempos, perhaps one on the half beat and the other on every other beat.

Projecting Cameraless Animation

Cameraless animation requires a lot of working time and yields relatively little viewing time. Here are some hints on how to stretch out the screening of your films and, in the process, extend their impact upon an audience.

Loops. If your piece of finished film is not too long (between 5 and 15 feet), you can thread it through the projector in a way that allows it to repeat itself continuously without rethreading. First thread the film normally and allow the front end to run out of the machine for 3 or 4 feet. Stop the projector. Take the front end (the "head") and splice it to the rear end of your movie (the "tail"). You will have to manually "feed" the film out the rear of the 16mm projector and into the front so that the film doesn't snarl up or touch the floor.

Silent Speed. The universal speed for 16mm sound films is 24 frames per second. This is an international standard. It is the slowest speed at which a film's sound track can move and still generate reproducible sound through the projector's amplification system. But many 16mm projectors are equipped with a switch that allows them to operate at a *silent speed* of 18 frames per second. At this slower speed our persistence of vision still works, so that visual continuity is maintained. When you project your cameraless film at silent speed, it takes longer going through the machine and hence it takes longer to see. The difference between 18 and 24 frames per second may not seem significant, but it is. This reduction in projection speed will add one fourth more time to a film's running time. A 15-second film at sound speed will run 20 seconds at silent speed. The difference is significant, at least to the artist.

Forward/Backward. Another way to extend the viewing experience is by projecting film in reverse. Most 16mm projectors have this capability. Simply thread and run the projector normally and then, when the last frame of your work has been exposed, shut off the projector, put it into reverse mode and see the entire film again, back to front. You will need at least a 3-foot tail on your film so that it doesn't come undone or pass through the projection gate before you reverse the projector.

Musical Accompaniment. Whenever you can, play music as you screen your cameraless animation. It's weird to discover that no matter what kind or what tempo of music you select, it always somehow seems to work with the visual segment. And if you experiment with enough different music tracks, you'll come upon one that will appear to have been made just for your film. Both records and audio tape recorders are easy ways of providing musical accompaniment to your movies. But it is also valuable to try creating your own original tracks to go with these movies.

Creating Sound Tracks

Using 16mm single-perforated clear or black leader, you can make your own sound track. The process is fun and it teaches a lot. It wouldn't be quite honest, however, to suggest that most people find the effect of a handmade sound track anything more than "interesting."

All commercially produced 16mm or 35mm films are equipped with sound tracks that have been placed on the actual surface of the film through a procedure that translates the frequencies of sound into a visual code system. The *optical sound track* that you see in Figure 2.15 is usually made by a laboratory at the time the film is printed. The actual process of turning recorded sound into an optical track need not concern you here. But it is important that you notice the placement of the track upon the edge of a piece of 16mm film and the visual characteristics of the optical track. If you study both these elements, you can create unearthly sounds of your own. For further information on making sound tracks for animated films, see Chapter 7.

Look again at the enlarged diagram of a regular 16mm film that has an optical track. You will notice that filling the space where the second set of sprocket holes would be if the film was double-perforated is a continuous column. It is very thin and runs the full length of the film. In the middle of this column is a white line that varies in width. If you look at it closely, you can see that this white line is jagged. Figure 2.16 is a simplified diagram of the standard 16mm projector. After the film has

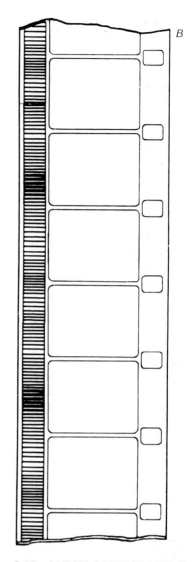

2.15   OPTICAL SOUND TRACKS: Diagram *A (opposite)*, enlarges a piece of 16mm film bearing an optical sound track—one or more clear lines, varying in width and running parallel to the edge of the film. This is a "variable-area" sound track, the kind most often used today. Diagram *B* shows an alternative form of optical track. It is called a "variable-density" track and consists of a series of ladderlike lines across the width of the track area. In creating your own track, it is easier to work in the fashion of the patternings shown in the variable-density optical track. *Diagrams courtesy Eastman Kodak Company.*

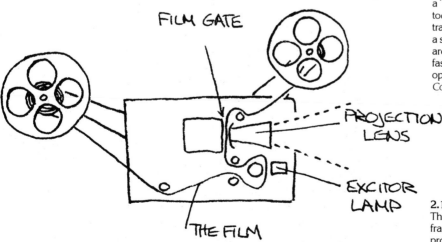

2.16   A STANDARD 16MM SOUND PROJECTOR: The excitor lamp reads the optical sound track exactly 26 frames ahead of the corresponding image as it is projected.

2.17 PITCHES AND TONALITIES: The musical tone middle C is heard when the air vibrates at the rate of 256 cycles per second. If you create this number of marks along the edge of 24 consecutive frames, the excitor lamp's beam will be interrupted precisely 256 times per second. When amplified and fed into a speaker, this signal will be heard as middle C. Twice the number of lines in the same area would produce a tone one octave above middle C and half the number (128 lines) would create a tone one octave lower. The diagram shows lines spaced to produce the 13 notes indicated on the musical staff. *Diagram courtesy Eastman Kodak Company.*

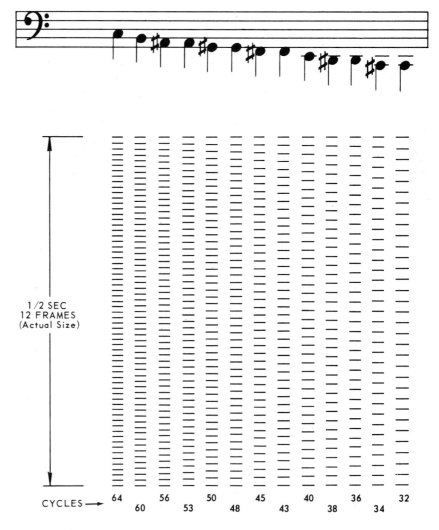

passed through the projection gate, it continues heading through the projector until it passes over the *soundhead* on its way to the rear of the projector and onto the take-up reel. As the film passes over the soundhead, an intense light is aimed at the sound track. The source of this beam is the *excitor lamp*. The patterns that the light makes as it passes through the optical track are picked up and amplified by the sound drum. The "read" sound is translated into electrical signals that are amplified and fed into a loudspeaker. Presto: music, voice, or whatever else was originally recorded.

You can make a sound track by hand by trying to duplicate along the unperforated side of 16mm black leader the kinds of patterns you see within an optical track. Here are some techniques.

Scratching on Black Leader. Using the sharp point of an Exacto knife or similar tool, scrape lines of varying width along the edges of a length of single-perforated black leader (Figure 2.17). Vary the closeness of the lines as well as their thickness. Project the film and listen to the sounds. You will discover how to make sounds of high and low pitch.

Rhythms. Create a rhythmic sound track by scraping repeated patterns of lines onto the edge of the black leader. First select a rhythm you can tap out and then time it with a stopwatch so that you can measure the duration of the beat and the silent intervals between beats. Because 16mm film is always projected at a constant 24 fps, you can easily figure out the number of frames a particular beat should occupy and the amount of time between beats. If earlier experimentation has shown you something about pitch, you should be able to create a melody, of sorts! Experiment with the chart in Figure 2.18.

Clear Leader. You can also create sound tracks by working along the edge of single-perforated clear leader. The projector's exitor lamp reads differences in light. Blocking out the light, therefore, will also cause a reaction and amplification. Use a black felt-tipped pen to see what kinds of sound it will produce. As above, experiment with rhythm and pitch. A variation would be to apply art materials called Zipatone patterns onto the film.

Project: The Complete Cameraless Sound Motion Picture. After some initial explorations in creating a sound track, it is fun to combine your sounds with your images. There is something else, however, that you will need to know in order to do this. As you are aware from watching movies, sound and images are synchronously perceived by the viewer's eyes and ears. However, while the corresponding visual element and the sound track are "read" by the projector at the same moment, they are "read" at different places within the machine. If you study the simplified diagram of a projector in Figure 2.16 you will see that the images are projected in the gate and that the sound is picked up by the exitor lamp that is located under the gate near the beginning of the film. *This means that the sound for any given frame is advanced exactly 26 frames ahead of its image.*

Create a sound track using a piece of either clear or black leader. Keep in mind that you will be adding images to your track—this may suggest to you particular rhythms and effects you will want to use. Begin with the sound, and when it's completed, lay the film on a white sheet of paper. Locate the specific frame at which the first sound of the film appears. Draw an arrow pointing toward it on the piece of paper. Count off 26 frames, moving toward the tail of the film. Mark the 26th frame with another arrow. In creating images for your sound track, keep checking between the optical mark at the first arrow and its corresponding image on the frame at the second arrow. As you move the piece of leader past the two arrows, you will be able to maintain a perfect registration of image to sound. When projected, your movie will be *in-sync,* that is, operating with a synchronous sound track in which images are matched to sounds.

Recycling Discarded Movies

All the skills you have developed through the preceding projects can be applied to experimentations with old or discarded films. And there are plenty of such films around. Inquire at a school or public library for old prints that they no longer can use or ask local TV stations or advertising agencies or businesses for their cast-off films.

Begin your creative work by projecting these films many times. Look for a sequence in which you see some "possibilities." Project this segment a number of times so that you are thoroughly familiar with it

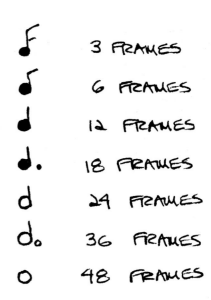

2.18 BEATS AND RHYTHM: To get the relative interval of standard musical notations, scratch or draw the indicated number of frames. The spacing between beats will create the rhythm.

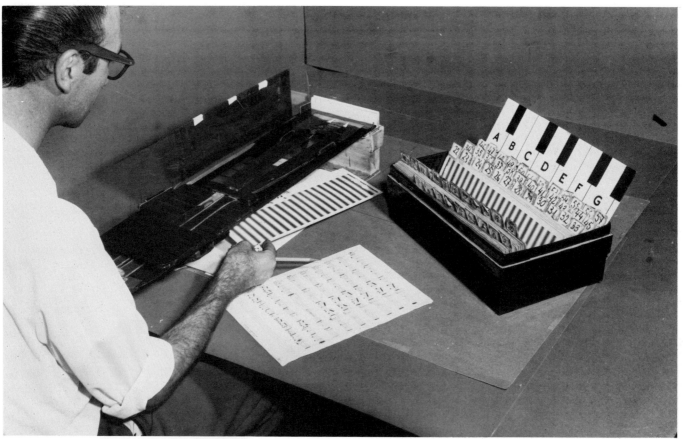

A

B

2.19   DRAWING A SOUND TRACK: Animator Norman McLaren (*A*) is seen with a file of precise measurements and samples from which musical notes can actually be drawn onto a strip of film. The enlargement *B* shows the edge of 35mm film leader with sound track markings created by Norman McLaren. *Courtesy National Film Board of Canada.*

and so that you have a detailed idea of how to alter it by scratching and doodling. A 16mm viewer can help in making a detailed study of the film. Or you can even hold a strip of footage up to a window for close inspection. Here are just a few of the things you can do.

Coloring. Black-and-white film can be colored with markers and ink.

Superimposition. Representational or abstract images can be superimposed on the existing live-action material of the old movies.

Scratching. Sometimes you can get a startling effect by simply scratching off specific pieces of the emulsion or scratching in a design or character of some kind.

Cloroxing. Using a Q-Tip and a solution of hydrogen peroxide, or a similar cleaning solvent such as Clorox, you can selectively bleach off a particular part of the image and thus create a true washday miracle.

Found Sound. With a Q-Tip you can selectively bleach off all the frames and substitute in their place new visual elements to go with the preexisting sound track.

New Tracks. You can try to bleach off just the sound track and then add your own hand-drawn sounds to fit the movement of the existing footage. Remember the 26-frame advance.

2.20   16MM OPTICAL MASTER:
Reproduced at full size, this strip of 16mm optical master shows a "boop-booped" melody. Remember that a hand-drawn image *follows* 26 frames behind its appropriate sound on the track.

Project: Old Flicks/New Mix. Project some film you've located with the objective of finding short sequences to alter and play with. The preceding list of possibilities should help you in locating a "promising" sequence or two. After you've selected a potential sequence, cut it out of the longer film, add head and tail leader, and project it a number of times so that you are really familiar with the material (see Chapter 18). Then to go work. Give the old message new meanings. Such a recycling of found materials is one of the traditional approaches to parody and satire.

Drawing to an Original Optical Track

As noted earlier, the optical track that you find on "real" movies is made through a laboratory process that begins with sounds that have been recorded on standard cassette or ¼-inch audio tape. Normally, the human eye cannot "read" an optical track. The squiggles do not obviously reflect the sounds they represent. You can't see the difference between a dialogue track and a music track, much less sort them apart just by looking at the edge of the film. But if you record a sound track that has only a single sound source, and if you leave pauses between parts of the track, it then becomes quite easy for the eye to observe both where specific sounds occur and how long they last.

Project: Boop-Boop Movies. Tape-record onto a ¼-inch, reel-to-reel audio recorder a very simple sound track. Be sure that each note or each sound is separated from the preceding and following ones by a short interval of silence. For example, a simple percussion piece or a short melody that is "boop-booped" provides tracks that will be easily read in the optical stage.

Take the finished tape to a film laboratory and ask to have it transferred to an *optical master track* (see Chapter 19). What you will get back is a piece of clear film with your sound track registered along the edge. Because you are already familiar with the sound track (you created and recorded it, after all), you should have no difficulty in identifying the beginning sound, which will appear as a squiggle arising out of a thin, white line that is always present down the center of the space on the film's edge (Figure 2.21). From the first identified sound, you should be able to locate all other sounds you have recorded.

You may find it helpful to begin your tape with three quick taps on the microphone with a pencil. The optical image of this sequence can leave no doubt about where the piece begins. Remember the 26-frame advance when you create images to accompany your sound track.

Double Printing

The major activity of a motion picture laboratory is the developing and printing of film footage that has been exposed by the filmmaker. There is a simple and effective way of halving the number of images

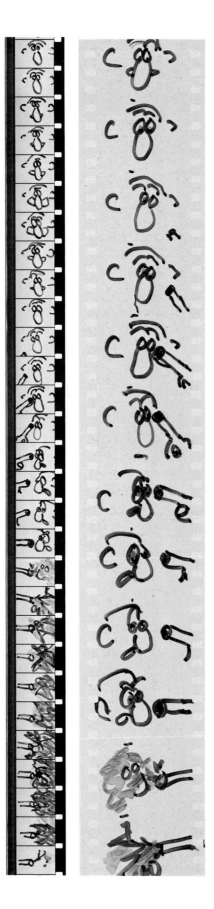

necessary to create animated movies if you have the laboratory print from a piece of leader you've worked on in a special way.

Scratch off and then hand-color a piece of 16mm black leader in the normal way, except that in this case work only on every other frame. When you take your finished film to the lab, ask the technician to print the film in the normal way and then print the entire movie a second time on the same piece of raw stock. In this second run-through, however, the printer must *advance* the original film precisely one frame in the optical printing machine. This means that every frame will be printed twice. It may surprise the lab personnel when you make this request, but they should quickly see why. Be sure to add that you do *not* want your original footage to be cleaned before it is printed. Cleaning an original is the standard procedure in many of the best film labs, and if it's done right, the process can wipe out all the drawing or coloring you've spent hours doing.

A special note of encouragement. The people who work in film laboratories are among the nicest and most patient you'll find anywhere in film. Even if you use laboratory services infrequently, take the time to get to know the person behind the desk. He or she can often explain to you why something isn't coming out the way you wanted it. The lab can also recommend a particular film stock or printing process that can save you hours of work. Lab personnel are terrific learning resources.

35MM Cameraless Filmmaking

Take a look at the piece of 35mm film printed in Figure 2.21. Next to all those 16mm frames you've been studying and working with, it will look pretty big. A gracious landscape indeed. Because it's so gloriously large (to the animator, at least) 35mm clear leader is the most effective and luxurious medium for creating drawn-on-film images and sound tracks. Anything that can be done on 16mm leader can be done better on 35mm leader because the larger size affords greater control, greater detail, and greater ease in drawing.

The primary developer and popularizer of hand-drawn films is the Canadian filmmaker Norman McLaren, who has worked for more than thirty years at the National Film Board of Canada. McLaren's wonderful movies are now commercially available (see Chapter 21), and prints of them exist in most school and public library film collections.

Because of the size of 35mm film, it is helpful to use an accurate registration system when you want to repeat or vary slightly an image from one frame to the next. Working carefully, you can draw a registration strip by hand, making a series of frames carry the same visual patterns and then placing a piece of fresh leader on top of the grid system as you work. A better system is to get hold of a piece of

2.21   35MM CAMERALESS ANIMATION: The size of a 35mm frame allows one to work with more detail than could be undertaken in 16mm format. Here are some samples of experiments by the author. The clips include a cartoon sequence drawn onto clear leader; designs scraped into the emulsion on black leader; abstract series of circular shapes on clear leader; drawings added to a "found" piece of film from a 35mm television commercial; a series of tracings from small photographs; and a 16mm reduction print taken from the same series of 35mm hand-drawn films.

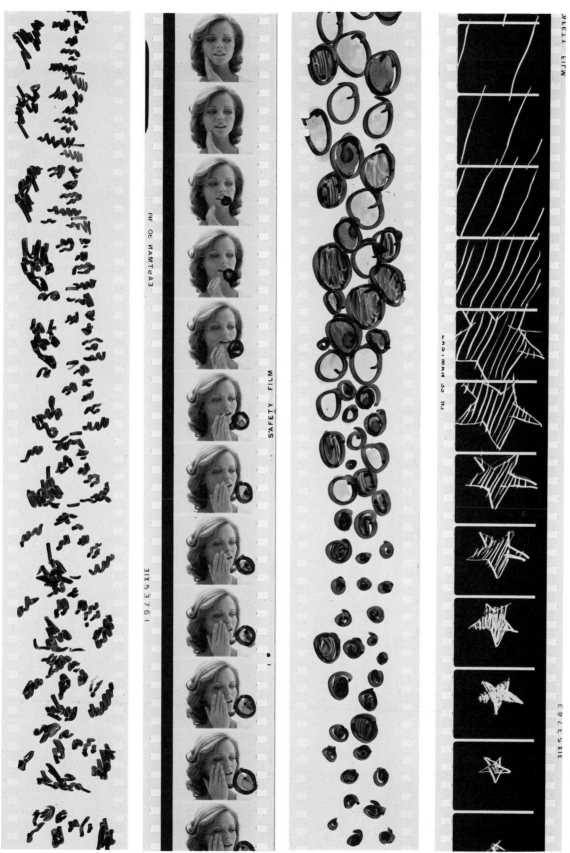

2.21

35mm film on which a grid has already been filmed. You can use any piece of used 35mm film (see Chapter 23) with whatever image exists as a registration guide.

The use of 35mm clear leader makes it far easier to create and control a handmade sound track. Here is Norman McLaren's own description of the technique he invented:

"I draw a lot of little lines on the sound-track area of the 35mm film. Maybe 50 to 60 lines for every musical note. The number of strokes to the inch controls the pitch of the note: the more, the higher the pitch; the fewer, the lower is the pitch. The size of the stroke controls the loudness: a big stroke will go 'boom,' a smaller stroke will give a quieter sound, and the faintest stroke will be just a little 'm-m-m.' A black ink is another way of making a loud sound, a mid-gray ink will make a medium sound, and a very pale ink will make a very quiet sound. The tone quality, which is the most difficult element to control, is made by the shape of the strokes. Well-rounded forms give smooth sounds; sharper or angular forms give harder, harsher sounds. Sometimes I use a brush instead of a pen to get very soft sound. By drawing or exposing two or more patterns on the same bit of film, I can create harmony and textural effects."

A

In order to project cameraless 35mm film it is necessary to have it *optically reduced* by a laboratory to a 16mm format. And 16mm can even be reduced to a super 8mm format, assuming, of course, that you don't have access to a 35mm projector—the kind of jumbo machine that you see in commercial movie theaters.

Reducing the film is a relatively simple process but requires a laboratory with special facilities. Be certain to check with your lab before you undertake a 35mm project. You may need to send your finished film to a lab that specializes in such work. Chapter 22 contains a list of such laboratories.

B

2.22 NORMAN McLAREN'S WORK: Although other artists had worked directly on film before him, Norman McLaren is recognized as the primary explorer, refiner, and popularizer of cameraless animation techniques. This series of stills shows his work and that of Evelyn Lambert, a colleague at the National Film Board of Canada. *A* shows McLaren painting directly onto a strip of 35mm clear leader; *B* shows Lambert applying patterns to the film's surface with ink and roller; *C* and *D* show frame enlargements from *Begone Dull Care,* a clear and opaque frame respectively. *Courtesy National Film Board of Canada.*

C

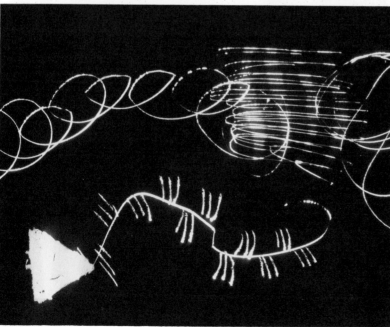

D

3
Tooling Up

A general introduction to filmmaking equipment is all that remains to be gone over before you're ready to begin animated filmmaking. This chapter will do just that, and quickly.

To get things under way properly, I'll first preview the basic hardware that you will need in doing almost all of the techniques described in the chapters to come. The goal here, however, is only to orient the reader. A far more comprehensive and detailed description of equipment will be found in Chapters 15 through 18. As mentioned earlier, I encourage you to flip forward in this book whenever you have a specific technical question or need further information about a particular tool or whenever you are just plain curious to know more.

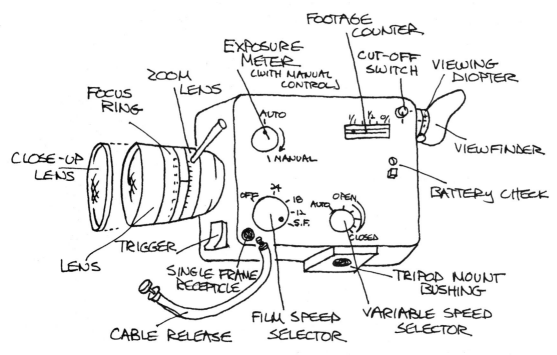

3.1   THE BASIC CAMERA: Whether you film with super 8mm or with 16mm equipment, the features indicated here are all basic to animated filmmaking.

The Basic Setup

Camera. A motion picture camera must have two features before you can animate with it. First, it must have the capability to make single-frame exposures, usually done by means of a cable release, a device that screws into the camera's trigger and allows the operator to release one frame at a time, as opposed to shooting the camera at full, live-action speed. An animation camera must also have a lens that can be focused on a relatively small field; 8½ by 10 inches is a working minimum, although some techniques will not require a field this small. Usually all motion picture camera lenses will take an auxiliary closeup lens or a diopter. These gadgets screw into place in front of the standard lens and act as magnifying agents. Figure 3.1 identifies these and other features of the basic camera.

Whether you work in super 8mm or 16mm format, your motion picture camera should have an exposure setting, worked either manually with the assistance of a light meter or by means of an automatic, built-in exposure metering system. Most super 8mm cameras have the automatic system. It's also helpful if the camera you use has a manual override, which allows you to set the lens opening or aperture by yourself. Other common features are a footage counter, a drive mechanism with a spring or battery-powered motor, and a variable speed setting.

Zoom lenses are almost standard on today's inexpensive movie cameras. Having one built-in or being able to mount a zoom on your camera will be helpful for various techniques in animation, although it's not essential. There are other special features and accessories, such as intervalometers, fade and dissolve mechanisms, variable shutters, frame counters, and backwind mechanisms that are nice to have, but they're gravy.

Tripods and Animation Stands. Common to every technique of animation is this inflexible requirement: The camera must be held in exactly the same position throughout the filming of a sequence. Great energies and endless gadgetry have gone into designing ways to hold a camera steady.

The simplest way of securing a camera is with a *tripod*. Generally, the bigger and stronger (and more expensive), the better. A good tripod will get you through every single filming requirement in this book. Beyond its requisite firmness, a tripod's best feature is its flexibility. Figure 3.2 shows three of the many positions in which a tripod holds an animation camera.

Animation stands are actually just sophisticated and specialized variations of tripods. Stands are less flexible but allow more precision and control in what is the most common camera position, pointing down onto a surface. Chapter 16 contains information on animation stands and their various features.

Lighting and Film. Animation almost always takes place indoors and thus requires artificial lighting. The precise kind of lighting depends on the kind of film stock that is being used. Most animators choose to use color film that is formulated for "indoor" or "tungsten" lighting conditions. There are many types of color (and black-and-white) films and each will require different degrees of brightness and different measurements of what is called color temperature. More on all this later. For now, however, you need to secure a light or set of lights that match the requirements you'll find printed on the film stock you select. Generally, you can fulfill these requirements by using photoflood bulbs—inexpensive bulbs that are very bright, have the required color temperature, and can be used in inexpensive and easy to mount reflectors with screw-in sockets. In most forms of animation, lights are mounted 45 degrees to the plane of the artwork being filmed. This positioning causes reflections from the photographed area to pass by the camera's lens. Most often two lights (both mounted at 45-degree angles) are used to insure even illumination of the filmed surface (Figure 3.3).

Other Paraphernalia. The basic equipment for making animated films has been covered: camera, tripod or stand, film and lights. But to see what you've filmed, a few additional items are required. Most

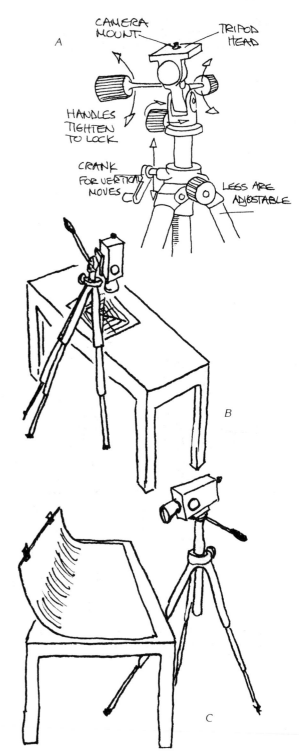

3.2 TRIPOD CAPABILITIES AND STANDARD POSITIONS: The only absolute requirement of a tripod is that it be able to hold the camera absolutely motionless during and between exposures. Line drawing *A* shows the directions in which a good tripod head should be adjustable. Drawings *B* and *C* suggests very different but commonly used positions for the camera-mounted tripod during filming.

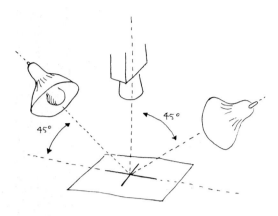

3.3 BASIC LIGHTING: For even illumination when shooting indoors, a pair of lights are mounted at a 45-degree angle to the camera's axis and to the surface being filmed. Pictured in this sketch are two photoflood bulbs that have been mounted in standard metal reflectors.

important (and expensive) of these is a motion picture projector. It's nice, of course, if you are able to project the completed film onto a screen, but this isn't really necessary. A white wall will do. Again, it's nice but not essential to record and then play back a sound track that accompanies the animated film.

If you want to edit your film or join two rolls of processed film onto a single reel, then a viewer and a splicer are required. Because each animation technique utilizes unique materials, I'll save discussion of them for the appropriate chapters.

Production Formats

As an independent animator, you have a choice of two production formats: 16mm and super 8mm. The following will provide you with a basic analysis of the similarities and differences between them. Incidentally, the word "format" is given a broad meaning here. It includes the film stock, film equipment, and even the process of filmmaking. In other words, format is an entire *system* for filmmaking. Selecting one of these two production systems is one of the most important decisions you will have to make.

Film Gauge. This refers to the actual physical makeup of what goes through the camera—the film stock. Paragraphs of discursive prose won't provide as clear a definition as you'll get by a quick look at Figure 22.1. Study the differences in width, perforations, image area, and sound-track area.

Width. The fundamental difference between formats is the *width* of the film stock. Super 8mm is half as large as 16mm. Sometimes it's easy to forget the obvious, and scale itself dictates much about a particular format's characteristics. The larger the area of film, the sharper the resolution of the image (given equal grain and projected image size). The larger the area of film, the faster the stock must move through the projection gate and, hence, the better the sound quality. The larger the area of film, the bigger the hardware that handles it, and the larger the equipment, the more expensive it will be. Finally, the larger the gauge, the easier it is to physically handle the film during the editing process.

Image Area. The actual projected *image area* on 16mm film has three and a half times as much area within a single frame as that of the super 8mm image. The proportions of the frame's rectangle are the same in both gauges—horizontal to vertical dimensions form a proportion of roughly 4 to 3. This is called the *aspect ratio* and it is usually written 1.33:1.

Cost. Sixteen mm stock is three to four times more expensive than the same screen time of super 8mm stock. In animation, however, the *cost* of film stock is less significant in overall budget terms than in live-action forms of filmmaking. Even the most prolific animator shoots a lot less film than his or her live-action counterpart. A standard shooting ratio of exposed footage to footage in a final edited film is something like 15 or 20 to 1 for documentary films and more like 2 to 1 for animation. Comparing costs of animated and live-action filmmaking is tricky, however. The expenses of preparing artwork, for example, may be far more than the live-action costs for what the camera films.

Quality. It's not easy to compare the *quality* of super 8mm and

16mm gauges because it's not easy to decide exactly what quality is. According to technical definitions that measure grain, sharpness, and color accuracy, 16mm is always of a better quality than its super 8mm equivalent. But to the naked eye, the quality of gauges is very difficult to measure. A well-projected and well-exposed super 8mm sequence is virtually indistinguishable from a 16mm image.

Selection of Films. Information on different kinds of film stock is provided in Chapter 19. In general, there is little difference between super 8mm and 16mm formats. The high-resolution and low-speed stocks that are best for animated filmmaking are available in both formats.

Equipment Systems. Up until the last few years, it would have been easy to claim that the 16mm format had a clear advantage over super 8mm in terms of sophistication and the technical quality of production tools. This is no longer true. The design, the workmanship, and the reliability of the best super 8mm filmmaking systems equals that of 16mm systems. This goes right down the line, from cameras to tripods to editors to sound systems to projectors to laboratory services.

Lenny Lipton, author of two highly recommended volumes on the technical characteristics and processes of filmmaking, has estimated that, by the time one adds up the greater cost of 16mm equipment, stock costs, and sound, one minute of 16mm color sound film is as expensive as a half hour of super 8mm color sound film. These figures may be inaccurate for the process of animation, but they are accurate enough to illustrate the considerable cost differential between working in super 8mm and 16mm formats.

In terms of entire systems for filmmaking, the most significant difference between formats has to do with the duplication and distribution of finished films. More on this later.

How to Choose a Format

If all beginning animators were forced to select between super 8mm or 16mm production, they'd face a confusing barrage of offsetting factors, different recommendations, and antithetical analyses of how and where and why to start. Fortunately, few neophyte animators ever face such a decision. For most independent animators it's not *which* format to go with but rather *how* to get going at all. Polemics are replaced with pragmatics. You use what you can afford and what you can get your hands on.

If you are faced with the decision of whether to work in 16mm or super 8mm format, use and trust your own common sense. Ask yourself the following questions.

What is available? If you already have some filmmaking equipment, you should certainly try to build your exploration of animation around it. Access to tools is a more important factor. Can you borrow a camera? Can you find a projector?

How much do you want to spend? Money matters. Take a cold, hard look at what you can comfortably invest in animated filmmaking. Part Three: Tools should help you to develop a rough working budget for whatever kind of film you have in mind. And there is more instruction on budgeting later in Chapter 14.

What kind of filmmaking will you be doing? Sometimes a

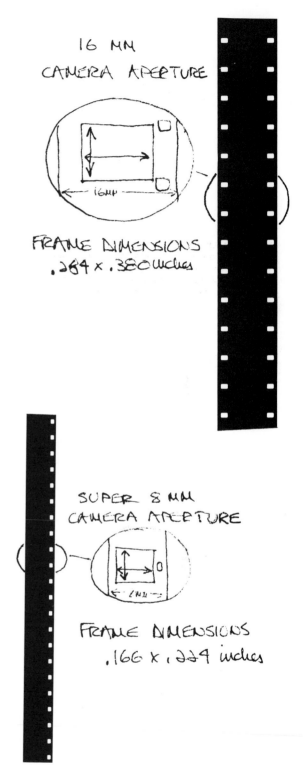

3.4 FILM GAUGE: The relative sizes of 16mm and super 8mm film are easily compared by lining up a strip of each format. The line drawings suggest the detail of the formats and give precise measurements for each.

A frame from *The Doodlers* by Kathy Rose. *Courtesy of the Serious Business Company.*

decision on format can be made by considering the alternate uses you'll want to make of your filmmaking gear. If it's only animation you are interested in, for example, an old-fashioned 16mm camera might suit your needs. On the other hand, if you know that you'll also want to use your camera for taking movies of family and friends, then the super 8mm might be a lot more versatile for your needs.

How deep is your commitment? You alone will be able to judge the level of commitment you want to bring to animation. Obviously this should be a factor in your decisions. If, for example, you know you're interested in animation as a hobby and avocation, then you might want to limit financial commitments to allow for other interests. If you intend to produce movies for commercial sale, you should consider working in 16mm format. Another consideration—artwork used in a super 8mm format can always be reshot in 16mm or even 35mm format if the super 8mm has really worked out well.

What animation techniques interest you most? The preceding sections have indicated distinctive requirements for different production techniques. In selecting a format, your experimentations and preferences will guide you. If you are interested in kinestasis techniques, for example, you'll probably want a super 8mm or 16mm camera that has capabilities for in-camera effects.

Who will be seeing your films? In today's marketplace the broad distribution of films is done through the 16mm format. Hence, if you intend to sell prints or place your movie into distribution by a commercial orgainzation, you should seriously consider working in 16mm format. Remember, however, it is possible to blow up super 8mm films to 16mm format. Also there is an increasing use of video cassettes to distribute film-based materials. Super 8mm and 16mm can both be transferred to various video-tape formats. In any television format there is certainly no difference in image quality between what began as either a 16mm or super 8mm production.

Can you identify special technical requirements? Let's say you want to do frame-by-frame synchronization of the audio track with the film's imagery. To do this well and easily, you must work in 16mm format. On the other hand, if you know that, at best, you'll want an unsynchronized track accompanying your animated films, then you should probably go with super 8mm sound systems or perhaps silent super 8mm technology.

Starting Out

I am a strong believer in inductive learning. I trust experience. All the questions and decisions that will face you as an animator are best taken on at that precise moment when the questions spontaneously present themselves, and not before. What is important is to get oneself under way, to begin working in animation. After that, matters take care of themselves as one tool or technique leads to another.

Whether your next step is to scrounge or borrow a basic animation setup, or whether you already own all the equipment you need to get started, it's my hope that you are now prepared to actually make some films, to explore techniques, to get deeper into animation. Your orientation is complete. The following eleven chapters stand ready to help you on your way.

PART TWO: TECHNIQUES

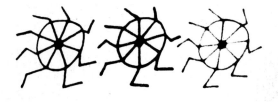

There are just about as many animation techniques as there are animators. A complete listing is impossible. Refinements and variations are being invented even as you read these words. In fact, someday you may well find yourself a contributor to the expanding universe of animation techniques. Before plunging into the next eleven chapters, I think it will help to know the criteria that have been used in identifying and describing the techniques of film animation.

Achievement itself is one criterion. Sand animation is a good example of this. This is a recent addition to recognized animation techniques, and it is included here because a few brilliantly conceived and widely acclaimed films have been made with sand. If you've seen any of the outstanding works by Caroline Leaf, you'll understand why sand is considered its own technique.

Another criterion has to do with what contemporary animators regard as currently interesting or significant. Collage animation, for example, is really just a variety of cutout animation. But the phrase itself is in such wide usage that the category has assumed its own validity. Such judgments are subjective and change with time. Pin-screen technique was in vogue some years back, but it's not singled out for special treatment because it is rarely done today and because it requires specially designed hardware.

Some techniques proclaim themselves because of a distinctive application. Pixilation is a perfect example. Pixilation is very similar to the technique of animating small objects. But pixilation's distinctive application is that it animates people. That's its raison d'être. It helps too that there have been outstanding achievements in this technique and that the phrase has become familiar.

Ways of using tools and even the tools themselves can sometimes provide the criteria for distinct animation genres. Rotoscoping is a technique that takes its name from a very fancy and specialized technological process. Computer techniques are now being employed in animation and they will undoubtedly yield a number of new techniques as the technology becomes more accessible.

In one way or another, however, most techniques are categorized as they are because of the materials they employ. This is true with cutout animation, clay animation, puppet animation, paint-on-glass animation, and cel animation.

Whereas most of the following chapters discuss techniques there are three that approach animation techniques from a different perspective. The chapters on working with sound, storyboarding, and production planning each deal with a set of problems encountered in any animation project.

As you study the various techniques in the following chapters, I hope they'll become much more than mere titles and categories, and that you will appreciate that the boundaries between techniques are arbitrary, that they are simply conventions. As you move toward real exploration and refinement in your own work, disregard all such schemata. It is in breaking out of the established categories that the best new forms of expression are found.

4
Animating Objects

Above all, animation is the art of *movement*. The accomplished animator can bring to life just about anything—a series of drawings or a tin can. Unfortunately, there are no prescriptions or formulas for animating an object. You just have to develop a feel for movement—what animators call "touch." It can be learned only through experience, despite the fact that there are some general guidelines that will help you along. One of the quickest and easiest ways to develop your understanding of the nature of animated movement is to experiment by filming a series of small objects.

Materials

It is an indication of the medium's power that even the most prosaic and ubiquitous of household items can be employed to create interesting films, films that move an audience in emotional and conceptual terms. And you can do this with anything—with pipe cleaners, pencils, pennies, pop-tops, pajamas, plates, penknives, pansies, peas, pills, and pins. With multiple sets of the same small objects, an exploration of geometric designs can become the focus of a short film. Or stories can be created. Or, if you're very good, small-object animation can delve into significant themes and topics—panic, pillage, phobia, puberty, pain, paranoia, and platonic love.

Setting Up

The object or objects that you decide to animate will dictate the setup required in filming them. Usually, however, the animation of small objects is accomplished by mounting the camera on a tripod and by carefully determining and controlling the area in which the filming will take place. A typical arrangement is illustrated in Figure 4.2.

The heart of animation, as we've been saying, is movement. Anything that detracts the viewer's attention from what is being animated works against the movie. For this reason, backgrounds in all forms of animation tend to be simple, nondistracting, and absolutely rock steady. Certainly this is true in animating objects. If the placement of the camera is to be vertical, that is, pointing down at the surface to be photographed, then a solid-colored piece of paper can rest underneath the objects themselves. Naturally, the color of this background should emphasize the objects on top of it. In some cases the camera will be mounted in a horizontal position and pointed toward what amounts to a small stage with both floor and backdrop. In this case, seamless art paper forms an effective background material that has no edges or structural details that can detract attention from the animation. Such backgrounds appear to recede into a depthless void. This kind of setup is called a diorama.

A

B

4.1 MATERIALS: That just about anything can be animated is illustrated by these two frame enlargements. In *Bags*, by Tradeusz Wilkosz, simple household objects plus a bag create a drama of aggression (A). Simple cookies with drawn heads constitute all the players in Frenc Varsanyi's *Honeymation (B)*. The films were produced in Czechoslovakia and Hungary respectively. Eastern European animators have developed strong traditions in animating objects and puppets. *Courtesy Pyramid Films.*

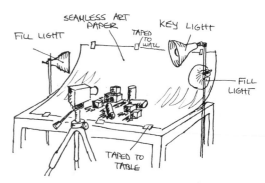

4.2 DIORAMA SETUP: The illustration suggests a common setup for animating small objects. Many lighting combinations are possible. Here a *key* light focuses on the objects while two *fill* lights illuminate the background. The use of seamless art paper, available at art stores, creates the illusion of a "limitless" background.

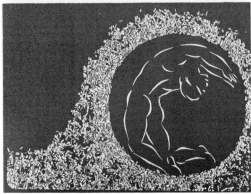

4.3 OVERHEAD SETUP: Canadian Laurent Coderre is shown working with tiny chips of wood in his film *Zikkaron.* Note the simplicity of the setup: a motionless camera held over a sheet of black matte board. *Courtesy National Film Board of Canada.*

A few words about lighting. Although different objects will present unique lighting problems, generally a form of "flat" lighting is used that minimizes the existence of strong shadows that overpower the movement of the object being animated. This is achieved by the use of at least two light sources. The illumination of one tends to eliminate the shadows caused by the other. Sometimes, however, lighting must be used more dramatically. For instance, it may be important to create a bright background against which the objects will stand out clearly. A controlled absence of lighting can create a similar effect. In this case the lights are focused only on the objects being filmed, while a black background, unlit, provides contrast for the animation itself.

Movement

Let's say that you've got a camera, loaded it with film, placed it on a tripod, surrounded it with lights, and pointed it down at the surface of a table. In your pocket there is a handful of loose change.

How can you make that money move? When is something moving too fast for the eye to follow? Is it possible to imbue objects with recognizably human kinds of movement? You'll have to find out the answers to such questions by your own experimentation. Here are some general parameters.

How Many Frames? The most thorough way of animating an object is to take a single photograph of it (expose one frame of movie film), then alter the object's position slightly and expose another frame. The camera and background must not move during this frame-by-frame shooting process. It is the absolute steadiness of the background and camera angle that permits us to perceive the illusion of movement brought about by incremental changes in the object's position. During projection of the film, the tiny incremental changes pile on top of each other and the persistence of vision effect lets us experience the illusion of movement on the screen. Changing the position of an object before each exposure requires 24 separate movements (and a corresponding number of clicks of the camera's shutter) in order to make one second of film. As mentioned earlier, 24 frames per second is the "standard" projector speed in filmmaking.

Fortunately, "smooth" movement can still be perceived when two exposures are snapped before changing the position of the object. This lets the animator create the same quality of movement in the same amount of screen time by making half the number of changes in the object's position. This process is called shooting-on-twos or, simply, *shooting twos.* It is a basic element of animation technique. Unless there is a special reason why single exposures must be made, animators will always photograph two frames before altering the thing that is being animated. After all, this saves half the work, and the visual results of shooting-on-twos or shooting-on-ones, as seen in the projected film, are not significantly different. So unless otherwise stated, *it is always assumed that filming will be done by shooting-on-twos.* This holds for every animation technique. The habit of clicking two frames at a time will become second nature.

Sometimes, however, it is possible and desirable to shoot-on-threes or -fours or even -fives. Extending the number of exposures for each position will cause a flickering or jumpy quality to the movement. The larger the number of exposures between movements, the greater the "visual stutter." But smoothness is not always appropriate. You may want to have objects moving in a jerky, high-energy fashion. You may find that radical shifts between the number of exposures and the direction of movement will provide just the quality you want. There is only one way to learn the different effects caused by exposing a different number of frames. You must experiment.

What Distance? What Speed? Because projection speed is a constant, the greater the physical distance you move an object between exposures, the faster it will appear to move. The less you vary positions, the more slowly and smoothly an object will appear to move when the film is projected.

Note that movement is always perceived relative to something else—usually the background or the frame of the image itself. "Relative" or "apparent" speed is worth elaboration. Figure 4.4 illustrates how to make an object move quickly or slowly. The example also shows the same size object within 2 frames of different sizes. Even if the actual physical movement between exposures is constant—say a quarter of an inch—the chess piece in the smaller frame will appear to move more slowly than it does in the larger one.

There is no limit to how smoothly or slowly you can animate an object. There is, however, a perceptual limitation on the maximum rate of movement you can use. If the object is placed in a position that does not permit it to at least partially overlap or touch its preceding position, its motion may appear to "flutter" when the film is projected. Figure 4.5 shows this problem of visual continuity.

Movement and Style. Here's where the real fun begins. In the final analysis, the effectiveness of animation is not simply a matter of how far or what number of frames a movement commands. What's more important by far is the *way* it moves and the *feelings* that this movement is able to evoke. Animation is really the art of making things move *with style.* And the common gift of all great animators has been an ability to observe and then re-create movement in ways that resonate deeply within all of us. To the good animator, movement becomes a concrete material. It is a material that has color, portrays mood and motivation, and is textured with overtones of human passion and human meaning.

Project: 15 Pennies and 15 Seconds. As a warm-up exercise, set up your camera so that it looks down on a horizontal field about the size of a standard piece of notebook paper. Get hold of 15 pennies and make a film that is exactly 15 seconds long. In your film, try the following experiments. Use the first 5 seconds (that is, 120 individual frames or 60 individual movements, each being exposed twice) to get all the pennies onto the field. Use the second 5 seconds to have all the pennies moving together in some way. Use the final 5 seconds to have different numbers of pennies moving under the camera at different speeds; that is, one cluster of pennies should move very quickly, another more slowly, and another just fast enough so that the viewer can see them moving. Find ways to make smooth transitions between each of the preceding sections of the film.

Project: 15 Pennies vs. 5 Nickels. The problem here will be to use movement as the sole means of embuing coins with a degree of significance far beyond their usual meaning. Create a short film that

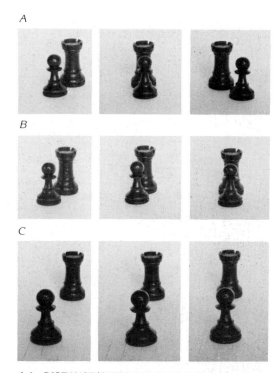

4.4 DISTANCE/SPEED RELATIONSHIPS: This series of photographs tries to suggest two aspects of relative movement upon the screen. Moving the same *real* distance, the pawn appears to move more quickly when it is passing a stationary castle *(A)* than when it passes a castle that is also moving, although not at the same rate *(B).* The proximity of the pawn to the camera in the third series *(C)* will cause it to appear to be moving faster than in the first series despite the fact that in both the pawn is covering an identical distance in real space.

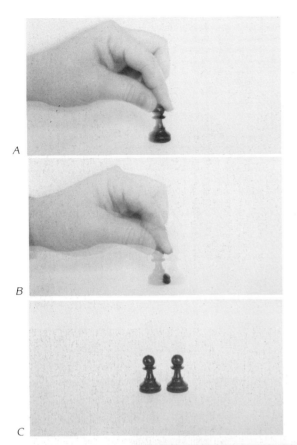

A

B

C

develops two unique characters, or groups of characters, and place these characters within a story that has an identifiable theme.

As you undertake this project, remember that it is only through movement that you will be able to give either the nickels or the pennies their own unique personality. It is often good to first decide the kinds of characteristic movement you can use to show contrasting personalities or emotions. From this, you ought to be able to make up a simple story, one that has a single dramatic conflict. As physical movement should lead to dramatic movement, so the story should lead to a theme, a recognizable, universal truth that will move your audience.

4.5 FLUTTER: A photograph shot with a long exposure time *(A)* suggests a very small change between an initial and a final position. If the first and last positions were shot on an animation camera (one wouldn't see the hand moving the piece), then the movement would appear very smooth and very slow. Photograph *B* suggests a larger change in position. This would be perceived as a faster movement if the first and second positions were filmed with an animation camera. Note the overlap of position—the dark area. Because of this overlap, the motion on the screen will appear smooth. Two stationary pawns *(C)* suggest a degree of change between the first and second positions that would create a "flutter," or "strobe," effect.

4.6 ANIMATING BEADS: Four frames from Ishu Patel's *Beadgame* suggest a more sophisticated style of animating small objects. Here tiny plastic beads, the kind used in beaded belts and costumes, become the medium creating complex transformations of line and color. The "ray" effect in photos *B* and *C* was created with a computer controlled movement of the camera while the shutter is opened on successive single frame exposures. *Beadgame* is the product of a highly sophisticated camera and stand in the hands of a highly experienced animator. *Courtesy National Film Board of Canada.*

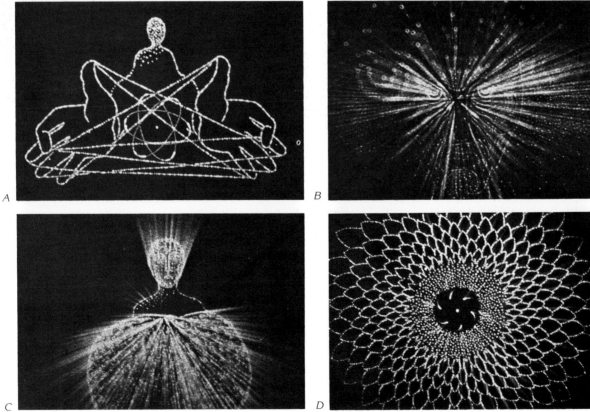

A

B

C

D

4.7   ANIMATING BLOCKS: *Tchou-Tchou* is a 14-minute adventure story featuring five characters that are created from children's blocks and inhabit a block world. In the film's climax, the hero and heroine *(A)* and a friendly bug *(B)* outsmart a ferocious dragon composed of a long row of blocks *(C)*. Animator Co Hoedeman and a colleague *(D)* help indicate the scale and complexity of this production's set. *Courtesy NFBC.*

5
Cutout and Silhouette Animation

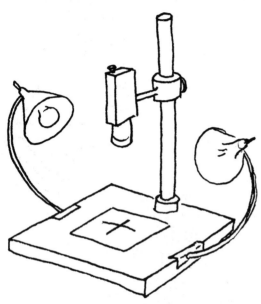

5.1 STANDARD SETUP: The camera is positioned directly above the background on which the cutout characters will be animated. A simple copy stand (as illustrated) or a tripod can easily hold the camera, and lights are mounted at both sides to provide even illumination.

Animation excels at telling stories, especially the kinds of stories that it is not possible to put on film using real actors and real locations. Fantasy landscapes and fantasy characters have dominated the growth of animation from its earliest days. Unfortunately, the full-cel techniques most often used by professional animators and commercial studios in developing such narrative films are time consuming and difficult for an individual animator to undertake. And so independent animators have invented "cutout" animation, a simplified form of cartooning that lets them work effectively with characters and stories.

Something is always lost when a simple technique replaces a complex one. So it is with cutouts. As you will see, the movements of the characters are restricted. Stories tend to be more concrete and simpler with this technique than with its full-animation counterpart. But the benefits outweigh the disadvantages. Cutout animation makes accessible to the individual filmmaker a broad and rich universe of creative possibilities. And it does so with simple techniques and inexpensive tools.

Stories

Cutouts work best with plots featuring lots of physical action that takes place on a broad scale. Conversely, it's difficult with cutouts to deal effectively with the nuances of story as revealed through the detailed movement of figures and backgrounds. An example will make the distinction clear. Say you have a story in which a character gets very angry at his parked car when a wheel falls off. In cutouts, the anger would have to be shown, for example, by having the character leap to the roof of the car and start jumping up and down on it. Cutout techniques would *not* be effective, for instance, in showing a slow flush building in the character's face or in catching a subtle kind of rage that builds in the character as he glares at his vehicle.

The natural bias of cutout techniques is toward broad action. Keep this in mind when selecting stories to work with. As with all kinds of animation, the limits and the unique characteristics of a particular technique are most often bound up in the materials that are used. This will become clearer as you begin to prepare the characters and background of your first cutout film.

Characters

As its name suggests, cutout animation is achieved by moving figures that have been drawn on a piece of paper and then cut out. The force of gravity (and a glass pressure plate, or *platen*) holds these figures flat against the background or "scene." The animator's own hand moves the cutout pieces across the scene. Positioned overhead, the animation camera clicks off two exposures between each movement. A typical cutout animation setup is illustrated in Figure 5.1.

Quite obviously, this technique saves the animator a great deal of work, since he can use one drawing again and again. But this also means that the figures themselves cannot be changed. This apparent dilemma is solved by the process of *jointing*. Depending on what a character will be doing in the story (and depending on the animator's patience), each cutout is designed so that it has some movable parts: arms, legs, hands, a head, and even some facial expressions.

There are three common ways of connecting the moving parts of a cutout character or object:

Thread and Tape. A piece of thread is attached with masking tape to the reverse side of each separate piece of paper. The thread keeps the pieces aligned and still allows them to move. The closer the thread is attached to the moving parts of the body, the easier it is to work the characters under the camera.

Metal Fasteners. A small metal fastener can be used to connect various portions of a character. Such clips are very effective and hold up well in use. But the connecting mechanism can be seen by the camera. In some films this matters, in some it does not. The choice is aesthetic.

Gravity. Plain old gravity can be used to keep one part of a figure aligned with another part. This is the easiest way to design characters, but you may find them difficult to manipulate because each part has to be moved individually during shooting.

There are times when the gravity method is the only way to go. It makes no sense, for example, to connect an eyeball with the eye socket in which it rests. The *overlay* is a generic term that refers to a series of separate cutouts that are used at different times within the same character or object.

Even in cutout animation you'll encounter situations where you will need to create a different version of the same character. Such moments occur when a character's physical appearance must change drastically for dramatic effect (for example, being scared suddenly) or when it is impossible for your cutout to accommodate a new body position that a character is forced to assume; for example, when a character stops walking across the scene and turns to face the camera.

Sometimes, too, you will need to draw and cut out a detail of your character that will subsequently be filmed as a closeup shot; when, for example, it is necessary to show an extreme close-up of a bug crawling on someone's nose, or a hand that is holding a bottle of poison, or a foot slipping on a banana peel.

In designing cutout characters, always keep in mind what your story requires a particular character to do physically. What sort of personality do you wish to create? Your story itself should help in determining where and how to use jointings, overlays, and close-ups.

Working Scale and Paper Stock

Cutouts should always be made to a relatively large physical scale. By using a 12- by 16-inch field, or larger, you can make characters

5.2   JOINTING: As this character walks, its arms and legs will move. The composite figure *A* is actually composed of four separate cutouts, as indicated in *B*. These movable parts can be fastened to the body by means of a piece of thread sewn through the cutout's body. The ends of the thread are then anchored with masking tape at the appropriate places on the reverse sides of both jointed elements *(C)*. Another joining technique uses metal fasteners that are punched through the cutouts and opened on the back side of the body section *(D)*.

A

B

5.3 OVERLAYS: This lopsided and toothy collection of mouths would give the creature in *A* a very wicked style of speaking. By placing the "explosion" overlay over the magician's hand in scene *B*, taking it out and putting it in again on successive pairs of frames and then overlaying the hand with the rabbit, an effective piece of magic can be achieved.

about 4 to 6 inches tall, with plenty of detail, and their moving parts will be easy to manipulate during filming. Furthermore, if you are filming with a camera that has a zoom lens, large-sized artwork allows you to zoom in for close-ups instead of having to create new drawings. Another tip: Stick with the same scale throughout your film. This way you can use the same characters within different scenes.

It makes things easier too if you draw your characters and overlays on heavyweight paper stock. This keeps the edges from curling, and the movable figures will last longer.

Backgrounds

While the location of a story is often an important element in a cartoon, it is best to wait until you have designed your characters and central props before you fashion the background on which they will move. One reason for this procedure is to insure that you end up with a background that is big enough for the cutouts you've made. But a more important reason has to do with design. You don't want to create a background that is so "busy" that your characters get lost in it. The exaggerated example in Figure 5.5 will help you to remember this point. One of the most common problems with cutout animation is the relationship of character and story to background scenes. It is important to balance all the graphic elements of your movie.

Make backgrounds simple. Use muted colors. Keep nonessential action to a minimum. It is always better to tend toward understatement in designing a background. Otherwise you risk upstaging your characters and the story they have to tell.

Don't, however, neglect the dramatic potential of the background either. And don't be afraid to cut into your background, literally. The two examples in Figure 5.6 show that sometimes you can use a cutout within the background to relay important information. A well-designed background can also solve key dramatic problems.

Special Effects

If necessity is the mother of invention, ingenuity is the father. The successful invention of a special technique to achieve a special effect is one of the greatest satisfactions an animator can have. So don't give up when your story calls for something to happen that seems impossible to achieve with cutout techniques. Improvise. To give you an idea of the difficulties that can be overcome, here are two ingenious inventions that have been rediscovered many times by independent animators.

The Stormy Day. Rain or snow is drawn or painted on a clear sheet of acetate and this is pulled across the background and characters as the camera is being used, a frame at a time. The effects of lightning are achieved by varying the positions and brightness of the filming lights. To show the effect of an earthquake, either the table holding the cutouts or the camera itself is given a healthy shake while film runs through the camera at live-action speeds.

20,000 Leagues Beneath the Sea. A glass tray filled with water is suspended between the camera and the artwork. The water is stirred with a fingertip before the shutter is released. You can also place a piece of blue acetate over the camera lens. Yet another alternative is to shoot

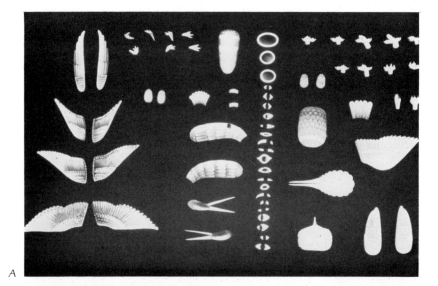

5.4 A CUTOUT PRODUCTION: These three photographs show the cutouts *(A)*, the working scale *(B)*, and a sample frame *(C)* from Evelyn Lambert's *Fine Feathers.* The animator herself is seen at work. A camera is positioned over her head and is activated by a foot switch. *Courtesy National Film Board of Canada.*

5.5 BACKGROUND DESIGN: Keep it simple.

the camera through the bottom of a colored glass jar. This has the effect of keeping part of the scene in focus and part out of focus as the jar is rotated during filming. A final possibility is to apply a series of greenish and bluish washes directly to the film after it has been shot and returned from the laboratory.

Sound Tracks. Just a reminder here that the Absolute Truth about creating sound tracks for your animated films is given in Chapter 7. Generally, the tracks for cutout films are created after the movie has been shot and edited completely.

Project: A Cutout Title Sequence. Make a 15-second film in which a single character (person, animal, object, or whatever) enters a black field and, in some appropriate way, produces the letters of your name, one at a time. This exercise will let you experiment in fashioning a character with movable parts, as well as teach you how to move the

5.6 BACKGROUNDS: Pulling down the single cutout (blind and hand) in *A* would provide a simple way to end a movie. Note that the windowpanes could be cut out so that the scene outside could be changed by simply sliding a different drawing under the window. The gum-ball machine background in *B* is slotted to allow the gum balls to tumble out of the black hole.

figure so that it has a characteristic personality. You will also learn to handle a series of nonjointed elements—in this case, the letters of your name.

Project: Park-Bench Scene. If you've already come up with an idea for a cutout film that you're burning to get on with, by all means do it. But if you want to try cutout techniques and haven't something specific in mind, here is a stock situation that is designed to provide plenty of creative possibilities. It's an open-ended situation containing lots of room for your own invention within each of the given elements. The scene is a park. You must use two different locations or backgrounds, and one of these must include a park bench on which your characters sit. The characters include one child, one old person, and one animal. The action involves a natural disaster—anything from a windstorm to an earthquake.

Felt Animation

Enough animated films have been made with felt to justify its coverage under cutout techniques. Both the texture of felt and its brilliant colors show up well under the camera. Felt techniques have been used most often in making simple story films for kids. "Cloth" animation is a variation on a variation. The techniques used in creating characters and moving them beneath the camera are the same for felt, cloth, and paper cutouts. But the character of the material adds special quality to the film because of how it looks and how it moves. For example, a king might be made of silk, while his serfs are made of burlap. This choice of materials would be symbolically accurate, but, best of all, the qualities of the different fabrics will themselves suggest unique styles of movement.

Silhouette Animation

There is a well-known group of animated films that have been made with the silhouette technique. This form of animation was pioneered by a German animator, Lotte Reiniger, during the 1940s. Ms. Reiniger is still actively working and teaching.

The great asset of silhouette animation is that any jointing of the characters is fully hidden from the viewer by the filming process. Characters may be intricately cut out and joined as in Figure 5.8. These are positioned on the top of a surface that is lighted from beneath. The contrast between the black cutouts and the brightly illuminated background easily camouflages jointings. Very effective representation-al movements can be created with this technique.

5.7 CUTOUT STYLES: For every general trend that one can observe within a particular technique, there are always plenty of contrary examples. The seven films sampled here make this point quite eloquently. All employ cutout techniques but each has a distinctive graphic style, and the last three don't have the kind of narrative structure that I've associated with cutout animation. The object lesson here is that it is always dangerous to generalize about art. The films cited are: *Cecily (A)* by Paula Reznickova—*courtesy Learning Corporation of America; Crocus (B)* by Suzan Pitt Kraning—*courtesy Serious Business Company; My Financial Career (C)* by Grant Munro and Gerald Potterson—*courtesy NFBC;* Our Lady of the Spheres (D) by Larry Jordan—*courtesy Serious Business Company; Shout It Out Alphabet Film (E)* by Lynn Smith—*courtesy Phoenix Films;* and *Spheres (F)* by Norman McLaren—*courtesy National Film Board of Canada.*

A

B

C

D

E

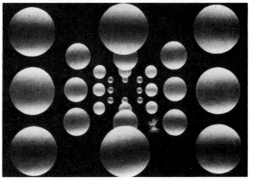

F

5.8 SILHOUETTE ANIMATION: The medieval love story of *Aucassin and Nicolette* has been animated with silhouette techniques by German animator Lotte Reiniger. The delicate characters are hand cut from black construction paper and have intricate moving parts. The design of the film and the construction of the cutout silhouette characters are similar to the techniques developed by Ms. Reiniger in 1923-1926 when she created *The Adventures of Prince Achmed*, the world's first full-length animated film. Two frames from *Aucassin and Nicolette* are shown in *A* and *B*. Produced recently at the National Film Board of Canada, the characters in the film are set against backgrounds of colored tissue paper and gels, lit from below a glass table and filmed from above, *C*. These simple techniques pioneered by Lotte Reiniger, *D* and *E*, are capable of tremendous detail and grace. *Courtesy National Film Board of Canada. Photo by Lois Siegel.*

Time Lapse and Pixilation

6.1 TIME LAPSE: In Derek Lamb's *Housemoving (A)*, a time-lapse technique records the disassembly, transportation, and relocation of an entire colonial home. Walerian Borowczyk's *Renaissance* shows the reconstitution of a room filled with mementos. The frame enlargement in *B* shows a photograph that is reconstructed in one sequence. Oskar Fischinger's *Motion Painting No. 1 (C)*, produced in 1949, presents the step-by-step evolution of an abstract painting. *Photo A courtesy Phoenix Films, B courtesy Pyramid Films, C courtesy The Museum of Modern Art Film Stills Archive.*

Our perception of the world and the things in it can be vastly extended through animation. Everyday processes that were once hidden from the naked eye are suddenly revealed as if by magic. Time-lapse animation lets us watch those progressive stages of evolution and change that normally occur over periods of time that are far too long for the eye to follow. Pixilation is a specialized technique that animates people in startling ways and also speeds up real time. But in pixilation the animator manipulates or directs what is happening in front of the camera and then produces special effects with a unique dramatic power. In this chapter we'll study both forms of magic.

Time-lapse Animation

In time-lapse animation every frame is exposed at a predetermined interval, which may range from a few moments to a few days. A familiar example will provide a handy definition of this technique. Out of a plot of earth we see a small green shoot grow and reach toward the sun. Within a few seconds of viewing time, this shoot becomes a plant with leaves. It continues growing. Then it buds and finally we witness the gentle explosion of a flower's blooming.

Essentially, the time-lapse technique alters our perceptions by collapsing time. This compression of the normal sequence of events will usually reveal either a process of generation or that of destruction. By thinking of this kind of animation in just these terms, and by seeing beyond the growing flower image, you will quickly find new and exciting possibilities. Here are a few.

Nature. The organic patterns clouds make as they sweep across the sky, the movement of shadows on a brick wall, the passing of a thunderstorm, the path of a snail, the arrival of a snowfall, the development of a chick embryo.

Man. Crowds of people moving in and out of buildings, the traffic patterns of a highway or an airport, the demolition of a house, the construction of a skyscraper.

Art. The development of an oil painting, the erosion of a sand sculpture, the decoration of a Christmas tree, the scribbling of graffiti upon a wall.

Many of the phenomena cited above have already become topics of films, and the experience of viewing any of these movies for the first time is pure revelation. Familiar things are discovered in startling new ways.

Intervals

The exact amount of time between exposures for time-lapse photography will depend upon the nature of the subject you select. For

6.2 WEEKS BECOME SECONDS: This series of key frames from *Organism* shows the demolition of an entire office building. In this film by Hilary Harris, time-lapse and pixilated sequences compare the flow of a city's life with that of the human body as seen through macrocinematography. *Courtesy Phoenix Films.*

example, filming the construction of a skyscraper might require just a few frames per day. Shooting could go on for months. On the other hand, it would take less overall time and smaller intervals between exposures if you wanted to catch the drama of a melting ice-cream cone.

Here's how to determine the interval you'll need. Begin by studying carefully the subject of your film. What is the movement or change you want to explore? Next, determine how much "real time" it takes for the action you've selected to complete itself. Now decide upon the best overall duration for your finished movie. This will be its "screen time." Because the projection rate of film is always constant (24 or 18 frames per second), you can now work out the correct interval between exposures. Multiply the *screen time in seconds* by the appropriate *projection speed.* The answer is the total *frame-count* for the finished movie. Calculate the *real time* of your subject in the smallest units of time that are practical (generally in seconds or in minutes). Divide the *real time* by the *frame-count.* The answer is the *interval between frames.*

An example will make this calculation process look less like a physicist's blackboard. Suppose you want to make an animated film about office workers streaming out of a building at the end of the workday. You visit the location and study the action (and select the best camera position), and you determine that most of the "action" takes place in a ten-minute period. In order to emphasize the "flushing" effect of the spectacle, you decide that the entire event ought to take place on the screen in just five seconds. You know you'll be projecting your film at 24 fps. Here are the computations:

step 1: 5 seconds × 24 fps = 120 frames
step 2: 10 minutes × 60 seconds = 600 seconds
step 3: 600 ÷ 120 = 5-second intervals

Setup

Camera Mount. Like all forms of animation, time-lapse techniques require a stationary camera. A solid tripod is generally used, although it's possible, with ingenuity, to mount a camera just about anywhere, even on the nose of a 747 in order to let the world see a transcontinental trip in only minutes.

Shutter Release. The actual exposure of each frame can be done either manually or by a specially designed motor called an *intervalometer.* If you are doing the filming by hand, you'll need a watch with a second hand and a cable release for your camera. With a motor, the shutter can be timed to trip at a predetermined interval. Some cameras include accessory gadgets that work as intervalometers. See Chapter 15 for more information about the hardware.

Exposure Level. One of the problems of filming over a long period of time is that the lighting of your subject is apt to change between the individually exposed frames. A built-in, through-the-lens light-metering system can help in keeping a relatively constant exposure value when filming outside. If you're working under lights, it's possible to get a timing device that will turn on your lights a few moments before the picture is taken and then turn them off. If you are dealing with a complicated lighting problem, be certain to do a thorough test before undertaking the entire filming. The color and temperature of the lights, as well as inconsistencies in the power sources you use, may, for example, give you additional problems and require voltage stabilizers.

Other Variables. Try running your film backward. By reversing the usual start to finish order, you can heighten the effect of your film. A flower can "run in terror" from an approaching blight by appearing to pull in its petals and shoot back into the earth. Try shooting out of focus on purpose. Shoot at night using a long exposure time for each frame. Shoot with the camera mounted in an unusual position. Shoot with different time intervals between frames, so that whatever you project will appear to be going faster and faster.

Project: Super Doodle. Set up your camera so that it looks over your shoulder at a blank page of paper. Using either a foot release, an intervalometer, or a friend, select a time interval of 3 seconds between exposures. Film for a period of 10 minutes. Begin doodling on the paper. Pay no attention to the clicking of the camera as you draw. Don't worry about arriving at a "finished" picture at the end of a given 10-minute period.

With a 3-second interval, your finished film will take about 8 seconds to project. Not only will you witness the evolution of the drawing, but the camera will also have recorded the motion of your hands and shoulders. With luck, you may be able to gain a fresh perspective on the style and energy with which you doodle.

Pixilation

Pixilation is a specialized technique for animating people. The camera records occasional frames of some "natural" or "real" event, but because of the intermittent filming, the effect in the resulting film is that of an "unnatural" movement somewhat like an old silent movie. What is impossible in real life becomes commonplace with pixilation.

In Europe the common expression for a cartoon is "trick-film." Pixilation is trick-film at its trickiest. And one of its best tricks is the way the term itself hides its own roots. I've been unable to locate even an unauthoritative explanation of how the term originated. But whatever that may be, and although the technique admittedly bears a close relationship to both time-lapse and small-object animation, the expressive function of pixilation is clear. The technique is almost always used for humor. And the effects one can create with it are absolutely astonishing.

In pixilation, a stationary camera records a stationary, posed subject, shooting-on-twos. Between exposures, the character in the film moves to a new position. The process takes patience and concentration. Sometimes great physical agility is needed. Because the subject is a living person, complete control of the pose is difficult, and this forces the animator to guesstimate much of the action. Trial and error rules pixilation.

Effects

What the technique lacks in precision, it makes up for in its sheer display. Here's a beginning catalogue of characteristic effects.

Locomotion. Pixilation permits weird ways of moving. A person

An enlarged strip from a student's 16mm film that includes both time-lapse and pixilation techniques.

C

D

E

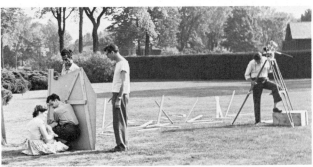

F

6.3 PIXILATION: Norman McLaren's Oscar-winning film *Neighbors* is credited with introducing the technique of pixilation in 1952. Described as the most eloquent plea for peace ever filmed, *Neighbors* shows how a neighborly misunderstanding escalates into genocide. The enlarged strips of 35mm film, *A, B, C,* show the positions that the two principal actors had to hold for the single frame exposures. The 360-degree sliding handshake soon turns into the 360-degree nose-to-nose staring battle. The duel with pieces of a picket fence, *C* marks the acceleration of hostilities during which both actors show grimmer faces with each sequence. *D* shows the final face worn by animator Grant Munro, who acted in the film. Interestingly, the movie's climax (in which wives and children are slaughtered) was cut from prints because the sequence's effect was so shocking to sensibilities of the time. Recently, however, the National Film Board of Canada has reinserted the original ending, *E.* The production still *F* shows the camera setup and the highly simple and stylized set. McLaren is wearing a white T-shirt. *Courtesy NFBC.*

can appear to transport himself by flight. This is achieved by having the subject jump into the air precisely as the camera clicks off a frame and repeating the action again and again. An individual may move like an automobile. Here the actor moves about on the ground but carefully assumes the same "driving" position during each shot, with hands holding an imaginary steering wheel and feet on an imaginary brake and an accelerator. There are endless variations: skidding, bouncing, floating, swimming, even flipping end over end.

Entrances and Exits. There are all sorts of tricks for entering or leaving the screen. People can come up out of the ground (a hat, clothing, and other props are required for the first few frames). They can appear through a wall. They can flash in and out of the picture; or they can just "pop" on and off.

Speed. Pixilation gives the effect of speeding up things. If a sidewalk crowd was filmed at 3 frames per second (instead of the usual 24 fps), the crowd would appear to be racing along in a jerky, old-time-movie style. The slower the rate of exposure, the faster the crowd will begin to move.

If you want to see just how fast you can make things go, point a camera out the front window of a car and expose a frame every couple of seconds as a friend drives you around town. Here is another special effect you might want to try. Have an actor walk with intentional "slow motion" within a crowd that is walking normally. With some experimentation, you can pixilate the scene so that the character will appear to move almost "normally" while others will appear hyperactive.

People with Objects. Coordinate an interplay of pixilation (animating people) and time-lapse or stop-action techniques (animating objects). The result will be animated bedlam: a vacuum cleaner swallows a housewife; a chair torments its owner; a necktie embarrasses an overly earnest suitor; a refrigerator produces the evening's meal automatically—then serves up the owner as the entrée.

Shooting

Here are some pointers for filming pixilated actions.

Continuity. Have someone do nothing more than make certain that each actor assumes a pose identical to his or her previous pose after relocating himself between shots. Precise registration is always a problem in pixilation. After all, it's not easy to hold an awkward position again and again as an animator laboriously builds a scene.

Camera Movement. The more frequently you take exposures, the less rigorously will you need to control the movement of the camera itself during shots, tilts, or zooms. As always, the steadier the camera, and the more accurately you can calibrate incremental changes, the better everything will work out. It is wise to use camera movement very sparingly.

Exposures. Pixilation is often done outdoors and the process of filming a scene can take long periods of time. This raises the danger that natural lighting will change significantly between the beginning and the end of shooting. The result can be a disturbing effect of arbitrary changes in the picture quality caused by uneven exposures. The best way to avoid this difficulty is to shoot on a clear, sunny day. Still, the shadows will change during the course of the filming.

A

6.4 PIXILATED HEROES: Not withstanding the serious topic and sobering impact of *Neighbors*, pixilation usually lends itself to humorous, zany animated productions. This is evident in *Blaze Glory* (A), a parody of the cowboy hero by Chuck Melville and Len Johnson. Andre Leduc's *Tout Ecartille* (B) is a surrealistic experiment in pixilation in which the hero, clad in a flowing black cape, travels the world. A, *courtesy Pyramid Films*; B, *courtesy NFBC*.

B

Background. The camera picks up and magnifies any movement in the background, so if you are planning to shoot outside, pick a day when there is no wind. Check your location to be certain that the background is devoid of cars, cows, or other objects that may suddenly move or disappear during the filming.

Project: The Skating, Snaking, and Skidding Film. Set up your camera in an environment that will have little background movement. Find a patient friend to assist in operating the camera. You will be out in front of the camera this time. Begin with a static frame (no camera movement or background movement) through which you "skate," even though you're traveling across the earth and there is no ice. Next, try to coordinate a camera pan that follows you "snaking" past the camera on your stomach. Place obstacles in your way so you can try to smoothly pass over them as a snake might. For a grand finale, you might attempt a short film in which you enter the frame in a live-action walk and then, through pixilation, start skidding as you appear to be trying to stop. Direct your skid toward a tree or similar obstacle. Add more and more "panic" to your body position as you approach the obstacle. Finish yourself off with a terrific crash—one that lifts you high into the air and throws you quite some distance before landing.

7
Working with Sound

Special bonds connect film images to film sound. But in animation, these bonds are *very* special. The visual elements and the audio track seem to share a more intimate and more creative partnership than exists in any other motion picture form. Before I discuss the techniques by which you will be able to exploit this dynamic union, a few comments are appropriate concerning its nature.

The technology of animated filmmaking itself encourages a higher degree of synchronization than is practical within other forms of moviemaking. As we've already seen, the animated film's images are designed and executed frame by frame. So it is with the accompanying sound track, which can also be studied and measured with frame-by-frame precision. Hence, the inherent nature of the technology encourages a closeness between picture and sound.

Images and sounds also appear to share many common elements of structure. A musical tune, for example, is often characterized by a simplicity that is a lot like the graphic simplicity and the familiar gestures we recognize in cartoon characters. In many animated films

7.1 SOUND RECORDING FORMATS: *From left to right*, these are full-scale samples of the formats and materials used in creating sound tracks for movies: (*A*) standard ¼ inch audio recording tape; (*B*) super 8mm film with a magnetic recording strip; (*C*) super 8mm full-coat magnetic recording stock; (*D*) 16mm film with an optical track; (*E*) 16mm full coat magnetic recording stock; (*F*) 16mm optical master film; (*G*) 35mm film with an optical track; (*H*) 35mm full-coat magnetic recording stock.

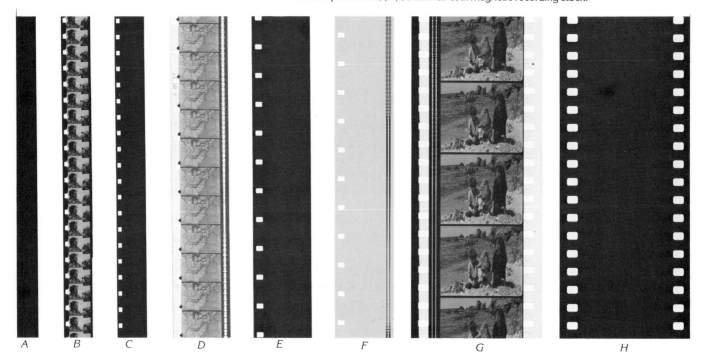

A B C D E F G H

there exist close counterparts for certain musical elements. Repetition in music is like repeating a set of drawings or camera movements; tempo is related to visual beat; dynamics in musical performances correspond to narrative and graphic exaggeration; orchestration relates to the overall coloring and structure of an animated sequence.

Music theorists have suggested that the fundamental power of music to move us as it does is a result of various psychological states we experience in listening to the music's structure. Our natural desire to anticipate the completion of various patterns that have been fashioned from individual notes, intervals, rhythms, and the like is of prime importance. Human beings are pattern seekers. In music we come to anticipate how a familiar melody or arrangement will work out. We wait for the expected outcome. When a tune follows the pattern we've come to anticipate, there is a satisfying sense of "release" or "accomplishment." If our anticipation is thwarted, we are disturbed and our attention increases. Delight also comes when a familiar pattern is embellished in a new and unexpected way.

These same effects can be created and controlled in animation through conscious manipulation of various patterns: visual repetition and rhythm; the movement of characters and background; the predictability of a story or situation that is familiar; and the pacing and editing of the film. To the degree that animation can create a flow of patterns, the medium appears to mirror the nature of musical expression.

Theorizing aside, there's no doubt about the terrific power that exists when a close synchronization of animated images and sounds is achieved. No advanced degree is required to appreciate just how rich the relationship is—all you need to do is see some animated films. You'll hear it. You'll see it. You'll feel it. And in case you still have any doubts about just how closely these two elements are related, buy a ticket for Walt Disney's *Fantasia* or George Dunning's *The Yellow Submarine* the next time they play near you.

7.2   A HORIZONTAL EDITING MACHINE: See chapter 18 for more detail concerning these and other editing systems that can be used for the analysis of recorded sound tracks in super 8mm, 16mm, and 35mm formats.

Selecting a Sound Track

In most forms of moviemaking, the sound track is completed after the film's images have been shot and edited. In animation this process can sometimes work in reverse. A particular piece of music or a particular sound effect will give birth to ideas for accompanying visual images. It is therefore important to consider the full range of sound sources when you begin planning a film.

Music. Original sources of music include conning a friendly orchestra into playing a score that you've written yourself, or asking a musical friend to record a favorite ditty, or just humming into a tape recorder some simple tune you think it would be fun to animate.

Effects. Just about anything you hear can be recorded. Or it can be artificially re-created. You can pick up a portable cassette tape recorder, go outside, and try to get the sound of a motorcycle accelerating loudly as it races up your street. For a different effect, however, you could mimic that sound yourself: varooooooooooom!

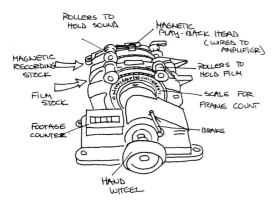

7.3 A TWO-GANG SYNCHRONIZER: This specialized piece of equipment is available in two-, three-, and four-gang models. Specialized synchronizers are also manufactured that combine formats, for example, 8mm with two 16mm gangs.

Voice. The usual forms of voice that appear with movies can be used in animation. There can be narration or voice-over. There can be dialogue that is lip-synchronous or non-lip-synchronous. Consider the potentials and the difficulties inherent in different uses of voice. Often you will be able to discover creative ways of avoiding the situations that call for precise lip synchronization.

Incidentally, you should attempt to create wholly original sound tracks. It's not just that there is something nice in the idea of drawing on one's own resources first. There may also be some legal complications if you don't. There'll be no problem if you want to use prerecorded sound for a movie that will be shown only for your own personal enjoyment. If you undertake various projects suggested in these pages, for example, feel free to "recycle" anything that appeals to you. But if you anticipate a possible commercial use of your animation, through sale or rental, or admission charges from a viewing public, then you'll have to acquire the "rights" to any prerecorded material you use. And that costs money!

More bad news. Say you've found a piece of music that you're just dying to use. Even if this is a classic piece that belongs in the public domain, you will still need to acquire permission in writing from the orchestra that recorded the music or from the recording company that has produced the specific album you're using. But here's some good news. There are a number of *music libraries* that will provide you with recordings that are already "cleared" for permission. And the rates for this service are reasonable. These organizations will mail you their catalogues of music, special effects, and voice recordings. See Chapter 22 for their names and addresses.

Adding Sound to a Finished Film

Adding sound to your film is most easily done after the movie itself is finished. Depending on your ability to find or create effective sound tracks, such an approach can be highly successful in extending the impact of the film's visual elements. Adding sound to a finished film is necessitated, of course, when you are working with equipment or budgets that preclude a frame-by-frame analysis of the sound track before filming starts. Here are a number of such techniques, ordered by accessibility to tools and relative simplicity.

Dropping the Needle. This is the easiest method of all. You simply locate a phonograph or a tape recorder, select a track that feels like it will work, and then turn on the movie projector and the sound equipment so that the recorded sound accompanies the film.

Coordinated Start-ups. In this technique you carefully coordinate the initial start of both the projector and tape recorder. At the beginning of the audio tape (a phonograph won't do), record a "countdown" ("5"..."4"..."3"..."2"..."1") that will lead directly to the first sound of your track. When the moment comes to screen the finished animation, you first turn on the tape recorder, listen to the countdown, and quickly stop the machine, or put it into the *pause* mode precisely at that moment when you anticipate the first sound of the track will be heard. Next, start your projector. Be certain that there is plenty of blank leader at the beginning of your movie to allow you to be watching the screen when the first image of the film is projected. At that moment, turn on the tape recorder. Within reasonable limits, the sound and picture should continue to be "synchronized" throughout the screening. Because film projectors and audio tape recorders tend to play at slightly different speeds, even though they are supposedly "standardized," you will get the best results if you always use the same projector and the same tape recorder.

Super 8mm Sound Stripping. With a special super 8mm projector that has sound recording and sound playback capabilities, it is possible to place a sound track directly on a thin strip of magnetic recording tape that has been attached to the edge of the film (see Chapter 18). Such projectors accept a number of different sound sources (microphone, line-input, etc.). Best of all, it's possible to record the same track over and over again until you have the timing just right.

16mm Optical Tracks. The most accurate sound tracks are achieved with the procedures and standard editing tools available in 16mm filmmaking. Comprehensive and detailed discussions of the 16mm editing process can be found in a number of publications (see Chapter 20). The discussion that follows will give you a basic outline of the steps that are used in creating optical sound tracks for 16mm movies.

Starting with a Sound Track

Now let's talk about techniques that allow you to harness *all* the energy that resides within sound tracks and animated images. The end product we're after is a frame-by-frame "map" of a preselected sound track. With such a guide, you'll be able to match, frame by frame, the images that you want to accompany the track. Here's a breakdown of the process.

The animator studies the possibilities for a sound track. The movie's theme, style, length, and technique are all factors within the equation. At this initial stage, the goal is to select those audio elements that will best fortify and extend the visual components of the movie. The outcome of the original design phase is a *sound treatment* that identifies in detail all the parts of the completed sound track.

Each track is recorded separately—voice, music, and effects. Sometimes as many as ten individual tracks are recorded on a ¼-inch audio tape. These audio recordings are usually done on a reel-to-reel tape recorder. The more sophisticated the recorder, the better. Quality

7.4 16MM PROJECTOR WITH MAGNETIC SOUND: Detail of a Bell & Howell model 504 projector. This versatile piece of equipment can both record and play back 16mm magnetic stock. It can also project standard 16mm prints with optical tracks. With simple modifications and using a special threading technique, this model can serve as an interlock projector, a specialized and expensive piece of equipment used to simultaneously project a 16mm print while playing a matched magnetic track in 16mm mag stock format. Occasionally, these classic Bell & Howell magnetic/optical projectors can be purchased used at reasonable rates.

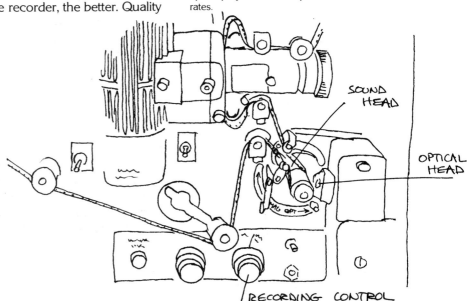

SOUND HEAD

OPTICAL HEAD

RECORDING CONTROL

is important, as you'd expect. Next the tracks are *transferred* from ¼-inch audio tape to 16mm magnetic recording stock, "mag stock" for short.

The use of a 16mm format for both film and mag stock is intentional. It allows the filmmaker to locate any given sound according to a specific frame. Each track of mag stock is studied carefully. Then the different tracks are played together and mixed onto a single "master" reel. In effect, the film's final track is being determined at this early stage, although it is usually possible to make some changes after the filming is completed.

Track analysis, the next step, is the heart of the process of building images according to a sound track. The master track (or individual, premix tracks) is now analyzed on a frame-by-frame basis. Over and over again the animator listens to the recorded track using special equipment that allows the sound to be played at various speeds. The exact location (by frame count from a "start" mark) is determined for every single piece of sound that is deemed significant—any words, any musical note, or any sound effect that the animator will want to know the timing of as he or she creates the movie's visual elements.

Perhaps the act of analyzing a recorded track with such precision sounds horrendous, an impossible, even unnatural act. And so it would be without the existence of two very common filmmaking production tools. The first, the *editing machine,* is a special and costly piece of equipment with a variable speed motor that will simultaneously project the film and "read" a recorded sound track that has been transferred to mag stock. By playing the machine at a slow speed and by going forward and backward over a particular stretch of sound many times, you can identify the exact place where a sound begins or ends.

The other tool used to analyze a sound track is called a *synchronizer.* It is equipped with a magnetic soundhead that reads the track and then amplifies it with a special speaker, sometimes called a *squawk box.* Figure 7.3 shows how the mag stock is run through the synchronizer. The filmmaker's control over the rewind reels allows him to run the track under the soundhead many times until the precise

7.5 A SAMPLE BAR SHEET: This format for analysis of sound tracks is based on the standard musical notation system. As indicated, *dialogue, action,* and *effects* are located relative to the musical score itself.

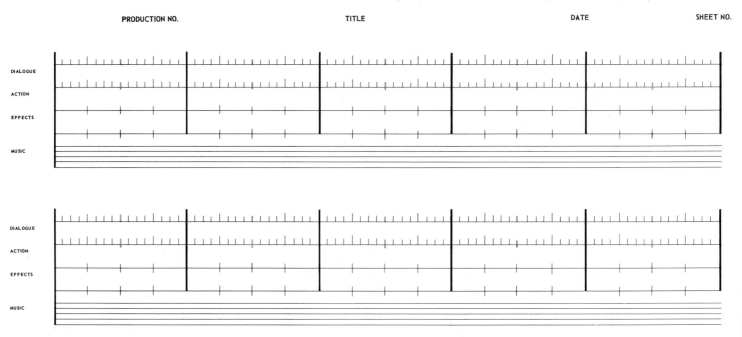

| PRODUCTION NO. | TITLE | DATE | SHEET NO. |

location of a sound is determined. Please look at Chapter 18 for a more complete description of these and other sound tools and processes.

Alternative Track Analysis Gizmos

While the preceding tools and methods are recommended, there are some alternative ways to find out where a particular sound is located on a prerecorded track. Here are three such techniques that, when mastered, can provide an accurate reading of a track.

Stopwatch. Use a stopwatch that is calibrated in tenths of seconds or smaller units if possible. As you listen to your track again and again, time the various sounds you'll want to work with. Note both the duration of these sounds and their elapsed time from the start of the film. Because you know the projection speed (24 fps in 16mm and 18 or 24 fps in super 8mm), you now can convert "stopwatch time" into a frame count.

Taping on Leader. Thread a roll of white leader into the film projector (super 8mm or 16mm) that you use in showing your films. Take the audio tape you've selected and prepare to play it. Position yourself so that you can make a mark on the surface of the leader as it passes through the gate of the movie projector. A grease pencil or felt-tipped marker will work well. Turn on both the projector and the recorder. Experiment first to be certain that your markings register on the leader as it passes through the projection gate. When both machines are going, simply "tap" a mark on the leader at the same moment you hear the sound. Use this technique to identify the specific "beats" within a musical piece or the beginning or end point of other sound elements. You may want to use different colors to denote different sounds. Finally, take the leader out of the projector and literally count off the frames from the starting point in order to determine the precise makeup of the track. If it's a complicated track, you may want to mark different elements on separate stretches of fresh leader.

16mm Magnetic Tracks. There are 16mm film projectors designed both to record and playback sound tracks on either fully coated magnetic recording tape or on thin strips of magnetic tape applied to one edge of a 16mm film (Figure 7.4). Although this system resembles the newer super 8mm sound projectors, it was actually developed a number of years ago and is generally no longer used in professional 16mm film production.

Thread a fresh roll of mag stock into the projector. Record your track on it. Play back the track, and marking on the "sound drum" with a marker, you can locate any sound you want. As you study the track and its markings, remember that the magnetic track is read by the soundhead at a point that is advanced 26 frames ahead of its synchronous image at the projection gate.

Lip Sync

The precision with which it is possible to analyze a sound track also enables the animator to locate individual words or parts of words. This makes it possible to create cartoon characters so that they appear to move their lips while talking. The effect, of course, is that the mouth you've animated will be speaking the voice you're hearing on the track.

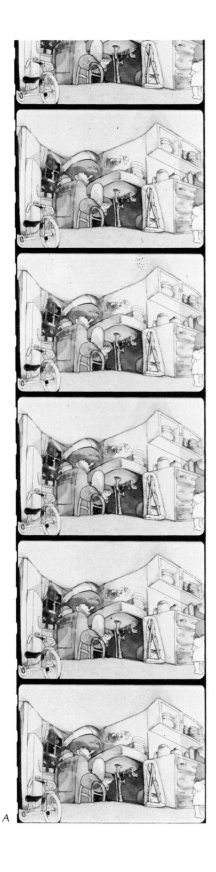

A

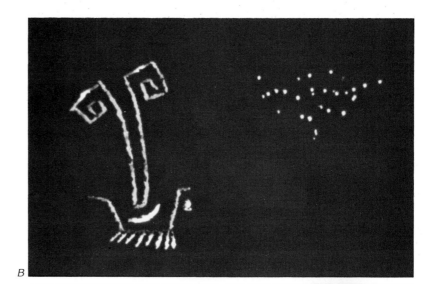

B

C

D

As you might imagine, lip synchronization is a pretty tricky business. A lot of patience and practice will be required if you want to become really proficient in determining the shape of mouth that goes with a particular spoken sound. Animators often sit in front of mirrors in order to study the shapes of their own mouths while they try to determine how to match an analyzed dialogue track. Over the years, animators have been able to figure out "standard" mouth shapes that accompany particular speech sounds.

Bar Sheets

A *bar sheet* is the standard notation system by which animators record the analysis of a sound track. A sample is shown in Figure 7.5, complete with an analysis of musical score, voice, and sound effects. There is nothing sacred about the particular bar sheet format illustrated here. You can create a recording system of your own design that will accommodate the special needs you find in a given project.

Project: Create-a-Track. Depending on the equipment and resources available to you, create a project that will test the parameters of your production system and also test your skills in analyzing a sound track. Start with a specific recording but try to choose one that won't go beyond your resources. If you are working with just a stopwatch, for example, select a simpler track than if you are working with sophisticated equipment, such as a gang synchronizer (see Chapter 18). Finish the analysis by constructing a bar sheet.

To test the precision of your analysis, take a piece of leader and scratch on it so that you will be able to see a flash of color, lasting just two frames, that matches the location suggested by your bar sheet. When you've finished marking the leader, project it with the track. Be sure to use the most sophisticated projection system you can get your hands on so that you can give yourself a fair test of your ability to break down a track.

Analyzing sound tracks for animated films is a highly specialized craft and in the major studios there are individuals who do nothing else. For further detail on the nuances, theories, and specific tools required for professional sound track analysis, consult one of the technical manuals cited in Chapter 20.

A selection of frames from cartoons with innovative sound tracks. In *Cockaboody* (A), John and Faith Hubley informally recorded the conversations of their two small daughters at play and based the entire film on an edited version of that sound recording. In Norman McLaren's *Blinkity Blink* (B), the animator hand drew both the images and the sound track directly onto 35mm black leader. Sound effects and dialogue by Eskimos constitute the sound track of Carolyn Leaf's *The Owl Who Married the Goose* (C). Highly amplified natural sounds are featured in the track for *The Animal Movie* (D) by Grant Munro and Ron Tunis. *Courtesy of the Learning Corporation of America (A), Pyramid Films (B), the National Film Board of Canada (C), and McGraw-Hill (D).*

8 Storyboarding

The storyboard, a conceptual planning aid used today in all kinds of filmmaking, was originally developed specifically for animation. Perhaps the first storyboard was made by a person who found it easier to draw a story than to write it out.

The basic idea is very simple. A storyboard is a film in outline form. The examples of storyboards on the following pages will provide a good definition in just a quick glance. For those who like to read their definitions, a storyboard is a collected series of single pictures, each of which represents a distinct sequence or narrative element within the film. The storyboard is thus a new system for conceptualization.

The use of small sketches gives the animator a spectacularly clear and inexpensive way to work out the style, continuity, and visual approach to a film. Unlike live-action filmmaking, in animation one doesn't want to risk creating scenes that may be discarded in the editing process. A storyboard provides the filmmaker with an extremely concrete outline for his or her further labors, and it eliminates to whatever degree possible wasted hours of drawing a shooting.

As you may have already experienced, it is difficult to explain the visual flow and texture of an animated movie—especially when the images tend toward the abstract and the fantastic. A storyboard can help here too. Not only is it useful in explaining a concept to people you

8.1 A SAMPLE NARRATIVE STORYBOARD: This solution to the suggested project bears analysis. The scene is set and our protagonist is introduced in panels *A* and *B*. A closeup shot is shown in panel *C*. In panel *D* the story's ingenue is introduced as she enters the frame and starts walking across it. Panel *E* shows the closeness of the characters and sets up the overall scene's dramatic tension. In panel *F* the same background is used as in panel *D*. A storyboard helps one to evaluate and refine a film's structure before preparation of the final artwork. For example, this storyboard points out that a more dramatic first scene should be developed, that a close-up of the heroine might be inserted between *D* and *E*, that *E* is unnecessary to the overall scene, or that the same background could be used in *A* and *D*.

A

B

C

D

E

F

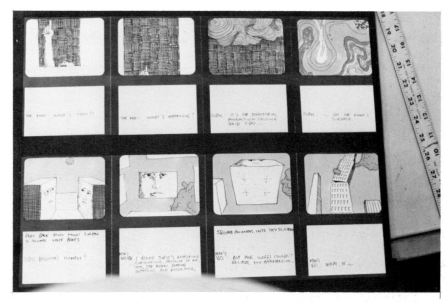

8.2 A "SHOW" STORYBOARD: Drawings and dialogue are formally mounted on a precut storyboard matte. This sample is from an unproduced project by George Griffin.

are working with (animator friends, camera people, writers, musicians, etc.), but a storyboard becomes essential in explaining a movie to producers. The storyboard has been termed the animator's mouthpiece.

Length and Detail

A matched pair of questions almost invariably presents itself as one prepares a storyboard. How many pictures should I use? How much detail should I show? To answer these related questions, it is necessary to consider the different functions that a storyboard serves.

The amount of visual detail within each individual drawing or *panel* depends upon the individual animator's desire to try out what is in his or her mind's eye.

The number of individual drawings within a storyboard will vary widely. Some shots can be adequately previewed by one or two sketches, along with associated notes and directions for movement. There should always be at least one panel for each new shot or sequence. In practice there are almost always two panels for even the shortest, most static shot—one to show the opening image and one to show the ending image. This allows the animator to study the transitions between shots and scenes.

In more complicated sequences, there can be as many as 30 or 40 drawings for a screen action that will take only a matter of 2 seconds. In such cases, the animator uses a single panel to indicate each important or *key* position (or movement) within the flow of images that will eventually make up the film. Determining the appropriate number of panels becomes a function of the complexity of a particular sequence and the animator's wish or need to previsualize precisely how a particular movement will work within the finished film. Before proceeding to a discussion of the fine points of storyboarding, I'd like to suggest that you take on the following exercise.

Project: Narrative Storyboard. Our antagonist is a comic-strip freak. He reads them all the time. Even on the way to his job. He dreams about being a hybrid of all the super-heroes in Marvel Comic-land. In the

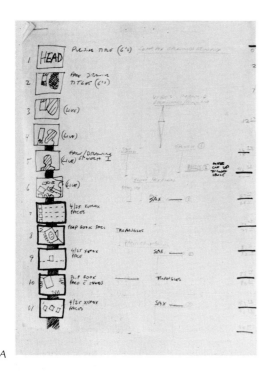

A

house next door lives a young woman with a thing about dogs. As she walks her poodle before going to the typing pool each morning, she studies the poodle's every movement. She dreams up stories about her dog—he saves lost children, is given his own television series, discovers ways to show the young woman's boss just how wonderful his mistress is.

Enough background. Our story deals with the inevitable: A collision of fantasies brought on by a collision of bodies. As she walks her dog and he leaves his house reading a favorite comic, they collide. Your assignment is to work out a storyboard that shows how you might structure an animated sequence that takes these two characters to the moment just before they walk into each other. A very simple solution to the problem is presented in Figure 8.1. Yours should be better.

Storyboard Styles

Commercial animation production houses and advertising agencies have made the storyboard into a "high" art form. Their renderings are done by well-paid specialists who mount each drawing on fancy, precut mounting boards. A typical "show" storyboard will also bear verbal notations (dialogue or descriptive information) that have been typed and mounted beneath appropriate panels. Figure 8.2 is a photograph of one such highly finished presentation.

For most independent animators, however, there is nothing precious about a storyboard. It is a tool and an aid, not a piece of art. Sketches are done quickly and they are revised often. In order to study the overall flow of the film a standard storyboarding procedure is to create each sketch on a different card or sheet of paper. All drawings

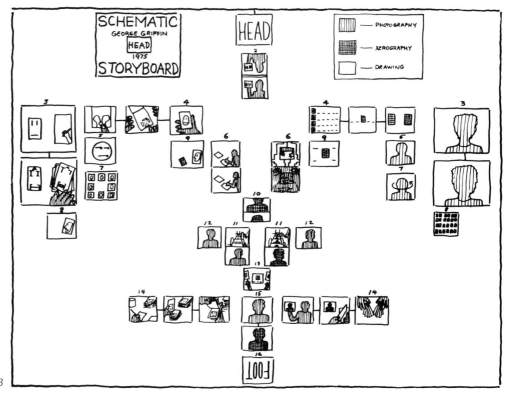

B

are then tacked upon a bulletin board. This technique makes it easy to change the order of scenes and to insert or delete an entire series of drawings. At the Disney studios in Burbank, California, there are entire rooms with cork-lined walls where the principal animators and directors of feature films mount and study thousands of individual sketches used in planning an animation feature.

How much detail does there need to be in an individual drawing? The right amount is the amount that works for you and for any others that you may want to see your plans. A few very rough sketches can do the trick, drawn so quickly and simply that you are the only person who can decode the storyboard. Or you may find that you just have to make renderings that will be every bit as finished as the style used in the final film—formal drawings with full color and complete detail.

Storyboard Function

Conceptualization is the essential function of the storyboard. And even when the idea you've got in your mind seems absolutely detailed and complete, getting it down on paper is always a creative step. The process of visual thinking releases new energy and new ideas. Best of all, developing a storyboard lets one see the "problems."

Many would say that the *real* creativity starts only after that inner idea has been given a visual and concrete first draft, however informal, via a storyboard. The idea of the movie suddenly becomes accessible in new ways. One is able to step back from the concept and study it with

8.3 STORYBOARD STYLES: Animators approach storyboarding with an endless variety of styles and techniques. Photograph *A* shows a working storyboard element from George Griffin's *Head.* The schematic in *B* represents the overall structure of the finished 10-minute film. Photograph *C* shows animator Mary Beams's simple plan for a sequence in her film *Seed Reel.* The National Film Board of Canada encourages its animators to use a standard format in presenting finished storyboards for approval prior to production. In *D,* the NFBC's format is used to present the beginning of a new film by Derek Lamb and Janet Perlman.

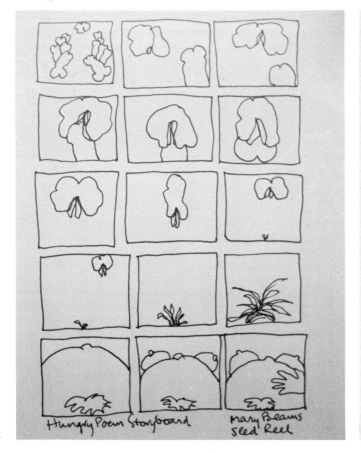

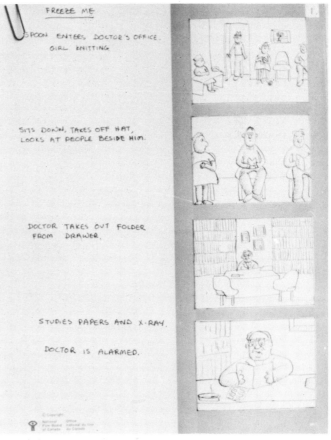

C

D

8.4 A WALL AS TOOL: The wall beside animator John Canemaker's drawing table is used as an impromptu (but important) planning/storyboarding tool. *Courtesy John Canemaker.*

more objective eyes. Various component elements are seen independently of the central concept.

A storyboard makes the idea accessible to others, too. It facilitates experimentation, messing around, revision, and those other steps that are required in making an idea work as a film. Take out the storyboard you did earlier in this chapter or one that you may be currently working on. Try to apply each of the following perspectives to it. Together, these perspectives represent functions a storyboard can perform in your service.

Depending on the detail you've included, the storyboard will indicate the film's *visual style.* Take a moment to consider if there might not be another graphic style that would better suit your idea. Also study the storyboard to determine if all the sequences in the film share the same visual "look." If different styles of artwork are to be used, do these fit together well?

The storyboard should represent the *key moments* of the film, whether it be a story or an abstract piece. If you can spot a number of drawings that don't represent what you consider an important development in the film, then you should consider deleting or altering this section. Check that your key moments actually represent all that you want them to. The advice of a friend can be helpful in this regard.

Your storyboard should direct your attention to two particularly tricky structural elements. The first of these is the order or *sequence* of individual shots and scenes. Do elements of the story possess continuity? Will the viewer be able to follow the sequence without getting confused? Is the pacing varied? A study of these different elements will lead to a study of the transitions between them. Here is one of the most difficult areas of animation or any other form of moving-image creation. Getting from one thing to another thing has to be done in ways that fit the flow of ideas and experiences that you are creating for your viewer. In some cases you may wish to make a "smooth" transition, one that effortlessly joins two elements. At other times, however, it may be important to structure a transition to create shock, disorientation, or sudden insight. Remember that there are some effects that shouldn't be overdone. Balance is an overall goal. The film's whole must be valued above the impact of individual sequences. Storyboarding will help you to see and control the overall structure.

Other things you should study through the storyboard include *sound, movement, composition,* and *color.* Is information clearly presented? Are characters sharply portrayed? Is the story clear? Is your basic concern or idea forcefully presented in the overall film?

Look at the storyboard with a practical eye, not an aesthetic one. Does the film call for techniques and tools that you don't have? Can you reasonably expect to finish the film in the time you will be able to put aside for it? What is the cost of this production? The list of questions can go on and on and on.

As you make different kinds of animated films, you will find yourself spontaneously adopting different styles of storyboarding as, film by film, you ascribe different functions and combinations of functions to the task of storyboarding. That, of course, is just the way it should be. After all, the film is the thing. Remind yourself that storyboarding is a technique for generating and refining ideas, not an end in itself.

Carolyn Leaf's animation table. The small drawings on either side of her filming area—six of which are shown are used to plan her technique of painting directly on glass.

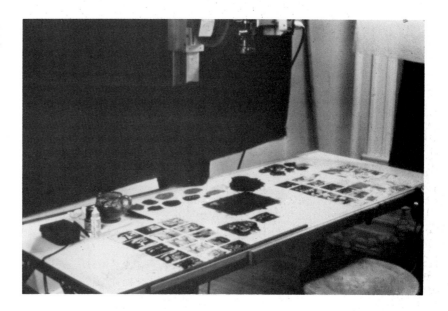

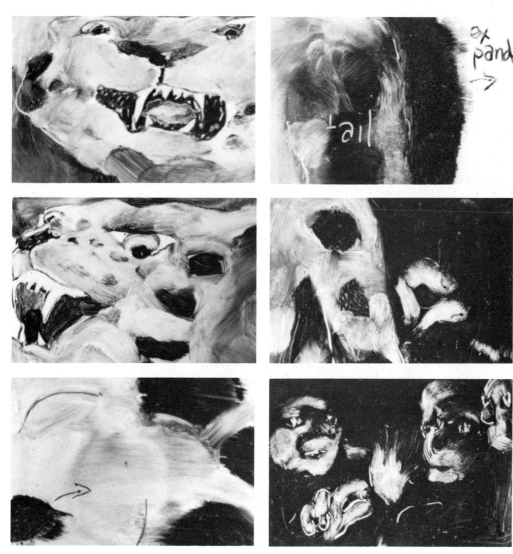

9
Kinestasis and Collage

This chapter discusses animating still images—usually photographic images of one kind or another. More sophisticated camera techniques will be called for in what follows than have been important up to this point. Conceptual demands will be greater too. Both these kinds of animation will give you opportunities to put into use the techniques of storyboarding and working with sound presented in the preceding two chapters.

In other words, the pace picks up now. We're moving into the more challenging domains of animated filmmaking. But as I think you'll find, with more demanding techniques will come more stimulating opportunities for expression.

Kinestasis

A host of awkward names have been attached to the technique of making movies from still images: still-scan, konograph, photoscan, filigraph, photomontage, kinestasis. We'll use the last of these as it appears to be the most frequently cited, and the word kinestasis accurately exposes the semantic roots and essential characteristics of the technique itself: kine=moving; stasis=stillness.

Whatever the name, an operational definition for this kind of animation would be as follows: A series of still pictures become animated through (a) variations of movement across them and (b) variations in the succession between them.

You may have experienced this kind of animation without ever knowing it. To the casual moviegoer, kinestasis is often considered a "normal" filmmaking technique, a fluid flow of images that incorporates panning or zooming effects and thus produces much the same perceptual experience as one has when seeing a live-action film.

Please try the following project. Its requirements are minimal—you're only asked to draw a few straight lines—but it will clearly illustrate the creative choices and the surprising power of kinestasis.

Project: A Photograph Becomes a Movie. Imagine that you are a live-action filmmaker standing, hidden, in a position that allows you to see exactly the same scene as pictured in Figure 9.1. Imagine also that you have a camera equipped with a zoom lens, allowing you to frame and film the smallest detail or the entire scene. One small limitation: The gear you are filming with won't let you zoom, pan, or otherwise move the camera while the camera is actually running, though you can recompose the image between shots.

As you've noted, of course, there are two prints of the same photograph in Figure 9.1. This is because this project requires you to make two different movies from the same single image.

The first is to be a narrative film. Study the picture until you see a story of some kind. Using a ruler and pencil, draw directly on the first

A

9.1   DOUBLE FEATURE IN A PHOTO: In choosing and marking off the five different sets of images in copy *B* and copy *C* of the photographs, try to use the rectangular frame that is standard in all forms of filmmaking. Note that in this project it is permissible to use the same area of the photograph in two or more individual frames that you select. The small copy of the picture, *A*, illustrates these ground rules.

B   C

copy of the picture at least five separate frames that capture the essence of the story or relationship you have seen. These individual frames should be sequenced and numbered. Part of your problem here is to determine an order for the images you've selected, and part of the challenge is to actually compose the individual frames themselves.

You'll have completed the first part of this project when you've framed at least five images within the larger one, numbered the sequence of your selections, and indicated the length of time in seconds that you would hold each of the "shots" you've been making.

The second part of the project asks you to use the second photograph in making an altogether different movie. This film cannot be a story in any way. Rather, you should select as your topic another kind of visual element or nondramatic quality in the photograph. Choose and arrange in sequence at least five completely new shots. Base the selection around something like your feeling of the scene's mood, a study of one element in the natural environment pictured in the photograph, or some purely intuitive connection that you can make.

In essence, the decisions you've been making are exactly the same kinds of decisions that are made in creating a kinestasis film. Were you, in fact, to actually film the individual frames you've marked, you'd be producing a simple kinestasis film. In full-scale kinestasis, there are many additional effects that could be added to either of the sequences you have selected, and we'll be discussing these options later in this chapter. But before we get to the nuances of different filming techniques, before we become encumbered in refinements, it will be valuable to break down the kinds of choices that I suspect you were quite easily able to exercise as you marked up the photographs.

9.2 THEMES AND VARIATIONS: Tokyo's Tsukiji fish market provides a rich location for testing the different criteria through which images can be selected and ordered. This series of photographs was selected from color slides photographed by independent filmmaker Michael Lemle. The first set *(A-F)* shows a narrative structure. The sequence that follows *(G-L)* shows a design structure, based primarily on geometric shapes, textures, and parallel composition in adjacent frames. The third sequence *(M-R)* is structured in a documentary mode—an establishing shot leads to closeups of hands and then to a series of portraits of shopkeepers. The final sequence of six images was selected by the photographer because it "felt right" in summarizing the Tsukiji market as he experienced it. *Courtesy Michael Lemle.*

A

B

C

G

H

I

M

N

O

S

T

U

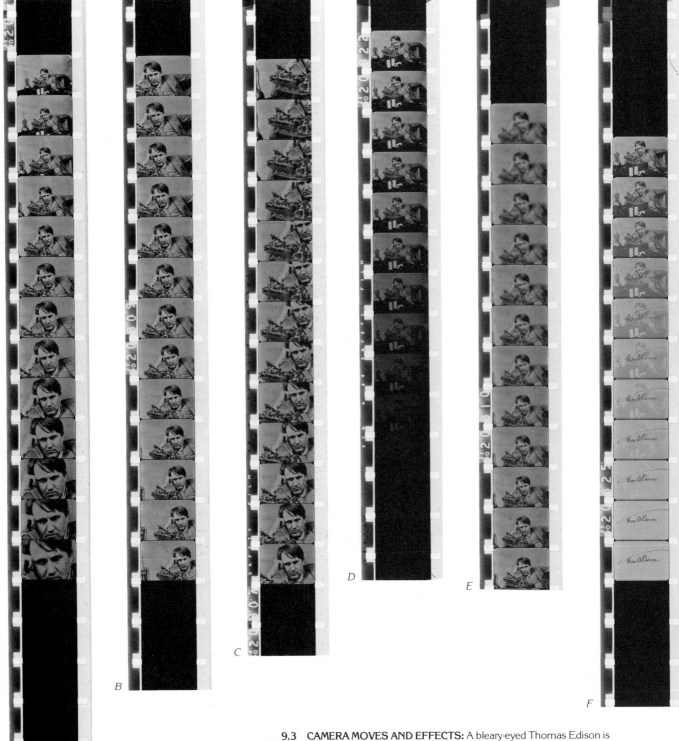

9.3 CAMERA MOVES AND EFFECTS: A bleary-eyed Thomas Edison is
rephotographed in six different ways using a professional Oxberry animation stand. Clip A
shows a direct zoom into Edison's face. Clip B is a pan—the photograph is moved under
the camera in precisely controlled increments. Clip C shows a complex camera
movement in which the stand's compound moves both horizontally and vertically to
produce the effect of a diagonal tilt. Clip D is a fade-out. In clip E, the series begins out of
focus. An in-camera dissolve is shown in Clip F as Edison's image cross-fades into his
signature. Note that the 16mm clips have been enlarged. *Photo courtesy Edison
National Monument.*

Four Design Genres

When all the fuss and glamour, all the technique and the tools are taken away, the craft of filmmaking boils down to the execution of two tasks. The first is to capture images that are forceful. This is the task of "filming" as it occurs in live-action production. Editing the selected images is the second task. The filmmaker must carefully order his or her individual shots so that they lead the viewer to see a particular relationship among the images. Sometimes the relationship that the filmmaker wants to show comes in the form of a story and sometimes it is something entirely different. All this corresponds to what you were asked to do in the preceding project.

Now, in animated filmmaking, the control of the artist is extended far, far beyond that which is normally available in live-action filmmaking. Consequently, animators are able to design or structure entire sequences with a precision and purity of concept that reveals the four basic genres of media design.

The most familiar basis for choosing and ordering images is that of a "real life" process or story. This is termed the *narrative genre.* Decisions follow a story line. A different kind of logic rules what has come to be termed the *documentary genre.* Here the criteria for selecting images and sequencing them have more to do with the nature of the subject matter than with an individual story or event. A film about a city, for example, calls for a different approach than a film that is set in the city. Totally different sets of criteria are at work when one operates in a pure *design genre.* In this case images are captured and ordered around a formal quality that links one image to the next. I'm referring here to qualities such as balance, tone, color, shape, texture, perspective, composition, graphic and photographic elements. These are elements of "pure" design rather than elements that are generic to a story or to the subject matter per se. Sometimes, however, the criteria for selecting and joining images reside beyond the logic of each of these genres. Sometimes it is just a gut feeling, an intuition, that guides the process of designing. A combination of images feels "right," it "works"—although it may be impossible to say just why. I call this the *intuitive genre.*

Certainly intuition plays a large role in fashioning any powerful film sequence, be it a documentary, narrative, or pure-design genre. In fact, all manners of design can all operate simultaneously within one film, even within one scene. The genres have been isolated here only because breaking things into parts is necessary for exposition. When you lay out a kinestasis film, these categories or "logics" are employed simultaneously, as you'll see in the following project.

Project: Four Variations on a Scene. Ask a friend to accompany you to some interesting environment, a park, a market, a fast-food restaurant, a downtown intersection. Take along a still camera and a couple of rolls of film. Your task will be to shoot a number of still images that can subsequently be used in making four 10-second kinestasis films. Each film will be structured according to a different design genre as introduced above. This project should bring into sharp relief the aesthetic decisions we've been discussing.

You should do a good deal of preplanning before deciding what images to shoot and how to direct your friend, who is to be an actor. It

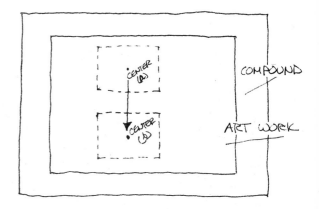

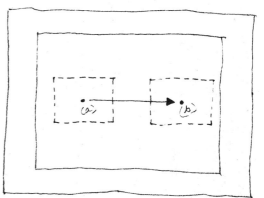

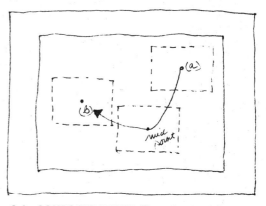

9.4 COMPOUND MOVES: These drawings place one in the camera's perspective, looking directly down onto a compound that holds the artwork. Three basic kinds of compound moves are suggested: vertical, horizontal, and complex. The dotted outlines represent what the camera is framed to film, the initial and final positions of each movement. Note that the entire compound surface can move and that the artwork itself can be moved across a stationary surface.

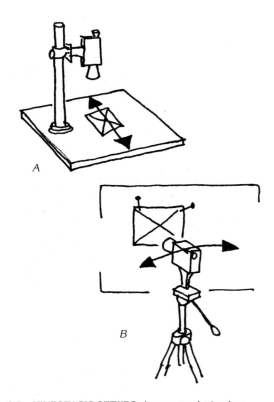

9.5   KINESTASIS SETUPS: A copy stand, tripod, or animation stand holds the camera above the artwork. In A the artwork itself moves to create pans, tilts, etc. A horizontally mounted camera, B, allows easy panning by the camera while the artwork remains stationary.

might be good to begin with the *narrative* treatment. Concoct a story, using your actor, that can be told in five or six images. Shoot these first. Next, photograph a series of *documentary* stills that record one event or theme or location within the general environment. Again, shoot at least a half-dozen such pictures. You should remain in the same location as you undertake the next approach, a *pure-design* treatment. Shoot a series of at least five images that are connected by one or more formal graphic qualities. Finally, take a few photographs on a purely intuitive basis. Shoot what feels right in capturing a tone, a feeling, or some other quality that you've come to associate with the environment in which you've been working.

After the photographs have been developed and printed, make four 10-second kinestasis films. Through the camera work on each film you will be able to explore more deeply each of the approaches you've taken. Look at the examples in Figure 9.2 before you take on this assignment. And read the rest of the chapter before you actually film the series of photographs that you finally select.

Image Sources

In the project above you will be animating still photographs that you yourself have taken. The process is one of rephotography, using an animation camera and stand. However, many other kinds of visual materials lend themselves to kinestasis.

One of the most satisfying characteristics of working with this technique is that you have an opportunity to use some of the most powerful images that have been created by our species. You can, for example, make a film from reproductions of photographs made by the world's best photographers. There are books full of these. Old family snapshots are another good source of material. So are drawings, paintings, and other pieces of artwork such as watercolors, pencil sketches, pastel and charcoal studies, silk screens, lithographs, and so on.

Although they require special equipment, 35mm slides can be turned into effective kinestasis films. You can project the still image on a screen and then rephotograph it with an animation camera.

Whether your source materials are new or old, original or borrowed, you'll discover that an enormous flexibility exists in the possible ways you can alter an image before filming it, by painting on photographs, for example, or mounting two or more slides within one frame, or tracing a silhouette from a photograph, or altering images with filters and focus variations.

As a general rule, anything that is reasonably flat can be used in making a kinestasis image, including three-dimensional objects, such as tapestry or wall hangings, oversized art in the form of posters or wall murals, or specially screened photographs that have been printed on clear acetate sheets for use in conjunction with brightly colored papers or gels.

Whatever the actual source and style of images, during the process of designing and filming animated films, all materials that go under the camera become "artwork."

Movement Within One Image

Imagine that a sophisticated super 8mm camera is fixed to a tripod and points at an 8- by 10-inch photograph. How could you bring movement to the photograph by moving just your camera?

Tracking/Planning/Tilting. The camera itself can move toward, away from, or parallel to the artwork during the process of filming. Figure 9.3 shows these and other camera movements and effects. If you're using just a tripod, however, it may be very difficult to calibrate accurately the distance and speed of such movements. The design of copy stands or animation stands accommodates such camera movements far more easily and accurately than a simple tripod.

Zooming. Most of today's cameras have excellent zoom lenses built into them. Registration of the zoom movement, in and out, during frame-by-frame filmmaking, is tricky. Chapter 15 provides some simple and inexpensive modifications you can make on your camera and stand in order to extend precision in panning and zooming.

Focus. Another way to alter an image and to give it life is by selectively changing the focus on your lens. One can go in or out of focus. This can be a good way to bring together images that have no logical connection built into them.

Filters. In addition to the built-in filter on most super 8mm cameras, it is possible to place accessory filters or other devices in front of the lens while filming. Special multifaceted lenses can produce kaleidoscopic effects, for example. Shooting through an irregular glass surface, like a Coke bottle, will produce weird forms of movement within stationary pieces of art.

In-camera Effects. Relatively sophisticated cameras produce a number of in-camera effects that can be forcefully incorporated into kinestasis films. In a *fade-out,* the picture goes to black over a specified number of frames. Or the screen starts black and the image smoothly *fades in.* A fade-out that is superimposed over a fade-in gives the effect of a *dissolve*—one image disappears or "melts" into a new image. Two images can be simultaneously seen on top of each other if your camera has the ability to expose the same piece of film twice. The technique of *superimposition* requires a backwinding mechanism and a variable shutter control, both described fully in Chapter 15. Superimposition is used in creating a dissolve effect.

As suggested earlier, panning or tilting the camera is particularly difficult to control with the kind of accuracy required in animation. For this reason, most animation setups are designed so that the body of the camera itself is never moved. Instead, the subject or artwork moves. Incremental movements of artwork under a fixed camera are termed *compound movements*—named after the movable surface of full-scale animation stands. Figure 9.5 places you in the position of a camera as it points down on a compound.

Registration of the artwork's movement can be controlled by your own eye as it estimates the right distance to move the artwork between exposures. Actual measurement can be employed as well. Use a ruler to record and direct the amount of movement between exposures. Both these systems work fairly well. But in both, precise control is difficult and the process of filming is painstaking and slow. So animators have invented special tools.

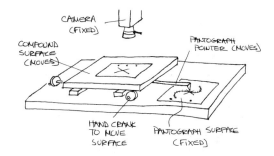

9.6 THE PANTOGRAPH: The pointer is connected to the compound surface and is positioned to indicate the center of the camera's field of view. The pantograph surface generally bears a field guide onto which a camera movement can be charted. Note that the pantograph's needle moves and the surface remains stationary. This is the reverse of the stand where the camera remains stationary and the surface moves. This drawing suggests that the pantograph is to be used with an expensive animation stand. Figure 9.7 shows an alternative, less expensive pantograph construction.

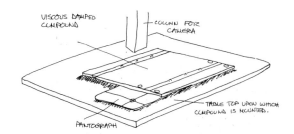

9.7 THE VISCOUS DAMPED COMPOUND: The line drawing is based on the Oxberry Corporation's Media Pro Animation Stand. The compound is entirely made of metal and rests in a metal carriage containing the thick lubricating substance.

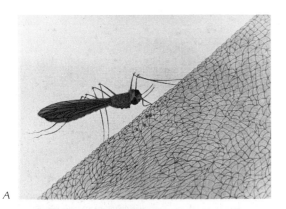

A

B

C

9.8   APPROACHES TO KINESTASIS: The first two frame enlargements *A* and *B* sample moments from *Cosmic Zoom*, a film by Eva Szasz and Tony Ianzelo. This film consists of a continuous zoom from the micro-universe of a human cell to the macrouniverse of galaxies. Photos *C* and *D* are from *City of Gold*, a 23-minute film produced primarily from old photographs showing Dawson City and the Canadian Yukon at the height of the gold rush. Directed by Wolf Koenig at the National Film Board of Canada, *City of Gold* was one of the first kinestasis films. Frame *E* is from *Enter Hamlet*, a takeoff on the famous "To be or not to be. . ."soliloquy by Shakespeare. Each word is represented by a humorous drawing by animator Fred Mogubgub. Frame *F* is from the film *Secrets* by Phillip Jones. This movie explores the changing moods achieved through graphic variations of the same basic image of a woman's face. *Photos A, B, C, D courtesy National Film Board of Canada; photos E, F courtesy Pyramid Films.*

Setting Up and Special Equipment

Cameras best suited for kinestasis techniques share these general features: the ability to film extremely close up, reflex focusing, a built-in light-metering system, a zoom lens, and both single-framing and continuous-run filming speeds.

Figure 9.5 shows two standard camera mounting arrangements. Both positions enable the camera operator to easily and quickly focus on different size fields or to reframe the composition of the scene between exposures. If one wants to use a great deal of movement within the filming of a single image (tracking, panning, zooming, in-camera effects, and compound moves), then it's nice to know about two specialized pieces of animation equipment, the pantograph and the viscous damped compound.

The Pantograph. A key feature of an animation stand is the control it provides the filmmaker in moving the surface beneath the camera. This surface is called the *compound* or *bed* of the stand. The most precise way to chart a complex movement is by using a *pantograph* (Figure 9.6). The animator draws a single line on a sheet of paper that fits a specially designed platform. This line represents the path that the camera is to follow as it moves across a static piece of artwork. During the process of filming, the animator simply places the sheet of paper into its special mount alongside the compound itself. A special pointing needle lines up the center of the camera's field with the starting point of the line that has been drawn to guide the camera. Now, as the operator moves the compound so that the pointer follows the line on the pantograph, the camera can trace a complex movement over the artwork. The operator pauses to make two exposures at points on the line that have been indicated by the animator. For more information on the pantograph, see Chapter 16.

The Viscous Damped Compound. Kinestasis filmmaking can be photographed in "real" time when the animator uses the continuous running feature of the camera to execute preplanned moves across the artwork. As you can see, this accelerates tremendously the process of filmmaking. In fact, the freedom to use the camera at "normal" speeds is one of the nicest qualities of kinestasis. With the right equipment, the move itself can be just as smooth and accurate as that achieved with a pantograph and frame-by-frame shooting. The "right kind of equipment" is a *viscous damped compound.* Figure 9.7 illustrates how this tool is made by mounting the flat surface of the stand in a tray-like device that contains a thick viscous lubricant. This dense fluid "smooths out" manual movements of the compound. After rehearsing the direction and speed that have been selected for a particular movement, the operator can simply turn on the camera at full speed (or something slightly less than full speed, such as 12 frames per second) and proceed to reposition the artwork while the camera is running. The damped compound facilitates a fluidity of all movements—jerks and jumps and other inconsistencies of movement are eliminated. The viscous damped compound is a special feature available on both the super 8mm and 16mm stands manufactured by the Oxberry Corporation (see Chapter 16).

Other Variables

We've discussed the conceptual dimensions of choosing and sequencing images. We've reviewed ways in which the animation camera and stand can add movement to an individual frame and how it can join different images through in-camera effects. We've looked also at simple camera setups and at the sophisticated and specially designed tools required in this kind of animation.

In planning an entire kinestasis film, there are a few other variables that you should know about. All of these must be employed with a purpose that matches the basic structure of the overall film. Lest all this begin to sound vague and abstract, here's a quick summary of the kinds of variables I am talking about here.

Duration is one variable, an obvious one. The camera can film any image for any length of time, ranging from approximately one twenty-fourth of a second (one frame) to as long as you wish, including several full seconds or even minutes. Because your camera will generally be able to focus on areas that are smaller than the boundaries of the single image you are filming, that image can suddenly become the primary source for a number of different secondary images. This is the process of *reframing*. The photograph of a landscape, for example, can generate additional images that present parts of the overall picture, a tree, a road, or some other detail. The same image can be used a number of times at different places within a single film. This is *reshooting*. The animation camera simply rephotographs the original art exactly as done earlier or with slightly different variations. Kinestasis techniques are particularly well suited for correlation with elements of a sound track. Precise *sound matching* is thus another variable. Finally, kinestasis lets the animator control the rate and style of *sequences*. The same basic movements (pans, zooms, fades, or whatever) can produce very different effects according to the rate of change that is given them in a particular scene or sequence. A slow zoom, for example, has a different feel from that of the exact same movement done very quickly. Similarly, the style of a particular movement—its smoothness or abruptness—alters its meaning. Depending on the subject matter, story, or feeling that is being developed, a set of quick pans, for example, can create a powerful effect. When you see a kinestasis film look for such patterns in the rate and style of movements as well as in the selection and sequencing of individual images.

Shooting Sheets

Your materials are assembled and the movie camera is loaded. You've studied each image and each movement. The first sequence starts well. The process of filming is slow, of course, because it takes time to work with precision. Unless you have a photographic memory, however, as the shooting proceeds you are bound to arrive at a point when, suddenly, you can't remember what's next or how to shoot it. You've lost your way.

That's a generous scenario. Chances are you will get lost quickly and hopelessly in making a kinestasis film unless you have some sort of

D

E

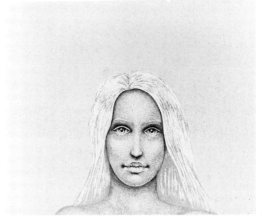

F

notation system that can be used while planning the film and, more important, during the process of filming itself. Otherwise you'll screw up.

The way *not* to become lost is to make yourself a map, a system that stores all the details of your film and helps you to work fast and accurately while at the camera. Figure 9.8 shows a portion of a *shooting sheet*. I highly recommend this system for keeping track of the detailed information required in kinestasis. You can modify your own shooting sheet to fit the capabilities of your own equipment. Categories you may need to include are identifying the artwork, the sequence of images, the framing or composition, camera movement, compound movement, the duration of each shot, in-camera effects, special effects such as the use of filters, sound-track information, and so on. Create and utilize shooting sheets as you plan and film the *Four Variations* project suggested earlier.

9.9 SHOOTING SHEET: This sheet details one way that the narrative images in Figure 9.2 might be animated. Note patterns of movement, tune, and composition.

SHOOTING SHEET

SHOT #	SOURCE	FRAMING	DURATION	CAMERA MOVEMENT	SPECIAL EFFECTS
1	A	FULL FRAME THEN ZOOM-IN	5 sec hold 3 sec zoom	AFTER HOLD, ZOOM IN 3 SEC TO C.U. MAN IN BKG.	DISSOLVE LAST 24 FRAMES
2	B	FULL FRAME ZOOM-IN	4 SEC	ZOOM INTO HAND AT SAME RATE AS #1. HOLD AT END	24 FRAME DISSOLVE IN (OVER ZOOM)
3	C	FRAME VERY TIGHT HAND/BRUSH	2 SEC	NONE	NONE
4	C	FULL FRAME	3 SEC	NONE	NONE
5	D	E.C.U. ON FISH ZOOM BACK WITH PAN TO FULL FRAME	6 SEC	WITH ZOOM OUT MOVE TO FULL FRAME IN 6 SEC.	NONE
6	E	E.C.U. MAN'S FACE	18 FR.	NONE	NONE
7	E	E.C.U. HAND	18 FR	NONE	NONE
8	E	E.C.U. BLADE	18 FR	NONE	NONE
9	E	E.C.U. FACE (WIDER FRAME	18 FR	NONE	NONE
10	E	MEDIUM - HAND, KNIFE, FILLET	18 FR	NONE	NONE
11	F	FULL FRAME	4 SEC	NONE	48 FRAME FADE OUT

Collage

Collage animation is a technique in which bits of flat objects—photographs, newspapers, cloth, pressed flowers, postcards, etc.—are assembled in incongruous relationships for their symbolic or suggestive effect. The technique is much like kinestasis in the kinds of images used and in the various ways that they can be given movement by means of the animation camera and setup. But the feeling that a collage film engenders in the audience is distinctive. There's often a special quality of zanyness in collage. There's often a feeling of being inside a visual maelstrom.

It's obviously difficult to find words that capture the essence of collage. So let's have the images themselves try to do it. See Figure 9.10.

There seem to be two basic styles of making collage films. The *impressionistic* style is the more familiar. A blitz of imagery fills the screen. The effect can be likened to that of a kaleidoscope, or we might call it an image bomb. The animator creates a flow of images (usually a very rapid flow) through his or her creative use of duration, association, proximity, and, of course, the selection of the images themselves. Full-sceen images can be used for this effect or just parts of images, image shards.

Collage techniques have also been used effectively in what I think of as a *narrative* style. In these films a story is acted out, but it's almost always a very surreal kind of story. Terry Gilliam's animation in the *Monty Python* television series provides a good example of how collage techniques can be used in a rich narrative style. Cutout images combine to create weird characters and weird landscapes. The movement of the characters is often realistic, although the logic of these changes defies description.

If you are drawn to this style of collage, I suggest that you reread the chapter on cutouts. It will give you ideas on how to create jointed figures, how to design backgrounds, and how to determine speed and distance as you film under the camera.

Here's a project that should demonstrate the potential of kinestasis and collage animation techniques. It also tries to give you an opportunity to experiment with both the narrative and the impressionistic styles of collage.

Project: Zookeenie Talk. From magazines or similar sources, find two heads, seen in profile. Select the largest ones you can find and be sure one profile is facing left and the other right. Position these characters at either side of the camera's frame in a way that suggests they are looking at each other. Next, joint the mouths of both characters so that they can be made to open and close.

Cut out and sequence a succession of images that present different foods—apples to ice cream to liquors. You will be animating a "dialogue" between these two characters. If it's possible, try to create an argument that the viewer will be able to follow. As the conversation evolves, you may also want to animate other features of your characters' faces—eyes, expression, whatever. Or you may wish to broaden the topic of the dialogue. Limit this project to a maximum length of 15 seconds.

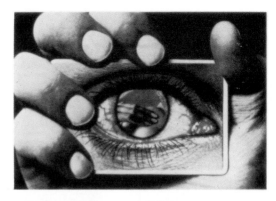

9.10 APPROACHES TO COLLAGE: Two frame enlargements from Frank Mouris's *Frank Film. Courtesy Pyramid Films.*

10
Sand and Paint-on-Glass Animation

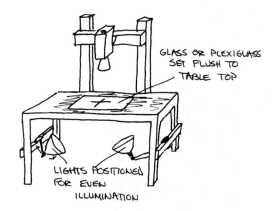

10.1 BASIC BOTTOM LIGHT SETUP: A fixed camera with fixed lens over a fixed, rear-lit surface: the sketch represents a basic setup for doing sand or paint-on-glass techniques.

10.2 SAND ANIMATION: Frame enlargements *A, B* and *C* are from Caroline Leaf's *The Metamorphosis of Mr. Samsa.* Based on a Kafka story, the film demonstrates the animator's abilities to achieve a full tonal range and sharp detail with sand on a rear-lit surface. Enlargements *D, E* and *F* are from Ms. Leaf's *The Owl Who Married a Goose.* Note the positive/negative reversals of figure and ground and note the emphasis on silhouette forms. The production still from *Sand* (also titled *Peter and the Wolf*) *(G)* reveals the way sand is piled up on the glass surface. This film was Caroline Leaf's first work in the sand technique. The photograph of Ms. Leaf, *H,* was taken in her office at the National Film Board of Canada's production headquarters near Montreal. *Photos A-F courtesy NFBC; photo G courtesy Phoenix Films.*

The brilliant work of one young animator, Caroline Leaf, has created two new techniques. This chapter describes her approach and samples the extraordinary effects of her films.

The Basic Setup

The way to animate with sand or paint is almost identical. A stationary camera is mounted above a piece of frosted glass or Plexiglas. A special light or series of lights is positioned beneath the compound so that the translucent white surface is illuminated evenly. (See Chapter 18 for bottomlighting gear.) The material is placed on the glass. In one technique, a fine sand is used and in other technique ordinary water-based inks or paints are used in combination with an agent that keeps the liquid from drying out. Because of the grueling demands of the animating process, it is valuable for the animator to have a foot pedal or similar release for exposing single frames of film in the overhead camera.

As you can see, there is nothing particularly special about the tools or setup. When the camera is loaded, work can begin. But beware the apparent straightforwardness of these techniques. Animating sand and paint is extraordinarily demanding. Hour after hour the animator sits at the working surface and makes minute changes in the art, exposes a frame or two, and then repeats this operation again hundreds and even thousands of times. If there are any mistakes, an entire sequence must be re-created from scratch.

Someone has observed that either technique requires the precision of a watchmaker, the endurance of a long-distance swimmer, the concentration of a mathematician, and the vision of a great artist. Each of these qualities is evident in Caroline Leaf's work.

Designing in Sand

Figure 10.2 carries frame enlargements from three of Caroline Leaf's films. Within these images perhaps you will be able to sense some of the special qualities that reside in animation with sand. Consider these elements as you study the samples.

Texture and Tone. Variations in the size of the sand grains or in the camera's distance from the surface affect the textural quality of the image. Caroline Leaf prefers to use an extremely fine white sand. By spreading it thickly or thinly with her fingers as she works, she can achieve a full range of gray tones. The full black tone is created, of course, by piling sand deep enough so that no light shines through it toward the camera. Conversely, any area that is not covered with sand will be photographed as pure white.

94

Positive/Negative Fields. The rich graphic power of sand animation is achieved, in part, by designing characters and objects in high contrast: white whites or black blacks. Using this flat, sharp-edged imagery, one can manipulate the positive and negative relationships. See, for example, how the shape of a bird (Figure 10.2) that has been used as black on a white field can suddenly be transformed into a white shape on a black field. Such transitions of figure/ground relationships are powerfully exploited in Caroline Leaf's films.

Planning and Execution. It is almost impossible to previsualize the form and pacing animation will follow when one is animating with sand. Through experimentation the animator develops a sense of the visual effects that can be achieved through various styles of moving the sand under the camera. Caroline Leaf works on a surface about the same dimensions as this page. Generally she uses her fingers to manipulate the sand, but occasionally a sharp point is employed to etch a thin line. Informal sketches are sometimes used to plan ahead for the next sequence or to record the appearance of an earlier sequence (Polaroid photographs could be used in recording what has already happened).

10.3   METAMORPHOSIS IN SAND: These fourteen frames indicate the bold and fluid style with which Caroline Leaf sets a scene. In this example from *The Owl Who Married a Goose,* the two prime characters are introduced and their relationship is established. The 7-minute film is based on an Eskimo legend and the sound track consists of sound effects and dialogue recorded by three Eskimo collaborators on the project. *Photos courtesy NFBC.*

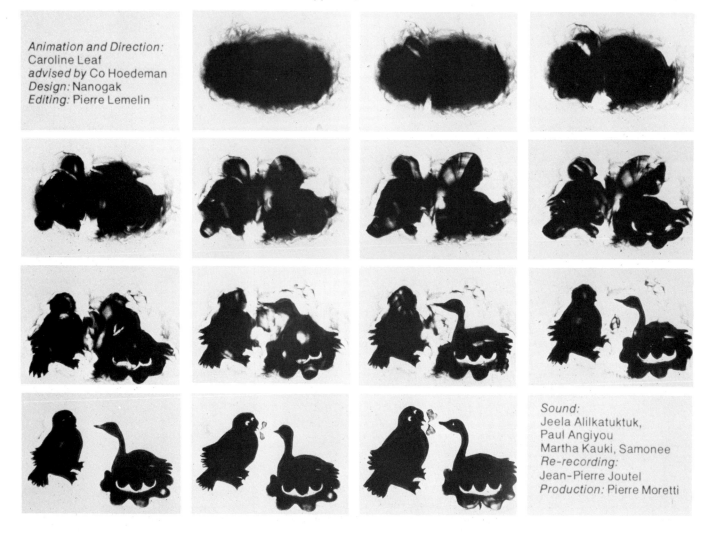

Animation and Direction:
Caroline Leaf
advised by Co Hoedeman
Design: Nanogak
Editing: Pierre Lemelin

Sound:
Jeela Alilkatuktuk,
Paul Angiyou
Martha Kauki, Samonee
Re-recording:
Jean-Pierre Joutel
Production: Pierre Moretti

But basically animation is improvised as the work proceeds. Great concentration is required, particularly in maintaining a steady rate of manipulation so that there will be a consistent flow in the finished sequence.

The laborious and painstaking nature of this technique does have its dividends. In order to keep one's mind alert, the animator invests each image with tremendous thought and care. He is absolutely conscious of every manual change, and this attention to the expressive quality of the smallest detail is clearly evident in the finished footage. Figure 10.3 gives you a taste of the improvisation process and of the significance that just a few details can yield.

Here is some advice that will help when you try the sand technique. Because the bottomlighting shines so directly into the camera, it is best to run some tests to determine the proper exposure. Whites should be their whitest and blacks their blackest. A sheet of clear glass can be used as the compound surface provided you rig a system that diffuses the light evenly. Try ordinary tracing paper to diffuse the lighting. It works best to judge evenness by eye. Also experiment with different field sizes until you find a scale that feels right to you.

As with all animation techniques, watch for variations that open up new boundaries. For example, you might try sand animation with toplighting only. Or instead of using regular sand, try gold, silver, and multicolored glitter. Substitute other sandlike materials: peas, seeds, rice, flour, and coffee. The material you select will dictate much about the best way to light and to animate.

Project: A Three-Day Improvisation. Set up your camera with lighting from the top or the bottom. Over the following few days, plan on working sporadically. Initiate a particular movement or subject in the sand. Play with it. Explore its parameters. Then leave it. During the next session at the camera, evolve the old image and idea into a new topic that exhibits a new style of treatment. Explore this for a while and then leave it. Repeat this process just as many times as you can. Vary the lighting, rates of movement, image material, tonal density, etc. The film that results may lack unity, but it should generate ideas for subsequent sand animations.

Designing with Paint-on-Glass

On the basis of a single film, universal recognition has been achieved for a distinct animation technique that involves working with paint on a glassy surface. Nominated for an Academy Award in 1977, Caroline Leaf's *The Street* represents in one step the discovery, exploration, refinement, and perfection of the technique.

The Street is actually not the first work in this mode. In fact, Caroline Leaf herself worked with ink on a glass field in an earlier film titled *Orfeo* (Figure 10.4). Other animators also experimented with similar effects prior to the completion of *The Street*. However, the scope and level of artistry within this 10-minute film clearly identifies and proclaims it as the source of a new technique.

The frames reproduced in Figure 10.6 can't do real justice to what is going on in this film, to the magic that makes it what it is, a masterwork. All the same, I'd like to describe a few of the major effects

10.4   INK-ON-GLASS: Two frames from *Orfeo*, a
simple and powerful telling of the myth by Caroline Leaf.
Courtesy Pyramid Films.

that can be achieved through this technique, and the most direct way to do this is by discussing how Ms. Leaf has designed *The Street.*

Caroline Leaf works small. Her painting surface is roughly 6 by 8 inches and she uses just her fingertips in applying the paint and then reworking it, frame by frame, as a particular scene develops. Because of the relatively small scale, the images themselves must be boldly rendered—there is not a lot of room for detail and this seems to facilitate a visual metamorphosis in which one image, scene, or movement is transformed into another.

Paint-on-glass animation has a distinctive look. Water-based inks and tempera colors are animated over the bottom-lit field, and thus colors have the quality of illumination rather than of reflection. Water-based colors present a major problem in that the artwork dries out quickly. To keep the paint or ink workable over extended periods, a wetting agent is required. Caroline Leaf uses Color-Flex, a medium that is commonly used in painting animated cels (see Chapter 19).

Two additional structural elements warrant special attention: *story* and *choreography.* Both these elements may be more generic to the personal style of Ms. Leaf than they are to the basic technique of painting-on-glass. Be that as it may, *The Street* forcefully displays these important elements.

Caroline Leaf's films depend heavily on a narrative structure. The story line is developed through the music, sound effects, and dialogue tracks. During the year and a half that it took to create *The Street,* Ms. Leaf followed a sound track that was recorded at the outset of the production and then was carefully analyzed before the shooting process began. (See Chapters 7 and 18 for more on sound-analysis techniques.) For me, a good measure of the artistry of *The Street* resides in the way that dialogue and sound effects are used as primary sources for constructing images and guiding transformations.

Caroline Leaf choreographs her films with distinctive flair. It is astounding to most people that she animates all "camera moves" (as they would be called in live-action filmmaking). A zoom, for example, is accomplished through manipulations in the artwork rather than by actually moving the animation camera. As a result, the movement within the frame is free in a way that could never be accomplished through real camera moves. In Leaf's work the viewer's point of view is totally fluid.

But the choreography goes further. As they move within the frame, *The Street*'s characters establish dynamic and dramatic spatial relationships between themselves and with their setting. Each scene is well "blocked," as someone in the theater might describe the positioning of actors on a set. Figure 10.6 shows key frames from one sequence in *The Street.* By studying it, I hope that you will be able to get a sense of the animator's structural design. And here is an activity that will extend that appreciation through induction.

Project: An Animated Through-Move. Create a simple scene by employing ink or watercolors. Use just enough detail so that the viewer can recognize the location—if the set is an exterior, for example, show a few trees. The "problem" of this assignment will be to animate the scene so that the viewer will have the same visual effect that would be achieved if a live-action camera mounted on a dolly was pushed through the set while film was being exposed at normal speed. Add a

10.5   CAROLINE LEAF AT WORK: *Courtesy National Film Board of Canada.*

10.6   KEY FRAMES: By sampling the flow of key frames within a sequence, the complexities of choreographic and dramatic flow are revealed. With great economy of form and movement, see how much information, characterization, and detail Caroline Leaf is able to invest in this series of paint-on-glass images from *The Street. Courtesy NFBC.*

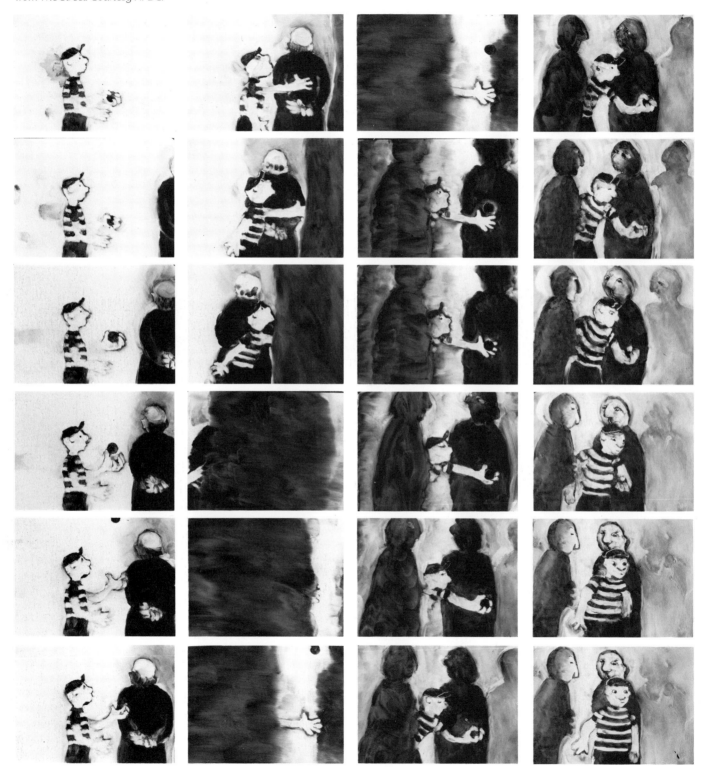

180-degree pan to the preceding move. This means that at the end of
the sequence the ink-on-glass painting should show the initial point of
view from which the scene began.

I admire Caroline Leaf's work. However, I want to temper my
celebration of her art by noting that I don't believe that this animator's
mastery of sand and painting-on-glass techniques in any way precludes
or discourages the work of others in these styles. Each animator brings
his or her particular gifts to each technique, as Ms. Leaf would agree. If
her particular gift is in telling stories through brilliant choreography and
metamorphoses, other animators may have different sensibilities for
using sand or paint to explore abstract imagery, different uses of color,
different relationships of image to sound, or another fresh dimension of
what is possible. Finding your own vision and fresh techniques is what
it's all about. Still, I believe it is also valuable to study others' work. And
nowhere is there more nourishing fare for an independent animator
than in the movies and techniques of Caroline Leaf.

11
Clay and Puppet Animation

Animation of three-dimensional objects has long fascinated film-makers and film audiences alike. "Trick photography" in films was one of the most important attractions for early movie audiences. When the animation of small objects became familiar, enterprising filmmakers found new sources of magic through allied techniques such as pixilation and time-lapse animation.

The ultimate refinement of three-dimensional animation is probably represented by puppet techniques that originated and were refined in Eastern Europe. This chapter will introduce puppet techniques through the newer technique of clay animation—a direct descendant of puppet films that had its genesis in North America.

11.1 **CLAY ANIMATION:** Independent animator Eli Noyes was one of the first to use clay in animation. The four frames below and the 35mm clip on the opposite page sample his stylistic range.

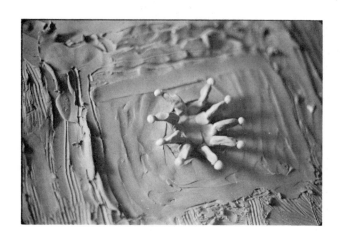

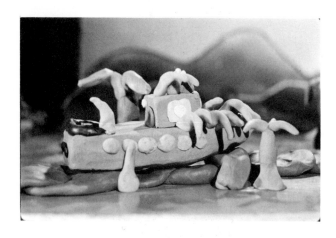

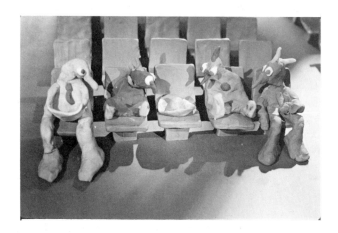

Clay

Few animation techniques more fully exploit the medium's power of metamorphosis than does working with clay. A three-dimensional object can form itself and then transform itself through endless variations. Clay lets us witness transformations in very concrete terms. The images are palpable. They have texture, shape, and weight.

Standard modeling clay works well. It doesn't dry out under hot animation lights, it is easily shaped, it stores well, and it comes in a variety of colors. A number of synthetic substitutes, such as Plasticine, also work well (see Chapter 19).

I recommend that you work large. It's far, far easier to manipulate relatively big clay models than to work with small ones. Generous size also gives you room to establish significant detail. Sheer bulk helps in maintaining the shape of your clay characters or background. However, you must be careful to design characters so that they will be able to stand independently over long periods of time. For this reason, the legs of animated characters are usually short and their feet large. Be certain to check the practicality and flexibility of the clay figures you want to use. Birds, you'll discover, are difficult to keep together and long flower stems are simply impossible.

There are dangers in working on a large scale, however. One is tempted to fill the entire surface of the character or the background with too much detail. Doing this will give you two headaches, one technical and one aesthetic. The constant handling of the clay figures between camera exposures is bound to flatten and obliterate fine detail. More important, complicated detail will detract viewers from seeing the essential movement and timing by which the characters and the story are revealed.

In shooting clay animation, mount the camera horizontally, or else it will point down from an angle of about 45 degrees. Artificial lighting is required, and by using different lights at different locations, dramatic effects can be heightened. The camera can also be mounted directly above the clay, and if the lighting is strong and comes from a sharp side angle, the surface can be seen in sharp relief. With this setup, the contrast between highlights and shadows and ridges and troughs encourages experimentation with abstract patterns.

Each technique of animation seems to have its own distinctive style of movement. As suggested earlier, clay techniques tend to lend themselves to transformation; that is, one shape turning into another. The series of frame enlargements in Figure 11.1 illustrates this quality. In order for the action to make convincing the metamorphoses inherent in clay animation, the action needs to appear relatively smooth. Changes between one position and the next should be very gradually revealed and, where possible, the evolution of one shape into another should be anticipated and exaggerated. Any extraneous source of movement should be eliminated.

Project: Spontaneous Generations. Clay animation can also be used for "character" animation—the art of creating highly anthropomorphic, humanlike characters and stories. This next project will help you get a feel for the tolerances of the materials and the possibilities inherent in transformation. Begin with a fist-sized ball of clay or

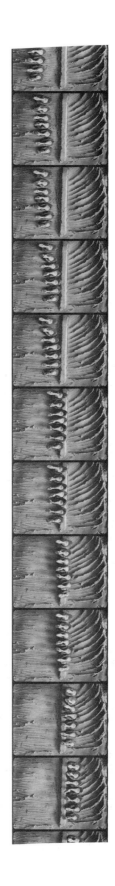

Plasticine. Place it on a simple background—a tabletop will do. Animate the clay as it rolls into the middle of the frame. Then, in exactly 10 seconds of film (240 frames) make your lump turn into five different objects. Plan ahead so that one shape will naturally transform itself into another. Each transition should be as smooth as possible. Shoot on twos. At the end of the 10 seconds, have the lump of clay leave the screen.

11.2 CLAY ANIMATION: The three frame enlargements, *A, B, C,* from the Academy Award-winning *Closed Mondays* illustrate the highly representational style of clay animation used by animator Will Vinton. *Courtesy Pyramid Films.* The production still, *C,* from the Yellow Ball Workshop shows filmmaker Mead Notkin, aged 8, working on *Moon Man.* Note the scale of the clay figures and the effective simplicity of the stage on which they are being animated. The clay apes in *D* were created by Amy Kravitz, aged 13, for a film entitled *Eden* from the Yellow Ball Workshop's reel *Plum Pudding. Photos courtesy The Yellow Ball Workshop.*

A

B

C

D

Puppet Animation

History's seven leading puppet animators have been identified as George Pal, Bretislav Pojar, Ladislas Starevitch, Jiří Trnka, Hermína Týrlová, Zenon Wasilewski, and Karel Zeman. Their names aren't exactly household words. For most of us, in fact, the names are terrifyingly difficult to pronounce, even to read. With the exception of George Pal, these master animators have done their work in Eastern Europe, four of them in Czechoslovakia.

Although the technique of puppet animation has been used widely throughout Western Europe, North America, and Japan, it is no coincidence that the major figures of the genre are Eastern Europeans. For within these countries there is a long-standing tradition of puppetry. National film production centers in Czechoslovakia, Poland, Yugoslavia, Hungary, and the Soviet Union have produced puppet films that exhibit levels of artistry, technical proficiency, and narrative power that are capable of capturing the most profound human experiences.

11.3 PUPPET ANIMATOR CO HOEDEMAN: In his work at the National Film Board of Canada, Dutch animator Co Hoedeman has experimented widely with puppet techniques. In *The Owl and the Lemming (A)* simple Eskimo dolls become characters in an adventure story. In a recent film titled *Sand Castle (B-D)*, Hoedeman combines claylike characters in a setting of sand dunes and sand structures. *Photos courtesy National Film Board of Canada.*

A

B

C

D

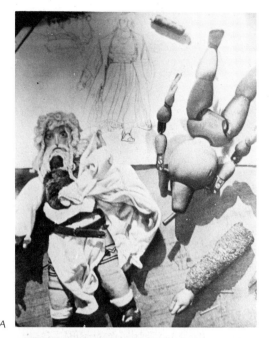

11.4   PUPPETS BY JIŘÍ TRNKA: The craft of Czech master animator Jiří Trnka is shown in A. Note the original sketch, the armature, and a finished puppet. Another Trnka puppet is seen with the lighting and set that complete the film's scene. *Photos collection R. Bruce Holman.*

Puppet Construction

The basic principles of single-frame movement and photography have been discussed. So let's focus attention on the "stars" of puppet films and study what they look like and how they are made.

Animation puppets share certain basic features. They are freestanding and able to support their own weight; they have movable body joints that can hold any position; they are all well executed with remarkable detail; and they can be viewed from 360 degrees.

The anatomy of a puppet begins with an *armature,* an inner construction that allows the puppet to be both sturdy and flexible. There are three basic systems for creating an armature. A wooden body can be crafted that has snugly fitting joints, but eventually the wood wears smooth and no longer holds its position. Flexible wire can be folded to create the basic body structure, though the armature must be padded and clothed, and the wires will eventually break from constant manipulation. Probably the best armature device is also the most sophisticated, a series of metal joints constructed from rods and combinations of ball joints and slip joints that are held together under tension. Figure 11.5 shows examples of various armature designs.

Armature systems help to define the different body types commonly used in puppet animation. The oldest of these is a simple wooden toy, a carved doll that can be moved with precision. Contemporary animators have used the modern equivalents of traditional wooden dolls. Any toy store can provide plastic-jointed dolls that can be used in puppet animation. Such modern toys can be used as they are or modified in varying degrees by an ingenious animator.

Another traditional body type is made by covering an armature with a padded and costumed body. These are often referred to as Czech puppets because of their association with the films of Jiří Trnka and other Czech puppet masters.

Finally, there is the molded body type. The most recent and technically advanced of puppets, a molded body puppet is created by placing an armature within a plaster mold, usually made from a clay or a Plasticine model, which is then filled with a flexible rubber or plastic compound. More specifically, foam rubber is injected into the plaster-of-Paris mold. After the body has "cured," the puppet is taken out of the mold and finishing touches are applied.

Set Design

Puppet animation techniques require special worlds for these special characters. The animator must build mini-sets that are appropriate for a particular story. Like a regular theatrical set, the stage and environment of the puppet film may need flats, backgrounds, props, and other details. Here are a few requirements that are unique to designing a set for puppets.

Scale. The set must match the size of the puppets. Select a scale in which characters and settings can be easily manipulated. As a general rule, don't try to animate a puppet that is much smaller than 6 inches.

Stability. Not only must the construction of the sets be very solid in order to stand up to prolonged use, but the set designer should be sure that "disturbable" items are few. Here are a few things that can provide migraine headaches because they are so easy to move unintentionally: billowy curtains, tables in the middle of a room, real or artificial plants, shag rugs, or any surface that shows dust easily.

Camera Access. Before designing a set, the animator should carefully consider what kinds of camera positions will be used. Will a high angle show the floor? Is it possible to shoot through a window? Can a wall be easily removed in order to get a reverse-angle cutaway? Can the camera get extreme close-ups? Is it possible to track within or past the set?

Lighting. Here is an opportunity to create special lighting effects. Various combinations of color, intensity, and placement can totally reshape an existing set. There should be a lot of experimentation with lighting possibilities that heighten the dramatic tensions of a particular scene or story.

D

11.5 ARMATURES: The wooden foundation of a Trnka puppet *(A)*; a simple wire armature *(B)*; a metal armature *(C)*; and a molded rubber puppet *(D)*. *Photo C courtesy The Yellow Ball Workshop; others from collection R. Bruce Holman.*

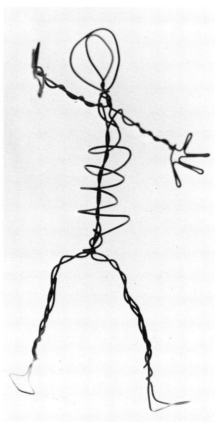

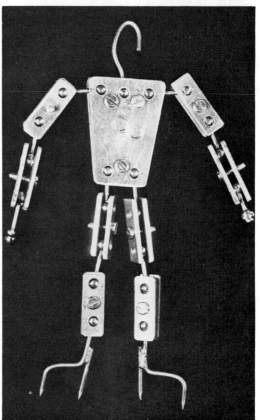

A   *B*   *C*

A

B POSITION 5

C POSITION 6

D POSITION 7

E POSITION 8

Production

There is no really satisfactory way to plot or plan the movement of an animated puppet. The best approach involves some careful observation and simple arithmetic. If you are trying to execute a puppet's walk, for example, time the duration of the overall movement with a stopwatch. Measure the distance to be covered in the walk and measure the average pace of the character. Divide the distance by the number of steps and determine the number of separate moves within each pace. Figure 11.6 illustrates the procedure.

You will still have to use your intuition in applying this system. There must be adjustments because puppet characters will be called upon to perform moves with subtle variations of tempo and emphasis, so that each individual puppet's mood or personality will be revealed through its movement.

If you can imagine the painstaking process of walking a puppet across a set, then you'll agree that the supreme requirement of the puppet animator is patience. But spontaneity is also required. The animator must have the patience to work slowly over long hours with great concentration, and he must have the spontaneity and ingenuity to project into the puppet those details of movement that bring a recognizable personality, a distinctive character to each of the handmade movie stars.

Project: Gulliver's Desktop. As a way to explore some of the characteristics of puppet animation, find a child with plenty of toys and borrow a doll for a few days. If you can, get one of those plastic puppets with full-jointed bodies—ankles, knees, hips, waist, arms, neck, and head. Film a set of tests that shows the doll walking, running, sitting down, and waving. Try various physical activities so that you can find the particular capabilities and limitations of the doll.

Now for a short movie. Mount your camera on a tripod so that it points at a desktop. Light the area in a dramatic way and distribute a normal sample of desktop paraphernalia; Scotch tape, pencils, books, a lamp, a coffee cup, whatever. Shoot a film in which your doll awakens to find itself lost on a giant's desk. Have the doll explore the surface and its implements. You might end this sci-fi saga with the giant's hand suddenly appearing and lifting up the terrified doll.

11.6 PLANNING MOVEMENT: In this example, the action calls for the Lego character to drive through the gate, past the camera, and out of the frame to screen right. If the real distance to be covered is 12 inches and the shot takes two seconds, then each position of the driver would need to be ½ inch farther along the trajectory of planned movement (24 positions divided by 12 inches—shooting on twos). Photo *A* suggests how one would visualize the plan. To exaggerate the drive past, however, spacing between positions might be varied—less space at the beginning and more at the end. The series of four photographs shows the positions 5-8. Note how the character's face turns toward the camera.

A

11.7 PUPPET VARIATIONS: The Yellow Ball Workshop in Lexington, Massachusetts, is a very special place. Under the direction of animator Yvonne Andersen, this center has for many years conducted workshops in practically every animation technique for children and adults. The variety of puppet styles and subject matter is suggested in these stills. Note the use of toys with a homemade puppet in *A*, the simple set in *B*, the use of soft, cloth puppets in *C*, and the huge production scale represented in *D* and *E*. *Photos courtesy The Yellow Ball Workshop.*

B

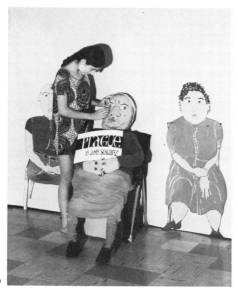

C

D

E

12
Line and Cel Animation

12.1 THE LOOK OF LINE ANIMATION: Nine frame enlargements suggest the breadth of drawing style and subject matter that have been used in animating with registered sheets of paper. Note that the last three in this series are from a single film, Ryan Larkin's *Street Musique*.

Mildred Goldsholl, *Up Is Down. Courtesy Pyramid Films.*

Geoff Dunbar, *Lautrec. Courtesy Films, Inc.*

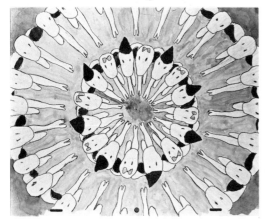

Sally Cruikshank, *Fun on Mars. Courtesy Serious Business Company*

Traditional American animation is cel animation. The technique has taken its name from the transparent sheets of celluloid that bore the likes of *Snow White and the Seven Dwarfs, Cinderella, Bambi, Pinocchio, Peter Pan,* and the special universe of *Fantasia.*

It is no coincidence that the classic animated feature films are almost all the work of the great Disney studios. More than any other individual, Walt Disney guided the development and refinement of cel animation techniques; its recognizable cartoon style, its perfect synchronization of movement with music and voice (called Mickey Mousing), its assembly-line system of production, its division of labor and massive logistics management. The Disney features are the penultimate achievement of cel animation techniques.

American cartoon animation, or *character animation* as it's now called, created not only a brand-new art and industry but also the first truly international audience for animated films. Cartoons have entertained viewers for almost half a century, and some contemporary psychologists might argue that the fantasy world of full-cel animation has reshaped the imaginations and the inner imagery of successive generations of children the world over.

Walt Disney is credited, and rightly, as being the father of classic American animation, but the body of work created with this technique was the business of entire studios of artists, filmmakers, businessmen, and technicians. While tributes are being handed out, here's just a beginning list of individual animators, those facile artists and storytellers and designers who contributed to the artistry and impact of full-cel animation: Walter Lantz, Oskar Fischinger, Winsor McCay, Max Fleischer, Paul Terry, Otto Messmer, John Hubley, Ub Iwerks, Art Babbitt, Bob Clampet, Tex Avery, Milt Kahn, Chuck Jones, Shamus Culhane, Frank Thomas, Tissa David, George Dunning, Grimm Natwick, Preston Blair, Ollie Johnson and many, many more.

In "big-time" Disney-type animation every movement is conveyed through acetate cels that lie stacked on top of each other under the animation camera. Each acetate cel has been painted by hand. The outline of the character is applied to one side and the interior colors to the other side. The number of layers of cels is determined by the number of moving parts in any particular scene. For example, if a character is motionless on the screen for a few moments, except for his mouth, cel techniques allow the animator to use one cel to show the body and head, and another set of cels to animate the various positions of the moving mouth. A background scene, of course, would rest under the stack of clear cels. In a nutshell, that's the cel technique.

Overview

The step from any other technique to full-cel animation is big. It's

Marcel Jankovics, *Sisyphus. Courtesy Pyramid Films.*

J. P. and Lillian Somersaulter, *The Light Fantastic Picture Show. Courtesy Films, Inc.*

Grant Munro and Ron Tunis, *The Animal Movie. Courtesy NFBC.*

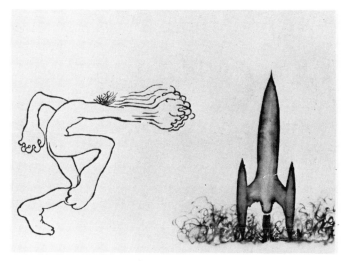

Ryan Larkin, *Street Musique. Courtesy Learning Corporation of America.*

Ryan Larkin, *Street Musique. Courtesy Learning Corporation of America.*

Ryan Larkin, *Street Musique. Courtesy Learning Corporation of America.*

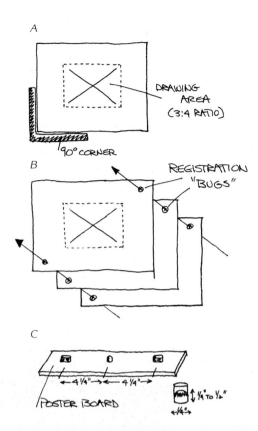

12.2 REGISTRATION DEVICES: A wooden molding, a 90-degree metal rule, or a similar structure is fastened to a wood or plexiglass drawing surface *(A)*. You can select any corner you prefer but note that the area used for drawing should not come too close to the edges of the paper sheets you use. In *B*, a simple pair of "bugs" is traced on successive sheets. These marks must be aligned in filming as well as drawing. Using a standard two-hole or three-hole punch (or a variation of your own), a sturdy registration peg system can be made with dowels and papers punched to match it. Measurements in *C* conform to the three-hole standard punch.

enormous, in fact. Although I don't want to scare you off from this most complicated of animation techniques, I do think it is important to point out that you are now entering a rugged domain. It's an area filled with as many new concepts, tools, and techniques as have been introduced in all the preceding chapters. The road beginning here is most challenging. The journey is not a short one. To get to the highest levels it's necessary to begin a lot further back In this case, you'll be starting with ordinary sheets of paper instead of acetate cels and with simple pencil lines instead of intricately drawn and painted artwork.

This chapter is complicated enough to require its own overview. It begins with an important discussion of the surface area on which animated characters are created. Next there is discussion of how to control movement and timing within a series of drawings. The problem of animating a bouncing ball is given here. It's a classic assignment and an important building block for technical refinements that follow. Central topics relevant to the aesthetics of animation follow. The terms of the discussion are neither vague nor abstract but perfectly concrete. You will design a character and then make it walk across the movie screen.

If you can get this far, you're practically home. Creating your first "walk" is probably the most difficult animation problem you will ever face. Once the technique is mastered, you'll have reached a wonderful plateau in which the refinements come easily and the parameters of your growth become wider than ever. The last part of this chapter (and the one that follows it as well) lets you chart this plateau.

Line Animation

Line animation is the technique of using registered sheets of paper with simple artwork to create a series of drawings that are then photographed by the animation camera. Line animation has only recently been recognized as a distinct and identifiable technique in its own right. An older cousin to this kind of animation is the *pencil test,* a familiar term around classic character animation studios.

The traditional pencil tests of the great animation studios were simply a stage in the development of full-cel sequences, whereby the initial drawings of an animator were quickly photographed right off the paper sheets used in developing such preliminary sketches. The pencil test was, literally, a test, a way of checking the flow and style of a series of drawings before they were laboriously (and expensively) transferred to transparent acetate sheets.

Today's independent animators often go no further than this paper stage of animation. In so doing, they design their movies in ways that make it possible to redraw the entire image (including background) on each subsequent sheet of paper. In the *line-animation* technique, the paper drawings aren't "rough" drafts to the final film. They *are* the finished drawings—fully articulated movements through finely rendered artwork in watercolors, charcoal, felt-tipped pens, or other graphic media. As we'll see, today's independent animators have made other modifications in paper-cel techniques that give their drawings the maximum impact with a minimum duplication of drawings.

The frame enlargements in Figure 12.1 and elsewhere in these pages should clearly indicate that enough significant work has been done with simple paper sheets to justify classifying line animation as a distinct technique.

Registration

A first requirement of line and cel animation is to keep all drawings in accurate alignment so that the projected image won't be jerky. A *registration system* is a way of establishing that the individual sheets of paper on which the drawings are made can be easily and precisely aligned. Here are four possibilities.

90-Degree Corners. It is possible to use the squared corners of paper sheets or index cards in developing an accurate registration system. The animator simply lines up the edges of the sheets, which should, of course, have the same dimensions. A corner of a wood or metal picture frame can be used to make a bracket to assist in the alignment. If you are using corner registration, work with the thickest paper stock available, index cards or heavyweight bond.

Registration Bugs. When using a light table or tracing paper, individual pages can be lined up visually by superimposing a "bug" drawn at opposite corners of each sheet of paper. This kind of registration system is recommended only for those situations in which the artwork is particularly large, unwieldy, or cannot accept a punched registration system.

Round Punch. The standard two- or three-ring punch that is used for school loose-leaf notebooks can be adapted to provide a serviceable and inexpensive registration system. A *peg bar* must be made that holds the sheets during the drawing and filming of paper cels. A simple way to do this is to glue ¼-inch in diameter wooden dowels, approximately ¼-inch long, to a piece of heavy cardboard (Figure 12.2). Sand the top edges so that the pegs won't rip the paper sheets.

Punch the outside holes at a distance of 4¼ inches from the center hole. In this way you can use standard three-ring notebook papers and you can always have your sheets punched to commercial specifications should you decide to shoot the drawings under a camera that accepts only professional registration peg systems.

Professional Peg Systems. Different standards have evolved for the placement and specifications of professional peg systems. The standard in widest use seems to be the Oxberry System, named after the firm that manufactures much of the professional caliber animation hardware. Specifications of the Oxberry pegs are to be found in Figure 12.3. There is another peg system that is used commercially today; the Acme system. Its dimensions are also given.

While these professional systems are accurate, they are also expensive. Metal sheets with a set of mounted metal pegs cost about $25 each. Paper has to be specially punched. Chapter 17 will give you more information about registration equipment and costs.

Field Size

While there's no universally accepted standard for registration, there is one for determining the area that lies below the camera. Figure 12.4 shows how the total field area and the pegs are placed on the

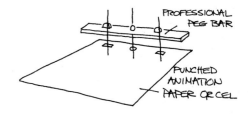

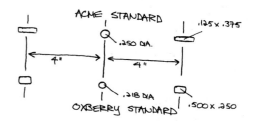

12.3   PROFESSIONAL PEG DIMENSIONS

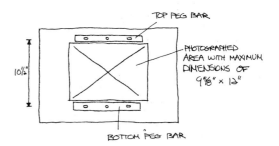

12.4   STANDARD FILED SIZE AND PEG-BAR ARRANGEMENT

compound bed of an animation stand. The dimensions cited are standard for the industry. This means that if you have your paper cels photographed on a professional stand, the camera operator will always be able to line up your artwork in the same way you've designed it.

In Chapter 23 you'll find an accurately reproduced *field guide*. A *field* is nothing more than the standard rectangular frame that the camera "sees." As you'll remember, there is a common aspect ratio for the film image. It is roughly 3:4, height to width, unless a special "wide-screen" format such as CinemaScope is being used. Camera fields are sized in common animation parlance with a simple number. A #8 field, for example, is exactly 8 inches wide. A #5 field measures 5 inches in width. The function of the field guide is thus to specify the area that the camera will be set up to photograph. A greatly reduced model of the standard field guide is shown in Figure 12.5. You may want to detach the guide in Chapter 23 and adapt it to whatever registration system

12.5   STANDARD FIELD GUIDE: In Chapter 23 there is a full-scale section of the standard field guide that you can detach and use in your own work. The circle beneath these coordinates: N-2/E-3. The heavy line shows a 4 field (4 inches wide).

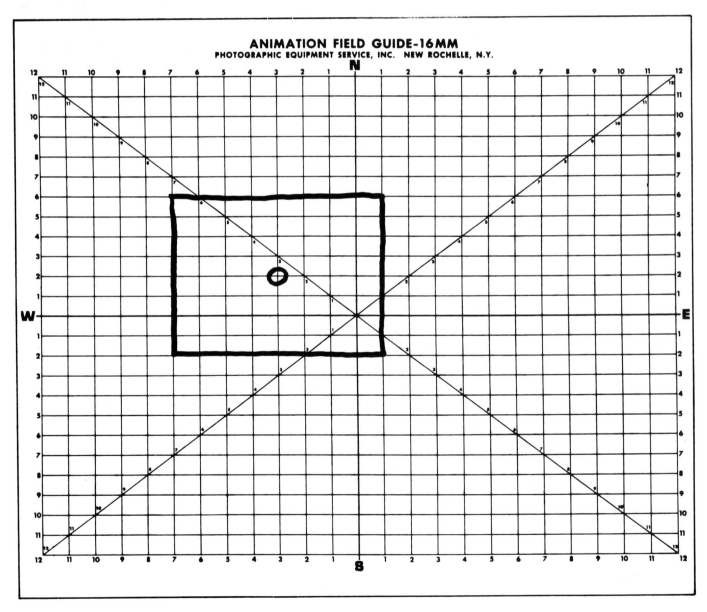

you're using. This tool will be immediately helpful in the projects to follow. Also, study Chapter 17.

There is a standard relationship of the field (and peg bars) to the animation camera. The center of the field guide is matched to the center of the camera's frame. This means that all directions for movement from the central position can be indicated by N (north), S (south), E (east), and W (west).

More now about the field guide itself. Its measurements are based on width increments of 1 inch. The smallest size field is called a #1 field and it is 1 inch wide by slightly less than ¾ of an inch high. A #12 field is the largest photographic area that is normally used. Its dimensions are 12 inches wide by a little less than 10¾ inches high. Here are a few important things to know about the standardized field guide.

Aspect Ratio. Regardless of field size, the dimensions of the frame must always assume the ratio of 4 to 3 (width to height). This is roughly equivalent to the standard format used in super 8mm, 16mm, and 35mm filmmaking, except for CinemaScope and other "wide-screen" configurations. The actual aspect ratio is 1.376 to 1.

Recommended Field. Typewriter paper, tracing tablets, quality drawing papers—almost every imaginable type and quality of paper stock—can be purchased in the common 8½- by 11-inch format. So often do animators use this size paper for their work that a practical field size has evolved that you may want to incorporate in your work. It's a #10 field, slightly smaller than an 8½- by 11-inch sheet, used horizontally.

Coordinates. When the standard field guide is *zeroed-out,* that is, when the center of the camera frame coincides with the center of the field guide, it's possible to specify any point within the field by stating the numerical value of its coordinates. This allows animators to specify precisely and universally the position of any point under the camera. For example, in Figure 12.5 the tiny circle would be indicated by N-2/E-3. If you wanted to begin a sequence with a small field located off center, you first mention the coordinates of the field's center and then the size of the field itself. In our example, N-2/E-3 is a #4 field.

This standardized system of coordinates permits an animator to provide very exact instructions for complicated movements. For example, the following would be immediately understood by any animation camera person: Initial position: #8 field 0-0. Final position #4 field N-2/E-3. Track and zoom in 40 frames.

Edges. Here is a practical note that is based on painful experience. Although super 8mm and 16mm reflex cameras are *supposed* to show precisely what the camera is seeing when you look through the viewfinder, often there is a slight discrepancy. For most forms of filmmaking this error is insignificant. But in animation, it matters very much. The precise location of frame lines is often critical. So be cautious. Always leave a little extra room between the edges of your drawing and the edges of the paper sheets you are using.

The Safe Area. When a film is broadcast over television, part of the picture area is always lost. As a matter of fact, some of the picture area is normally lost in 16mm or super 8mm projection. In any event, if you think your film might end up on television, you should design it so that the action takes place within the *safe area.*

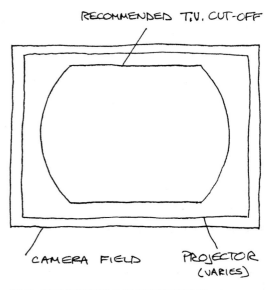

12.6 PROJECTION AND TV CUTOFF: The degree to which the edges of the field are masked during film projection will vary with the specific projector being used. Similarly, television sets differ in how much of the full picture they cut off. This illustration suggests rough limits for both projection and TV cutoff. Special field guides are available to indicate the recommended "TV Safe" area for various field sizes.

STEP 1

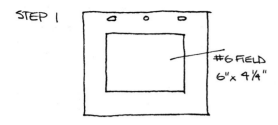

#6 FIELD
6" x 4¼"

STEP 2

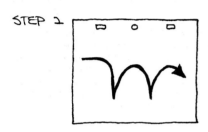

STEP 3

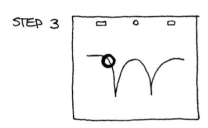

12.7   THE BOUNCING BALL

The Bouncing Ball

It's easy to despair in the face of field guide coordinates, registration pegs, aspect ratios, and safe areas. In fact, there's probably something wrong with you if you're not inundated with detail. However, all this information can be effectively assimilated if you put the information into real operation. Complete the following project. The challenge is to use paper sheets to animate a bouncing ball. This is one of the two classic exercises in animation. The other is the walk. As best you can, try to follow these instructions. You'll make mistakes—anticipate that at the outset. But you'll be familiarizing yourself with the basic process. And that will help you to understand the more detailed explanations and refinements yet to come.

Step 1: Field. Using a field guide and whatever registration system you have (the edges of the sheets will do), draw the outside perimeters of a #6 field. Center the field so that the coordinates are 0-0.

Step 2: Path. Using either tracing paper or a light table to help you see through more than one piece of paper, place a fresh sheet over the one showing your field and draw the path a bouncing ball might take if it were to enter the frame from the left and then hit the ground twice as it moves across the field and disappears off the right side of the frame.

Step 3: Ball size. Select a size for the ball you will animate. Don't make it too small or too large—something in the area of 1 inch in diameter ought to work well in this project.

Step 4: Timing. In this exercise you should try to pace the drawings so that the ball will hit the ground at intervals of exactly 1 second. You will be shooting-on-twos so that twelve drawings are required to make 1 second of screen time.

Step 5: Draw It. Without further explanation, try the problem of the bouncing ball. Use the path diagram as a guide and use a different sheet of paper for each new position. Try to have twelve drawings between each bounce of the ball. Remember, there should be two bounces as the ball moves across the screen. Number each sheet of paper in the upper-right-hand corner. Attacking this problem will require about thirty-six pieces of paper and several minutes of your life, but it will prepare you for the discussions to follow and for all the fine points of animating with line drawings and finally with plastic cels.

Step 6: Preview. After you've completed the problem, hold the stack of drawings in one hand and flip through the pile with the other hand. This will let you preview your work.

Controlling Movement and Time

It is, of course, the amount of change in position between one drawing and the next that creates the illusion of movement. But how can one tell how much to change each drawing from the ones preceding and following it? How is it possible to plan ahead so things end up where you want them and at the right moment as well? Is there a way to speed up the process of drawing? And how can one get a real feeling of character or personality into a particular movement?

If we were to undertake a structural analysis of the bouncing-ball problem, we would divide the distance to be covered by the time required for a particular movement. If you looked at a single, complete bounce of the ball, you would have a series of drawings that were symmetrically placed. The plotting of the balls in Figure 12.8 has been determined through straight arithmetic.

In real life, a ball accelerates as it approaches the ground and decelerates as it reaches the top of its bounce. This change of speed has to be designed into the animation. More than that, this nuance in the reality of a bouncing ball must be accentuated. There is a way to help decide where to place each drawing of the ball. The key lies in the analysis of the time for any given movement.

By now it should almost be second nature for you to change time in seconds into time measured in drawings. The process becomes almost unconscious once you've done it a few times. The camera shoots-on-twos. Therefore, each drawing will become 2 frames of film. Therefore twelve drawings are needed for 1 second of finished film.

To always know the number of frames comprising a given amount of "screen time" mount a *time chart* close to the work area where you

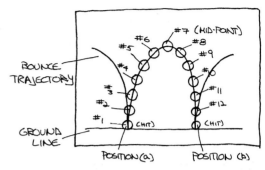

12.8 A MATHEMATICAL BOUNCE: A one second duration means there are 24 frames between each contact of the bouncing ball with the ground. Shooting on twos would thus require the animator to produce 12 drawings that start with position A and end *just before* position B. The ball hits only once per second and here we start each second with that hit.

ANIMATION TIMING CHART

FILM FORMAT	SUPER 8MM		16 MM	35 MM
PROJECTION SPEED (FRAMES PER SEC.)	18		24	24
	24			
RUNNING TIME AND FILM LENGTH	FEET+FRAMES	FEET+FRAMES	FEET+FRAMES	FEET+FRAMES
SECONDS 1	0 | 18	0 | 24	0 | 24	1 | 8
2	0 | 36	0 | 48	1 | 8	3 | 0
3	0 | 54	1 | 0	1 | 32	4 | 8
4	1 | 0	1 | 24	2 | 16	6 | 0
5	1 | 18	1 | 48	3 | 0	7 | 8
6	1 | 36	2 | 0	3 | 24	9 | 0
7	1 | 54	2 | 24	4 | 8	10 | 8
8	2 | 0	2 | 48	4 | 32	12 | 0
9	2 | 18	3 | 0	5 | 16	13 | 8
10	2 | 36	3 | 24	6 | 0	15 | 0
20	5 | 0	6 | 48	12 | 0	30 | 0
30	7 | 36	10 | 0	18 | 0	45 | 0
40	10 | 0	13 | 24	24 | 0	60 | 0
50	12 | 36	16 | 48	30 | 0	75 | 0
MINUTES 1	15 | 0	20 | 0	36 | 0	90 | 0
2	30 | 0	40 | 0	72 | 0	180 | 0
3	45 | 0	60 | 0	108 | 0	270 | 0
4	60 | 0	80 | 0	144 | 0	360 | 0
5	75 | 0	100 | 0	180 | 0	450 | 0
6	90 | 0	120 | 0	216 | 0	540 | 0
7	105 | 0	140 | 0	252 | 0	630 | 0
8	120 | 0	160 | 0	288 | 0	720 | 0
9	135 | 0	180 | 0	324 | 0	810 | 0
10	150 | 0	200 | 0	360 | 0	900 | 0

SUPER 8MM — 72 FRAMES PER FOOT

16 MM — 40 FRAMES PER FOOT

35 MM — 16 FRAMES PER FOOT

12.9 ANIMATION TIMING CHART

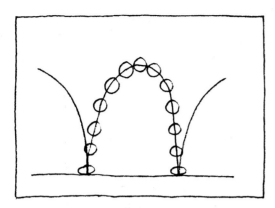

12.10   AN EXAGGERATED BOUNCE: Field, trajectory, and ball size are identical with those in Figure 12.8. Note however the different placement of individual positions on the arc. This bounce will look and feel "right," but even greater exaggeration would read correctly when filmed.

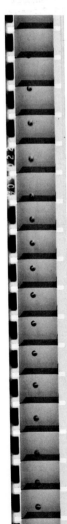

12.11   A LIVE-ACTION BOUNCE:
This enlargement of a 16mm film clip shows the positions of an actual rubber ball as it bounces in real time. In this example, the ball appears to be hitting at roughly a half-second interval—each 10½ frames.

draw and shoot your animation. Such a chart is shown in Figure 12.9. You'll find a larger version of the chart in Chapter 23. If you'd like, you can cut this out of the book, put it into an ornate rococo frame, and hang it over your drawing table.

Back to the bouncing ball. The given time in the problem is 1 second between bounces. The second-to-drawing computation is easy; shooting-on-twos, you need twelve individual drawings to fill the 24 frames of 1 second. Figure 12.10 shows the same bounce trajectory as used in Figure 12.8. Note, however, a different selection of positions for the twelve individual balls. This new spacing plan takes into account the unique way in which a ball really bounces; slower at the top of its arc, faster as it approaches the ground. Look at the ball's positions on the curve. Although these points are symmetrically placed on either side of the bounce (after all, things go up and down with the same flow), the positions of the six ascending and the six descending locations are asymmetrically arranged. This arrangement will accommodate the varying speed of the ball.

Study Figure 12.10 carefully. The slower you want the ball to appear to move, the *closer* must be the positions of consecutive drawings. Remember that in filming and then in projecting, these closer images will show *less* change over the same period of time than would wider-spaced images. Speed is always relative. To make the movement appear faster, the positions are spaced farther apart.

The series of positions in the arc actually exaggerates the positions of a real bouncing ball. In Figure 12.11 you'll see frame enlargements of a bouncing tennis ball from an actual film taken at live-action speed. Compare the difference in spacing in the real version with the animated version.

The spectacular squashing of the ball as it bounces summarizes the difference between an animated movement and the real thing. As gross as the squash may appear in the spacing guide (Figure 12.10), its effect will "feel" right in the finished movie. Exaggeration is the single most important quality in giving "personality" or "character" to an animated movement.

Here's another fine point that you can study through experimentation. Movement is always perceived relative to the size of objects and background, as well as to the speed of other objects. Different-size balls will seem to move at different speeds. Smaller balls look faster than larger ones even if the different balls are traveling the same trajectory for the same period of time. A similar effect exists with field sizes. The same set of drawings will be perceived differently according to the composition and size of the field in which they are placed.

Extremes and In-Betweens

If you have tried to animate the bouncing ball, you have probably found yourself beginning with ball #1 and then working steadily through the remaining drawings in numerical order. Somewhere in the process, I suspect, there may have come a moment when you realized that you must plan ahead so that things would come out right. In this case, the thirteenth drawing would show the ball hitting the ground as it initiates the second bounce. Getting to the right position at the right time is a universal problem in animation. With those techniques that demand precise timing, planning ahead is absolutely essential.

The best way to animate fluid movements that must arrive where you want them when you want them is to employ a process called *extremes and in-betweens.* The process generally begins not with one of the actual drawings but with a schematic sketch that outlines the course of a movement and the relative positioning of the entire set of drawings. This is called a *spacing guide.* A sample has been introduced already in Figure 12.10.

There is a second notation/planning device that animators often use before they start drawing. It's called a *breakdown count,* and it gives the animator an order in which to do the individual drawings. In the bouncing-ball exercise, the ball was to hit the ground at the beginning of each second. This is called a *24 beat,* one hit every 24 frames. As we've seen, the sequence requires twelve drawings. The animator begins by writing out the numbers of all the drawings required in the first beat (Figure 12.12).

The numbers representing the beats are circled. In our example, #1 and #13 represent the start of the first and second beats. These become a first set of *extremes* and should be drawn first. Next, the midway points between these extremes are located and drawn. In the example in Figure 12.12 this is #7. The midway points between the new extremes—#4 and #10—are drawn next.

Whatever the length or speed or quality of a movement, the extreme positions should always be drawn first. Because the light table enables the animator to see through at least three sheets of paper at the same time, extremes become very concrete guides to where to place and how to draw the remaining images—called *in-betweens.*

Only after the extremes have been drawn does the animator finish up the series by doing the remaining drawings. In our exercise, the in-betweens are numbers 2, 3, 5, 6, 8, 9, 11, and 12. While independent animators generally draw these themselves, in large studios the chief animator often does just the extremes and an assistant animator finishes off a particular movement or scene by drawing all the in-betweens.

Project: Bouncing Ball Revisited. To assimilate all this information and master the awkward process it requires, you should undertake another bouncing-ball problem. Use a #8 field, have the ball bounce on a "beat" of every 20 frames and use a very small size ball, about a ½ inch in diameter.

First make a spacing guide and select a trajectory within the field. Next, make a breakdown count in order to determine the order for drawing extremes and in-betweens. After you've completed the animation, film the registered sheets of paper, shooting-on-twos.

If you feel up to it, try this more difficult bounce problem. Select a large field and have the ball hit three times as it moves from deep in the distance toward the foreground. Use a beat of 16 frames. Have the ball begin small and end up very large in size. In fact, have it fill the screen in the last drawing. Film this shooting-on-twos. Figure 12.14 provides a rough planning chart for this more difficult problem.

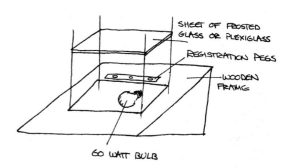

12.12   **BREAKING DOWN THE BEAT**

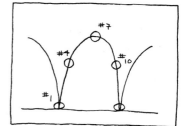

12.13   **A REAR-LIGHTED DRAWING TABLE:** The sketch suggests the features of an animator's drawing table. The raised angle makes it easier to draw. Light tables can be easily jerry-rigged. For example, a sheet of glass with tracing paper on its underside can be suspended between two piles of books allowing a desk lamp to light the surface of the glass from underneath.

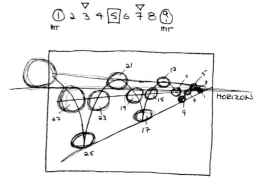

12.14   **A PERSPECTIVE BOUNCE:** This sketch suggests the loose working style that many animators use in roughing out a spacing guide and in breaking down a given time-distance problem.

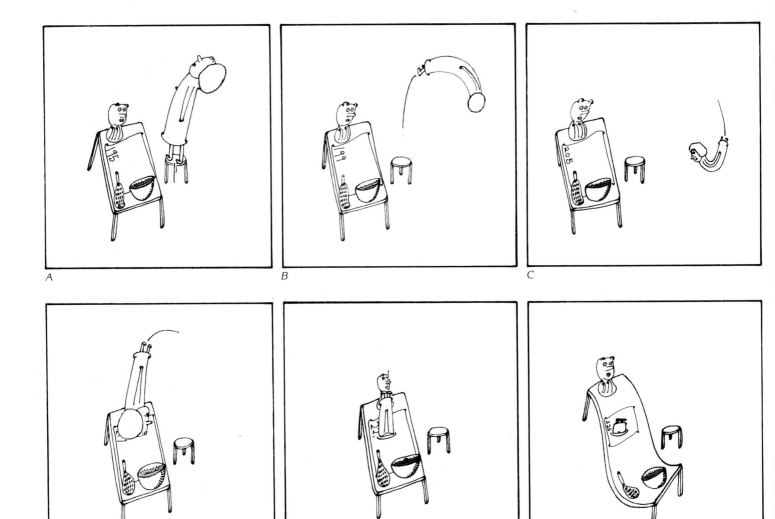

12.15 KATHY ROSE'S RULES: Lest the process of extremes and in-betweens or the value of motivation, anticipation, and exaggeration become too strictly interpreted, study this sequence of key frames from *The Doodlers* by Kathy Rose. Ms. Rose breaks all the rules. Some 6,000 drawings comprising the movie were all drawn upside down on paper. Voice, sound effects, and music were added after the filming. In all her films, Kathy Rose does the animation "straight ahead," very rarely using extremes or in-betweening. Most of the work is done using a basic storyboard, with a great deal of improvisation. *Photos courtesy Kathy Rose and Serious Business Company.*

D

E

F

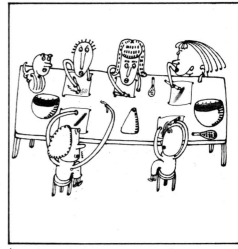

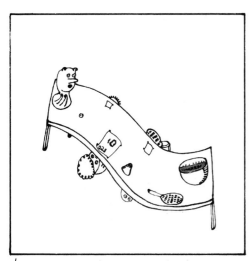

J

K

L

STEP ONE: CHARACTER DESIGN: Easily drawn circular shapes are used as the foundation of the character. All nonessential details should be eliminated. The rear leg is shaded to help distinguish right and left legs.

STEP TWO: ANALYSIS OF MOVEMENT: Spend time studying how different kinds and degrees of movement will best express the distinctive personality you wish your walking character to exhibit. This is a critical step.

12.16   ANIMATING A WALK

Anticipation, Exaggeration, and Motivation

In reading all this, and in trying it, you may begin to feel that the technique of animating with registered sheets has become its own end; that figuring out and then executing a series of drawings is the highest goal and most prized competency an animator can attain. But in animated filmmaking as in all other art forms, technique is meant to serve the primary goal of expression. How something is realized is never more important than what is being realized. Execution should never be of more importance than content.

As you are laboring with your spacing guides and extremes, try to keep part of your mind focused on the following kinds of questions. Is this movement right for the character? Does it have the same qualities as real movement? Does the movement reveal subtle qualities about the character or about the story? In the final analysis, does the movement "move" the mind and the feelings of the viewer?

Learning how to block out and animate a bouncing ball is only a means in that by mastering the process you'll be able to bring to life a drawing of your own design and make it move in ways that are unique and fitting to it.

Anticipation and *exaggeration* have become special concepts in character animation. Wherever and whenever possible, the animator tries to give a character a distinct physical movement in anticipation of what is to be a major movement. If Porky Pig is to walk toward screen-left, that movement is first prefaced and anticipated by a small movement toward screen-right. You've probably noticed how cartoon characters always seem to pause miraculously in midair before they begin their fall after walking over the edge of a cliff. This pause is "anticipation." And then the fall itself is often exaggerated. The fox chasing the roadrunner seems to fall off cliffs that are at least 5 miles high. And the impact of the fall causes the poor fox to disappear into a deep hole. Exaggeration again.

So central is the use of extreme anticipation and exaggeration in classic American cartoon animation that the matched concepts have taken on more informal names. When talking about the aesthetics of

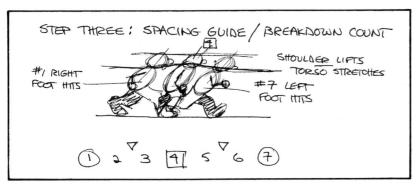

STEP THREE: SPACING GUIDE/BREAKDOWN COUNT: A foot is to hit the ground each half second or every 12 frames. This happens to be the timing of a "normal" walking step.

STEP FOUR: EXTREMES: In animating a walk, it is necessary to simultaneously see through at least 3 sheets of paper. Common tracing paper will allow this, or you can use a simple light table like the one shown in Figure 12.13. In drawing extremes, remember that if the character has weight, the position of whichever foot is on the ground will remain fixed throughout an entire step (in this case, for 6 drawings).

their craft, animators will speak generically of *stretch* and *squash*. The terms are synonymous for "anticipation" and "exaggeration." The bouncing-ball problem should have introduced both of these quite clearly.

One of the animator's most creative acts is the study of real movement. Hours must be spent watching how a friend walks, studying the mannerisms of animals, peering with concentration at one's image in a mirror. Yet understanding how and why things move as they do is only part of the creative process. If a movement is to "work" it must be properly *motivated*. The animator has to convince the audience that the only possible kind of movement for a given situation is precisely that movement the animator has created. Developing motivation for a particular sequence and movement becomes another central aesthetic concern.

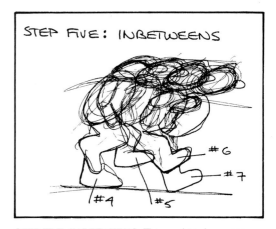

STEP FIVE: IN-BETWEENS: This ought to be an easy step. A registration system is required, of course, in steps four and five as well as in the eventual filming of the drawings.

The Walk

Needless to say, a ball is a lot easier to draw than even the simplest cartoon character. The bouncing-ball classic project is often followed by another classic, "the walk." Animating a walking character for the first time just has to be one of the most difficult and challenging problems you'll ever set for yourself.

The illustrations in Figure 12.16 clarify some basic principles about animating a walk. Note that the process of planning the drawings is exactly the same as the process used in executing the bouncing-ball problem.

Project: Your Very Own First Walk. This project assigns you the same specifications as the sample walk just presented: a #10 field size, a 12-frame beat, and a figure of approximately the same height and width of gait. But this time it's *your* character, a creation of your own mind that will move with the style you draw into it. The degree of exaggeration and anticipation that you select for your walking person is for you alone to decide. You can, if you want, even have the character look a little like yourself.

Here's a simple narrative framework for this walk sequence. Your

STEP SIX: CLEANUPS: Depending upon how roughly you work, it may be important to redo each drawing quickly so that the clarity and simplicity of the original design (step one) is maintained consistently throughout the walk. This is also a good time to check the details of movement and characterization that you've designed in step two (anticipation, exaggeration, motivation, stretch, and squash).

12.17   SPACING GUIDE FOR WALK PROJECT

character enters the screen from the left and takes two full paces (four steps) into the middle of the field. Plan this so that when the character comes to a standstill after the second full pace, he or she will still be within the given field size. At this point, have your character pause for a ½ second and then, in another ½ second, turn the character so that it faces the camera. Let there be another pause, this time for a full second. Finally, raise your character's arms in a move that takes a ½ second. In the last drawing of the sequence have a "bubble" pop onto the screen beside your character with this written inside: "I'm terrific." This project should require in the neighborhood of thirty-five drawings on separate sheets of paper. Figure 12.17 gives a scaled-down suggestion of how your spacing guide might look.

Easing-in and Easing-out

It's the moment for an important digression. In animating a pan, or any other movement, it is necessary to move *gradually* up to the full speed of the movement. A character can't suddenly appear to walk at full speed any more than someone in real life can suddenly jerk into full movement. A transition is required.

In animation, this transition from stasis to a steady rate of movement is called *easing-in* and *easing-out*. Complex formulas have been invented to help the animator chart the initial movements in this transition. At this level of exploration, however, it is enough to improvise easing-in or easing-out of a pan by gradually increasing the distance between positions during the initial phase of filming.

Cycles and Holds

Animators love shortcuts. It's not surprising. Shortcuts allow one to make the longest film for the least labor. Shortcuts stretch the impact of an animator's art. You'll grow to love shortcuts too!

In doing the walk problem, you can use a single drawing for a full twenty-four frames at the pause before the character lifts his or her arms. Such a moment is called a *hold*. This shortcut enables the animator to avoid drawing the stationary figure twelve times.

E   F   G   H   I

A

12.18 RYAN LARKIN'S WALKING: In Ryan Larkin's deceptively simple film, the screen shows us beautiful studies of people in motion. Done with sheets of paper, not acetate cels, *Walking* explores different walking gaits, different kinds of walkers, different angles of observation, different moods and different—boldly different—styles of animation. *Stills courtesy NFBC and Learning Corporation of America. Film strips by the author.*

B

D

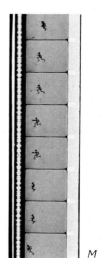

C

J

K

L

M

N

A *cycle* accomplishes the same thing, increasing the number of times a single drawing can be used. But a cycle does this with movement. In the walk, you were asked to draw two full paces, which was accomplished in twenty-four drawings (the "beat" was twelve, which required six drawings for every step). A cycle allows you to accomplish the very same visual effect with just twelve drawings, half the total number normally required.

The principle of a cycle is based on the ability to design a series of drawings so that the last drawing leads smoothly back to the position of the first drawing. This means, of course, that the same set of drawings can be used again and again as long as you want the sequence repeated.

In order for the last drawing in the cycle (#6) to lead smoothly into the first drawing (#1), the drawings must be modified so that there is no forward movement. The character's head stays in the same position, although the legs continue to move as before. This means that the character's feet must "slide" somewhat between drawings so that the walking figure always returns to the same initial position.

No matter what kind of character or object you are animating (a car, an animal, a spaceship) or how many drawings comprise the cycle, the movement will appear correct if the last position leads smoothly back to the first position.

To get a feeling of *forward movement,* a separate background is made, which will pass under the walking figure while it remains in exactly the same place. To achieve this effect, it is necessary to see through the top paper sheets to a background sheet. This is most effectively done with clear acetate sheets, as opposed to paper sheets. However, by using a rear-lighted surface under the camera, it's possible to see through more than one page of the paper sheets (Figure 12.19).

12.19 CYCLING WITH PAPER SHEETS: The sketch shows an animation disc that has been mounted into a table and then lit from beneath. In addition to the frosted glass or plexiglass insert in its center, the disc bears two sliding peg-bars. In filming a cycle, one set of pegs remains stationary (it bears the cycle of drawings) while the other set of pegs (bearing the same background) is moved incrementally between exposures.

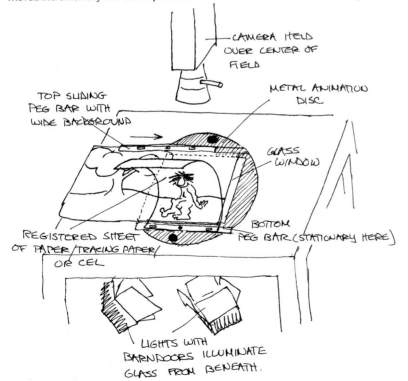

12.20 CYCLING SOMEONE IN MOTION: As only a master animator could do it, these variations have been created by Preston Blair. Mr. Blair worked for many years at the Disney Studios where he contributed to *Pinocchio, Bambi,* and *Fantasia.* (In the latter he designed the hippos.) Later working for MGM, Mr. Blair designed and animated *Little Red Riding Hood,* and directed cartoon shorts. *Material here is gratefully reproduced from* Animation—How to Draw Animated Cartoons *by Preston Blair, published by Walter Foster.*

MOVEMENTS OF THE TWO LEGGED FIGURE

HERE IS A COMPARISON OF THE VARIOUS TWO LEGGED FORWARD MOVEMENT CYCLES -- I HAVE
DRAWN ONE-HALF OF EACH CYCLE BELOW -- REVERSE HANDS + FEET FOR THE OTHER HALF --
-THESE CYCLES CAN BE USED AS "REPEATS" - (THAT IS THE DRAWINGS MAY BE REPEATED OVER
+OVER IF THE FIGURE REMAINS CENTERED ON THE SCREEN AND THE BACKGROUND MOVES.

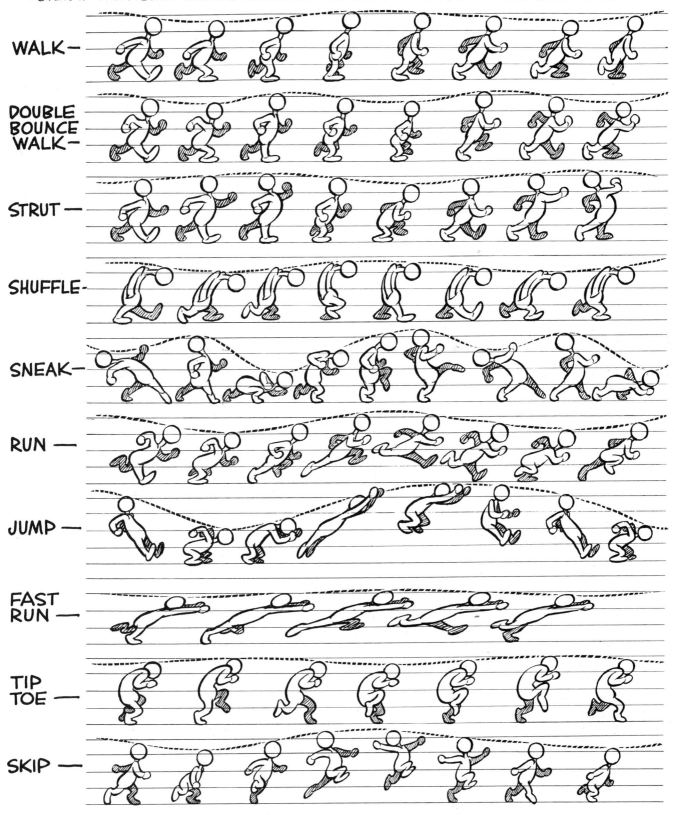

WALK—

DOUBLE BOUNCE WALK—

STRUT—

SHUFFLE-

SNEAK-

RUN—

JUMP—

FAST RUN—

TIP TOE—

SKIP—

Try to cycle the animated walk you designed in the last project. Create the effect of forward movement by panning a background beneath the walking figure, using rear lighting, or by simply advancing the drawings of the cycle under the camera without a background of any kind.

Numbering

You have already discovered how important it is to consistently number the separate sheets of paper that hold your drawings. This is especially important when you get into cycles and holds. The more complicated your film, the greater the need to keep accurate records of how many times to expose a particular drawing or how many times to repeat a particular cycle.

With the paper sheets of line animation, the numbering system can be relatively simple. Informal notation devices can be used. But the problem becomes much more complicated once you start to use layers of paper cels, or when you incorporate a camera or compound movement with the use of paper sheets. A sophisticated system for numbering is discussed later.

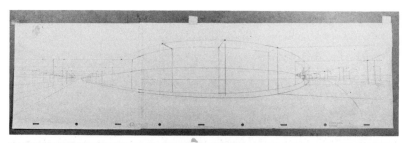

12.21   PRECISE PLANNING: These four photographs show a sophisticated spacing guide, planning elements, and final art used in Al Jarnow's *Autosong. Courtesy Al Jarnow.*

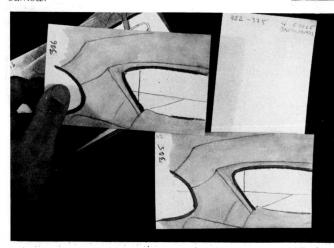

Refinements and Special Effects

Although we've not yet reached the use of acetate cels, I'd like you to know that once you have mastered the walk, you've dealt with animation in its most complete and most elegant state. The differences between line techniques and cel techniques are differences in execution, not conceptualization. In fact, cel techniques are designed to make simpler, easier, and faster the sort of complete animation that we've been working through thus far.

Line techniques yield "full" animation. Each element of the image can be modified in the twelve drawings required for each second of screen time. Unless one chooses to film separate drawings for each frame, there is no way to pack more movement within a second of film. You've reached the saturation point. Here are some quick notes on simple modifications of line-animation technique through the use of registered paper sheets.

Multiple Layers with a Light Box. A rear-lighted surface allows one to see through a number of sheets of paper. This helps in doing in-betweens once you've drawn extremes. If you use *tracing paper* you'll be able to get a clearer illumination for more layers of paper sheets.

A

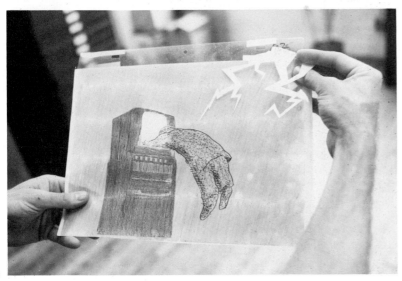

B

C

12.22 CEL/LINE HYBRIDS: George Griffin demonstrates a few innovative techniques that combine line and cel animation. In *A* an acetate sheet with lines and a paper sheet with textured color are cut so that a third level of material can show through the character's eyes. Also from *Candy Machine, B* shows how a paper lightning bolt has been mounted on an acetate sheet and then placed on top of other artwork. George Griffin stands beside an extended pan background that combines cel and paper levels, *C.* In his hands the animator holds cutout paper figures used in this scene from *The Club.*

12.23 USE OF LINE AND TEXTURE: A sketchbook's black pencil drawings come to life in George Geersten's *The Men in the Park*. Animation is sporadic but intense. Facial expressions change. A figure of a man rises and shambles off screen. There is a blur of nearby traffic. Note the texture of the lines. *Courtesy NFBC.*

Die-cuts. One paper cel can be used as a "frame" for those cels placed under it. The effect is quite pleasing—a frame within a frame.

Cel-Over. An easy way to show a very simple background without redrawing it is to create a single *acetate* cel with a few background lines drawn on it. This cel is placed *over* the sheets of paper before each shutter release. A set of top pegs and bottom pegs are helpful to ensure good registration.

Special Papers. Don't overlook the creative effects inherent in different kinds of drawing paper. You can take good advantage of variations in texture and color.

Graphic Media. There are also creative possibilities in using different marking tools. Experiment with watercolors, felt-tipped pens, pastels, crayons, colored pencils, charcoal, acrylic paints, drawing inks, and so on. Each dictates a special kind of drawing. Discover, if you can, which drawing media best fortify and extend the unique character of your own personal drawing style.

Dissolve Series. If your camera has the capability to execute in-camera dissolves, you can produce very powerful effects by "dissolving" between drawings. When used appropriately, this technique can save you the work of doing in-between drawings. For example a twelve-frame dissolve (which lasts ½ second) requires only two drawings, while full animation during the same ½ second would require six drawings. Experiment with dissolves of different lengths.

Multi-Image. With registered paper sheets you can easily create multi-image movies. For example, the camera can be positioned so that there will be a large field that accommodates two different sets of drawings. A masking device can be used to create a regular frame for different cycle drawings.

Cel Animation

Believe it or not, cel animation was invented because it saves work. The transparent surface of the plastic sheet makes it unnecessary to draw *all* the parts of a scene every time there is to be a change in *one* of the component parts. In turn, this means that the imagery of animation can become far more detailed and finely rendered than would ever be possible if every single element of the drawing had to be completely redrawn each time a change is required, as it is in line animation. The term "cel" comes from celluloid, the chemical substance of the early plastic sheets. *Acetate* is the proper chemical name of the sheets in use today, but the old name has stuck. Today, the word *cel* refers to transparent plastic sheets, regardless of material.

The heart of the process of working with cels has already been introduced: registration, extremes and in-betweens, cycles and holds, stretch and squash. The discussion that follows deals with the unique characteristics, potentials, and problems of using acetate sheets, and of the system of animation that has developed around them. Let's begin with the cel itself.

The standard animation cel is a transparent plastic sheet that is .005 of an inch thick and measures 10½ by 13 inches. The sheet is slightly larger than a #12 field and it is usually punched to fit one of the two standard registration systems, Oxberry or Acme.

The surface of the cel is very soft. It scratches, bends, rips, and smudges easily. It collects dust like a magnet. For these reasons, cels are handled with great care and usually the animator will wear cotton gloves while painting or handling them.

If you try to remember that the function of the cel is to save work, it becomes easy to see how the cel is used. Whenever and wherever possible, an animator will save the labor of redrawing. An example or two will make this clear.

Imagine that we want to animate that famous moment in prehistory when one of our ancestors discovered fire. We'll first create a scene, perhaps the mouth of a cave. Our character might be sleeping when a huge lightning bolt zaps the ground beside him. Let's say that this dim-witted caveman fails to stir during the first smashing bolt. He snores on. A second blast manages to burn off his fur clothing. He continues sleeping peacefully. Eventually, however, our ancestor starts shivering in his sleep from the cold. A third lightning blast awakens him and he notices a burning branch. His curiosity is aroused. He crawls over for a look, a very close look. He burns his nose and discovers the meaning of fire. It's an elevated moment—one small sniff for man, one giant waft for mankind.

The drawings in Figure 12.24 present the opening scene of this drama, plus quick sketches for key moments within the story: the first zap of lightning, the burning clothes, the awakening, the moment of glorious discovery.

The largest saving of work comes right at the outset. Using cels, one never has to redraw the background. The same drawing can be used throughout the entire sequence. The opening moment, for example, requires just one layer of cels for our sleeping friend. If the animator wants to have him snoring, then there might be a cycle of, say, three or four cels that would show the body moving slightly as our caveman sleeps. These few drawings could comprise the first five seconds of the film.

But greater economies are in store thanks to cel techniques. During the first blast of lightning, the animator could use a second layer of cels to show the lightning itself as it blasts onto the scene. No need to redraw our hero if the lightning is carried on a second level of cels.

In the sequence where our ancient relative sleeps peacefully as his loincloth is burning off, the animator might use one cel for the naked body, while a different cel level shows, in stages, the fur being singed away. Executed as a close-up, this sequence might bear further refinements. The great discoverer's face might reveal a sensual smile as his body is warmed for the first time by a flame. In this case another cel level could be used to show the changing facial expression. Without the use of cels, the entire body and background would have to be drawn twelve times for each second of screen time. With cels, only the burning cloth and perhaps the eyes and mouth would need to be redrawn for each exposure.

Skipping now to that moment of triumph, the animator could design the sequence so that the caveman's body remains motionless once he has crawled over to investigate the burning branch. Only his head and nose would actually be extended with suspicion toward the novel sight. At this moment three cel levels would be used: one for the

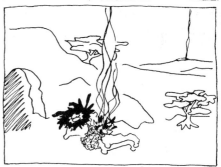

12.24 HOW ACETATE CELS SAVE WORK

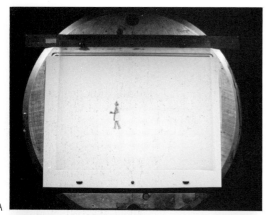

A

B

C

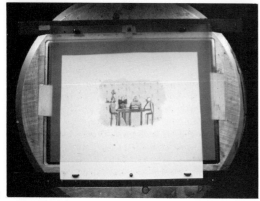

D

12.25 CEL LEVELS: Two cel levels (*A* and *B*) combine with a background painted on paper (*C*) to compose a frame (*D*) in Janet Perlman's *Lady Fishbourne's Complete Guide to Better Table Manners*. Frame enlargements *E* and *F* show other moments in the film.

E

F

body; one for the head and nose, stretching and sniffing; and one for the burning branch, the latter probably a cycle of three or four cels. The original background would still be used.

A maximum of four layers of cels can be used at any given time. The animator must study and plan the action carefully in order to break down the overall image into no more than four layers.

Each acetate cel has a small degree of optical density even though a single plastic sheet appears transparent. If you hold one cel over a picture you may not be able to make out the slight fading of color. But if you hold three or four cels against a background, your eye will easily detect a major change in color intensity and in the definition, or clarity, of the image.

Any change in the number of cels covering a given background will be noticed. Hence, if there is a scene in which four cels are used—even for a short sequence—four cels will have to be used throughout the film. In our example, three cel levels are required for the finale. This means that two *blank cels* are required for the first part of the scene in order to provide a consistent optical density. Otherwise the background will appear to change intensity and color.

Wherever possible, of course, the animator uses previously prepared cels or opts to hold particular cels under the camera for as long as possible. The latter is termed a *held cel.* And if there's a way, the animator will always keep one level of cels for use with a *cycle* of drawings that can be repeated again and again. When there is full movement, of course, everything that moves must be redrawn. For such movements the animator generally consolidates all the action into one cel level. This is simply for economy and drawing convenience.

As noted before, animators usually first try out complicated movements with a pencil test—a film of the first rough sketches that have been done on paper. It is after the animator has been able to review this rough cartoon that drawings are transferred to transparent cels. The necessity and value of the pencil test is easily understood when one learns how much work goes into preparing a cel.

First, the pencil drawing is covered with a sheet of acetate and the outline of the character is traced. At this stage the "roughness" of the pencil drawing is cleaned up and a smooth continuity between drawings is developed. The traced line is usually varied in thickness to provide emphasis to the character it portrays. This operation is called *inking.* In large animation studios there are teams of assistants called *inkers* who perform only this task. It's a demanding job and it requires great precision.

In order to keep the lines of the drawing as strong as possible, colors are applied to the reverse side of the acetate sheet. This work is done by another set of assistants called *opaquers.* Their job consists of carefully painting the correct opaque paints on the appropriate parts of the character. Figure 12.26 illustrates the processes of inking and opaquing. They are every bit as laborious as they look. And the materials are expensive too.

When there is no need to redraw a background for every scene in the finished film, it becomes practical to fashion detailed and delicately rendered backdrops against which the animated action will take place. In classic American cartooning, there are individual artists, and even

12.26 INKING AND OPAQUING: By flipping over a completed sheet of cel art, it is possible to see how the process works. Because the black outline of the character has been inked onto the front of the cel, the process of opaquing on the rear side can be somewhat imprecise. This frame is taken from *The Dog Who Said No,* an animated segment done for *Sesame Street* (The Children's Television Workshop) by animator Derek Lamb.

entire production departments at the larger studios, who do nothing but design and execute backgrounds.

Backgrounds are fashioned with care. A fine quality paper stock is used and art materials are also of the best quality. Watercolors are the medium most often used. All backgrounds, however, must be styled to fit the graphic quality and look of the characters. Backgrounds must also, of course, conform to the needs of the story. And, as pointed out earlier, it is important that the background not be so busy as to obscure or draw attention away from the movement of story and characters.

One of the most interesting effects of cel animation is experienced in *traveling scenes.* The use of transparent cels, combined with the principle of a cycle, allows the animator to create a long, exciting chase with very little work. The secret lies in a *panning background,* an extra long strip of background artwork that is moved underneath the cels and joins up with itself so that the pan can go on forever.

Project: A Long Way to Tipperary. Using commercially punched cels or a makeshift set of acetate sheets that have somehow been registered, copy (ink) the outline of the walk cycle you designed earlier. After the inking process, turn each cel over and color in the character using paint or felt-tipped pens. For this project you will be making a cycle of six different cels.

Design a panning background. It will be the same height as the field on which you are working, but it will be much, much wider (Figure 12.27). On this background draw and then paint a road upon which your character will eventually appear to be walking.

Once the background and cels have been completed, place them under the camera. The cycle drawings are placed over one set of pegs, and the background will be constantly moving between exposures. In order to provide a smooth registration for this panning movement, punch the background drawing and place over a *sliding peg bar,* a set of pegs that can be moved between exposures to carefully established positions. The sliding peg bar is usually located at the bottom of the animation disc. Chapter 17 will show such equipment in detail. It's possible, however, to use a common ruler in calibrating and controlling the movement of a background.

With some experimentation you'll discover how the speed of the

12.27   A PANNING BACKGROUND

walk is a factor in determining how much the background is panned between exposures. The movement of the character's legs must visually match the speed with which the background passes underneath the walker.

An illusion of depth can be created with the use of a second and closer moving background. An additional element can be placed over the cel sequence. It is moved at a relatively faster rate than the distant background. The combined effect mirrors the perceptual experience of real life, in which objects nearest one appear to pass more quickly through the field of vision than objects in the distance.

The background you've designed can itself be a cycle. If your drawing is long enough you may be able to reconnect it with itself so that the left edge of the drawing joins the right edge.

Special Problems

Working with cels is difficult and time consuming. It requires special care and it is expensive. Employing cels is certainly worth the trouble, however, when you want to present dazzling backgrounds and full movement of characters. There is a lushness to cel animation that cannot be equaled by any other technique or production shortcut. It *is* rigorous, however, and filled with special problems. Here are a few of them.

Reflection. Acetate sheets will reflect light into the camera lens. You must be particularly mindful of glare from the side lights, even if they are mounted at a 45-degree angle to the artwork. The glass platen that holds the acetate sheets flat on the compound should control such reflection. Problems nonetheless persist.

Shadow Board. Even with a platen and angled lighting, the cels can act as mirrors and reflect an image of the camera itself from the cels back onto the film's surface. To remedy this, a black, nonreflecting cardboard matte can be rigged to mask the reflections of the camera body or lens metal. See Chapter 18.

Newton Rings. It is important that there is just the right amount of pressure on the cels piled beneath the camera. If there is too little pressure the cels will wrinkle, causing ephemeral shadows that are very distracting. Too much pressure produces an effect known as Newton rings. This is partially caused by the thickness of the paint on the cels, and treatment of the problem may involve a very light dusting of the cels with face powder so that they won't adhere to each other under the pressure of the platen.

Cel Paints. As suggested earlier, there is often an appreciable loss of definition and color caused by the density of the acetate itself. This cel thickness causes a 5 percent loss of light and this shows up most clearly with color paints. If a red is used on the top cel and then the same red is used, say, on the fourth cel layer, these reds will have a different hue in the final film. This problem is solved by using special sets of commercially prepared paints in which the same colors are supplied in four different hues to compensate for the change in color caused by the cels themselves (see Chapter 19).

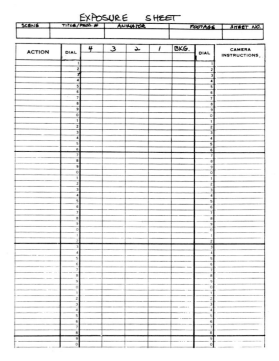

12.28 AN EXPOSURE SHEET

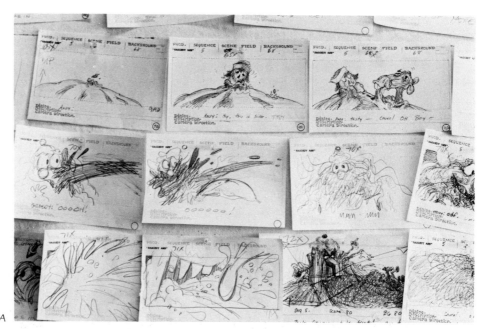

A

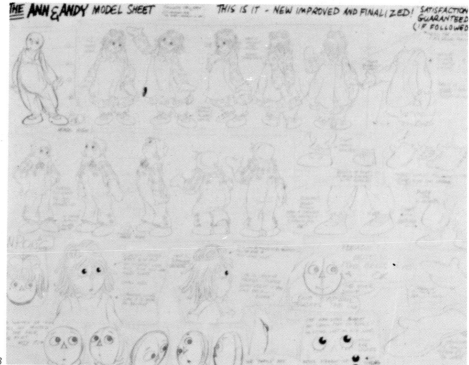

B

C

12.29 RAGGEDY ANN & ANDY: Many individuals, processes, and artifacts must come together creatively in the making of an animated feature. These photographs from John Canemaker's book *The Animated Raggedy Ann & Andy* show the personalities and the workings that went into Richard Williams' production of *Raggedy Ann & Andy*. Pictured are an early storyboard for the Greedy sequence (*A*); the Ann & Andy model sheet (*B*); a sequential set of cels showing Andy (*C*); cameraman Al Rezek at work (*D*); director Richard Williams (*E*), pictured here designing a character for another feature in production titled *The Cobbler and the Thief*; cels and paints from *Raggedy Ann & Andy* (*F*); and finally animator Tissa David (*G*), seated at the drawing table where she created the feature's central character, Raggedy Ann. *Photos courtesy The Bobbs-Merrill Co., Inc., 1976. Raggedy Ann and Raggedy Andy and all related characters appearing in this book are trademarks of The Bobbs-Merrill Company, Inc.*

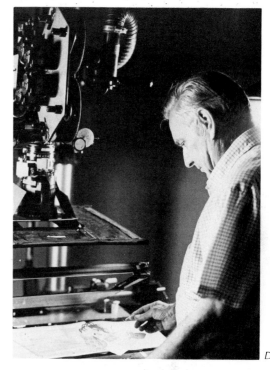

D

E

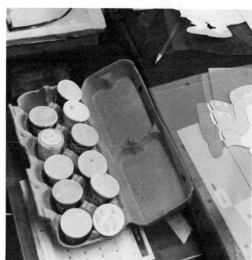

F

G

Dust. Tiny pieces of dust will settle on the glass platen during filming and these, unfortunately, show up as specks on the finished film. Dirt and dust particles also tend to adhere to the surface of cels, helped along by static electricity. A solution of vinegar or ammonia dissolved in water is a recommended cleaning solvent for the platen. Polaroid filters can be used to optically remove the glare caused by specks of dust and dirt (see Chapter 15).

Shooting Complexities. The more complicated the arrangement and number of cel layers, the easier it is for the camera operator to screw up during filming. There is simply too much to remember, too many changes to make, and too many variables for any individual to keep track of without some kind of written aid. And this leads us to exposure sheets.

Exposure Sheets

Full-cel animation requires a fastidious and precise system for recording the sequence and order of various cel layers, the number of exposures given to these layers, and the movements of camera, background, or compound. In practice, all this information is written down by the animator on an *exposure sheet.* Figure 12.28 provides an example of this record-keeping device, and in Chapter 23 you'll find a full-size exposure sheet that you can detach and have duplicated for your own use. Only a few comments about the exposure sheet seem necessary. *Dial* is a special term that refers to the consecutive numbering of each and every frame within the finished movie—24 frames to the second, 40 to the foot (in 16mm), 1,440 frames to the minute, and so on. In order to keep a running count of frames, the animator adds the appropriate prefix numbers before each zero. Cardinal numbers reading from left to right (4, 3, 2, and 1) refer to the order of *cel layers.* If possible, the animator positions those cels that require the most frequent changing at the top of the pile. The *background* (Bkg) is usually given a letter reference or a short descriptive term in order to differentiate between the various backgrounds used in a single film and even in a single sequence.

The exact timing and position of each cel is indicated by the individual cel's number, and this is placed on the exposure sheet in a box beneath its appropriate cel layer. Usually the animator employs both a letter and a number in marking individual cels. The letter is chosen to indicate the subject matter of the cel series. "H" might be for "head," "F" for feet, "HA" for hat, etc. The number beside the letter indicates the order of cels for each layer (F1, F2, F3, F4, etc.).

The exposure sheet has space for *camera instructions* such as fades, dissolves, superimpositions, and for camera/compound movements such as pans, zooms, and spins. In addition, the animator can requisition space on the sheet to indicate where a special sound exists on a prerecorded track or to note for further reference any item that might easily be forgotten or wrongly executed.

Treat this aid informally. Modify the standard form to suit your own particular needs and the capabilities of the production tools that you will be using and the particular techniques being employed.

Lip Sync

You can create animated characters that appear to talk, whose mouth movements precisely match the voice track. It's not easy, but you can attempt and eventually master the process if you have the required equipment for analyzing recorded voice tracks (see Chapters 17 and 18).

In order to create lip sync for cel animation, a *bar sheet* must be filled in with a frame-by-frame analysis of each vowel and consonant sound in a given piece of dialogue. With this information, the animator is able to match each utterance with the appropriate mouth shape.

Both track analysis and lip-sync drawing are laborious processes, as you can imagine. Doing it right requires patience and perseverence. A real mastery of lip-sync animation requires a control of head and body movement and of gestures appropriate to individual words, to the character's personality, and to the dramatic requirements of the film as a whole. If you are interested in pursuing this specialized technique, obtain one of the advanced manuals on the subject (see Chapter 20) and be prepared for a lot of work.

To get you started, however, look at the chart in Figure 12.30. It has been created over the years as a standard simplified guide for animating lip movements. In application, modify the style of each given mouth shape so that it matches the graphic style of your cartoon character.

The Studio Cel System

Your understanding and your appreciation of the technique of cel animation can be extended by studying the assembly-line hierarchy developed at the large animation studios in the heyday of character animation in the 1940s and 1950s. Incidentally, the same system, or one close to it, is being used today in the production of contemporary animation features and, to a lesser extent, in the production of animated TV spots. In doing your own independent animation, of course, you have to cram these separate jobs into a single job—*yours*. Anyway, here's a rough breakdown of the studio system of traditional cel animation.

The *producer* is the individual responsible for the overall development of the animated film. He selects personnel, raises capital, manages expenditures, arranges for distribution, and much more. The producer is everyone's boss. The *writer* is assigned or chooses the subject, defines the characters, and begins shaping story line and dialogue. The *storyboard artist* breaks down the story into component scenes. The storyboard provides a visual system for making a detailed analysis of the film's development. The storyboard includes a detailed study of character appearance and movement, a detailed work-up of backgrounds, and a delineation of scenes and sequences within scenes. The producer and all "creative" personnel (writers, designers, animators, directors) work with the studio's sound crew and the "actors," or voices, and the musicians and composers in recording the full sound track for the finished movie, including music and dialogue. Special sound effects can also be placed on the track at this point or added later in the final editing and sound-mix process. A *track analysis*

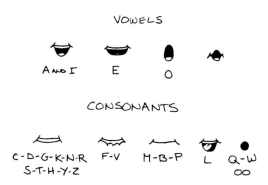

12.30 COMMON MOUTH SHAPES: This simplified set of vowel and consonant shapes must be styled to your particular character as well as the kind of emotional delivery the lines are being spoken with. Some animators like precise and fully articulated lip synchronization while others feel a "loose" technique is quite adequate. An alternative to such shape charts is for the animator to sit facing a mirror so that he or she can study the visual movement of his or her own lips in saying particular phrases with particular inflections.

A

B

C

is then made. A specialist will make a bar sheet from the sound track. All words, beats, and music are identified with the utmost detail and precision. Working with the bar sheets and the layout/design models, the *director* begins filling in an exposure sheet for every moment of screen time. Decisions made at this point shape the remaining work; the timing of movement, the stretch and squash of characterization, and the amount of time devoted to particular bits of action. Working from the layout drawings and in consultation with the director, the *background artist* creates each background that is required in the film. When full-cel animation is being used, backgrounds are lavishly executed pieces of art. Different *animators* are now assigned to different scenes or different characters within the overall movie. If the film is short, the animation may all be done by one individual. It's the animator's job to create the extremes for the cels that make up the film. These are drawn roughly on paper sheets. The animator is given the background against which he or she is to bring the story to life. The *assistant animators* prepare the in-betweens, also completed on paper sheets. Generally, the assistant smooths out the actual drawings of the animator and refines the animator's working sketches. At this stage the completed paper drawings may be filmed in a pencil test.

Once the animator and director are satisfied with the pencil test, the drawings go to the inking department where *inkers* trace the outline of every drawing onto an acetate sheet. At this stage decisions are made on how and where to break down the drawings in order to save work, time, and expense by using different cel layers. Now the *opaquers* flip over the acetate cels and paint in the colors of the characters. There is always at least one *checker* to be sure that all the cels and layers and exposure sheets and bar sheets and backgrounds are properly executed and marked and registered prior to the actual filmmaking. Working from the exposure sheets, a *camera operator* or team of operators films the entire movie. Then a *film editor* cuts together the pieces of exposed film and matches the images to the sound track. The editorial department will also prepare the original footage for duplication and printing at the laboratory.

That's the general process for making a cel animation film. But the work isn't over once the film is made. For if everyone involved wants to make more movies, then the finished film must generate revenue. It's the American Way. So there are always a host of other people involved in the studio animation system—accountants, publicity people, film programmers, distribution agents, and more.

The Limited-Cel System

The costs are tremendous for full-cel animation, and the process is slow. It requires a lot of people, most of whom must be highly trained and experienced. The equipment and supplies are costly too.

Just as the use of cels was originated in order to save production time, which equals money, in recent years a technique that seeks to cut even more corners and save more money has been developed.

The technique is termed *limited-cel animation*. To the purist, it is animation with a limited power and effectiveness as well as a limited technique. Samples of limited-cel animation are plentiful within

D

G

E

H

F

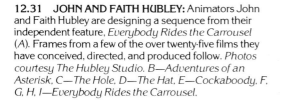

I

12.31   JOHN AND FAITH HUBLEY: Animators John
and Faith Hubley are designing a sequence from their
independent feature, *Everybody Rides the Carrousel*
(*A*). Frames from a few of the over twenty-five films they
have conceived, directed, and produced follow. *Photos
courtesy The Hubley Studio. B—Adventures of an
Asterisk, C—The Hole, D—The Hat, E—Cockaboody, F,
G, H, I—Everybody Rides the Carrousel.*

A

B

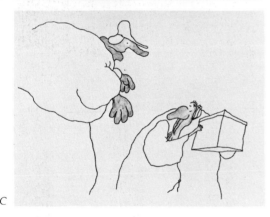

C

12.32   THE LOOK OF CEL ANIMATION: Seen in proximity with each other, these nine frame enlargements indicate the wide range of graphic styles and subject matters that have been used with cel animation techniques.

A—John Leach, *Evolution. Courtesy Learning Corporation of America.* B—Stephen Bosustow, *The Legend of John Henry. Courtesy Pyramid Films.* C— Paul Driessen, *An Old Box. Courtesy National Film Board of Canada.* D—Vincent Collins, *Euphoria. Courtesy Film Wright.* E—Zdenek Miller, *The Mole and the Music. Courtesy Phoenix Films.* F—John Halas and Joy Batchelor, *Animal Farm. Courtesy Phoenix Films.* G—Walerian Borowczyk, *Game of Angles. Courtesy Pyramid Films.* H—Bruno Bozzetto, *Opera. Courtesy Films, Inc.* I—Zlatko Grgic, *Courtesy National Film Board of Canada.*

American television, especially in the almost indistinguishable programs produced for kids on Saturday morning.

In planning their films, directors of limited-cel productions try to hold particular cels wherever possible. Typically, a character's face will be frozen while only the mouth moves in talking, or a body will be stiff while an arm performs a task. In full-cel animation, the entire body would move, as it does in life. Limited animation stresses the use of cycles, of course. Characteristic of limited animation are endless camera pans over static backgrounds. In order to recycle drawings from program to program, silhouette chases are often used and scenes are consistently drawn from an identical perspective.

The Simplified Cel System

The aspect of cel animation that requires the most tedious work, takes the longest time, and is the most expensive is the process of inking and opaquing. In looking for ways to simplify the cel process, some animators have simplified the graphic quality of their animation rather than the amount or quality of the movement itself.

The husband and wife team of John and Faith Hubley have done just this and their work's quality and integrity, as well as its technical structure, have served as an important model to many aspiring independent animators.

Up until his untimely death in 1977, John and Faith Hubley produced films of exceptional quality at the Hubley Studio, their New York-based production company. John Hubley was a Disney-trained animator who went on to become a major figure at the UPA Studios, where the first major reaction to and competition with the Disney style of animation began in the late 1940s.

The Hubleys and other character animators of recent years have developed a number of techniques that produce the full-cel look without all the full-cel work. We might call these techniques "simplified" as opposed to "limited" cel animation. The best trick of the simplified cel system is its new way of mounting paper drawings on a regular acetate cel, thus eliminating the requirements of inking and opaquing. Using standard registered paper sheets, the animator carefully draws the character. A background is prepared as in full-cel animation. The same coloring techniques are generally used for figure and background. Watercolors, crayons, or felt-tipped pens can be used. In this simplified cel technique an outlining of the character is not required.

The paper drawings are now mounted on cels. A thin layer of rubber cement is applied to the back of the paper sheet. Then each paper sheet is quickly placed on top of an acetate cel bearing identical registration holes. The paper cel is smoothed out and allowed to dry. In the final step, the sharp point of an Exacto knife or a similar implement cuts away the surplus white paper from the outline of the character. The completed cel can now be placed over its background.

Such simplified cels work well. There are some significant limitations to the technique, however. The number of layers one can use is confined in practice to three or, better, to two levels. This technique, like all others, must be tailored to the style of the individual artist. It works better for some artists than for others. The appearance of

D

E

F

G

H

I

paper figures creates its own unique "feeling" and "space." It is well suited for some stories and types of films, but not for others.

There are many more production shortcuts that ingenious independent animators are developing for their work in basic cel and character animation.

Drawing directly on the cels, as opposed to "rehearsing" first with a drawing on paper, is one such idea. In this variation markers or grease pencils are often used. It requires a practiced eye and a confident hand to work this way. But the technique may yield a spontaneous and unrehearsed quality that is often lost as pencil drawings are transferred to cels.

Airbrush coloring and painting can speed up the process of creating backgrounds. The airbrush has a characteristic style that can be employed for special effects of one kind and another. Transfer lettering, shading, and lines can all be adapted to cel techniques.

Reframing is often employed. The same set of cels are photographed against different backgrounds using a different frame composition each time. Typically, the animation camera or zoom lens is focused closer to the artwork when reframing.

Ultra close-ups are being used more and more in today's simplified animation. There are two reasons for this. Close-ups require less intricate drawing, and they also "work" well on the TV screen. Television is rapidly becoming the prime distribution medium for animated films.

There are other effective tricks and shortcuts for working with cels: the use of cutaways, silhouettes, die-cuts, color xerography, video keying, rephotography, and many, many other special techniques. Many of these are discussed in the following chapters.

A Graduation Exercise

As a final project, let me suggest that you use full-cel techniques (or simplified techniques as described above) to reanimate one of the characters or stories that you developed in one of earlier projects. Find a favorite, one that really interests you and that feels within reach of your present level of skill. The reason for suggesting that you repeat the same problem is that you'll discover in the process things about the characteristics of both techniques. A second try at the same basic material will also give you a chance to redesign the characters and reshape the story. You'll be able to experiment with new variations in timing, emphasis, dramatic flow, and plain old physical movement.

Limit this last film to a maximum length of 15 seconds. In the process of executing the full-cel film, allow yourself to begin sifting through all the projects you've completed. Search for images you enjoyed or transformations that excited you or interesting audio ideas. Begin studying the parameters of your tools. Determine what they are capable of doing and what their limitations exclude you from doing.

And as you sift through earlier projects on your sample reel, look for an idea or for a technique that can become your first magnum opus. Part Four of this book is designed to assist you in realizing this important first film.

Raggedy Ann and Andy by Richard Williams. *Courtesy of the Bobbs-Merrill Co., Inc.*

The Family That Dwelt Apart by Yvon Mallette. *Courtesy of the Learning Corporation of America.*

13
Other Techniques

13.1 XEROX REDUCTION: A cutout character can easily be reproduced in various sizes through repeated reductions on special copying machines having this feature.

This catchall chapter is unified by three elements. Each of the techniques that will be introduced here requires specialized tools, each incorporates new technologies into the process of animation, and each provides an exciting new "look." Together, these other ways of animating have infused important new sensibilities into the pictorial realm of animated filmmaking.

The techniques in this chapter have been grouped together because of their newness as well. For example, the evolving techniques incorporating *Xerox* duplication are so new that it is impossible to determine what the eventual applications will be. *Computer* animation is placed here rather than in a chapter of its own because it requires relatively sophisticated equipment, hardware and software, that at this time is realistically beyond the reach of independent animators. *Rotoscoping* and work with *optical* printing are often considered too technically advanced for an individual film artist to pursue. In fact, however, they are not, as I will try to show. Some techniques are in this chapter because, well, I don't know where else to put them. *Pinscreen, pastel,* and *matte effects* all deserve at least mention within these pages, although they are not in the mainstream of animation—at least not at this time.

"But is it animation?"

That question is invariably raised by many of these new techniques. It's an interesting point, too. I would answer the question this way. Animation is more than frame-by-frame filmmaking. For me, at least, the *control* that is brought to the creation of a movie has a lot to do with whether or not it is animation. The emphasis falls on what can be called the *designing process* by which individual artists approach their work. Whether something is animated or not doesn't have anything to do with the kinds of images and tools that have been used and it doesn't have anything to do with the artist's motives or goals. It has everything to do with the consciousness and precision with which the film is created.

The frame-by-frame process of design and manipulation that I feel is so central to animation is most accessible in the act of execution. That's why it is valuable to study the way a person makes a film. By extension, that's why it is so very important for each of us to explore actively many different techniques on our own. Playing around with techniques, exploring the boundaries of the medium, can extend your designing skills and sensibilities and ultimately your artistry.

The techniques discussed in this chapter should help you forge your own definition of animation. Your view certainly need not match mine. Many people, for example, wouldn't want to include computer-generated images or optical printing. Others would deny that approaches such as time-lapse or kinestasis belong with the same art form that includes drawing-on-film, pixilation, or animating by a series of drawn images.

For me, however, a designed and controlled execution of the

filmmaking process determines whether the resulting work can be classified as animation. Sometimes, of course, it's hard to decide how much conscious design there must be or what degree of manipulation is present in a particular film. Such gray areas test one's own definition and are valuable just because of that. So you will just have to work out and live with your own definition. I hope this chapter will stimulate you to do so.

Xerography

The ubiquitous office copying machine is a good example of how new technologies are being incorporated into animated filmmaking. Xerox machines and other copying machines offer a number of creative possibilities that can be sampled quickly here.

Preparing Cels. The first use of a Xerox copying machine in animated production was established by the major cartoon studios

13.2 XEROXED PHOTOGRAPHS: When a black and white photograph is duplicated much of the gray tone is lost. However, an easily recognizable image can be achieved and duplicated many times at low cost. In this example a cycle of four photographs would show the subject, Emily, covering and uncovering her face. In addition to the representational and more abstract variations shown here, many treatments are possible: backgrounds can be animated, a position can be held, time-lapse photography can record changes, collage images can be superimposed, and, of course, there are endless possibilities with color. Stills from *Family Spots*, a work in progress by the author.

13.3   LIVE-ACTION XEROX: Photograph *A* shows Xeroxed materials that were used in George Griffin's *Head.* The elongated or smeared faces were "mistakes" in the photocopying process that the animator used effectively within the finished film. In Griffin's *Candy Machine (B)* Xeroxed material shows a New York City subway platform as background to paper cels that were mounted onto acetate. Sample materials from a film in progress by Al Jarnow *(C)* and *(D)* suggest more abstract uses of Xeroxed imagery. *Photos courtesy George Griffin and Al Jarnow.*

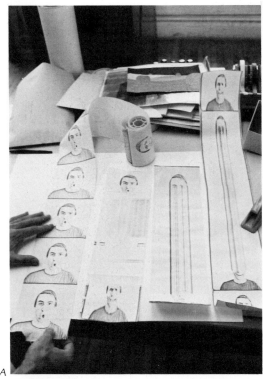

A

B

when it was discovered that pencil test drawings done on paper could be duplicated directly on clear acetate sheets. By eliminating the necessity for inkers to recopy every pencil drawing, this copying method represented a major labor- and money-saving step.

The use of Xerox processes proved to have an aesthetic impact as well. The quality of lines becomes more dynamic. The texture and shape of the animator's lines are preserved. The steps of inking and of cleaning up original art had tended to obliterate nuances of line. Furthermore, the mechanical transfer of the animator's drawings gives the animator a very direct control in styling the final image in full-cel animation. The process is not without drawbacks, however. When all factors are weighed, a Xerox process is almost as expensive as a crew of inkers. Often, in fact, cels produced by a Xerox process must themselves be cleaned up and reregistered.

Reduction/Enlargement. Occasionally an animator will find himself or herself faced with the need to repeat a single drawing or a short cycle of drawings in sizes that are smaller or larger than the original. For example, a simple cycle would be copied many times in different sizes if a character was to walk directly toward the vanishing point in an animated horizon.

Sophisticated office copiers have the capabilities of reducing or enlarging original materials. Thus it's easy to make a series of accurately scaled reproductions of a drawing or a cycle of drawings. Figure 13.1 will provide an example. The same reproduction technique eliminates the need for photostats and can be applied in almost all kinds of animation.

Reproduction of Line Drawings. A very simple yet effective use of the Xerox machine is the duplication of multiple copies of a single piece of artwork. For example, a line drawing of a landscape can be reproduced hundreds of times with precision, and then, a page at a time, the animator can draw and color in any number of different ways. White paint or ink can block out areas of the background if one wants to draw in new lines. Line drawings work particularly well with photocopying technologies, but solid areas of black do not copy well.

Reproduction of Photographs. Other graphic forms—including photographs—can be used with xerography. The examples in Figure 13.2 show one application of this technique. A series of four still photos was taken with a conventional 35mm camera. When mounted on a single sheet, these photographs create a simple cycle that can then be copied mechanically and subsequently cut apart and colored and manipulated by the artist. Some copying machines seem to work better with photographs than others. It is sometimes necessary to test a few different models to see which yields the clearest reproduction.

Photocopying Live-Action Footage. A special Xerox machine called the Copyflo has been developed to transfer microfilm information onto paper. The process involves reproducing and enlarging the individual panels of microfilm on a roll of paper that is later cut on the frame lines to separate the individual microfilm images. The animator can exploit this technology by reproducing pieces of live-action 16mm or 35mm motion picture film on a roll of paper. Negative film stock is used so that the final image will be positive. The size of the enlargements can be controlled—from a frame that is a #10 field down to a #3 or #4 field. The Copyflo machine can enlarge original materials by a factor of 22x. Contact your local Xerox representative to find the location and rates for Copyflo reproduction. Applications of the Copyflo technique are shown in Figure 13.3.

Other Possibilities. Color xerography has many potential applications within animation. One of them is described in the pastel technique discussed later in this chapter. Remember that office copying machines don't necessarily require the use of white paper. Experiment with other colored and textured papers. For example, heavy-weight papers can be used to duplicate cutouts. Xerox duplication can also help a designer to achieve some fantastic effects in the area of collage. Xerox machines capable of copying color make it possible to duplicate storyboards. And a Xerox machine capable of creating an 8- by 10-inch color print directly from a 35mm color slide is now available. Such technology has obvious uses in kinestasis techniques.

Allied reproduction technologies that can be incorporated easily into a number of animation techniques include the standard school ditto or stencil machines. And standard photostat services are often useful in creating positive and negative versions of artwork.

Rotoscoping

Rotoscoping originated as a technique to combine live-action and animated images. The process involves projecting a piece of live-action film, frame by frame, onto a surface so that the animator can create a new series that will eventually be inserted into the original live-action footage. Once the drawings have been transferred to cels (with perfect registration remaining vis-à-vis the live-action footage), the animation and live action can be combined on a single strip of film. This is done in one of two ways. The resynthesis can be achieved with an animation stand by rephotographing each rear-projected frame of the live-action film at the compound surface along with the appropriate cel from the animation sequence. An alternative technique is to photograph the animation sequence by itself and then combine it with the live-action footage in a process involving mattes and double-printing techniques (see optical printing, below).

Although it may sound quite complicated, traditional rotoscoping is not beyond the technical reach of independent animators. Expensive optical printers and rotoscope projection units can be rented. Inexpensive printers are available commercially, or a home-made rig can be constructed. A comprehensive description of various techniques is beyond the parameters of this volume, however. Consult the bibliography in Chapter 20.

The term "rotoscoping" has come to have a broader definition. Today's independent animators use different variations of the original technique to create images that are based on live-action film sequences but are not intended to be combined with live-action scenes.

Rotoscoping in this broader sense involves a simple three-step process that can be quickly outlined here.

Step One: Original Filming. Shoot or acquire some live-action footage that you would like to manipulate on a frame-by-frame basis. If you do your own filmmaking in either super 8mm or 16mm format,

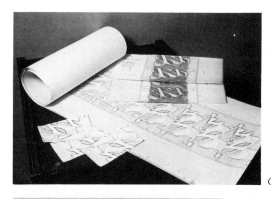

C

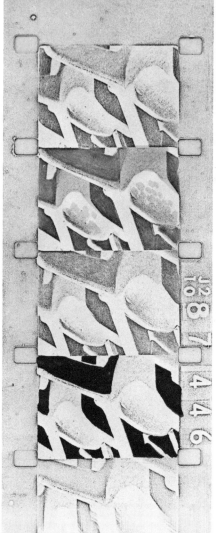

D

13.3

13.4   ROTOSCOPING STEPS: A section of live-action footage *(B)* is selected and alternating frames are traced off a rear projection surface *(C)*. The animator may make a series of tests *(D)* to determine what graphic style or styles best suit the original material and the nature of the film. A complete set of images is created *(E)* and filmed. The resulting footage will bear similarities to the original footage, but it will have a distinctive, animated look *(A)*. The illustrations are from *Family Spots*, a work in progress by the author.

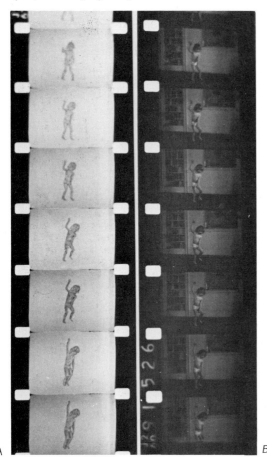

A   B

C

consider the background against which you shoot. It is often helpful to film against a solid-colored background (light or dark) because this makes it easier to discern and trace the image when it is projected in the second step (see Figure 13.4).

Step Two: Projection and Tracing. The live-action footage must be rear projected in such a way to allow the animator to place a piece of tracing paper over the image and trace it. This is not merely mechanical work; the artist must make important aesthetic decisions about how much detail to record, what style of representation to use, and so on.

Two common pieces of filmmaking hardware can be used in the projection and tracing step. A simple movie-editing machine (Chapter 18) casts a small image of a single frame onto a glass surface against which a piece of tracing paper can be placed. The difficulty with this technique is that it's hard to maintain registration between images (generally registration is established after the series of images has been traced). Furthermore, if the image cast on the rear-projection screen is small and relatively weak, it is often difficult to clearly see it through a sheet of tracing paper.

A movie projector throws a much brighter image that can be enlarged to any size. You must use, however, a 16mm or super 8mm projector that can hold and advance single frames without burning them at the projector's gate. Only a few projectors have this feature, but many older projectors can be modified for rotoscoping. A mirror is often used in the projection setup as indicated in Figure 13.5. Even with a projector, the set of tracings must be reregistered before they can be refilmed.

Step Three: Rephotography. Using a standard light box, redraw the tracings on sheets of paper. At this stage they can be colored or manipulated, and this is, of course, the most creative step in rotoscoping. What may start out as quite representational tracings are simplified and modified according to the artist's vision.

When the redrawn images are as the animator wants them, the series of drawings is filmed in the standard way with evenly distributed toplighting and two frames per drawing or whatever the exposure sheet indicates.

In a strict sense, what has just been described is not rotoscoping as

D

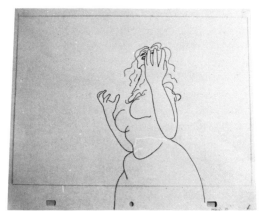

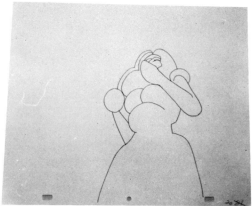

A

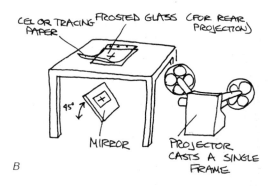

CEL OR TRACING PAPER — FROSTED GLASS (FOR REAR PROJECTION)

45°

MIRROR

PROJECTOR CASTS A SINGLE FRAME

B

13.5   TRACING SETUPS: If rotoscoping from a viewer *(A)*, select a model with as large a viewing screen as possible. Also see if you can use a brighter light source so that the illumination of the selected frames will be bright and sharp. Be careful, however, that the light doesn't burn the film in the viewing gate. Precut tracing paper to match the dimensions of the screen. Setup *B* illustrates how a film projector can be used in rotoscoping. Note that one can adjust the rig to get an image of almost any size. Old projectors can be modified for rotoscoping so that a single frame is advanced and so that the image is very bright.

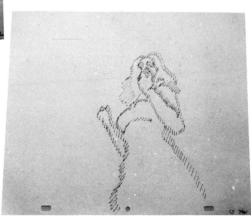

13.6   ROTOSCOPED IMAGERY: Four variations on a single style show the creative breadth of rotoscoping. Each of the graphic approaches sampled here will appear in *Odalisque*, a work in progress by Maureen Selwood. *Stills courtesy Maureen Selwood.*

A

B

C

D

13.7 OTHER ROTOSCOPE STYLES: Frame
enlargements, *A* and *B*, from Mary Beams's *Paul Revere Is Here* show how positive and negative versions of the same material can be used. Two stills from *I Never Sleep* by Yvonne Andersen *C* and *D*, show another rotoscoping style. The latter film is part of a reel titled *I Saw Their Angry Faces. A, B, courtesy Serious Business Company; C, D, courtesy The Yellow Ball Workshop.*

Hollywood knows the term. The original live-action footage is never combined with animated footage. Rather, an entirely new flow of imagery and movement is created. Yet even when the animator has highly manipulated the image and pacing of the basic material, a rotoscoped sequence will carry a distinctive look that is different from that produced by other techniques.

Figure 13.6 provides a set of examples of rotoscoping created by animator Maureen Selwood. Figure 13.7 samples the technique of other independent animators.

Pinscreen

The term "direct animation" refers to frame-by-frame image creation that is achieved during the process of filming, not before it. Many different techniques qualify as direct animation: clay, puppet, pixilation, painting-on-glass, and some forms of cutout and collage techniques. One factor common to all these approaches is that nothing—or almost nothing—remains after the film has been shot. In direct animation techniques, the act of shooting is not merely mechanical. In fact, much improvisation is required by the animator during the filming process as small incremental changes in the subject are slowly built into sequences, scenes, and the completed film.

Among the first of the direct techniques to achieve broad critical awareness was that of the pinscreen. This technique is truly astounding both in the process of its execution and in the special tool through which animation is accomplished—the pinscreen.

The pinscreen (Figure 13.8) is a sturdy frame holding a white board into which thousands and thousands of black pins have been inserted. These pins are very thin—much like wire. By adjusting the pins so that the length exposed to the camera varies from a few millimeters to nothing when the pin is shoved completely into the board, the animator can create various shadings from black to white. The variations of gray tone that, in composite, form the image itself are often attributed to the shadows caused by light striking the pins. This is not the case, however, for it is actually the density of the pins against the white board that causes the contrast between light and dark tones.

The pinscreen is the invention of Alexander Alexieff, who conceived and refined the technique through many years of independent film production in which he often collaborated with animator Claire Parker. A few years ago, Alexieff gave a pinscreen to the animation unit at the National Film Board of Canada in Montreal. There animator Pierre Drouin has carried on the Alexieff/Parker tradition. Figure 13.9 shows a few scenes from a recent film by Pierre Drouin, and Figure 13.10 shows this young animator at work.

The pinscreen is an anomaly among animation techniques. Because the pinscreen creates a monotone image with soft-edge definition, the elements of design are more restricted than in most direct animation forms. The pinscreen itself is very difficult to construct and it seems doubtful, therefore, that the technique will ever be extensively employed. And yet the body of work done with pinscreen demands its recognition as an independent animation technique. This odd tool seems quite capable of catching the enthusiasm and creative vision of new generations of animators.

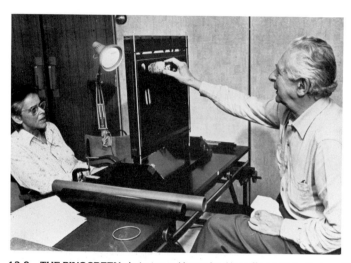 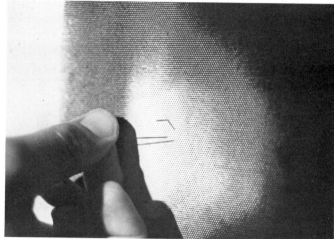

13.8   THE PINSCREEN: Animators Alexandre Alexieff and Claire Parker at the pinscreen. The close-up illustrates the size of a pin and how in aggregate it forms a full tonal range from light gray to black as it sticks out of the white board. *Photos courtesy NFBC.*

13.9   JACQUES DROUIN'S MINDSCAPE: Four frame enlargements. *Courtesy NFBC and Pyramid Films.*

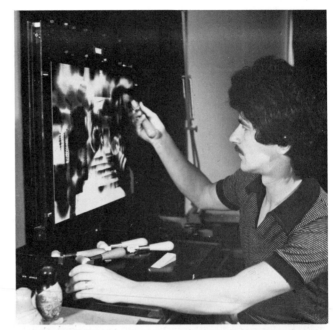

13.10 PINSCREEN TECHNIQUE: Animator Jacques Drouin is pictured at the pinscreen. The animation camera films the work head-on and is activated by a remote switch. The close-ups show the sorts of tools that are used to push the pins. These specialized tools are required because pins must be worked by pushing motions from both sides of the board rather than with the familiar strokes of most other graphic forms. *Courtesy NFBC.*

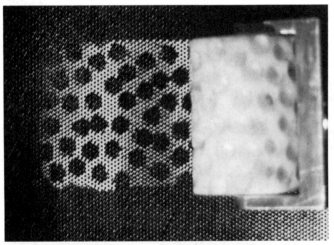

Pastel

Pastel animation, a technique being born at this writing, is being developed by Lynn Smith, a young animator working at the National Film Board of Canada. Her innovation deserves mention here because of its artistic force and also because it illustrates so well how the exploration of new graphic forms can produce what may become a distinctive new technique for animated filmmaking.

Lynn Smith was initially attracted by the brilliant color and the subtle graphic qualities created by smudged pastels. Through a series of experiments that led to some surprising refinements, the following technique has evolved and is currently being used to create a finished film. Here is a quick summary of the setup, materials, planning system, and visual style of the pastel technique.

Pastel colors are applied to a lightly sanded paper (sometimes referred to as snuffing paper). Available at art stores in a number of weights, the paper used by Ms. Smith is the heaviest because a single sheet of paper is used throughout an entire sequence: pastels are applied, a few frames are exposed, the artwork is smudged, new lines or colors are applied, a few more frames are exposed, and so forth.

Pastels create a great deal of dust. To deal with this special problem, an electric vacuum machine has been installed at the top edge of Ms. Smith's compound surface. Using a small hand air bulb and this low-powered vacuum pump, the animator periodically clears excess pastel dust off the drawing/filming surface. Special polarizing

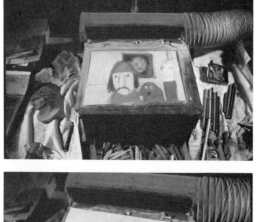

13.11 PASTEL TECHNIQUE: Lynn Smith *(A)* sits at the setup used for the technique of animating with pastels that she is pioneering. Note the special vacuum that is mounted at the top of her working surface. This helps the animator remove excess dust. Photograph *B* looks onto the working surface and *C* shows how Lynn Smith uses cels occasionally to record the composition of the surface. *D* shows the exposure sheet that the animator follows during the protracted process of direct animation. The sheet breaks down a prerecorded sound track. *Photos by the author.*

A

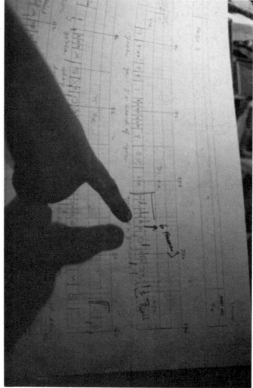

D

13.12   PASTEL IMAGERY: Two scenes from Lynn Smith's *Why a Museum* (working title) in production at the National Film Board of Canada. *Stills courtesy Lynn Smith.*

filters are hung between the lights and the compound to minimize the refraction of light off the dust.

Another unique feature of the pastel technique is that it incorporates color Xerox. Sometimes the image of a familiar painting or piece of artwork is Xeroxed on the lightly sanded paper. From this color image, a particular scene is built through successive alterations and additions of pastel. The Xerox foundation provides the animator with a highly representational image that can then undergo a series of frame-by-frame transformations.

Lynn Smith periodically places a sheet of acetate over the pastel drawing and quickly traces the outline of the image underneath. This is then used to help the animator keep track of the development of characters and scenes. Ms. Smith works improvisationally from an exposure sheet that bears a breakdown of the film's overall sound track. The latter has been written and recorded prior to under-camera animation, although changes in the track can be made to fit the evolving footage of the movie. The basic setup is illustrated in Figure 13.11 as well as the animator at her work. Figure 13.12 contains frames from the film.

Optical Printing

Optical printing is the process of rephotographing one strip of film onto another strip of film. In essence, a movie projector is pointed into a movie camera. The two machines must be carefully modified to insure perfect focus and registration during the frame-at-a-time rephotography process.

It's well beyond the scope of this volume to detail the specific refinements of technique that are required in doing one's own optical printing. Suffice it to say that specialized knowledge is necessary and that thousands of dollars can be spent on an optical printing "bench" as it is called—hundreds of thousands of dollars if the bench is computerized (Figure 13.13).

A simplified optical bench is available commercially at a price that is more realistic for independent animators. Figure 13.14 shows a 16mm model manufactured by J-K Engineering. Note also, however, that with persistence, ingenuity, and some technical facility, it's possible to use standard filmmaking and electronics gear in building optical printing setups that are capable of many different effects. One such home-made optical printer—albeit a very sophisticated one—is illustrated in Figure 13.17.

Hardware aside, here is a brief listing of optical printing effects:

Step-Printing. Instead of rephotographing one piece of film frame by frame onto another piece of film, some frames can be omitted and others printed again and again for as long as the designer wants. A common example of step-printing is the effect achieved when the key frames in a live-action sequence are held for a half second or so. The resulting staccato effect resembles what one sees when projecting a piece of film at, say, 2 to 6 frames per second instead of the usual 24 frames per second.

Colorizing. A colored gel can be inserted in the space between the lens of the camera and that of the projector. In this way it is possible to colorize an image as it is being refilmed. This effect is often used when

13.13 **OPTICAL BENCH:** One of a number of computer linked optical printing machines that are used in the French and English animation sections at the National Film Board of Canada. *Photo by author.*

the footage being duplicated has been filmed against a solid-black background.

Changing Formats. A well-known use of the optical printer is to enlarge or blow up a super 8mm to 16mm format, or to go from 16mm to 35mm. Optical printers are built on a modular basis so that filmholding and claw mechanisms can be inserted for different formats. The process of enlargement can easily be reversed, of course—a 35mm strip of film can be reduced to 16mm or even super 8mm format.

Photography from Slides. Many optical benches have attachments that allow the operator to place a 35mm color slide in front of the camera element and, with proper backlighting, to refilm from it. The precision of some benches will even allow one to film just a portion of a 35mm frame or, if the machinery is very accurate indeed, it is possible to do camera moves such as pans and zooms within the frame of a 35mm slide.

Matte Effects. Every imaginable kind of matte effect can be created through an optical printer. In fact, in commercial film production—from feature films to industrials to TV spots—it is usually in an optical printer that all special effects are achieved. By way of example, here is how a simple circular matte would be used to combine two different film elements. As a strip of film is rephotographed, a solid circular shape is placed in front of the camera lens to mask off a portion of each frame and keep it from being exposed. In a subsequent run through the printer, the negative of the circle matte would be inserted between the projector and the camera so that, in our example, a new piece of imagery would be inserted into the unexposed portion of each frame, and the new matte protects the previously exposed portion of each frame from being double-exposed. (Figure 13.15).

Bi-Paking and Traveling Mattes. The positive and negative versions of a matte, say, a wipe effect, can be filmed and developed and then loaded in the camera directly on top of the raw stock. When this "bi-pak" is run through the camera, a controlled set of shapes are left unexposed on the raw stock. The negative of the same traveling matte is subsequently placed on top of the same strip of raw stock. The new

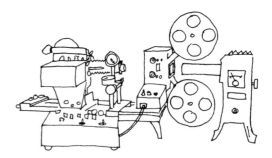

13.14 **J-K OPTICAL BENCH:** A relatively inexpensive optical printer that is available commercially from J-K Camera Engineering. This model, optical printer K-103-2, costs almost $2,500. Less expensive (and more expensive) printers are available.

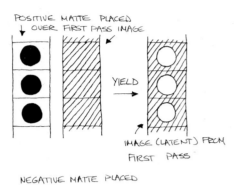

POSITIVE MATTE PLACED
↓ OVER FIRST PASS IMAGE

YIELD →

IMAGE (LATENT) FROM
FIRST PASS

NEGATIVE MATTE PLACED
↓ OVER SECOND IMAGE

YIELD →

COMPOSITE MATTE
IMAGE
(DEVELOPED AFTER THE
SECOND PASS)

13.15 MATTES: Whether the process is done "in camera" (with a matte box) or in the printing process later, combining two different images with a static matte requires two passes through the camera before the composite image can be processed and printed.

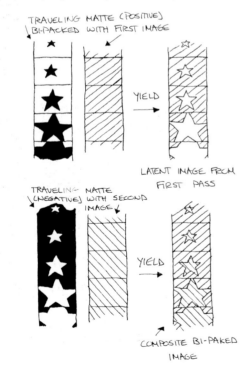

TRAVELING MATTE (POSITIVE)
BI-PACKED WITH FIRST IMAGE

YIELD →

LATENT IMAGE FROM
FIRST PASS

TRAVELING MATTE
(NEGATIVE) WITH SECOND
IMAGE

YIELD →

COMPOSITE BI-PAKED
IMAGE

13.16 BI-PAKING: A traveling matte also requires two separate passes to create the finished image. Bi-paking techniques are used in both passes through the optical printer.

bi-pak element is exposed to a new section of film and thus new visual material is inserted into each frame without double exposing the image previously recorded (Figure 13.16). Bi-paking provides for very precise registration among the different passes through the camera.

In a nutshell, that is the traveling matte technique. It is used in many kinds of transitions and in other optical effects that join different elements onto a single strip of film. This can include rotoscoping, the insertion of the image of an animated character into a normal, live-action scene, as discussed above.

Multi-image Effects. Optical printing allows one to divide a single frame of film into a number of different frames, each of which can contain different visual information. This effect is usually created with a series of mattes and multiple exposures of the same piece of film or different film elements. Figure 13.17 provides an example of multi-image work that has been done with a home-made optical printer. If you spend any time watching TV commercials you will come across countless examples of multi-image work and combined optical printing techniques.

Multiple Exposures. If original footage is shot against a black background, the image becomes its own matte. That is, the same strip of original film can be used in the optical printer so that the image itself can be repeated again and again in different locations in the same frame. This technique is a lot less complicated than it sounds. In practice, a single piece of film is duplicated, the raw stock is rewound to the starting point, and the same single piece of film is again printed on the raw stock—only the sequence is started on a different frame than in the first pass through the camera. The effect of multiple printing is dazzling. Figure 13.18 illustrates the effect.

It should be obvious that the techniques and hardware capable of producing the kinds of images sampled here are also capable of producing "standard" optical effects: fades, dissolves, freeze-frames, and superimpositions.

Matte Effects

With the use of a matte box some of the preceding effects can be achieved without the use of an expensive optical printer. A matte box is an inexpensive tool and it is quite easy to use in super 8mm and 16mm animation. Just a few modifications to standard animation procedures are required in order to do in-camera matte effects.

First, a matte must be designed and cut out of black matte board (actually, two mattes are created—one is the negative of the other and both are used in the process). One of the mattes is carefully positioned in front of the camera (the matte box itself holds the newly cut matte). Figure 13.19 shows matte boxes used with super 8mm and 16mm cameras. The box and the matte work together to keep light from striking a specific portion of the film surface within every frame.

After the film is exposed with one matte in place, the camera is rewound and the "reverse," or "negative," matte is mounted in the box and a new scene is shot. The resulting footage thus exposed will combine the appropriate elements of each shot without superimposition.

13.17   A HOMEMADE OPTICAL PRINTER: Frames *A* and *B* are from *Analogies: Studies in the Movement of Time*, a work near completion by Pete Rose. The first of these is an original live-action frame and the second enlargement shows the basic visual material reworked into 25 images, each of which shows a different moment of the original action. In Pete Rose's hand-built printer the camera (*C*) is mounted on a carriage that is free to move up and down on two vertical columns. These columns, in turn, are bolted to a second carriage that is free to move horizontally on a lathe bed. The flashlight illuminates a razor blade, whose shadow on the white tape of the lathe bed gives a positional indication. The apparatus on the camera consists of a remote control line to start the motor, a mirror mounted on the sync shaft, which reflects a light beam into a light cell when the shutter is closed, lenses to magnify the frame counter on the camera, a baffle in front of the lens instead of a lens cap, a cable release, and a power cable. Photograph *D* shows the Synchronopticon, a device for synchronizing the camera with the projector in any one of a number of ways. The control box for the projector (*E*) can be operated continuously at a range of speeds, or operated a single frame at a time by means of a push button. Photograph *F* provides an oblique top view of a slide projector, two fans, and a movie projector with motor, all part of the rig. The entire system is pictured in operation (*G*). Finally there is a portrait of Peter Rose with his camera and control setup (*H*). *All photographs courtesy Peter Rose.*

A

B

C

D

E

F

H   *G*

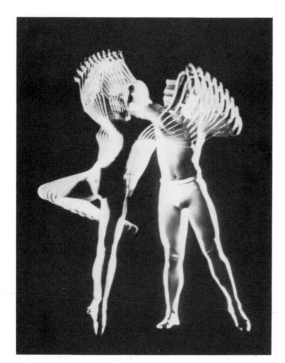

13.18   MULTIPLE PRINTING: A frame enlargement from Norman McLaren's groundbreaking film, *Pas De Deux*—winner of over two dozen awards. *Courtesy NFBC.*

13.19   MATTE BOXES: Adjustable matte boxes can be used with either super 8 mm or 16mm cameras. In *A (right),* the super 8 sound matte box is shown with a Nizo 801 camera. The matte box costs $150. In *B (below),* the Bolex matte box (around $400) is shown with a Bolex 16mm camera. Matte boxes are basically quite simple devices and can be jerry-rigged for most cameras and applications.

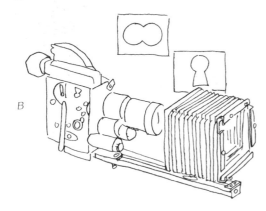

13.20   IN-CAMERA MATTE EFFECT: A frame enlargement at right from George Griffin's *Head.* In this scene, live-action footage shows the animator at work. By means of a matte, the actual drawing he is making appears as part of an animated sequence in the same frame. The matte inserts the animation footage into the live-action footage by placing it over a black book just to the left of center of the screen. *Still courtesy George Griffin and Serious Business Company.*

A few technical notes: Most 16mm cameras have a backwinding mechanism, but the film can also be rewound manually in a dark room and replaced in the camera for a second run. A system must be worked out, however, so that the starting position of both camera runs is known. It is sometimes difficult with super 8mm cameras to rewind film within the super 8mm cartridge. Single 8mm format makes this possible, and with a special device that is available today, an ordinary cassette can be taken out of the camera, rewound as much as is desired, and then be replaced in the camera for a second exposure run with a matte box and matte.

It is quite difficult to get sharp edges between matted areas of the final composite image when doing in-camera matte effects. If you want to try a matte sequence, design the effect so that a distinct separation or sharp edge is not critical. Figure 13.20 provides an example of such planning ahead for an in-camera matte effect.

Computer Animation

Only a limited orientation can be given here to the burgeoning field of computer animation. As one would expect, this is a specialized area that requires access to sophisticated and expensive tools. It also requires specialized knowledge about how to use those tools.

Probably the most important thing to know about computer animation is that it's not one thing. The field includes a surprisingly large number of very different techniques. Each of these in turn requires different approaches and each results in different sorts of images and kinds of movement. Here is a quick orientation.

Digital Computer Animation. Some computer technologies require the understanding of a specific computer language in order to write a program that will eventually render images or to work with someone who does. Digital computer systems generally follow the same set of procedures: Punch cards are created or a typewriter is used to give directions to the computer; as the computer processes the instructions it creates a series of single images, which are usually displayed on a black-and-white television monitor or other cathode-ray tube. A motion picture camera takes single-frame exposures of each new variation of the image as it appears on the video screen (the program directs the successive changes in the image), and the resulting film footage is often colored through optical printing steps.

Pioneers working in this area include John Whitney, Stan VanDerBeek, Lillian Schwartz, and Ken Knowlton. Schwartz and Knowlton have done their work at Bell Labs in New Jersey. Figure 13.21 illustrates the imagery produced by digital computer animation. In general, animation created by these digital modes tends to be abstract. However, the exploration of the technology and technique is at such an early stage of development—and new discoveries are being made so fast—that generalities about the look or effect or even the technique are inappropriate at this time.

Computer Interpolation. Figure 13.22 samples frames from a very different sort of computer animation system. Popularized by animator Peter Foldes, the "in-betweening" technique basically works as follows: The animator creates "key" drawings. The lines of these drawings are then broken down into small segments and coded. The computer is programmed to turn one image into the next by moving the coded segments of line from one position to another given position. In completing this change, the computer is also assigned a specific number of intermediate positions or moves. The result is that the computer itself generates the in-between positions of the line drawings.

As in most computer modes, generated images are displayed on a video screen and then filmed. Figure 13.23 shows this process. Films created by this in-betweening technique have distinctive transformational qualities. The line drawings can be easily colored with an optical printer. Although this technique seems to lend itself to narrative material, it is, again, much too early in the development of the technique to generalize meaningfully about its application.

Analog Image Synthesis. Another form of computer animation might better be called video synthesis. In this mode a given piece of graphic information (usually a high-contrast drawing but sometimes a piece of video tape with moving images on it) is scanned with a video

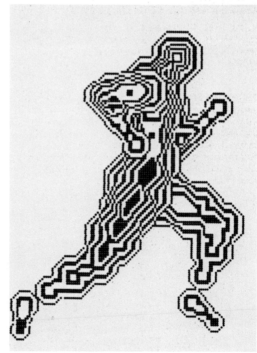

13.21 DIGITAL COMPUTER ANIMATION: Three stills (above and on following page) from work done at Bell Labs by Ken Knowlton and Lillian Schwartz. *Courtesy Ken Knowlton.*

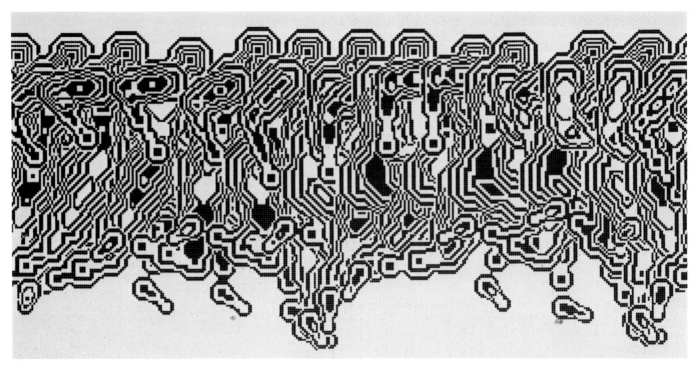

13.21

camera. (The video image, called a "raster," is composed of a number of electronic scan lines that form 30 "frames" of video information in 1 second. Each frame is made up of two fields, one representing the even-numbered scan lines, the other, the odd-numbered lines.)

The resulting electronic information is processed in a variety of ways, using electronic controls that make up the synthesizer. The image can shrink, oscillate, spin, and achieve other visual effects. These manipulations with the synthesizer can be executed in real time—a distinct advantage of this form of computer-assisted image generation. Colorization is done in a later step in the process while the information is still in its video state. Finally, the images are rescanned onto an especially high resolution cathode-ray tube from which 35mm film is shot. Dolphin Studios in New York specializes in this technology (Figure 13.24).

For the present at least, such forms of computer animation seem outside the reach of independent animators. But the continuing proliferation, sophistication, and miniaturization of computer technology suggest that what now appears as very exotic and inaccessible will be, within just a few years, within the reach of independent animators and artists.

It's an exciting prospect.

13.22   COMPUTER INTERPOLATED ANIMATION: Frames from two films by Peter Foldès suggest the graphic range of this computer technique. *A* and *B* are from *Metadata* and *C, D,* and *E* are from *Hunger. Stills courtesy Learning Corporation of America.*

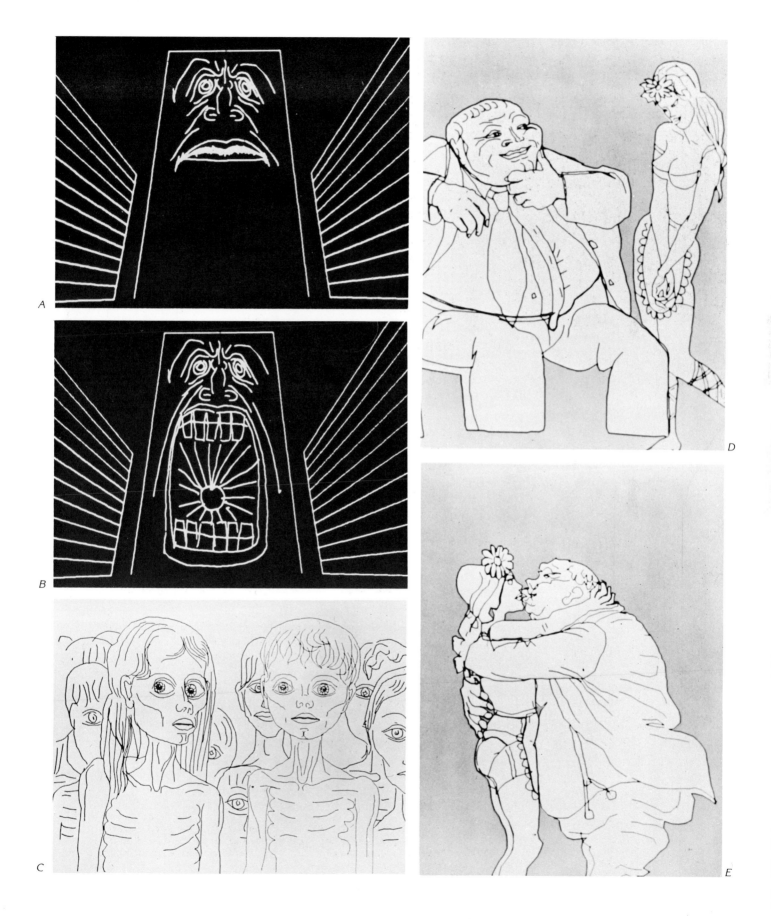

13.23   KEY FRAMES AND INTERPOLATIONS: The first and last images are drawn by the animator and the computer creates the three "in-betweens." Materials from Peter Foldes's *Hunger. Courtesy Learning Corporation of America.*

13.24   ANALOG IMAGE SYNTHESIS: Sample frames from works produced at Dolphin Productions in New York City. The diagram *(on opposite page)* breaks down the processes that are involved in animating in this mode. *Courtesy Dolphin Productions, Inc.*

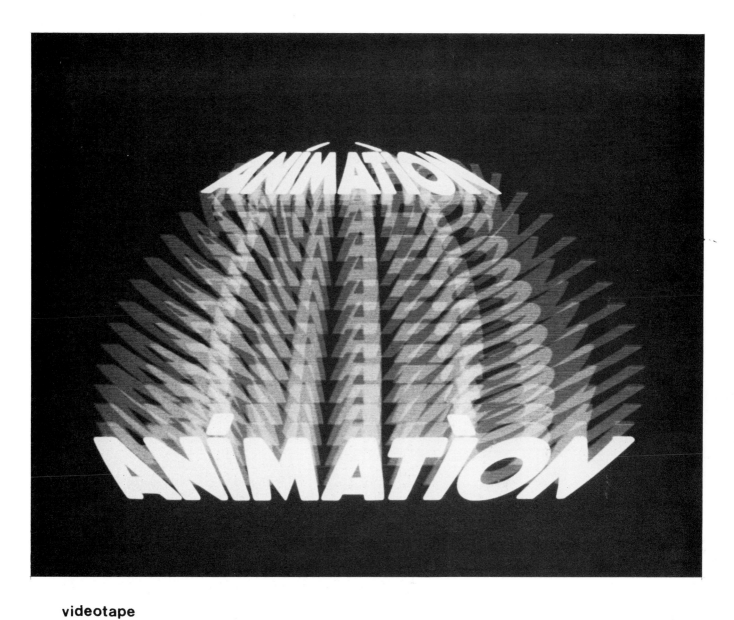

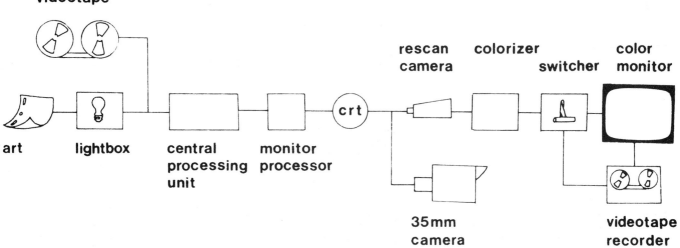

videotape

art lightbox central processing unit monitor processor crt rescan camera colorizer switcher color monitor

35mm camera

videotape recorder

14
Production Planning

The author's pictures of the wall provided production guidance to these young Thai students making films under the auspices of the United Nations.

Having read your way and, hopefully, having also worked your way through all the animation techniques described thus far, you ought to be ready for a film that is more ambitious, more intense, and more personal than any you've undertaken before. It's time for that larger film you've been wanting to animate.

This chapter's purpose is to lend a hand in getting under way. It tries to break down the complicated and interrelated series of questions you must ask yourself, and the problems you must solve, if you're going to get that movie made. As this chapter should demonstrate, production planning is an art in itself. Pulling together everything that is required is a major feat of logistics. Just as there are useful procedures to break down the sound track of an animated film, so too are there useful and proven techniques for structuring the overall process of producing an animated film.

While the following methodology is comprehensive and logical, don't put too much trust in it. Don't ever assume that any planning technique is capable of ensuring that everything will emerge in the right form at the right time. The unexpected is to be expected, and troubleshooting is the job of the producer. As a producer you'll constantly be improvising and you might as well begin doing that right now. In order to get your own independent production off the ground, some of the following steps can be easily omitted, while others will require major expansion.

Conceptualization

Without a good idea, there can't be a worthwhile movie. Chapter 1 presented some of the sources of ideas and some rituals that, if followed conscientiously, can be expected to yield the kinds of insights, questions, observations, and impulses that form the starting place for a film.

Production planning begins with a thorough shakedown of your basic idea. I recommend the following steps in this process and, for each, I urge you to take a lot more time and energy than you may initially feel is necessary. Remember what is at stake: You are going to be spending weeks and months breathing life and form into a single concept. So you had better be working with an idea that is rich enough to keep you interested and dedicated when the going gets rough and the initial infatuation of the idea has worn away.

No matter how complicated your concept is, you ought to be able to state it in one simple sentence. If you can't do this, you haven't yet really worked your way through your idea. It's absolutely critical for you to clearly understand what your movie is about. Its integrity and its unity demand just such precision.

To squeeze your concept into a simple sentence may seem

unreasonable. It is difficult to reduce into one sentence a multi-leveled conceptualization. *Romeo and Juliet* is a dazzlingly complex play. But the reason it works is that it has at its core one simple, classic concept: It is a love story. The play is, of course, many other things as well—a treatise on vengeance, loyalty, and the generation gap. But first and foremost *Romeo and Juliet* is a love story. And that single theme produces a structure that contains everything else. Take a single sheet of paper and complete the following sentence, "The movie is about . . . ."

Now that you really know what your movie is about, it's time to study and expand the central concept and elaborate on those concerns or interests that the idea represents.

Over the years there has evolved, for all kinds of filmmaking, a basic written format, about two pages long, that summarizes what the film is about, whom it is for, and how it will work. This format is called a *story treatment.* It traditionally starts with a concise statement of the film's idea—the sort of one-liner described above. This is followed with a paragraph or two that provides a more thorough analysis of the film's purpose: the kind of tone or feeling the film will hopefully convey, its major content requirements (information it must carry, if any), the film's projected function (to entertain, inform, instruct, provoke, etc.), and its audience. Of these four elements, an analysis of your audience may be the most important.

For if your movie is to have the impact you want, it must be carefully tailored to the specific audience you intend to reach. This may seem obvious enough. But many films fall short of their potential impact just because the producer never took the time and trouble to carefully consider who the film's audience was to be and, most particularly, what the audience would bring to the movie in terms of taste, expectation, and prior experience.

Let's take an example. Say that you want to make an animated film about the influence of television on people's fantasy lives. If you want this film to reach a broad audience, you'll surely have to deal with images that are "safe" for a general viewership. There are many topics that are simply unacceptable to most people. If, however, your film was to be shown only on college campuses, you could count on an audience that would give you far greater latitude in the sort of fantasies you might want to deal with. Knowing one's audience may call for far more sophisticated distinctions than this example suggests. In a movie about TV and fantasy, it would be important to know what kinds of shows your audience watches if you are really to resonate with their experiences.

The major service of a story treatment is that it forces you to be certain that the animation technique you've selected is the one best suited to the basic concept of the movie. This is a part of the story treatment that is usually called the "approach." Does the style of the

14.1 BUDGET OUTLINE: While this checklist should cover almost all the direct costs for a film, it doesn't take into account indirect expenses such as studio overhead, insurance, legal fees, equipment depreciation, storage, equipment repair, festival entry fees, and a number of incidental office expenses including mail, telephone, as well as standard supplies and working tools.

EQUIPMENT
CAMERA
LIGHTS
TRIPOD
ANIMATION STAND
CABLE RELEASE
MOTOR
LIGHT BOX
PEGS
PROJECTOR
SCREEN

SUPPLIES
FILM STOCK
PAPERS / CELS
FIELD GUIDE
OTHER ART MATERIALS
DRAWING TOOLS
PROPS
LIGHT BULBS

SOUND
1/4" RECORDER + TAPE
MAGNETIC RECORDING STOCK
STRIPING
SOUND TRANSFER
SOUND MIX
FEES: MUSICIAN, COMPOSER,
        RECORD LIBRARY, ACTORS.
TRACK ANALYSIS
OPTICAL TRACK

LABORATORY
FILM PROCESSING
WORKPRINT
ANSWER PRINT(S)
RELEASE PRINT(S)
OPTICAL EFFECTS
REELS + CANS

EDITING
FILM SPLICER + TAPE
VIEWER
REWINDS
EDITING CONSOLE
SYNCRONIZER
SOUND HEAD + AMPLIFIER
HOT SPLICER + CEMENT
CORES / REELS
LEADER
GLOVES / MARKERS

SPECIAL SERVICES
NEGATIVE MATCHING (A+B ROLLS)
TRANSFER TO VIDEOTAPE
FILM / TRACK CODING
TITLES PREPARATION
PHOTOSTATS

14.2 SAMPLE CAMERA TEST: This grid was developed in testing a 16mm Bolex camera, with a motor, that was to be used in top and bottom lighted filming. With appropriate modifications the same test can be used with nonreflex 16mm cameras and with super 8mm cameras. This test also explores variables of the compound, in this case an Oxberry disc with sets of moving peg-bars at top and bottom. Testing begins with a list of equipment being used:

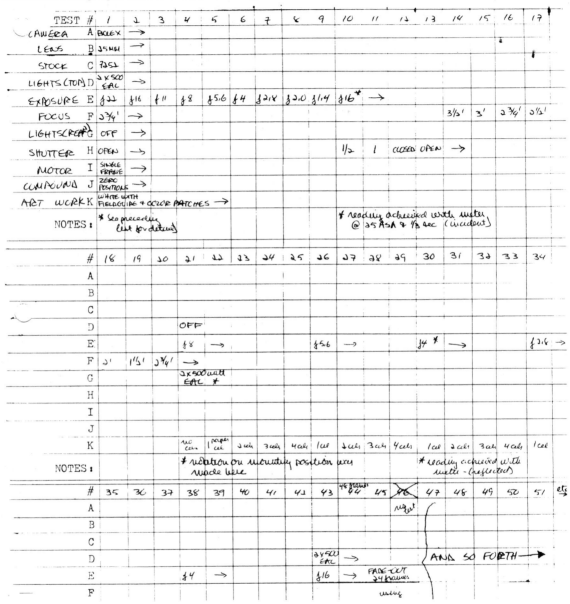

TEST #		1	2	3	4	5	6	7	8	9	10	11	12	13	14	15	16	17
CAMERA	A	BOLEX	→															
LENS	B	25MM	→															
STOCK	C	7252	→															
LIGHTS (TOP)	D	2×500 EAL	→															
EXPOSURE	E	ƒ22	ƒ16	ƒ11	ƒ8	ƒ5.6	ƒ4	ƒ2.8	ƒ2.0	ƒ1.4	ƒ16*	→						
FOCUS	F	2¾'	→												3½'	3'	2¾'	2½'
LIGHTS (REAR)	G	OFF	→															
SHUTTER	H	OPEN	→								½	1	CLOSED	OPEN	→			
MOTOR	I	SINGLE FRAME	→															
COMPOUND	J	ZERO POSITIONS	→															
ART WORK	K	WHITE WITH FIELDGUIDE + COLOR PATCHES →																
NOTES :		*See preceding list for details									# reading achieved with meter @ 25 ASA & ⅓ sec (incident)							

#		18	19	20	21	22	23	24	25	26	27	28	29	30	31	32	33	34
	A																	
	B																	
	C																	
	D			OFF														
	E				ƒ8	→				ƒ5.6	→			ƒ4*	→			ƒ2.8 →
	F	2'	1½'	2¾'	→													
	G				2×500 watt EAL *													
	H																	
	I																	
	J																	
	K			no cels	paper cel	2 cels	3 cels	4 cels	1 cel	2 cels	3 cels	4 cels		1 cel	2 cels	3 cels	4 cels	1 cel
NOTES :					*rotation on mounting position was made here									*reading achieved with meter (reflected)				

#		35	36	37	38	39	40	41	42	43	48 frames 44	45	46	47	48	49	50	51	etc
	A											no cut							
	B																		
	C																		
	D										2×500 EAL	→		AND SO FORTH →					
	E			ƒ4	→						ƒ16	→	FADE OUT 24 frames						
	F												using						

A. CAMERA—Bolex Rex 5—mounted 33 inches above field.
B. LENS—Switar 25mm.
C. STOCK—Ektachrome Commercial #7252 (double perf) ASA25.
D. LIGHTS (TOP)—2 x 500 watt EAL photofloods—3200K mounted at both sides 45 degrees.
E. EXPOSURE—openings range from 1.4 to 22—test all.
F. FOCUS—set at 2¾' (checked by reflex).
G. LIGHTS (REAR)—2 x 500 watt EAL photofloods—3200L mounted on SE and NW legs.

H. SHUTTER—set at open (to test ½ and 1 and closed positions).
I. MOTOR—trigger at M, motor disconnected, speed at 64fps, single frame shutter speed valued at ⅓ sec.—using foot pedal for single and continuous exposures.
J. COMPOUND—fixed at slightly over an 11 field, disc rotation at 0. Top and bottom pegs centered.
K. ARTWORK—White paper with colored and black lines beneath Oxberry field guide. Also to test gray card.

The above list is used with the chart . As you will see, all facets remain constant for any given test save one. All tests, in this case, were 24 frames long using the foot pedal to the animation motor. A small square of paper with the test number was placed under the camera during each test.

animation match the content? Are you the best person to execute the required techniques?

Different animation techniques lend themselves to different approaches. For instance, if the imagery of "real" TV ads was to provide the central material for parody, then kinestasis or collage techniques might provide the best approach. If one wanted to explore the implicit promises that TV advertisements use as they try to connect a product with a fantasy, then perhaps the best approach might be through rotoscoping, or by drawing directly on found TV spots. Either technique would allow you to transform a recognizable TV character or product into the fantasy object it really becomes for the average viewer. Still another approach might be to use cutout techniques in creating a parody of, say, one of the standard soap commercials. If one wanted to suggest that TV has the effect of totally overwhelming the intelligence of the average viewer, then clay techniques might provide the best approach. A TV set could literally suck up a family of viewers.

Much of animation's appeal resides in the fact that, as an art form, it presents so many techniques, each of which has its own subtle bias. Consider it a great challenge (and satisfaction) to select or to invent just the right approach to a given concept.

The most tangible and explicit way of refining a concept is by storyboarding it. As a conceptual tool, the storyboard lets you preview the look and the structure of the film you'll be making. As a practical tool, the storyboard indicates quite precisely many of the production requirements that lie ahead of you. As a promotional tool, the storyboard provides just about the only way that you can let other people in on the film you have in your mind.

Preproduction

Here's a quick list of things you must attend to as you prepare to make the film you've conceptualized and designed.

Hardware and Setting Up. Make schematic sketches of the particular stand or setup you will be using. These sketches can carry notations of the specific camera capabilities your production will require. Add other notes about technical demands and problems you are able to anticipate.

Software. List the materials you will need in creating the visual images for your film. List the amount and kind of film stock you will be using in the camera itself. Review other supplies you should have on hand: extra lights, batteries, and so on.

Budget. Determine exactly what the film is going to cost. Few things are worse than starting a film and then being unable to finish it because you've run out of money. Begin with concrete estimates of hardware and software expenses. In Part Three of this book you'll find estimated prices for just about every piece of production hardware or software that you'll need. In Figure 14.1 I've given you a sample budget outline against which you should check your own plans. I recommend that you keep all budget information, including receipts, in a special place. Over the course of a number of films you'll develop accuracy in projecting what things will cost. By having a fully itemized budget you'll also be able to spot and remember those inevitable hidden costs, things

14.3 PRODUCTION MAP: A well-executed storyboard is best of all planning devices. These samples represent the beginning of a 128 panel storyboard for a film that is sampled further in Figure 14.4.

FREEZE ME

SPOON ENTERS DOCTOR'S OFFICE. GIRL KNITTING.

SITS DOWN, TAKES OFF HAT, LOOKS AT PEOPLE BESIDE HIM.

DOCTOR TAKES OUT FOLDER FROM DRAWER.

STUDIES PAPERS AND X-RAY.

DOCTOR IS ALARMED.

PRESSES INTERCOM BUTTON

DOCTOR - NURSE, SEND IN MY NEXT PATIENT, PLEASE.

SPOON.

GOOD AFTERNOON, DOCTOR.

DOCTOR -

AH YES... ER... COME IN, MR. SPOON, COME IN, YES, HMM... ER....

....SIT DOWN...PLEASE.

SPOON - THANK YOU, DOCTOR.

(SITS DOWN)

(DOCTOR TAKING OUT CIGARETTE)

DOCTOR-

HUM HM...ER...MR.SPOON,
I HAVE SOMETHING IMPOR-
TANT TO...ER... TO TELL
YOU...ER...I'M AFRAID IT'S
GOING TO BE SOMETHING
OF A SHOCK.

(SPOON SITS FORWARD IN SEAT)

SPOON-

I-IS SOMETHING WRONG,
DOCTOR?
(DOCTOR LIGHTS CIGARETTE)
DOCTOR.

..ER... YOU'VE BEEN MY
PATIENT FOR SOME TIME,
MR. SPOON....

(TWO OTHER CIGARETTES BURNING)

····IT'S NEVER EASY FOR A
DOCTOR TO HAVE TO TELL
A PATIENT..ER...I WON'T
BEAT ABOUT THE BUSH....UM.
··I...ER···

SPOON-

·YOU CAN BE FRANK,
DOCTOR.

(DOCTOR WIPING FOREHEAD)

DOCTOR-

MR. SPOON, IT'S LIKE THIS-
YOU...ONLY HAVE A LIMITED
TIME LEFT TO LIVE.

(DOCTOR DROPS ARMS, RELIEVED)

SPOON- LIMITED TIME?

···HOW- HOW LONG DO I
HAVE?

DOCTOR- YOU HAVE EXACTLY.
     FIVE MINUTES.

     (PAUSE)

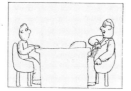

that come up that you'd never have been able to anticipate.

Sound Treatment. A detailed analysis of your film's sound track is important. If you are planning to synchronize your images to a sound track, then you will need to do a frame-by-frame analysis of the recorded track prior to any specific planning of artwork or filming. More information about sound tracks has been given in Chapters 7 and 18.

Schedule. Estimate how long each task will take and bring this information together in a comprehensive production schedule. Be sure to check the schedule against your budget and against your analysis of technical requirements. You may be working in an environment where access to equipment is limited. A production schedule ought to include all aspects of the production from conceptualization to preparation of materials to filming, editing, and laboratory work. Be certain to leave enough time for the various jobs and check with labs regarding their time requirements. Every aspect of animated filmmaking seems to take precisely five times as long as one projects that it will. That is Laybourne's Law. Keeping a careful record of the production schedule will help you in structuring time requirements for the next film you make.

Ego. Is the amount of personal dedication that you are going to invest in this film appropriate to the film? Take stock of what making each specific film means to you as you complete the preproduction phase. Is it the concept behind the film that is compelling your work? Is it what others will say when they see the film? Is it what you expect to learn through the process? Is it the doing of artwork or is it the filming that is most important to you? All these are significant questions. Generally it's a combination of them plus other incentives or compulsions that get us through creative projects. Try to figure out what it means to you. Watch how this changes from film to film and from production phase to production phase within one film.

Testing

It is recommended practice, as they say, to do a camera test whenever you begin working with a new camera. A camera test is sometimes the only way you can locate production problems that will eventually show up.

Technical Testing. There's no set procedure for designing and carrying out a test of your production equipment. Basically, what you want to do is identify all of the possible variables and then, systematically, keep all other factors constant as you test one specific variable, whether it is related to camera, stand, lighting, or whatever. The key word in all this is *systematic.* Clear reasoning and patience are required. In Figure 14.2 I've shown an actual camera test that I've used. In designing your own test, you will obviously need to specify the variables of your camera and of the stand that you are using.

When actually conducting a series of camera tests, I place small slips of paper bearing each test's number in a corner of the frame. I also shoot a few frames of black between each test, for this helps to distinguish one from another when I'm screening the footage after it has returned from the lab. My own tests are usually 24 frames long, sometimes more. Each individual test, of course, explores only one change in the overall technical setup. It might be a lens opening, a change in lighting, different focus, or any other single element that is being tested. All other variables must remain constant so that one can distinguish effects produced by the single change or variation being tested. Thus a camera test is really a series of tests.

Content Testing. It's a good idea to make a test for any effect that you will be trying for the first time in your movie. Similarly, it's good practice to run through any effect that you've learned from experience is difficult to control with the camera and stand at your disposal. It's often valuable, for example, to preview complex camera movements or any of the various in-camera effects such as dissolves and superimpositions. Depending on the movie you are making, there will be other things worth trying out before you proceed with full-scale production. It may be a style of movement. It may be a lighting effect. It may be a new material that you need to mess around with. In all cases, you should carefully write down what you are testing as you do the test. Be sure to add to that notation your comment on how the test came out.

Production

I want to urge you to keep a special *production book* for every film you undertake. There are at least four compelling reasons for doing this. First, a production book will facilitate the process of conceptualization as outlined above. It should contain your story treatment and you may want to store your storyboard here as well. Second, a production book can provide the literal framework from which you will organize the production. By means of a checklist, the book will insure a thoroughness in planning. It will help the movie come out the way you want it. Third, a production book can provide you with a comprehensive and detailed set of notes for use at a later time. That is, you can make sure that what you discover while making one film is not lost when you need that specific knowledge for a different film. A related function is that the book will help you isolate particular difficulties. Finally, a production book can have an important spiritual function. Sometimes it's important to have a place where one can voice frustrations or expectations or any of the other emotions that are experienced in the course of making a film. A production book can be a receptacle for all such observations and comments. In a sense, it can become a diary through which you stay in touch with the overall process that you are experiencing.

Postproduction

A great deal remains to be done after the film returns from the laboratory and you've had a chance to screen the results of your work. Briefly outlined, here are the postproduction stages that most animated films should pass through.

Editing. If you've worked out everything perfectly and if there are no unexpected problems during the production phase, editing will be easy. All the individual sequences of the film are assembled into their final sequence. Chapter 18 reviews the editing process more thoroughly and it will also show you the specialized tools you'll need. If you have

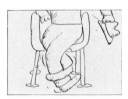

.... MY HOROSCOPE SAID
NOTHING ABOUT THIS!

(HUMS A TUNE, WALKS
OVER TO WINDOW)

.... NICE WEATHER TODAY,
ISN'T IT?...ER...UH UH. I
CAN'T BELIEVE IT....

(STORM OUTSIDE)

DOCTOR —

    ER...MR. SPOON....

SPOON—

    THAT'S IT, DOCTOR!

YOU'VE GOT ME MIXED
WITH ANOTHER SPOON.
THERE'S LOTS OF SPOONS
IN THIS TOWN.

DOCTOR —

IT WOULD BE NICE TO
BELIEVE THAT, BUT WE
MUST BE REALISTIC.

(SPOON PICKS UP REPORT, WALKS
SLOWLY BEHIND DESK, STUDYING IT)

SPOON—

DAM.... DAM....NO NO
NO NO!

WHY ME? WHAT'D I DO?

...WHY ME WHY ME WHY
WHY WHY (SOB). I HATE
YOU!

some problems in your footage, you'll want to try to fix them by rearranging the structure of the film during the editing process. Often it seems that the problems one finds in looking at the *rushes* (the unedited film just as it returns from the processing laboratory) simply cannot be solved through editing. Or if they can, such reediting of the original concept would force you to change the plan of your film in a way that you are unwilling to accommodate. In these cases, postproduction means:

Reshooting. The complexities of animated filmmaking make it common to reshoot a particular sequence. This may be for technical reasons (a light flare or the wrong exposure, for example). More often, reshooting is required because of human error. It's easy enough to make a mistake during the protracted and demanding process of filming. Unless you are very certain of your equipment and you are very practiced in the technique you are using, schedule extra time and budget extra funds for reshooting.

Sound Editing. When you've got all the footage just as you want it, go to work on the sound track for your film. Depending on the production format, different tasks are required in creating the sound track that will accompany your movie. Various levels and approaches to working with sound have been introduced earlier. The catalogue of sound equipment that follows in Chapter 18 will help you plan the sound editing tasks that will be required.

Screenings and Evaluation. It's a thrilling moment when you show your finished film for the first time. The lights are lowered. The audience becomes quiet. The projector stands poised. Your artistic vision is about to be communicated and, believe me, it *is* thrilling. All your work must now pass the scrutiny of an audience.

Somehow everyone lives through the anxieties of a film's first public showing. Living through it isn't enough, however. You've got to learn through it as well. I suggest that you arrange some screenings for people with whom you'll feel comfortable in asking for reactions. Find out what they liked. What did they think the film is about? Whatever reactions and feedback you can glean should be used in evaluating the film in terms of its original goal. Did it do what you wanted it to do? What were your movie's strengths and what were its weaknesses?

A rigorous and candid evaluation of the film's success is essential if you are to grow as a filmmaker. It's not a question of being hard on yourself. It's a question of being hard on the film. After all, you've put a great deal into the production and now you can gain a great deal from it. As you gauge the merits of the film, try to differentiate between the film as an object and the film as an extension of your ego. It's always both, of course, but to the extent that you can keep your ego in check and see the film as just one experience within a continuing process of mastering the craft, to that extent you'll mature as an animator. More and better films will lie ahead.

Distribution and Exhibition. If you like what you've made, you should try to get the film into distribution. One way to go about this is by entering the movie in festivals that showcase work by independent filmmakers. Chapter 21 lists a number of these. If you think that your movie might have a market in schools and public libraries or with other institutions and organizations that rent and purchase films, contact one

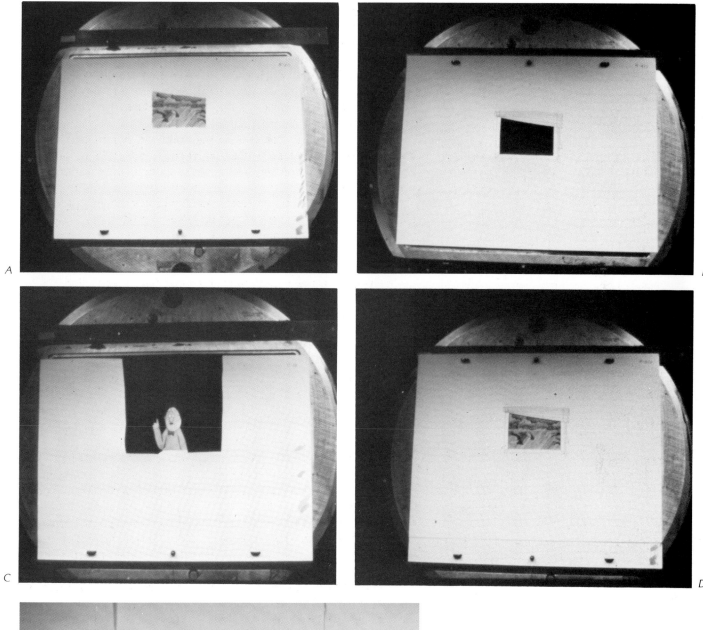

A

B

C

D

E

14.4   ANATOMY OF A FILM: Here are the production stages of *Why Me?*, the working title for a film by Derek Lamb and Janet Perlman that is being produced at the National Film Board of Canada. Using broad humor and irony, the film traces the clinically determined stages of emotional acceptance that are experienced by someone who knows he or she is terminally ill. The film's technique incorporates watercolors that are done on punched heavy-weight animation bond and then cut out and used in combination. No acetates are employed, yet the overall effect is just like that of full cel animation. Photos *A, B, C,* and *D* show individual elements with *E* representing their composite image.

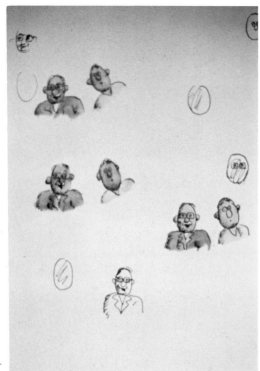

F

G

H

14.4   Photograph *F* shows a detail from preliminary character studies. In *G* a pile of finished drawings stands ready for filming. The storyboard panels in Figure 14.3 suggest the detail in which the film was written by Derek Lamb. Janet Perlman, who is single-handedly animating the film, is seen at work in her studio at the Film Board's production center outside Montreal (*H*). An exposure sheet bearing the track breakdown is shown in *I*. Janet Perlman follows such exposure sheets as she methodically works her way from the first scene to the movie's conclusion. *Photos by the author.*

PROD'N 30-340	SEQ.	SHOT	LENGTH					
		ACTION		FR.				
U				4 01	B-785 A-800			
L				02				
T				03	B-784 A-801			
I				04				
				05	B-785 A-800			
				06				
				07	B-786		ONE LEVEL	
				08				
I		BREATH		09	B-787			
M				10				
G				11	A-802 B-788		TWO LEVELS	
O				12				
N				13	A-803 B-789			
N				14				
A				15	A-802 B-790			
S				16				
U				17	A-803 B-791			
E				18				
Y				19	A-802 B-790			
O				20				
U				21	A-803 B-792			
				22				
				23	A-802 B-793			
				24				
				25	A-803 B-794			
				26				
				27	A-802 B-795			
				28				
				29	A-803 B-793			
				30				
				31	A-802 B-794			
				32				
				33	A-803 B-795			
				34				
B				35	A-802 B-789			
L				36				
A				37	A-803 B-792			
C				38				
K				39	A-802 B-796			
				40				
W				41	A-803 B-79			
H				42				
				43	A-802 B-794			
				44				
				45	A-803 B-791			
				46				
				47	A-802 B-793			
				48				
T				49	A-803 B-797			
E				50				
				51	B-798		ONE LEVEL	
				52				
				53	B-799			
A				54				
N				55	B-800			
D				56				
				57	B-801			
				58				
B				59	B-802			
L				60				
				61	B-803			
				62				
				63	B-804			
				64				
				65	B-805			
				66				
U				67	B-806			
E				68				
				69	B-807			
				70				
				71	B-808			
				72				
				73	B-809			

1

of the nontheatrical distributors listed in Chapter 21. Some independent animators distribute their own films. At the very least, you should try to show your film in as many places as possible and to as many different kinds of audiences as possible. Certainly include the finished film in a sample reel. Most animators keep at least one print of all their work so that they have a reel to show potential sponsors and investors.

The Next One. In a sense, the final step in the production of one film is the first step toward another film. You should always keep thinking of the next movie. Sometimes an idea will emerge from a test you've tried. Sometimes an idea comes from a mistake or an accidental discovery. Sometimes a particular technique of animation will spawn the next movie. Sometimes you'll learn as you work on one film that it is within a totally different approach that your real interest lies.

There is no such thing as a valueless production or a wasted film. Every sequence that you undertake teaches you something. And this makes film production a regenerative process. One thing always leads to the next thing, although it's often impossible to know what lies ahead. Nor is that really important. For it's the getting there that makes the journey worthwhile. Animation, like anything that matters, should be viewed as a dynamic process in which the goal is excellence, not just one excellent piece of work. The end of one movie marks the beginning of the next.

John Canemaker: *The 40's*

Paul Driessen: *Le Bleu Perdu*

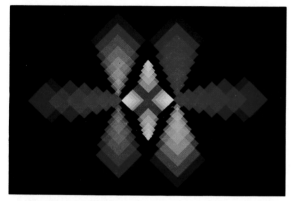

Ishu Patel: *Perspectrum*

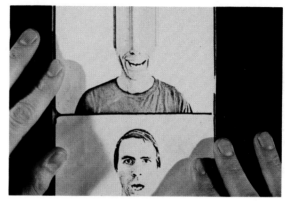

George Griffin: *Head*

Lillian Schwartz and Ken Knowlton: *Metamorphosis*

Maureen Selwood: *Odalisque*

Co Hoedeman: *Tchou Tchou*

Lynn Smith: *Teacher, Lester Bit Me!*

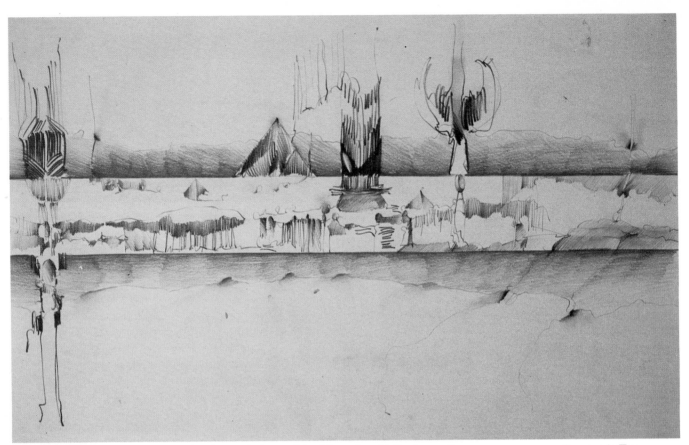

Dennis Pies: *Sonoma*. One of a cycle of backgrounds that are joined through rapid dissolves as the camera pans across the artwork. The horizontal lines indicate top and bottom of the field.

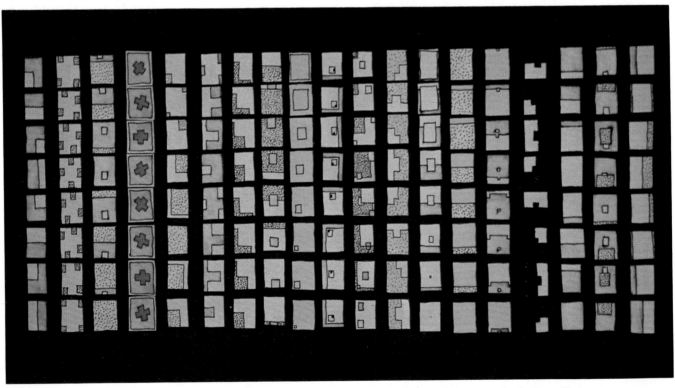

George Griffin: *Thumbnail Sketches*. Composite of 19-cycle sequences, ink and dye on paper, that make-up the 3-minute film.

The Films of John and Faith Hubley: for more than 20 years the Hubley Studio in New York has produced films that have won every award in the international field of animation. The Hubleys' work as independent animators ranges from segments for The Children's Television Workshop to the feature length, *Everybody Rides the Carrousel.* Sampled from top to bottom are *The Hole, Cockaboody, The Hat* and *Everybody Rides the Carrousel.*

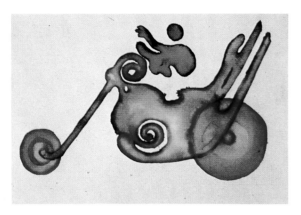

Ryan Larkin: *Street Musique*

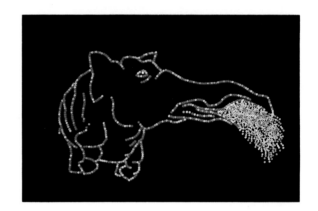

Ishu Patel: *Bead game*

Queasy the Parrot: a series of finished sequential cels from Richard Williams's *Raggedy Ann & Andy*.
Queasy was animated by Charlie Downs. Copyright The Bobbs-Merrill Co., Inc. 1976.

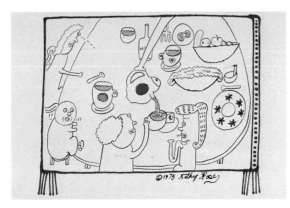

Kathy Rose: *The Doodlers*

Caroline Leaf: *The Street*

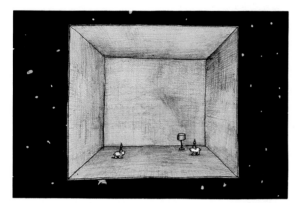 

Robert Mitchell and Robert Swarth: *K-9000: A Space Oddity*

Co Hoedeman: *Sand Castle*

Released in 1977, the feature film *Raggedy Ann & Andy* represents the contemporary extension of the traditions of full-cel character animation as it was developed by the Disney Studios. Directed by Richard Williams, the production includes work by many of the master animators from Hollywood's golden era of cartoon animation. Photos provided courtesy of the Bobbs-Merrill Co., Inc. Copyright 1976.

Right and center:
Caroline Leaf: *The Street.* These 26 frames represent just over one second of screen time. Note the animation on "one's" where the action is fastest.

Far right:
Lynn Smith: *Why a Museum* (working title). A new technique that combines direct animation of pastels with color Xeroxes. This and the other clips show full-scale 35mm footage.

Below:
Three frames from *Why Me?*, a work-in-progress at The National Film Board of Canada. The film is by Derek Lamb and Janet Perlman.

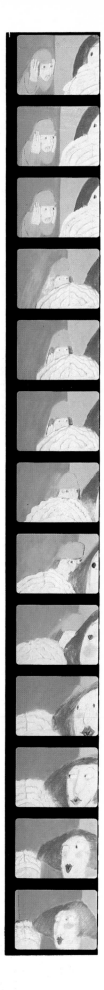

Joyce Borenstein: *Traveller's Palm*

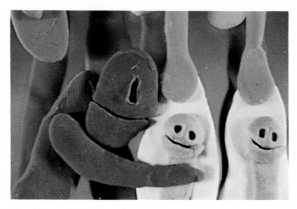

Eliot Noyes, Jr.: *Fable of He and She*

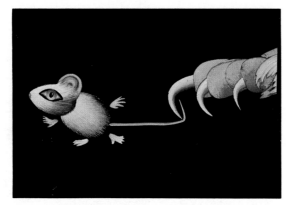

Evelyn Lambert: *The Lion & The Mouse*

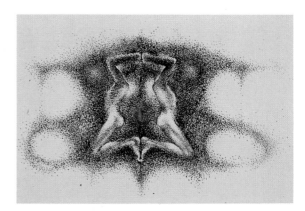

Ryan Larkin: *Street Musique*

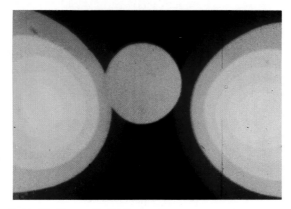

Oskar Fischinger: *Radio Dynamics*

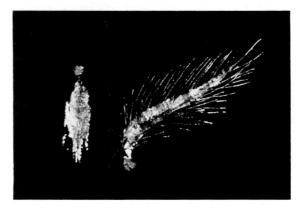

Norman McLaren: *Blinkety Blank*

Paul Driessen: *An Old Box*

Janet Perlman: *Lady Fishbourne's Complete Guide to Better Table Manners*

PART THREE: TOOLS

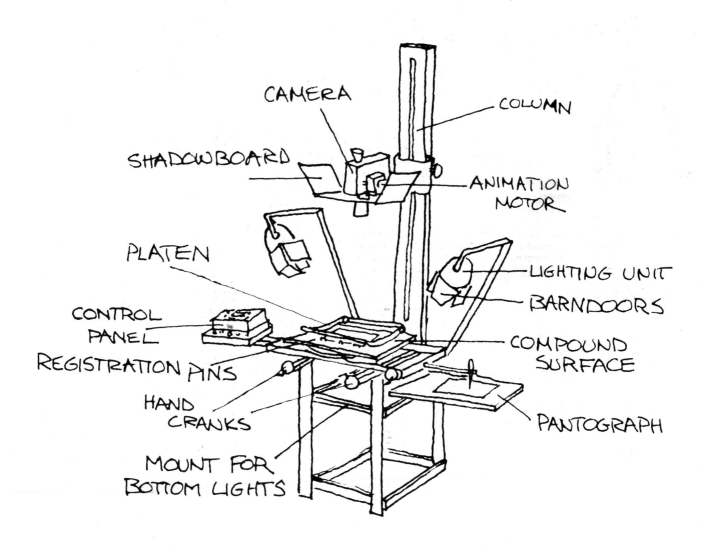

CAMERA

COLUMN

SHADOWBOARD

ANIMATION MOTOR

PLATEN

LIGHTING UNIT

BARNDOORS

CONTROL PANEL

REGISTRATION PINS

COMPOUND SURFACE

HAND CRANKS

PANTOGRAPH

MOUNT FOR BOTTOM LIGHTS

The next five chapters comprise a catalogue of animation tools. Collectively they provide a comprehensive list of every kind of tool you will need; a discussion of both super 8mm and 16mm production formats; a sampling of tools appropriate to different production levels from the most sophisticated to the simplest; an indication of the costs involved; and a description of the major features and basic utilization of each animation tool.

These chapters do not reveal the Absolute Truth. You will not find complete listings of all available models of various pieces of equipment. Technical specifications are left for each manufacturer's operating manual. The prices are illustrative only. By the time you read this, the cost of tools and services will surely have risen. Still, it's my conviction that ball-park figures can be helpful if only on a comparative basis.

It's important to amplify these limitations a bit further. The scope of this volume precludes even a simplified discussion of all the techniques common to live-action as well as animated filmmaking. Thus, for example, there is no description of standard film-editing techniques, nor is there a detailed explanation of camera and projector shutter mechanisms. An evaluation and discussion of microphones is omitted entirely. Such information is, of course, very important. And happily there are a number of large and inexpensive volumes you can consult for a general background in the medium or for a full discussion of any particular production tool or facet of filmmaking.

Part Four: Resources is designed to provide recommendations on where to go for more information. So when you come across a problem or you have a question that falls outside the parameters of these pages, check Chapters 20, 21 and 22.

A Caution for Hardware Freaks

It is very, *very* easy to become enamored of the tools of animation. Component parts and features, the beauty of a well-made tool, curiosity about special effects, the pride of technical competency—each of these honest responses can become a seductive mania that draws the animator further into hardware and further away from creativity and meaning.

I'd like to issue a warning. Check the impulse in yourself toward becoming a hardware freak. It may help to be reminded that no matter what tools you begin with, you will eventually outgrow your equipment. The desire to purchase the next level of equipment is never satiated. There's *always* another level. Besides, if you begin with the fanciest and most versatile hardware, you may find you never use some of the capabilities you've paid the most for.

So in the beginning, try to get along without the complicated gizmos. You'll find a great deal of creative energy is released when one works with limited hardware and is forced to explore the capabilities of relatively simple tools. That may sound weird, but it's a truism many have experienced. It's especially true for those who can picture themselves at the beginning of a long process of exploration and growth.

As your interest in animation advances and matures, you'll most likely find yourself shopping for new tools and making decisions about which techniques and formats are essential to the kinds of animation that fascinate you. Building one's equipment base can be one of the most rewarding aspects of being an independent animator. And this is most true when the acquisition is done patiently, carefully, and with a sense of creative as well as financial ecology. Here are some general tips for tooling up.

Shop Around, Widely. Familiarize yourself with all the camera shops and other hardware/software institutions in your area. Also familiarize yourself with mail-order sources of animation tools (see Chapter 22).

New vs. Used Equipment. Serious filmmakers take good care of their equipment. For this reason it is often very wise to consider purchasing used equipment. Also, you may be able to get a trade-in on a piece of hardware you yourself have cared for and have outgrown. Unfortunately used animation equipment is exceedingly rare. Journals and filmmaker associations can be helpful for establishing contacts and locating used gear.

Borrow or Rent. When you are ready to try out new levels and types of hardware, see if you can borrow before you buy. Or rent. The place to put one's real investment is with the software and the time for making lots of movies. Don't overextend yourself so far in acquiring hardware that you're left with nothing for software.

Get Warranties. You should never be forced into purchasing an expensive piece of animation equipment without the assurance that it will work properly. This is particularly true with cameras, even brand-new ones. So don't purchase any piece of equipment without some kind of warranty that allows you to return the item to the dealer if you discover a problem with it soon after purchase.

Always Test a New Tool. The first thing you should do when you acquire a new tool is to test it as thoroughly as you can. This will help you spot any malfunction, and it will help you to learn the full operational limits (and idiosyncrasies) of the particular tool. Some details on testing and keeping notes on the technical aspects of animated filmmaking have already been discussed in Chapter 14.

Enough of warnings and tips. The next three chapters ought to thoroughly orient you to the animator's world of tools and processes, gadgets and supplies, hardware and software.

Lady Fishbourne's Complete Guide to Better Table Manners by Janet Perlman. *Courtesy of the filmmaker and Carousel Films.*

15
Cameras and Accessories

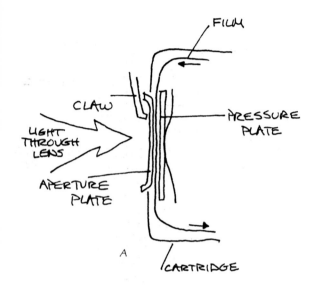

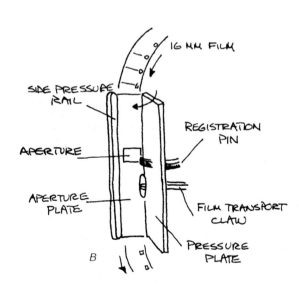

15.1 **CAMERA REGISTRATION:** Drawing *A* represents the cross section of a super 8mm camera. It shows the four elements that provide registration: the *aperture plate*, a channel through which film travels; the *claw*, which advances the film by pulling down on successive sprocket holes; the *pressure plate*, built into every super 8 cassette; and the *film stock* itself, bearing a precise configuration of sprocket holes. Drawing *B* shows the registration system of a 16mm motion picture camera.

The most important tool in animation is the camera. Its mechanical precision and its range of image-making capabilities set the parameters within which the animator must work.

Literally hundreds of super 8mm and 16mm cameras are capable of animation. These vary greatly in their relative costs, sophistication, and quality of workmanship. Yet there are certain basic elements common to all movie cameras, and there are special features that operate much the same regardless of camera size, format, or cost. Because of manufacturing standardization, it is possible to talk in general terms about cameras and accessories. In identifying and describing the elements that make a camera work, I've placed emphasis on those features that are especially critical in animated filmmaking. This chapter also presents three representative models of super 8mm cameras and then 16mm cameras. My selections represent simple to sophisticated models, inexpensive to costly ones, and models that can be used for all filmmaking needs as well as those designed only for animation.

If you can combine the data catalogued here with your own handson inspection of different cameras, you'll quickly forge a working knowledge that should get you quite far along. When it's useful, information becomes data. Otherwise it's Dada. Eventually, you are going to encounter a problem, question, reference, or demand that forces you to expand and refine your understanding of animation cameras. When that happens, return to these pages.

General Features: Cameras

The movie camera is a lot like a still camera except that it takes its pictures in rapid order instead of one at a time. But the movie camera *can* expose individual frames one at a time. In fact, that's what makes animation possible.

The mechanics of the camera are relatively simple. A *claw* device interracts with the *perforation holes* on the film surface to pull successive frames into the *camera gate,* where the frame is exposed. All this happens quickly—twenty-four times in one second when the camera is running at sound speed.

In order to use a motion picture camera for animation the *registration system* that brings the film into place during the exposure must be very accurate. In sophisticated and specially designed animation cameras there is a set of *registration pins* that holds the film precisely in place during exposures. In any movie camera, however, the claw device combines with both the aperture plate and the sprocket holes to produce a fairly accurate registration system.

All movie cameras require a source of power to advance the film. A power system is often required for other mechanical tasks—to operate a power zoom lens, for example. In most super 8mm cameras, electric current is used to power the camera. Its source is a set of alkaline batteries. Many 16mm cameras are also powered by batteries of one form or another, sometimes mounted in the camera and sometimes carried independently and attached to the camera by a cord. Some 16mm cameras, however, are powered by *spring-wind motors*. Either power system will work, yet both have liabilities. Animation drains batteries very quickly and there is a tendency for spring motors to vary somewhat in the length of exposure time they provide for each frame of film. For these reasons and others, animation is often done with *auxiliary motors* that are attached to the camera and are themselves powered by electric current from a normal wall outlet. Auxiliary motors are discussed later.

In both 16mm and super 8mm formats, the execution of an exposure of a single frame of film is often achieved by use of a *cable release*—a cloth or plastic tube that has a metal cable running through it and a plunger device at one end. The plunger activates a metal pin in the other end of the cable. This pin is inserted into the camera body and it triggers the release of a single frame of film. The cable release usually screws into a threaded receptacle that is located either within the camera's trigger or at some adjacent location on the camera body.

Some cameras employ an alternate method of executing single-frame exposures. Many cameras have a *single-frame position* marked on the camera's variable speed control. With this design, the trigger is pressed by hand (as in normal filming), but the action releases just a single frame. Because even the lightest touch of a trigger can cause a change in the relationship of camera to subject, this mode of single framing can mess up the stable registration required in animating. Note, however, that many of today's super 8mm cameras have *remote contact mechanisms* that allow operation without applying any pressure to the camera body.

Movie cameras have *standard filming speeds*. For 16mm this is 24 fps and for super 8mm it is 18 fps. Actually, the super 8mm format has two standard speeds. Eighteen fps is the silent speed and, increasingly, 24 fps is becoming the standard for super 8mm sound filming. At the present time both 18 and 24 fps are considered standard and many cameras have settings for both. Depending on the particular

15.2 VARIABLE SHUTTER: The drawings represent four positions of the variable shutter on a 16mm Bolex camera. Pictured to the right in each drawing is the *shutter blade* and *aperture hole*. Drawing *A* shows the shutter in its normal position (open) and in drawing *D* it is seen in its fully closed position. To the left in each of the four drawings is the corresponding position of the variable shutter *control*, which is located on the outside body of the camera.

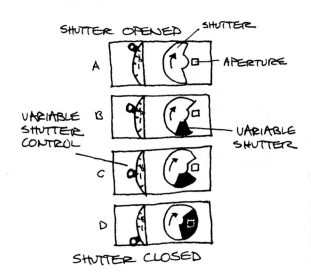

15.3 UNIVERSAL 16MM CAMERA: Following loosely the design of the Bolex 16mm camera, this drawing identifies all the standard features of 16mm cameras. This model contains elements from many different camera makes, and for convenience all its features are conveniently located on the visible side of the camera body.

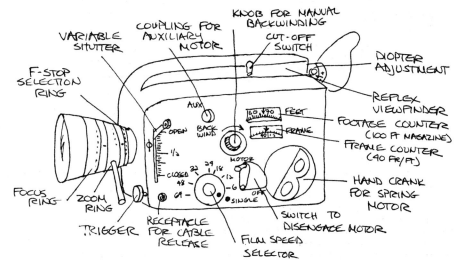

15.4 SUPER 8MM CAMERAS: On this and the following pages you'll find drawings of seven super 8mm cameras. These are ordered according to increasing levels of sophistication and, with that, greater cost. Prices vary so much between individual models and between retailers that there is no purpose in listing them. An inexpensive camera capable of single frame filming will cost between $150 and $300. Super 8 cameras in the $300 to $500 range should include all the animation features available. The highest priced cameras (such as the Beaulieu 500S that costs over $1,000) have features that are probably *not* particularly valuable in animated filmmaking. Note that the recent popularity of XL (low light) filming capabilities and of sound recording directly on super 8 film have actually *reduced* the value of expensive super 8mm cameras for animation. Good used super 8 cameras (without XL or sound) represent an excellent value. Keep your eye out for any of the models pictured here. Check your local dealer for the latest models from all the major super 8 camera manufacturers (like cars, new models come out each fall) or for excellent used cameras.

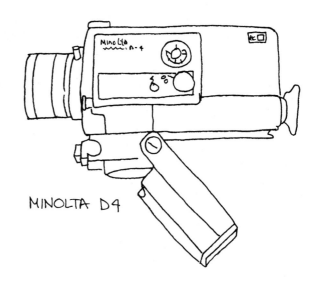

MINOLTA D4

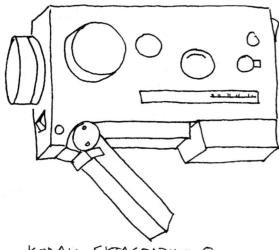

KODAK EKTAGRAPHIC 8

FUJICA SINGLE 8

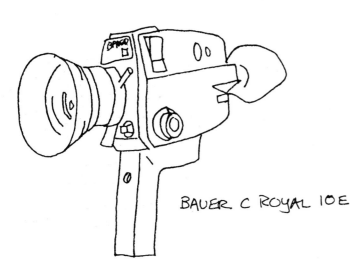

BAUER C ROYAL 10 E

16mm or super 8mm camera, the filmmaker may be offered additional speed options. The fastest speeds are generally 64 fps and the slowest 6 or 8 fps.

When the camera is running at the standard live-action speed, the actual *exposure time* for a single frame is approximately one fiftieth of a second. For various mechanical reasons, however, the exposure time for single framing is always somewhat longer. Usually the shutter is open for one thirtieth of a second per frame. Check the operating manual of your camera for specific calibration data.

Obviously it is of absolute importance for the camera to expose the film to just the right amount of light to get the proper image. Achieving the *correct exposure* requires the control of two factors: f-stop and shutter.

The *f-stop* or *aperture* is a function of the lens, which permits the filmmaker to control how much light will pass through the camera onto the film. This is done by means of an adjustable *iris* or *diaphragm* that is built into every lens. In almost all super 8mm cameras there is an *automatic metering system* that measures the light reflected from the object at which the camera is pointing. These metering systems compute and mechanically select the f-stop setting that will give the correct exposure. In doing this, the camera automatically makes an adjustment for whatever *film stock* is being used. Different stocks require different amounts of light (see Chapter 19).

If possible, animators always try to use a camera that has a *manual override* in addition to an automatic light-metering system. Animation techniques such as line or paint-on-glass (or anything with backlighting) require the camera operator to film relatively thin lines and small markings against very bright backgrounds. In this situation, an automatic exposure meter tends to let in too much light. Most 16mm cameras used for animation do not have automatic metering systems and require manual light readings and manual setting of the camera's f-stop. For more information on achieving correct exposure, see Chapter 18.

In animation, the f-stop setting is an extremely important variable because it controls *depth of field,* the amount of distance in front of the camera lens in which things are sharply focused. More about depth of field in the next chapter.

The *shutter,* a rotating metal disc, is the second factor controlling the exposure of each frame of film within the camera's gate. The shutter is mechanically linked with the claw mechanism to insure that light passes onto the film only at that moment when the film is being held motionless in the camera's gate.

A *variable shutter* allows the animator to use a number of *in-camera effects.* A *fade-out* is accomplished by closing the variable shutter gradually during a successive number of single-frame exposures until there is no light hitting the film as it passes through the gate. The reverse procedure accomplishes a *fade-in* effect (Figure 15.2).

Superimposition also requires a variable shutter—a feature available on many but not all super 8mm and 16mm cameras. To create a superimposition, the shutter is set so that roughly one half the normal amount of light passes onto the film during a first "pass" through the camera. The film is then rewound within the camera. To get

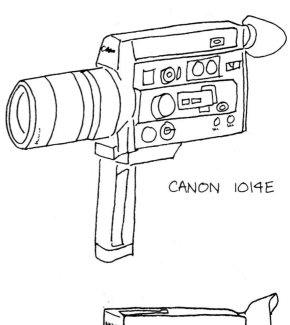

CANON 1014E

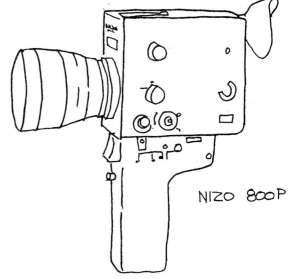

NIZO 800P

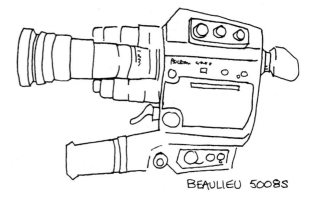

BEAULIEU 5008S

15.4

15.5   16MM CAMERAS: The following six illustrations will give you a quick introduction to specific 16mm cameras. As with the sampling of super 8 cameras, the list here goes from simple to complex, from older models to newer ones, from less expensive to more expensive. Independent animators often get into 16mm production through used equipment. Although prices vary wildly according to the demand, original cost, and condition of used cameras, it should be possible to get a good used Bolex or Kodak K-100 for under $500. I acquired the 16mm cassette model shown below from a pawnshop for $35. New equipment costs more, of course. A new B & H 70-DR is roughly $700 and a new Bolex Rex 5 is around $1,000. Special process cameras such as the Oxberry and Forox models are sold with their stands.

the superimposition, the film is advanced through the camera a second time. Half the normal exposure is again used in this second pass. Many of the more recently manufactured super 8mm cameras offer the special feature of an *automatic dissolve control.* This device enables the animator to superimpose, fade, and dissolve using the standard super 8mm film cassette. The best dissolve controls also allow manual control of the shutter. Check your instruction booklet to find out if your camera has this feature.

A close relative to the superimposition or "super" is the *dissolve.* Here a fade-out is precisely superimposed over an equally long fade-in. If the dissolve covers a long period of time—say 2 seconds (48 frames) or more—it is called a *lap dissolve.*

Doing supers and dissolves requires two additional camera features. *Backwinding,* as the name suggests, refers to the ability to run film through the camera in reverse. In order to achieve accurate fades and dissolves the camera must be equipped with a *frame counter,* a device that lets the animator keep an accurate count of the

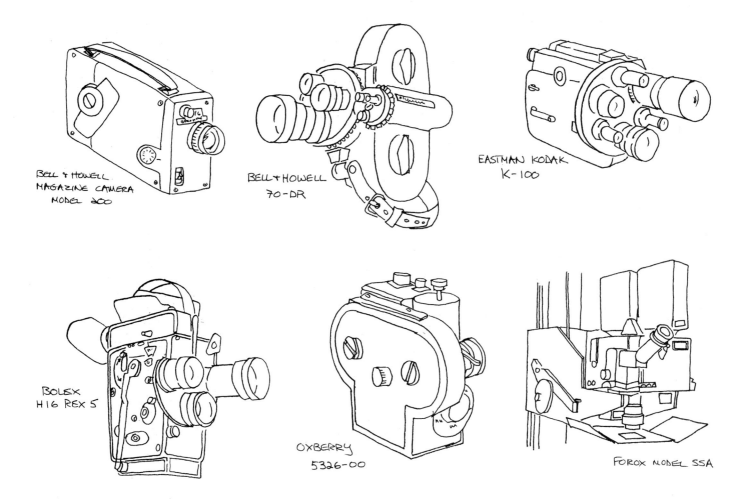

BELL & HOWELL
MAGAZINE CAMERA
MODEL 200

BELL & HOWELL
70-DR

EASTMAN KODAK
K-100

BOLEX
H16 REX 5

OXBERRY
5326-00

FOROX MODEL SSA

frames as they are exposed or backwound. *Footage indicators* are common to all cameras in all formats.

And every camera must have a *lens,* a combination of glass elements that reduces the image in from of the camera to that small, exact replica that is recorded on the emulsion of the film stock. A more detailed discussion of various lenses follows. It bears noting in this context, however, that some cameras are equipped with a built-in *zoom lens,* some cameras have a *fixed lens,* and some cameras accept *interchangeable lenses.* An important requirement for most animation techniques is for the lens to focus on objects very close to it. This is accomplished by means of a built-in *macrofocusing* capability and the use of a special *closeup lens* or *diopter,* which can be attached to the front of a normal lens.

The close proximity of camera to artwork makes it particularly critical in animation to have precise *framing* and *focusing.* A *reflex viewing system* is a built-in feature of most super 8mm cameras. It allows the camera operator to view the image exactly as it will fall on the film stock. Sharp focusing and accurate framing are made possible with this ability to view through the same lens that will expose the film. However, there are a number of excellent 16mm animation cameras that don't have reflex or through-the-lens viewing. Instead, such cameras have a *viewfinder system.* This kind of design presents the animator with a problem called *parallax.* What the lens records on the film is not precisely what the viewfinder shows to the camera operator. Many such nonreflex cameras have some sort of a calibrated system to assist the filmmaker in compensating for parallax.

Even *with* reflex systems there can often be a slight error between what is seen on the camera's viewing screen and what is actually being recorded on film. Animators should always test the framing and focusing mechanisms of their cameras (see Chapter 14). Another note: Reflex viewing systems require a *cutoff* mechanism that prohibits light from entering the camera body via the viewfinder when film is being exposed and the filmmaker's eye is not pressed to the viewfinder as it normally is in live-action filming.

These remarks are not intended to itemize all motion picture camera features. Nor do they describe in complete detail the listed items. It would take volumes many times longer than this one to explain fully how a camera works and what features extend the tool's capabilities. Annotated citations of such reference works are provided in Chapter 20.

The series of drawings that accompany this overlook of animation cameras will introduce you to some of the more standard models of both super 8mm and 16mm formats. The model number and manufacturer of each has been indicated, but I recommend that you check with your local dealer for current models—with the newest features and accessories. Note that the cameras are listed in order of increasing cost.

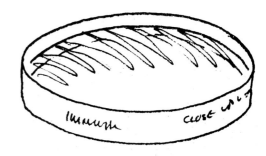

15.6 CLOSEUP LENS: A set of closeup lenses is available for virtually all super 8mm and 16mm cameras.

Lenses

Imagine that you've painstakingly designed and executed a 5-minute film using, say, paint-on-glass technique. Everything has been

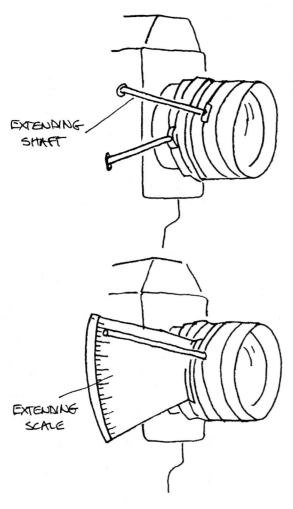

EXTENDING
SHAFT

EXTENDING
SCALE

15.7   ZOOM EXTENDERS: Most zoom lenses are equipped with short metal shafts that stick out of the lens and are used as levers in adjusting the lens before or during filming (many super 8 cameras have automatic zooms, a feature of little use to the animator). By replacing the short shaft with a longer one of metal or wood, the animator gains greater precision in causing the incremental changes that are required in executing a frame-by-frame zoom. Registration of the zooming action is further extended by attaching a reference scale to a fixed part of the lens shaft or the camera body. The scale allows the animator to control precisely a zoom movement and it also helps in planning ahead—for example, in estimating what change is required for a zoom that covers the entire zoom ratio in exactly 5 sets of two-frame exposures.

done under the camera—no artwork exists after your labors. OK. You rush home with your processed film and thread it through the projector. The lights go off and the image appears on the fabled silver screen. Just as you are about to grin with pride, you suddenly notice that the focus is soft. Part of your image is fuzzy. No matter how hard you work the focusing knob, the image remains blurred. The film is ruined.

This little horror story could be prophetic. It's happened to me, and if you are not careful, it can happen to you. I recount the tragedy as a reminder that optical precision is essential in animation. If a lens is even slightly out of alignment, the image will be sharp in places and out of focus in others. Indeed, any imperfection in a movie camera's lens system will show up most clearly when you are screening animation.

Most of today's super 8mm cameras have built-in lenses. When purchasing or using this kind of camera, you should conduct a thorough test to verify the optical quality of the lens. But whether you are using a built-in lens or a removable lens, the comments that follow are particularly important. They pertain to five facets of lens control and lens modification.

Closeup Filming

Many of the techniques described in this book require a focusing distance that is *less* than standard lenses will accommodate. The majority of super 8mm cameras, for example, cannot be focused on a subject that is closer than 4 or 5 feet. As an animator, you will constantly be required to operate inside this minimum focal range. The process of closeup filming, also called *macrofilming,* is achieved through one of four procedures or attachments.

Built-in Macrofocusing. Many of today's super 8mm cameras have built-in zoom lenses that can be operated in a macro-range. A manual adjustment is made on the lens or camera body that allows the variable focal mechanism of the zoom to act as a focusing device in ultra-closeup cinematography. A standard zooming motion is not possible when such a macrofeature is in operation.

Plus Diopter Lenses. By placing an auxiliary lens in front of the regular camera lens, one can simply and effectively achieve closeup filming. *Plus diopters* is the technical name for such closeup lenses. These accessories are generally sold in sets of three, and they are sized according to the threading within the metal housing on the front edge of the normal camera lens. Measurements for the diameter of the diopter, given in millimeters, must match that of your specific camera lens.

Diopters are rated according to their magnification power: +1, +2, and +3. The threading on each lens holder permits the filmmaker to stack two or more lenses simultaneously. This achieves various multiples in magnifying power. When more than one diopter is being used, the highest-power diopter lens is positioned closest to the normal camera lens. Note that the use of too many diopters can have deleterious effects, including soft edges and "barreling" of the field of vision.

Although simple in construction and use, plus diopters must be ground and mounted with extraordinary precision. For this reason, quality diopters are expensive. A set of three diopters for super 8mm cameras will range from $12 to $20; 16mm diopters are usually sold separately and, because they are bigger, cost more. Prices range from $7.50 to nearly $200. The manufacturers of diopters provide charts to help you determine how a particular closeup lens will affect the effective minimum focal length of the lens it is attached to.

Bellows. A bellows is an accordion-like extension that is used to move the lens farther away from the camera's focal plane in order to produce extreme close-ups. This device, available only on some 16mm cameras, permits continuous closeup focusing because the distance between the lens mount and the lens is completely adjustable. The function of the bellows is like that of an extension tube.

Extension Tubes. Some 16mm lenses can be made into closeup lenses by the use of extension tubes, simple hollow cylinders that physically extend the focal length and hence decrease the minimal distance required between lens and subject. The extension tube is threaded into the camera body and then the lens is threaded on the other end. Bolex makes a set of extension tubes for "C" mounts. The lengths are 5, 10, 20, and 40 millimeters, and they can be used in combination. Note that extension tubes affect exposure. Consult your dealer or the manufacturer's instructions for more complete information.

The Zoom Lens

A *variable focus lens,* usually called a "zoom" lens, can be one of the most technique-extending tools an animator can acquire for his or her camera. The popularity and usefulness of a zoom lens is shown quite graphically by the fact that it is almost impossible to find a super 8mm camera that is without one. Because 16mm cameras are usually sold without a lens of any kind and because these cameras generally accept different lenses (unlike super 8mm cameras), most animators will try to acquire a quality zoom lens.

The zoom lens permits the animator to quickly adjust the size of the field being filmed beneath the camera. A zoom lens also permits an effective camera "movement" toward or away from the subject. A special home-made device can be easily attached to almost any zoom lens in order to provide the animator with precise control of the lens during frame-by-frame filming (Figure 15.7).

A zoom and a set of diopters combine to produce the most versatile lens system for animation. It is possible, for example, to add enough magnification so that one can zoom within a field the size of a standard 35mm slide. Obviously, the "stronger" the zoom the more flexible it will be. Zoom lenses are measured by the ratio of their minimum to maximum focal lengths—a 12mm to 120mm zoom lens has the ratio of 1:10.

Zoom lenses for 16mm cameras come with different types of camera mounts (Arri Standard Mount, Arriflex Bayonet Mount, Bolex Rex Mount, Bolex Bayonet Mount, "C" Mount, Cinema-Products (CP) Mount, and more). Zoom lenses come in different sizes (9.5mm-57mm all the way to 12mm-240mm). Zoom lenses can be acquired with built-in metering systems and they come with reflex viewfinder attachments.

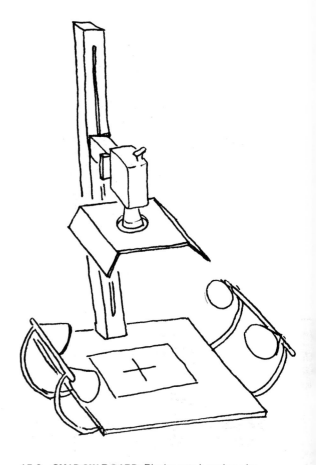

15.8 SHADOW BOARD: Black matte board can be used to construct a shadow board for your camera. The hole through which the camera shoots should be sized close to that of the lens' diameter. The wings can be made to bend by scoring the board rather than cutting it clean through. These wings help to ensure that ambient light doesn't reflect up into the camera lens. There are many ways to mount a shadow board: it can be attached to the camera body, to the tripod or stand, to the structure that holds the lights, or it can be independently hung.

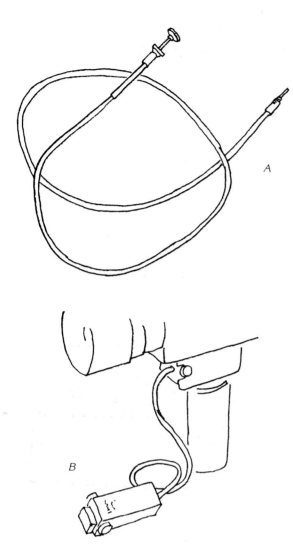

15.9 CABLE RELEASE: The familiar cable release *(A)* can cause the camera to jiggle. The newer electro-magnetic release systems *(B)* do not require any external pressure to trigger the camera. Pictured here is a Minolta remote release. The Minolta super 8mm camera system is particularly well designed for animation and its price is relatively low.

Here are a few sample models and prices. Kern 17-85mm, f/3.5 zoom lens with Bolex Bayonet Mount, $375; Cannon 12mm-120mm macrozoom lens with Arri Standard Mount, $2,200; Angenieux 12mm-120mm zoom lens with f/2.2 automatic iris, $3,500.

Lens Features and Problems

Depth of Field. As noted earlier, depth of field refers to the amount of physical distance in front of the camera that will appear in focus. Depth of field is a complicated phenomenon—a function of a number of elements, including lighting, film speed, distance from subject to lens, focal length of the lens, and f-stop. The f-stop is the easiest variable to control—the higher the f-stop (say f/16 or, better, f/22), the greater the distance in front of the camera that is in focus.

As you can clearly see, depth of field is a critical factor in many animation techniques. For example, in clay, puppet, or time-lapse techniques, the animator may want to blur the background by using a low f-stop and less lighting, thereby reducing depth of field. Sometimes it may be important to have as much territory in focus as possible, with a high f-stop and lots of lighting. More times than not, animators try to shoot at a high f-stop in order to maximize the distance in which everything will be in sharp focus.

Other important factors affecting depth of field include the focal length of the lens (wide-angle lenses give greater depth of field than telephoto lenses); the distance from the art to the camera (the farther away, the greater the depth of field); and the film speed (the slower the film stock the greater the depth of field if lighting is constant). Note that the shutter speed is not a factor in depth-of-field control because, in animation as in all live-action filmmaking, the shutter speed is fixed at roughly 1/50 second (live action) or 1/30 second (single framing).

Light Reflections. Even when the lights of an animation stand are mounted at the proper 45-degree angle (see Chapter 18), a glass platen or the shiny surface of a cel can cause the camera to record a reflection of the lens itself. A *shadow board,* a *sunshade,* or just a liberal application of black electrical tape will effectively mute such reflections. Incidentally, any shiny surface within range of the camera can cause reflection of light.

Aperture. A final and very critical quality of every lens has to do with the range of its *aperture settings.* For most moviemakers, the "faster" the lens the better. The lowest possible f-stop opening is desired in order to extend the camera's range when shooting under minimal lighting conditions. For animators, however, it's the other end of the scale that is most significant. Because of the artificial lights under which animation is filmed, it is easy to get bright, even illumination. Therefore the animator selects a lens because of its *highest f-stop*—f/16, f/22, or even f/64. It's nice to celebrate pleasant serendipities when you find them. It's much cheaper to buy a lens that does not have a low f-stop, and for animators, low f-stops aren't really needed.

Filters. There are many different filters that operate as camera attachments. Filters provide effects such as stars, multi-images, and just plain weird colors. An introduction to filters will be found among the comments about lighting tools for animated filmmaking (see Chapter 18).

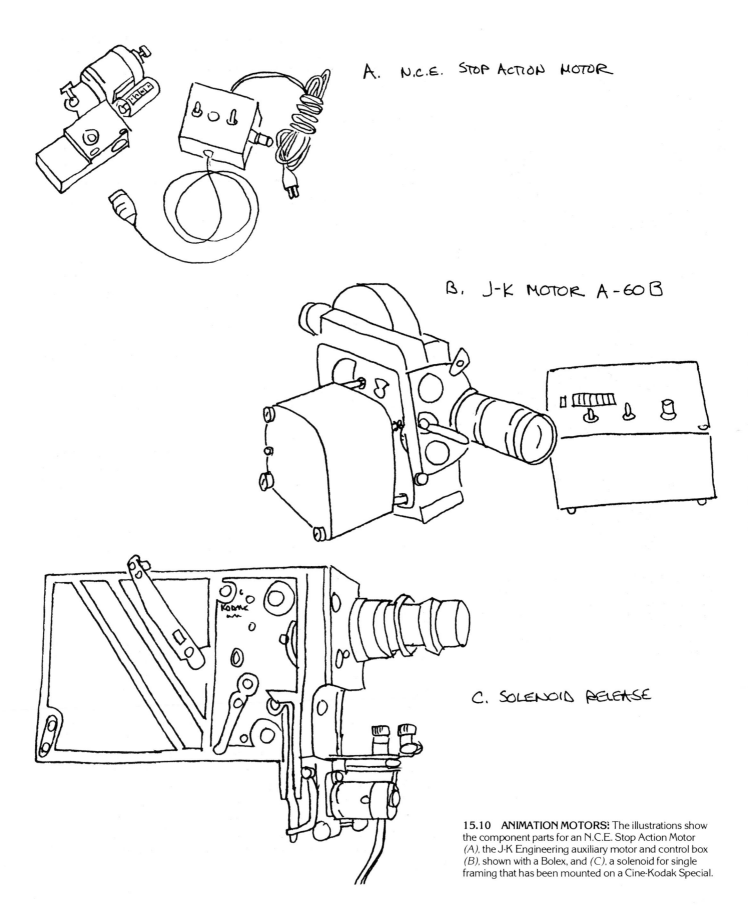

A. N.C.E. STOP ACTION MOTOR

B. J-K MOTOR A-60B

C. SOLENOID RELEASE

15.10 ANIMATION MOTORS: The illustrations show the component parts for an N.C.E. Stop Action Motor (A), the J-K Engineering auxiliary motor and control box (B), shown with a Bolex, and (C), a solenoid for single framing that has been mounted on a Cine-Kodak Special.

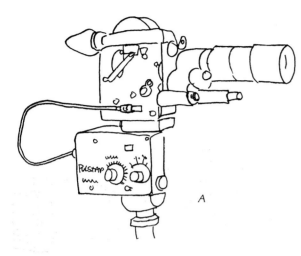

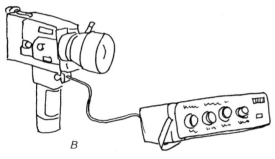

15.11   INTERVALOMETER: A Bolex is mounted on top of a PulsAR intervalometer in *A*. Increasingly, super 8mm manufacturers are beginning to offer inter- valometers among accessory items for their cameras. Pictured in *B* is the Minolta system. Minolta also offers a more compact intervalometer that can be mounted on top of the camera itself.

Cable Releases

To most live-action filmmakers, single framing means nothing more than the technique of exposing one frame at a time. To the animator, however, single framing is a matter of tremendous concern. Animators perceive single framing as an act filled with many hazards and nuances.

The registration between the camera and the artwork has to be perfect in animation. This means that the process of exposing a frame must be done with a feather touch. The duration of the exposure must be precise too—down to a hundredth of a second. All frames in an animated sequence must have an identical exposure time as well as a perfect registration.

In order to minimize the pressure on the camera during filming, a *cable release* can be used to trigger the advance of single frames. The cable release provides a sheath in which there is a metal pin and a spring. One end of the release threads into a single-frame release socket usually found in the trigger of the camera or nearby. The other end of the cable release has a plunger. Manual activation of the plunger causes the metal pin to trip a frame release mechanism inside the camera. The spring returns the pin quickly to prevent the exposure of multiple frames.

Cable releases come in different qualities and different lengths. Some 16mm cameras such as Bolex require a special form of cable release. A useful feature on some cable-release systems is a foot pedal or air bulb that allows the animator to operate the release by foot. The hands are then free for work under the camera.

In recent years, the more sophisticated super 8mm cameras have been designed with electronic rather than mechanical single-framing devices. These electromagnetic systems expose single frames by means of a remote cable attachment that bypasses the trigger and permits the animator to advance the film without touching the camera at all. This is a preferred method, because while cable releases push the camera in some degree, electromagnetic operation is accomplished without the application of any physical force to the camera body.

Animation Motors

Many 16mm cameras, and a few super 8mm cameras, will accept an *auxiliary animation motor.* When such a motor is used, the built-in power system is disengaged. These auxiliary motors, powered with electric current, are linked with the camera body by means of a coupling device. The drive wheel of the animation motor connects with the frame advance mechanism within the camera.

Auxiliary motors are designed to fit particular cameras and there is no standardization of design for the coupling system, the exposure time, the triggering device, or other specific features. Here are some notes on a few common animation motors.

The *Arriflex single-frame animation motor,* for example, is used with Arriflex 16-S and 16-M cameras. It has a built-in frame counter and flash synchronization, an 8-volt DC outlet to operate a torque motor on the Arris S magazine, and exposure times of ⅛, ¼, and ½ second. The basic motor costs approximately $1,300. An auxiliary *capping shutter* is available for an additional $450, and an *intervalometer* that provides exposure times from 1 to 11 seconds and intervals between exposures of from 3 seconds to 1.75 hours is available for use with the single-frame motor. The intervalometer controls both camera and light operation and costs $325.

National Cine Equipment Company produces an animation motor with remote control. It has a built-in Verdeer counter, on-off and continuous switches, a function indicator light, and a manual motor release for threading. The remote control has function and running direction indicators and an outlet for either hand- or foot-actuated switches. The motor costs roughly $1,200, and it must be used with an adapter, costing from $65 to $500, depending on the 16mm camera that the motor will drive. NCE animation motors can be adapted to the Eastman Cine Special I or II, the Mitchell 16mm camera, Bell & Howell Filmo cameras, Arriflex 16S camera, Bolex H-16 camera, and other brands and models. NCE also produces a time lapse control unit.

The J-K Camera Engineering Company manufactures a number of motors for animation and optical printing. The most often used is the J-K Animation Motor (Model #A-60D), which is designed for use with Bolex cameras and costs approximately $300. It features a 60-frame-per-minute synchronous motor, and all the operating controls are located in a remote-control box that is connected to the motor by an 8-foot cord. J-K has six other motors, including a more expensive model ($720) with an electronic preset memory, bright digital display, a self-contained intervalometer, and other features.

Solenoid releases operate much like the more complicated animation motors. A solenoid is an electric device capable of activating camera shutters and film transports from remote locations. Samenco solenoids are available for mounting on Beaulieu R16B cameras ($65), Eastman Cine Kodak Special Cameras ($110), Bolex H-16 or H-8 cameras ($50), and many others. The control box provides intervals of 1 second through 10 hours with 1 frame to 10-second bursts, and with a lighting control and 12-volt-DC motor control ($400).

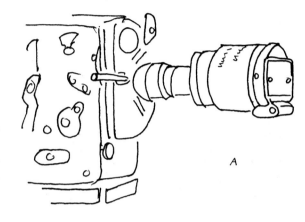

15.12 SLIDE COPIERS AND FRAME ENLARGERS: The Duplikin III slide copying lens can be mounted into 16mm cameras *(A).* A simple device designed for the Bolex Macrozoom 155 super 8mm camera is illustrated in *B.* Incidentally, the Macrozoom 155 was one of the best super 8 cameras ever manufactured in terms of its suitability for animation. Drawing *C* shows Duplikin Model IV, used to make freeze-frames and step-printing effects.

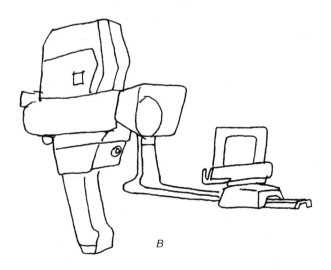

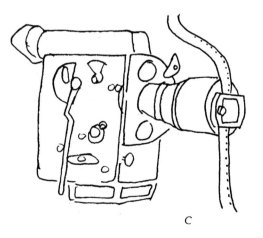

Intervalometers

Intervalometers are specialized auxiliary motors that are used only for time-lapse cinematography in order to activate exposure of a single frame at predetermined intervals. For most models of intervalometers, the timing intervals vary from less than a second to a number of minutes or even hours between exposures. Actuation can be mechanical or electronic. Some intervalometers can activate an electronic flash or tungsten lighting arrangement just prior to filming. Others have a remote-release feature that is activated by a cable or radio system.

An intervalometer is a highly specialized piece of equipment, and unless you're doing a lot of time-lapse photography, you'll probably want to rent it. Recently, however, manufacturers of super 8mm cameras are designing intervalometers as an accessory within their camera systems. Minolta is one such camera manufacturer (see Figure 15.11). Harmony Electronics is a firm that manufactures inexpensive intervalometers—one model under $50 and another under $100. Science Dimensions, Inc., offers a time-lapse intervalometer that can be used with any cable release or electronic release super 8mm or 16mm camera. Prices run $45 and up. Sixteen mm intervalometers combine timing units with stop-action motors and remain very expensive. The NCE Time Lapse Control Unit, for example, is priced at $950.

The Matte Box

The matte box is an awkward-looking device that is positioned in front of the camera lens to shield it from undesirable light that could possibly interfere with proper exposure. The matte box is also used as a filter or matte holder during the filming process. Usually a rail or set of rails holds (and allows adjustment of) a *bellows* that masks out the ambient light. One end of the matte box fits snugly around the lens and the other is fitted to hold gelatin filters of all kinds.

Mattes are used for a number of special effects, including split screen, keyholes, wipes, and other optical feats. See Chapter 13 for greater detail and for illustrations of matte boxes that are available for both 8mm and 16mm cameras.

Slide Copiers and Frame Enlargers

Most super 8mm and 16mm cameras with built-in macrofocusing can be used to film from 35mm slides. The manufacturers of many such cameras sell slide copiers—attachments that place a plastic or metal holder at a carefully predetermined position in front of the lens. During filming, the slide is backlighted with an evenly illuminated source. Such slide copiers range in cost from $35 to $75 (Figure 15.12).

Duplikin is the brand name of a line of camera accessories that allow refilming of 35mm slides and of 16mm single frames. Use the Duplikin II enlarging device ($190) to transfer 16mm images to 35mm slides. The Duplikin III ($190 for the "C" mount and $235 for the Arri mount) is devised to reduce 35mm slides to 16mm film. The Duplikin IV ($230 for the "C" mount, and $275 for the Arri mount) is for 16mm freeze frames and step printing with 16mm cameras.

The cheapest way to get photographic enlargements from a single frame of 16mm or super 8mm film is with a special enlarging device called a Cine-enlarger that costs $25 and takes size 120 roll film.

Lens and Camera Cleaning Supplies

Cleanliness is next to godliness. Finger smudges are the work of the Devil. Be pure. Be virtuous. Use lens *cleaning tissue,* lens *cleaning fluid,* and a can of compressed air to blast the dust out of camera openings and from animation-stand compounds and platens. Costs of tissue and fluid are minimal. An 8-ounce can of Dust-Off (canned air) with a pinpoint and variable control button costs less than $5.

The rewards for tidiness are manifold—quality work, preservation of equipment, rushes of satisfaction, accomplishment, and goodness.

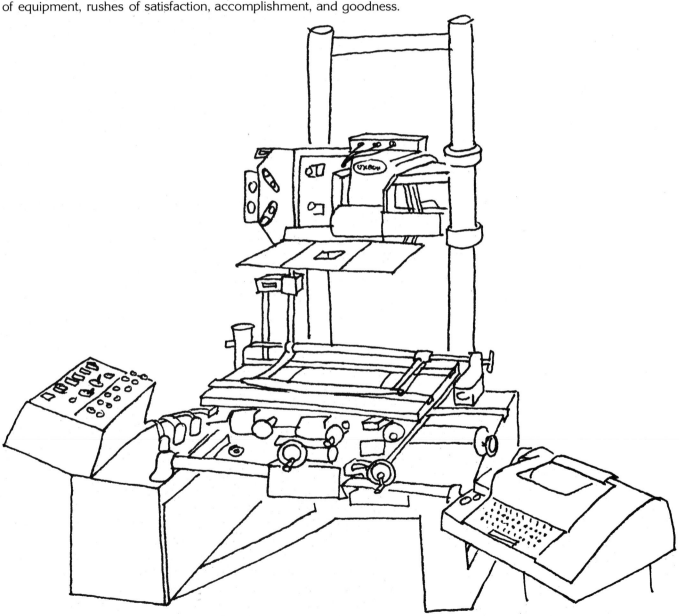

15.13 OXBERRY "MASTER" SERIES ANIMATION STAND

16
Animation Stands

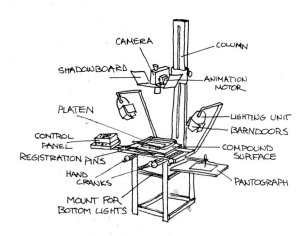

16.1 UNIVERSAL STAND: Comprised of elements from many different commercially produced animation stands, this single sample exhibits all the basic features of an animation stand.

CAMERA
COLUMN
SHADOWBOARD
ANIMATION MOTOR
PLATEN
LIGHTING UNIT
BARNDOORS
CONTROL PANEL
COMPOUND SURFACE
REGISTRATION PINS
HAND CRANKS
PANTOGRAPH
MOUNT FOR BOTTOM LIGHTS

Animation stands come in all shapes and sizes. You can build your own rig or you can purchase a professionally designed and commercially manufactured "system." The cost of an animation stand can vary from a few dollars for 2 by 4's and plywood to something well over $100,000 for the top-of-the-line, fully computerized animation stand. But whether you are in the market for a sophisticated tool or just planning to make do with whatever is available, a familiarity with the general features of animation stands will extend your competencies as an independent animator.

General Features

The main feature of any animation stand is its *structural stability*. It must hold the weight of the camera in an absolutely steady position in relation to the artwork being filmed.

Requirements of stability extend beyond the stand itself. Check the room in which you are working for vibrations that can come from other sources. If you can, place the stand in some out-of-the-way spot to avoid accidental bumps or jarring. Once the stand is in position and the camera is mounted, try to avoid moving the stand or having to take it apart. The location you select ought to have good security.

Obviously, every animation stand must have a *camera mount*. Every super 8mm and 16mm camera has a threaded receptacle called a *bush* that receives the standardized screw of the tripod or other camera-mounting hardware. Naturally, any stand must be able to mount the camera you will be using. But because of variations in design, not all stands accept all cameras. Sometimes a stand's manufacturer will sell adapters especially designed to fit a particular camera to a particular stand.

An animation stand will often be designed for a specific camera. Whether you are building a stand or buying one, check carefully to determine what kind of camera is recommended, or required, for the stand you are considering. The preceding chapter should help you to identify those features you'll need to meet your own working objectives. Items to check include the camera type, film selection, viewfinder system, lens, filters, film advance, a single-frame device, film speed, film rewind, footage and frame counter, shutter, aperture and metering system, and available lens and camera accessories.

All stands hold the animation camera over a flat surface on which the artwork is placed during filming. Some stands can also be turned on their sides to present a horizontal puppet stage. An important thing to check for is the ease with which you can sight through the camera's viewfinder during filming. Also, make sure that the stand's height permits easy access to important camera controls, such as a fade/dissolve lever.

Many stands feature a vertical column that is engineered to allow the entire camera mounting arm to be adjusted to various heights above the table. Usually there is a single column (the larger stands have double columns), which carries inside it a ball-bearing system and counterweights. Such *column movement* permits the operator to adjust the camera's height with ease and accuracy.

Vertical movement of the camera toward or away from the artwork produces a *zoom effect,* sometimes also called a *vertical truck.* The precise height from focal plane to film surface is often calibrated right on the column and there must be a locking device to hold the camera 100 percent steady at any position along the column. Some vertical movement mechanisms are motorized. The fancy expensive stands also have an automatic focusing device that keeps the lens sharply in focus at any height.

The "look" of a vertical movement toward or away from the compound is identical to the effect produced in using a zoom lens within a two-dimensional setup, but this is *not* so with 3-dimensional animation techniques in which the actual change of distance between camera and subject creates a subtly different effect (greater depth) than the effect achieved by zooming the lens of a stationary camera.

All animation stands require a registration system, a way to insure that the camera holds a constant relationship to the surface below it and that artwork can be precisely aligned. Registration on both these matters is generally attained with an Oxberry or Acme pegging system. These industry standards are discussed in detail in Chapter 17. It is possible and sometimes necessary to use alternate registration systems. But whatever the system, it must be used consistently in preparation of artwork as well as for filming.

On commercially manufactured stands, the surface bearing the registration device may have two sets of pegs—one on the top and one on the bottom. In some stands, there are as many as four sets of pegs— including moving peg-bars, calibrated in twentieths or even hundredths of an inch.

The surface that holds the artwork is called the *compound.* In many stands the compound can be moved laterally in any direction. Compass coordinates are used to indicate horizontal directions: north, south, east, and west. Such N/S and E/W movements are usually done by cranking mechanisms, often calibrated in hundreths of an inch. While compound movements are usually done with hand cranks, sometimes the drive mechanism is electrically powered. A locking system is always present.

As noted earlier, the movement of artwork beneath the camera can be facilitated by a *viscous-damped compound.* This device makes possible ease-ins, ease-outs, and constant-speed panning at real-time filmmaking speeds. The viscous-damped system yields an omni-directional compound with a grease-based braking action. It is tremendously useful in composing the frame over artwork.

Many compounds also provide a rotational movement through the full 360 degrees. The *rotating disc* always has a lock mechanism, and its spin movement is calibrated in degrees.

The *platen* consists of a metal carriage that holds an optically pure sheet of glass. It is used to force artwork flat on the compound table. Because of differing thicknesses created by cels, cutouts, and other artwork, the platen is designed to "float." The glass is mounted on a

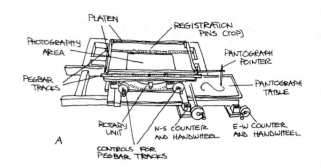

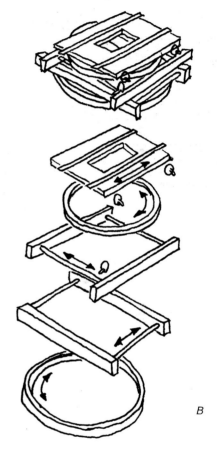

16.2 THE COMPOUND: Illustration *A* shows the individual elements of a professional caliber animation stand. Illustration *B* indicates five component pieces and the direction of movement each facilitates. The latter drawing is based on an illustration of a rostrum com-pound in *The Animation Stand* by Zoran Perisic, Focal Press Ltd. London. Drawing *A* is based on an illustration in *Animated Film* by Roy Madsen, Interland Publishing, New York.

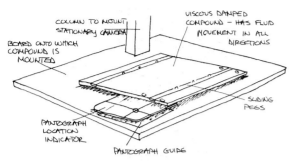

16.3 VISCOUS DAMPED COMPOUND: The line drawing shows the basic features of the Oxberry "Media Pro" compound. Oxberry also manufactures a viscous damped compound for its "Animator 8" stand.

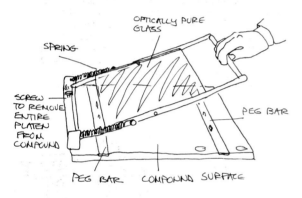

16.4 PLATEN: The platen illustrated here bears features common to all platens: pure glass that floats in a center mounted framework; spring mounting; a handle for manual operation; and a removable mount on the compound surface.

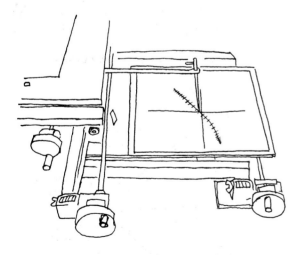

16.5 PANTOGRAPH: The pointer on the pantograph is attached to the movable compound surface. The pantograph surface never moves itself but, rather, carries plotting lines that the camera operator will follow in filming a complicated sequence of moves during an animated scene.

pivoting center and hinged on spring-loaded brackets. Platens are operated manually, even on the most expensive stands, and they are generally removable for oversized artwork. A standard size for platens is a #12 field. There are #10 and #16 field platens as well. A commercially manufactured platen will cost between $50 and $100. Note that an ordinary sheet of glass can be easily rigged to form a platen.

Animation stands must have toplighting. The lights themselves are color corrected and mounted at a 45-degree angle to the plane of the camera. This prevents reflection of the light directly into the camera. A useful feature of animation stands can be a capability for bottomlighting or backlighting. More information is provided in Chapter 18.

The *pantograph* is a device that allows the animator to execute complicated camera movements. In using a pantograph, the movement is first planned out on a separate sheet of paper. Often this pantograph grid is somewhat smaller in total size than the full compound field. However, the planning graph, like the pantograph table on which it sits, is accurately aligned to the camera tracking mechanism of the compound. The physical movement the artwork will make underneath the fixed camera is represented by a thin line that the animator draws on the pantograph. Often the positions at which the animation camera will take exposures are represented by cross-hatchings on the camera direction line. During the actual filming, a pointer or a cross-hair device follows the line of movement.

Depending on the camera and the sophistication of the stand itself, there will be a correspondingly complicated *control system*. The simplest control is a cable release (to expose a single frame) and a footage indicator (to measure the amount of film that has been shot). Some super 8mm cameras carry both features a bit further by means of a foot pedal for the cable release and a frame counter as well as a footage counter. Additional camera controls such as forward/reverse, lighting, focusing, and exposure switches are required when using a specially designed animation camera or when using an auxiliary animation motor. In many of the more expensive stands, all the camera controls and stand controls for automatic column and compound movement are presented on a single control panel, which also provides an accurate frame count (Figure 16.6).

One respects an animation stand for its precision. But what makes a stand lovable is its idiosyncrasies. Almost every stand, manufactured by oneself or by a commercial company, also has its own unique features, which represent, really, the personal biases and passions of its designers. You'll have to check instruction booklets or each home-made-stand builder for what passes as special features or plain quirks.

Tripods

The tripod is an accessible and highly versatile tool. It constitutes a relatively primitive yet effective sort of animation stand. Note, however, that all tripods are not alike. The ones that can be used for animation must have these three qualities. They must be strong enough to hold the weight of the camera and its accessories. They must be sturdy enough to keep the camera absolutely steady when shooting. Tripods must also adjust easily but hold various positions firmly.

The following animation techniques *require* a tripod: time-lapse, pixilation, puppet, clay, and small object animation.

Often the technique will call for *controlled movement* of the tripod through pans, tilts, and even dollies. Such movements can be plotted out most accurately if the animator improvises a marking system right on the tripod itself.

For closeup photography, tripods can be "tied down" with gaffer's tape against a raised surface. (In case you are unfamiliar with it, *gaffer's tape* is a standard supply in filmmaking. It is a super-sticky and super-strong tape that is cloth-backed, usually gray in color, and comes in widths up to 2 inches. It is sometimes called "duct" tape.) With some tripods, it is possible to reverse the head of the model entirely. A collection of tripod positions is illustrated in Figure 16.7.

The least expensive tripod you can use with a super 8mm camera will cost in the neighborhood of $60 to $100. Brand names to investigate include Testrite, Bogen, and Husky.

Top-of-the-line 16mm tripods are purchased in two parts. There are the "legs," or the "tripod," usually made of wood with metal-fortified joints; and there is the "head," made of highly machined metal. In live-action filmmaking a fluid head is desired for professional 16mm work. However, this viscous-cushioned design is not required for animation. A high quality "friction" head is recommended. Costs for legs are $150 to $300 and a tripod head runs from $200 to $400. Note that tripods and tripod heads are not standardized. Be sure the units you get are compatible.

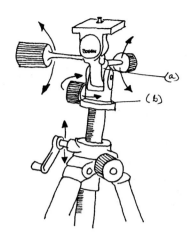

16.6 TRIPOD HEAD: The arrows indicate directions which different elements of the tripod allow (or limit) movement. To calibrate a particular movement, measurement lines can be taped onto or etched into a fixed piece of the hardware at a place where it meets the corresponding area of movement. The model pictured here is a Bogen 3030, costing around $100. It is manufactured with calibrations at points *a* and *b*, as indicated.

Copy Stands

Although originally designed for still photography photocopying work, commercially manufactured copy stands can be used for animated filmmaking too (see Figure 16.8). Their structure is simple. A metal column is firmly mounted on a solid baseboard. A bracket allows the mounting head to be moved vertically up and down the column. Copy stands generally come with a pair of lighting fixtures that are mounted at 45-degree angles to the camera plane. A good copy stand, like a good tripod, is one that is strong, steady, and adjustable. The least expensive copy stand is priced around $25. Top-of-the-line copy stands will cost hundreds of dollars.

I should point out here that unless it's been specially modified, using a copy stand for animation requires one to work upside down because of the camera mount. This can be a real inconvenience with those techniques that require manipulation of materials directly under the camera.

Home-Made Stands

If there were ever an international contest to search out the best examples of human cunning—of the inventiveness, tenacity, and resourcefulness of the human mind—there's no doubt that an animator would get the Grand Prize. For nowhere, it seems, is there a greater manifestation of sheer inventiveness than in the design and development of home-made animation stands. Here are three very simple examples:

16.7 TRIPOD POSITIONS USED IN ANIMATION

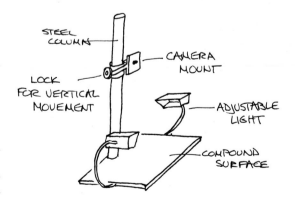

16.8 COPY STAND: Ranging in price from less than $50 to many hundreds, copy stands must be strong enough to hold firmly your particular motion picture camera.

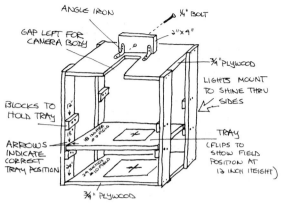

ANGLE IRON

¼" BOLT

GAP LEFT FOR
CAMERA BODY

2"×4"

¾" PLYWOOD

LIGHTS MOUNT
TO SHINE THRU
SIDES

BLOCKS TO
HOLD TRAY

ARROWS
INDICATE
CORRECT
TRAY POSITION

TRAY
(FLIPS TO
SHOW FIELD
POSITION AT
12 INCH HEIGHT)

¾" PLYWOOD

16.9   LAYBOURNE'S BOX STAND: Selection of heights for the removable tray are determined by the minimum focal length as marked on the lens of the particular camera being used. If this is a nonreflex camera, remember that a test roll must be shot to determine the precise location and size of the fields at the selected heights. In such a situation, once the camera is mounted it is removed only when absolutely necessary. Modifications may be required so that the camera can be loaded and adjusted without dismounting.

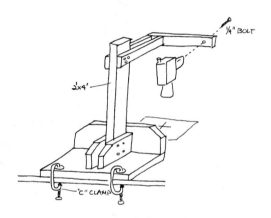

¼" BOLT

2"×4"

"C" CLAMP

16.10   N.F.B. SUPER 8MM STAND: This drawing is based on a sketch of a wooden stand specially designed for super 8mm cameras that was used in a workshop coordinated by Co Hoedeman of the National Film Board of Canada. You'll have to experiment with heights and other measurements so that the stand will suit your camera and your animation plans. A nice feature is that the stand "reverses" the camera so that the field is not inverted as it would be if a super 8 camera were mounted on an ordinary copy stand.

Laybourne's Box Stand. A box design is particularly well suited for a nonreflex camera. The frame holds the camera in a fixed position, but allows it to be loaded, wound, and single-framed. The heights of a movable shelf are determined by the focal length of the camera's particular lens. Because the camera we are discussing has no through-the-lens focusing, there is no way to determine the precise focus at close distances without relying on the distance indicator marks on the lens casing. In order to locate the precise boundaries of the fields at the preselected heights, a camera test must be shot. In this test a field guide is placed on each level and film is shot of it. Only when this film returns from the lab and is screened can the exact frame demarcation be determined. This is marked on the surface for future reference.

NFB Super 8mm Stand. I encountered another simple and inexpensive stand at an animation workshop conducted by the National Film Board of Canada. In constructing your own version, determine the vertical height of the column after you've played around with your own super 8mm camera. You'll need to select a height that affords the largest range of field sizes, using the zoom at a wide-angle setting all the way to the telephoto position with diopters or macrofocusing. Like the box stand, this design is portable. The reflex camera can be easily removed for live-action filmmaking or for those kinds of animation that require a tripod.

Kodak Copy Stand. The Eastman Kodak Company circulates information on how to build a simple wooden copy stand that is sturdy and features a vertically adjustable column. Figure 16.11 provides a detailed breakdown of the Kodak stand.

Other Designs and Commercial Components. There are endless variations. Depending on the range of animation techniques that you want to do and on your camera, various building materials can be combined in any wondrous concoction.

Slotted steel angle irons can be used to create a strong and adjustable framework. It's like a giant erector set. Modified photographic enlargers, lathe beds, X-ray machines—all have been used to create successful animation stands.

As you begin to plan your own stand, you may want to consider integrating into its design some of the commercially produced elements that have been introduced here, such as backlighting units, an auxiliary motor, a zoom-lens extender arm, and so on. For example, the J·K Engineering Company offers a compound table for do-it-yourself animation-stand builders. The compound mounts on two metal pads and its features include a black anodized aluminum tabletop, 360-degree rotation, traveling peg-bars, #12 or #16 field platens, rear lighting, graduated handwheels for 20 inches of east/west movement and 12 inches of north/south travel, and mechanical counters. The unit costs just under $2,000.

Commercial Stands

The commercial stands listed here are arranged according to price, from lowest to highest. A standard format used to summarize the features of each stand should help you to compare models. The specifications for all the stands have been taken from the appropriate manufacturer's sales materials and equipment specification sheets. All prices are fall 1977 list prices, provided by the manufacturers.

OX PRODUCTS SUPERMATION STAND

Structure: Tubular steel columns mounted on a wooden base. Camera platform and two light brackets.

Camera Mount: Unique design of camera platform allows 360° rotation (calibrated). Platform 18 inches above base. Bracket attaches to camera's tripod bush. Can remove camera.

Camera: Will take virtually any super 8mm camera that has zoom lens with thread-in closeup diopters, reflex viewfinding, and single-frame capabilities. Stand requires a +2 diopter.

Column Movement: None.

Registration: Model 74.5 has one set of fixed pegs. Model 75.5 has one fixed set and one moving set of scaled pegs. It uses a #9 field Ox two-peg system.

Field Size: A 9-inch field guide is supplied with the stand. Diopters and zoom lens give rough extremes of #9 field through #2 field.

Compound Movement: A two-stage compound is mounted on the base and gives calibrated N/S and E/W movement. Movement is done manually.

Platen: Hinged glass platen.

Toplighting: Brackets take two photofloods—75 to 500 watts.

Bottomlighting: None.

Pantograph: None.

Controls: Cable release or other camera attachment.

Miscellaneous: Model 75.5 features a special wipe attachment. A kit is available for $2,800.

Price: Model 74.5 (1 set peg-bars) $120; Model 75.5 (2 sets of peg-bars) $160.

OXBERRY ANIMATOR-8

Structure: Welded-metal camera support attached to a wooden base, which takes a compound and circular disc. Entire stand can be turned on its side to provide a puppet stage.

Camera Mount: Stand is designed for three different cameras. Check to see if other cameras can be used. Special mounting brackets are available for Nizo and Beaulieu super 8mm cameras.

Cameras: The Animator-8 system comes with a choice of three cameras. All are removable. *Camera A:* 4:1 zoom, f/1.8, power or manual zoom, reflex, 18 to 32 fps, single frame. *Camera B:* Same as A with time-lapse of .5 to 60 seconds and strobe synchronization. *Camera C:* Same as B with in-camera fades, dissolves, and superimpositions.

Column Movement: None.

Registration: System has its own ¼-inch registration pegs, punch, pads, and hole strengtheners. The system will mount Oxberry or Acme peg plates.

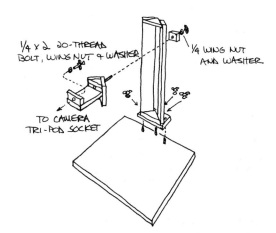

16.11 **KODAK COPY STAND:** For approximately $15 you can build a copy stand with an adjustable column. Pamphlet T-43 from the Eastman Kodak Company (Rochester, New York 14650) provides further specifications for the stand illustrated here. *Reproduced with permission of Kodak.*

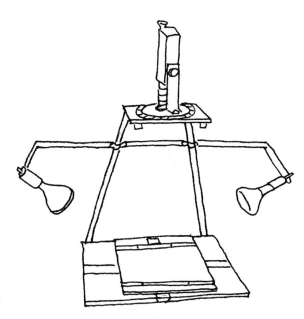

16.12 **OX PRODUCTIONS "SUPERMATION STAND"**

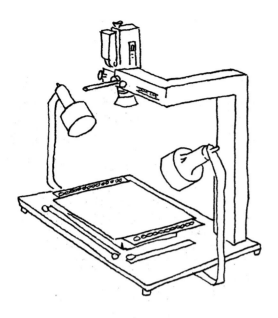

16.13   OXBERRY "ANIMATOR 8"

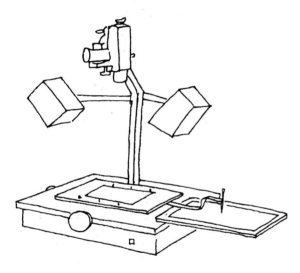

16.14   ANIMATION SCIENCES MODEL 1000

Field Size: A standard 12-inch field guide is supplied. Diopters and zoom permit use of #12 to #2 fields.

Compound Movement: This stand's outstanding design feature is a viscous-damped compound. This consists of a special tray-like device that used thick grease to "smooth" the manipulation of the compound in N/S, E/W and complex moves. The viscous-damped feature facilitates ease-ins, ease-outs, and constant-speed panning at real-time filmmaking speeds. The compound permits live-action zooms to be combined with continuous artwork pans. This is very useful in kinestasis techniques. Compound movement is calibrated in twentieths of an inch. A heavy-duty aluminum spinning disc can be placed on the base (viscous-damped compound can be removed) for 360° rotations (calibrated in degrees).

Platen: A spring-mounted plate-glass platen, 12 inches square. Removable.

Toplighting: Two 75-watt flood lamps used in conjunction with an 82C filter or photofloods.

Bottomlighting: None.

Pantograph: The compound is consistently tracked by a pantograph with registration arm pointer.

Controls: Camera's single-framing release and film counter.

Miscellaneous: The Animator-8 comes with an art kit containing a lettering font of ½-inch characters, six 5- by 7-inch paper animation pads, and four colored felt-tipped markers. Heavy-duty clear plastic panning guides and panning sheets help accurate panning of large artwork.

Price: Model 2000-00 (without camera), $630; Model 2000-10 (camera A), $910; Model 2000-20 (Camera B), $1,000; Model 2000-30 (camera C), $1,030.

ANIMATION SCIENCES MODEL 1000

Structure: A steel column is connected to a metal base. An extension post increases camera height and shooting range. Measurements are 29 by 20 by 25 inches.

Camera Mount: The stand is designed for a Minolta D-4 super 8mm camera but the manufacturer has mounting brackets for other cameras. With the extension post, the stand can take a 16mm camera.

Camera: The stand comes with a Minolta D-4 featuring solenoid-triggered single-frame or continuous shooting reflex viewing, a zoom lens with 4:1 ratio. Camera can be dismounted.

Column Movement: None.

Registration: Model 1000 uses round pins in all locations. Registration is compatible with Oxberry and Acme pegs. There are two floating peg scales mounted on the stand base.

Field Size: Built-in zoom permits use of #3 through #9 fields, or with extension post, #5 through #15 fields.

Compound Movement: The compound has N/S and E/W movement calibrated in twentieths of an inch and controlled with rack-and-pinion gears. 360° rotation is achieved by disc in center of the table (calibrated in degrees). The compound table moves 4½ inches in the east-west direction and 3¾ inches in the north-south direction.

Platen: None.

Toplighting: Two quartz or tungsten halogen lamps rated at 200 watts, 3200°K, and life of 1,500 hours. Lamphousings are fan-cooled and shielded with heat-absorbing glass.

Bottomlighting: None.

Pantograph: The stand bears a pantograph table of the same dimensions as the compound surface. This makes panning easier.

Controls: Single-framing release and film counter. The recommended camera, a Minolta D-4, offers a foot switch.

Miscellaneous: An aluminum puppet stage is provided.

Price: Model 1000 (with camera), $1,800.

OXBERRY MEDIA PRO

Structure: The basic Media Pro stand (Model #2500-00) has an aluminum column mounted on a Formica-laminated baseboard measuring 28 by 40 by 1¼ inches. A five-outlet junction box is provided.

Camera Mount: The camera mounting bracket adapts most quality cameras and supports animation motors as well. An animation dissolve linkage and scale attaches to a variable shutter on the 16mm camera. Camera arm is box-welded.

Camera: The stand can be purchased with a modified Bolex H-16 SBM (reflex viewing, variable shutter, ground-glass focusing, automatic diaphragm, zoom lens, 100 feet-plus film capacity, full rewind), a single-frame animation motor, a Vario-Switar 100 POE-4 lens (with 16mm–100mm, f/l.9 to f/16, automatic metering with manual override), closeup diopters, dissolve linkage and scale, Kelvin Correction Filter, and an 18-inch cable release.

Column Movement: The heavy-duty aluminum column measures 3 by 3 by 36 inches, and can be adjusted vertically by a spring-balanced ball-bearing camera carriage and lock.

Registration: A standard #12 field registration system is used. The stand comes with a registration kit consisting of a ¼-inch single-hole punch, twelve ¼-inch brass pegs, pads, and hole strengtheners, suitable for a wide variety of registration problems. The system also accommodates Oxberry, Acme, or Signal Corps pegging systems. Two dovetailed brass rules are built into the aluminum compound table. Calibration is in twentieths of an inch.

Field Size: Vertical adjustments permit photography of artwork ranging from under a 35mm slide-sized area to a #16 field, depending on the lens.

Compound Movement: The compound features the same sort of viscous-damped movement discussed under Oxberry's Animator-8 model. A center rotation pin and locking screw provide 360° of viscous-damped rotation. The compound table is made of aluminum and measures 16 by 20 by ⅜ inches. As noted above, the table has two movable, brass peg-bars.

Platen: A #12 field platen holds artwork flat with a ¼-inch float glass,

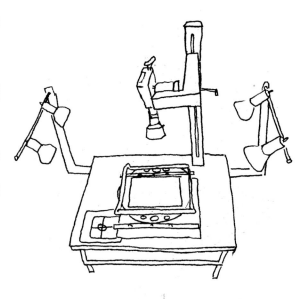

16.15 OXBERRY "MEDIA PRO"

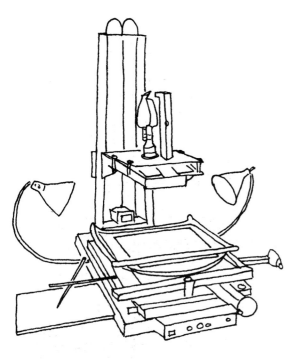

16.16 "FAX-JR." ANIMATION STAND

which is mounted on a pivoting center and hinged on a spring-loaded platen bracket. The platen can be removed.

Toplighting: Two adjustable lighting brackets carry four long-life lamps that are filtered at 3200°K.

Bottomlighting: The Media Pro takes a 17-inch cast-aluminum disc with two peg tracks cut to match the movable peg-bars included with the compound table. There is a #12-field opal-glass insert over a #12-field 3200°K, cold cathode backlight. The backlighting stage is on legs that raise it above the compound during filming. When the stage is removed and the legs are detached, it can be used as a standard drawing desk for preparation of art, tracing, inking, and opaquing.

Pantograph: The system has an #8-field pantograph, which provides accuracy via a factory-aligned cross-hair registration device. The pantograph comes with four #8-field Mylar registration tracing guides.

Controls: The single-frame motor, which is used with the recommended Bolex 16mm camera, has a baseboard console with function controls (forward, reverse, continuous, and single-frame modes), a digital frame counter, and a foot-switch operation.

Miscellaneous: The Media Pro is a system-designed, high-precision tool with great flexibility. It can be used for super 8, filmstrip, and photocopying work. It can be modified and upgraded in many ways and combinations. Optional accessories with the Media Pro stand include a filmography table (a heavy-duty table that positions the stand at optimum stand-up reflex-viewing height).

Price: Basic Media Pro #2500 (no camera), $2,300; #2500-32 with camera as described, $6,300.

FAX-JR. ANIMATION STAND

Structure: A welded-steel frame of baked black enamel with two vertical columns, camera platform, and two lighting brackets.

Camera Mount: Separate camera-mount pedestals accommodate most quality 16mm cameras. Super 8mm custom-made pedestals are also available. Pedestals rest on a cast-aluminum camera support with an adjustable camera plate.

Camera: The stand will accommodate virtually any 16mm or super 8mm camera.

Column Movement: Variable heights of camera are achieved with cast-aluminum brackets, which move vertically on a pair of 40-inch columns. The vertical guides have ball bearings and there is a spring counterweight system. There is a lock system to secure vertical positioning.

Registration: A combination #12/#16 field disc is attached to the frame, and it carries sliding peg-bars at top and bottom. These take interchangeable pegs (Oxberry or Acme) and are calibrated in twentieths of an inch. A unique and patented "magnabar" system uses magnetic strips to secure E/W moves with either top or bottom sliding peg-bars.

Field Sizes: All standard sizes are achieved. The smallest depends on the particular lens being used. There is a field position tape indicator and pointer.

Compound Movement; The Fax-Jr stand has full N/S and E/W compound movements controlled by hand cranks. The disc rotates 360° (calibrated in degrees).

Platen: The #12/#16 field disc has an attached platen of the same size, manually operated and removable.

Toplighting: Two brackets for toplights are attached to the steel frame. There are outlets for both lamps and a cord to an outlet box.

Bottomlighting: A large Plexiglas opal window is mounted into the disc. The open framework under the compound permits backlighting, including mounting rails.

Pantograph: A full pantograph plate with mounts and pointers is carried on the stand.

Controls: There is a front-mounted control panel for connection to animation motors and for connection to an optional drive mechanism that raises and lowers the camera. No frame counter on the control panel. Fax also makes auxiliary animation motors for certain 16mm and 35mm cameras, including Kodak Cine, Bolex, etc.

Miscellaneous: The basic stand may be purchased with special support brackets for floor mounting. A full #16-field platen is available.

Price: Basic Stand (fixed #12-field disc), $1,195; Basic Stand (rotating #12/#16 field), $1,615; "Jr" Stand Complete (motor, control panel), $2,895.

More Expensive Stands

THRIFTFAX ANIMATION STAND

Features: self-standing with twin columns, adaptable to every camera type, vertical 32-inch truck by motor drive, 360° rotation, #12/#16 field disc and platen, optional counter, pantograph, front-mounted control panel, master N/S and E/W compound movement via hand wheels, 18-inch top and bottom peg-bars, underlighting with lamp assembly, Veeder-Root counters optional. Entire system without camera or camera mount: $5,530.

J-K ANIMATION STAND

Features: modified Bolex H-16 camera and A-200E motor and controls synchronized with a J-K optical printer for rear-screen projection, two 3-inch steel columns, carriage positions capable of #1½- to #12-field zooms by motor or manual adjustment, automatic follow-focus, adjustable compound, control panel with full control, 500-watt halogen lamps. Entire system with camera: $7,700.

OXBERRY FILMMAKER ANIMATION STAND

Features: 16mm Oxberry process camera, automatic focus mechanism, self-supporting structure, motorized tracking, automatic remote controlled reticle projection shows size of artwork covered by camera, shadowboard with hinged wings, quartz-halogen top and bottom

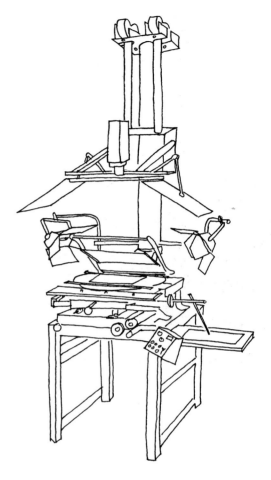

16.17 "THRIFTFAX" ANIMATION STAND

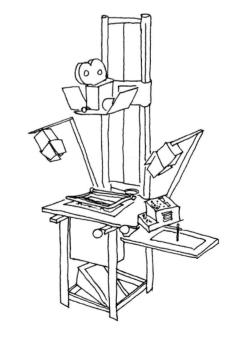

16.18 J-K ANIMATION STAND

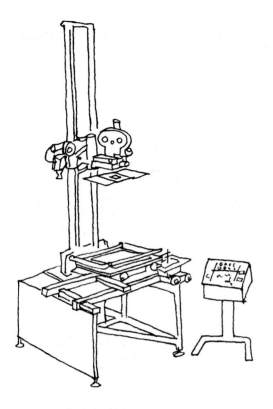

lighting, compound with four peg tracks (two at #12 field with hand wheels and counters, two push tracks at #18 field), N/S and E/W compound movement with hand wheels and digit counters, rotation units, pantograph, full control consul, rotoscope attachment. Entire system with camera: $14,900.

FOROX SSA SLIDE-STRIP ANIMATION CAMERA AND STAND

A unique form of specialized animation camera is manufactured by the Forox Corporation (see Chapter 22 for address). This camera has interchangeable movements for 46mm, 35mm, 16mm, super 8mm, 110mm, and 120mm films. Other features include: fixed-pin registration, remote-controlled reticle projection, 400-foot magazine, rotary dissolving shutter, remote-control direct-viewing eyepiece. The stand on which the camera is mounted features an automatic focus, a variable motor controlling carriage movement, and a compound surface that allows top and bottom lighting, off-center zoom, N/S and E/W movement with hand cranks and counters, a rotation pantograph, two peg tracks with #12 field standard #12 field platen, a front-mounted control console. Entire system with camera: $17,000

16.19   OXBERRY "FILMMAKER" ANIMATION STAND

OXBERRY MASTER SERIES (COMPUTER CONTROLLED)

Features: Twin precision ground steel columns, field range of #30 to #3 fields, mechanical counter registers camera movements in hundredths of an inch, automatic focus, electric operation of camera allows filming of complex moves at constant speeds, reticle projection, full rotoscope possibilities, multispeed stop-action motor ranges, fixed-pin registration, allows bi-pack operation, variable shutter calibrated in 10-degree increments, automatic fade-dissolve mechanism, all operations controlled at a master control, compound allows all movement with either manual or electric control, two pantographs, moving peg-bars with counters calibrated in one-hundredth of an inch, #12 field platen, Oxberry underneath Aerial Image projection system permits combination of live action and animation without making traveling mattes, computer model controls all operations and requires no knowledge of programming, Teletype terminal and paper punch-tape render program information. Entire system without computer control: $38,800; entire system with computer control: $80,000.

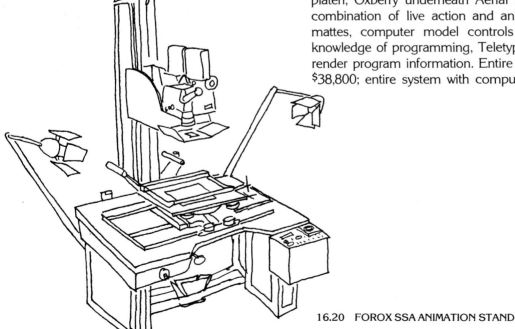

16.20   FOROX SSA ANIMATION STAND

17
Registration Devices

Registration is the animator's mania. Throughout the long hours of preparing artwork, the animator must be focused—physically and mentally—on keeping things lined up, keeping them registered. This awareness is intensified during the process of filming—the artwork must stay perfectly aligned under the camera.

Almost every piece of animation equipment exhibits a technical preoccupation with registration. Cameras must advance single frames with perfect registration; zoom lenses must be modified if the animator wants a fully registered movement; the stand itself is nothing more than a mechanical system that provides fully controlled registration of all filming variables.

So total is the registration obsession that this chapter can't even begin to cover all aspects of the topic. What it can do, however, is to list and illustrate those specific tools that are essential in letting an independent animator establish and maintain registration.

General Features

The animator's choice of different *pegging systems* has been discussed fully in Chapter 12. Improvised registration systems for individual sheets of paper or acetate include the use of: (1) a standard ¼-inch ring punch, the type employed with loose-leaf notebooks; (2) 90-degree corners on sheets of paper and acetate cels to provide a simple way of lining up successive images; (3) index file cards, a variation of the corner method, and (4) some kind of "bug," a continually redrawn mark that is consistently employed. To review these pegging systems, see Figure 12.3.

The specifications of commercially produced pegging systems have also been discussed earlier. The two major peg systems bear the names of the companies that first developed them: *Oxberry and Acme*. Both systems are illustrated and full-scale models are provided in the last chapter of this book.

Animating with either paper sheets or acetate cels requires the artist to make continual comparisons between the position of a drawing on one sheet or cel and the positions of that drawing's variations on other sheets or cels. In order to work easily, an animator needs to combine a pegging system with a lighted drawing surface. Hence, the evolution of special drawing discs and other underlighting devices, which will be discussed shortly. All these registered drawing aids also, of course, provide a standardization and registration of specific areas that will be filmed by means of a field guide. As described earlier, the field guide is used in conjunction with the pegs and drawing surface (see Figures 12.4 through 12.7).

A catalogue of these tools, along with other items that help an animator plan and plot and polish his or her work, follows.

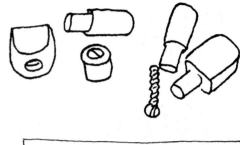

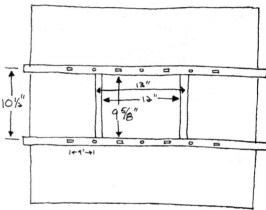

17.1 LOOSE PEGS: Metal pegs can be purchased unmounted. These loose pegs are equipped with screws so that you can mount them onto a drawing or filming surface. Whether Oxberry or Acme pegs are used, the distance between both round and flat pegs is always exactly 4 inches (center to center). Also illustrated is a conventional arrangement of pegs on a compound surface. Note that a number of peg sets can be mounted both above or below the drawing surface. This eliminates much of the need for sliding pegs.

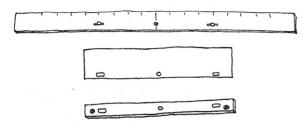

17.2 PEG-BARS AND PLATES

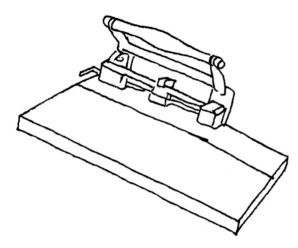

17.3 COMMERCIAL CEL PUNCH

Pegging Devices

Loose Pegs. Sets of three loose, removable, screw-in pegs (Figure 17.1) are available for Oxberry or Acme systems. Each set contains two oblong and one round peg. A set of three: $10.

Peg-bars. The standard peg-bar is made of aluminum and is ³⁄₁₆ by ¾ by 10½ inches. Available with either Acme or Oxberry pegs, the bar is mounted on a wooden board or light box. Note that a channel for accepting the bar must be routed out of the surface. A bar with nonremovable pegs: $16.50. A bar with removable pegs: $30.

Extra long, black, anodized-aluminum peg-bars are available in Oxberry or Acme systems. These long bars carry three round and two flat pegs and are scaled in twentieths of an inch. They can be glued or taped to a surface. Dimensions: ⅛ by 2 by 18 inches. Price: around $30.

Peg Plates. A particularly flexible pegging device is an aluminum tape-on peg plate bearing either Oxberry or Acme pegs. It can be easily mounted on a light board or under the camera by simply taping the thin plate to the surface. The plate, which is also easily removed, is ¹⁄₃₂ by 2 by 10½ inches. Price: $21.

Cel Punches. High-precision cel punches can be purchased that allow the animator to punch Oxberry or Acme registration systems (holes) into paper or acetate sheets. The design of the most expensive punch is "progressive"—the system can be used with extra-long backgrounds, pan papers, and cels. Oxberry's punch costs $900. Another heavy-duty punch is manufactured by George Randall ($650). Tabletop versions that are hand-operated with lever action and have hardened steel punches are available for somewhat less. Fax makes an Oxberry punch for $285 and J-K Optical makes an Acme punch for $275.

Oxberry also sells a two-hole, ¼-inch cel punch to go with the Media Pro animation stand's simplified pegging registration system. Price: $80.

¼-Inch Wooden-Dowel System. Lumber and hardware stores sell round wooden dowels that are ¼ inch in diameter. These can be used to create an inexpensive, home-made registration system that is accurate enough for most work. Pegs can be cut from the dowel and inserted into drilled holes on a drawing or shooting surface. Similarly, short pieces of doweling can be cut and glued on heavy poster board or matte board. In either case, the exposed portion of the dowel/peg must be sanded carefully to prevent the scratching or tearing of paper and acetate sheets.

The distance between holes on such home-made peg plates and peg-bars should be carefully selected so that it matches one of the standard two-ring or three-ring spacing distances that are used in standard school loose-leaf notebooks. I recommend the three-ring system in which ¼-inch diameter holes are exactly 4¼ inches apart. If the pegs are placed correctly, the animator ought to be able to use rotary cut and punched loose-leaf papers. One's own cel punch can be purchased for just a few dollars; single ¼-inch-hole punches and bar punches that make two or three holes at a time are available.

Drawing Devices

Animation Disc. The Oxberry Corporation manufactures and sells a series of high quality animation discs that feature a $^{\#}12$ field translucent glass window mounted within a machined cast-aluminum disc. These discs can be clamped to a baseboard for under-camera cel registration and background moves. It is better, however, to mount the disc in a 16⅜-inch diameter hole in a drawing table or surface to be placed beneath the camera. When so mounted, the disc can be rotated for drawing, tracing, inking, opaquing, or for 360-degree rotation moves under the camera. The disc's outside dimension is 17⅜ inches.

On such drawing discs, sets of pegs are mounted top and bottom, 10½ inches apart, and accommodate up to a $^{\#}12$ field. An Oxberry brand animation disc with fixed pegs (bearing either Oxberry or Acme pegs) costs $125. A disc of the same design and construction but with one set of pegs mounted on a sliding ruler marked in twentieths of an inch, with a lock, costs $145. A disc with two sets of movable pegs (used to simulate panning moves of cel or paper sheets) will cost $165 (Figure 17.4).

A special Oxberry Media Pro disc with two moving peg-bars is drilled for the attachment of four legs and a photographic quality backlight that is mounted behind the glass window. The assembly can also be used for cel preparation and pencil testing. Price: $170.

The Fax Corporation makes a similar disc with an outside dimension of 20 inches. It is unique, however, in that it is capable of accommodating either a $^{\#}12$ or $^{\#}16$ field layout (accomplished by reversing the position of the top and bottom peg-bars). Magnetic strips eliminate thumbscrews and permit easy and secure positioning of the movable peg-bars. The Fax disc has a Plexiglas opaline window with dimensions of 15½ by 9½ inches. The disc itself is made of cast aluminum with a baked-enamel finish. There is a pencil slot in the top half and a turning hole in the lower center. It accommodates Oxberry or Acme pegs. Price: $175.

Heath Productions offers a sturdy ¾-inch flakeboard disc that has two 18-inch pan peg-bars with metal pegs calibrated in twentieths of an inch. The wooden disc has a window of ¼-inch translucent, shatterproof Plexiglas. Its outside measurement is 18 inches and it requires a 16½-inch hole for mounting. It accommodates either Acme or Oxberry pegs. Price: approximately $70.

Ink and Paint Boards. The Fax Corporation produces simple boards for use in drawing, tracing, inking, and opaquing. Choices include size ($^{\#}12$ field or $^{\#}16$ field), material (clear Plexiglas, aluminum, or white opaque plastic), and top pegs only or top and bottom pegs. Available with Oxberry or Acme systems. Price range: $14 for a clear Plexiglas or white plastic $^{\#}12$ field with top pegs; $30 for an aluminum board with top pegs; $45 for a $^{\#}16$ field aluminum board with top and bottom pegs.

Oxberry manufactures a thick, black, anodized-aluminum inking peg board—11 by 16 by ⅜ inches—with three permanently mounted Oxberry or Acme pegs. Price: just over $50.

Light Tables. Oxberry has a light table that mounts any Oxberry aluminum drawing disc. There is an instant start, fluorescent backlight. The table is recommended for preparation and registration of paper sheets and acetate cels (Figure 17.5). Price, without disc: $130.

Fax Corporation markets a drafting table with a 16½-inch cutout hole to flush mount all fax discs. Price: $72.

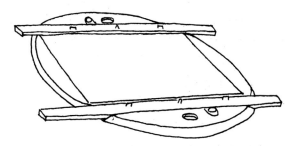

17.4 ANIMATION DISCS: This drawing is of an Oxberry disc.

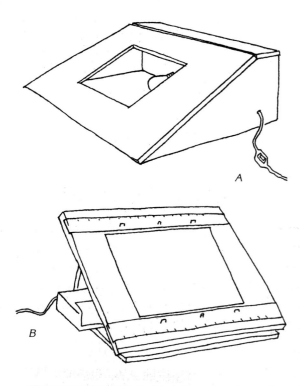

17.5 LIGHT TABLES: Ordinary plywood can be used to make a simple light table such as that in *A*. The square hole is sized to accommodate a #12-field sheet of white Plexiglas. Standard wooden molding keeps the drawing surface in place and mounted flush to the wooden surface. A porcelain socket is mounted for use with a 60-watt incandescent bulb. A peg plate can be taped to the wood or to the Plexiglas and then repositioned beneath the camera where the registered sheets or cels are subsequently filmed. Illustration *B* shows a portable light table from Heath Productions. It has two 18" pan peg-bars and a removable fluorescent lighting unit.

For $75, Heath Productions will sell you a portable light table that features a translucent Plexiglas window and a collapsible, hinged construction of composition board. Rubber feet prevent sliding. Two 18-inch pan peg-bars (Oxberry or Acme) are mounted and calibrated in twentieths of an inch. A removable fluorescent unit is included. Heath also sells a single sheet of ¼-inch-thick Plexiglas that can be used in drawing or inking over a light. This lighting board has built-in metal pegs (Oxberry or Acme) and measures 11½ by 14 inches. Price: $20.

An alternative to the specialized animator's light table is a professional designer's table that features straight edges, an adjustable top surface, steel construction, and a translucent glass top 25 by 21 inches that can be used for inking/opaquing in conjunction with a tape-on pegging system. The overall size is 46 by 32 by 37½ inches. Price: $390. Less expensive secondhand designer's tables can provide the same services at considerably less cost.

Another variation of a light table is the portable steel tracing box. Its 16- by 20-inch glass surface has a light diffuser and either two or three 15-watt bulbs with a three-way switch. The metal stand allows the top surface to be tilted. This kind of tracing box has to be used with a tape-on peg plate. Price, with two bulbs: $75.

Field Guides. The standard reference for the area beneath the animation camera is the Oxberry field guide. Field guides that are printed on .02-inch plastic sheets provide #1 through #12 fields. They are available punched to Oxberry or Acme standards. Price: $8, on unpunched plastic sheets, $6. (See Chapter 23.)

Field guides that indicate TV cutoff areas—that familiar rounding of the rectangular shape of the television screen, which can mean a loss of up to 20 percent of the screen's area—are also available. These clear plastic sheets are like a field area chart, but they show the precise cutoff line that exists when a film is projected on television. Such TV charts show a #14 field through a #12 field and are available punched or unpunched (Figure 17.6).

Other Aids

Exposure Sheets. Should you not wish to detach and duplicate the exposure sheet provided later in Chapter 23, you can purchase 80-frame exposure sheets that are printed on 11¾- by 18½-inch yellow stock from Heath Productions. Price: 10 cents each.

Footage and Timing Charts. A 16mm-35mm footage and timing chart, printed on thick plastic, can be purchased from the Fax Corporation. Price: 50 cents. Or use the one in Chapter 23.

Spur Wheels. Spur wheels, which mark points at regular distances, are used on pantograph plates to follow varied camera movements, such as French curves, diagonals, circles, etc. In following these dots with the pantograph's pointer, you eliminate hours of layout time, and a smooth filming action is assured. Spur wheels are available in a set with three spurs and 15 to 21 dots per inch. Cost from Cartoon Color Company: $6.50.

Stopwatches. A stopwatch is often useful for determining the precise duration (and subsequent number of frames, number of drawings) of a particular movement or portion of a movement. A standard stopwatch will work, but for those with *everything,* Fax will sell you a stopwatch with time-footage scales for 16mm, 35mm and super 8mm animation. Price: about $100.

Animation Platen. If you are building your own stand, you ought to know that you can purchase an Oxberry #12 field platen that is designed to hold cels and other artwork of variable heights flat on the compound table. The glass sheet is ¼-inch thick, float-mounted on a pivoting center, and hinged on a spring-loaded platen bracket. The glass itself is optically pure. Since the entire assembly fastens to the surface with knobs, it is easy to mount and then remove completely when filming large art. Price: $168. Platens are critical for registration in many cutout and collage techniques (for illustration, see Chapter 16).

17.6   FIELD GUIDE WITH TV CUTOFF (not to scale)

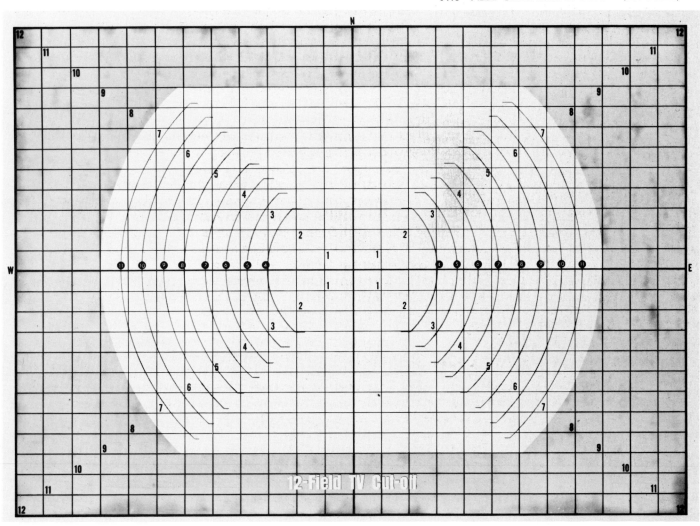

18
Lighting, Audio, Editing, and Projection

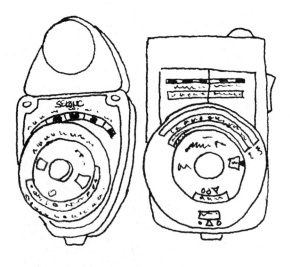

18.1   LIGHT METERS: At left is an incident light meter (Sekonic model #L 280), which measures radiated light directly, whether it comes from the sun or a flood lamp. On the right is a reflectant meter (Gossen Luna-Pro) that can also take incident readings. A reflectant meter measures light that bounces off a surface.

Because animated films are almost always shot indoors and under controlled situations, the element of lighting is less problematic for the animator than for the live-action filmmaker. If you set up the right lighting system once, you may never need to think about it again.

With that incentive in mind, the following discussion of general lighting requirements should clarify for you the choices you will have to make and the options open to you. As always, the selections you make for your own work will depend both on your equipment and on the range of animation techniques you'll want to undertake. And as always, remember you can extend and upgrade the capabilities of your lighting system whenever you feel you are ready.

General Lighting Requirements

The human eye and brain are always making compensations to allow us to perceive colors as constant under various lighting conditions. It is different with film. The same colored surface—say a white piece of paper—will film with very different hues, depending on the source of light and the characteristics of the kind of film stock that is being used.

Motion picture film is manufactured with different chemical balances. These produce different measurements of *color temperature* —the sensitivity of the emulsion to whatever light falls on it. *Daylight* film stocks are structured so that a white sheet of paper will appear white when filmed under normal daylight—the light provided by the sun. *Tungsten* film stocks are designed to be used with artificial lighting. As far as color balance is concerned, there are two variations of tungsten stocks (also called *indoor* stocks). Type A film is balanced to one specific measurement on a temperature scale (3200°K), and Type B film is balanced to a slightly different reading on the same scale (3400°K). Daylight films, by the way, have color temperature of 5500°K.

You may remember from your science classes that light, at least in part, behaves like a wave, and that these waves occur at different frequencies within the electromagnetic spectrum. For the filmmaker, the practical result of this phenomenon is that different kinds of light sources—the sun, an incandescent bulb, fluorescent lights—will produce different colors even if the same object is being filmed on the same film stock.

So how do you get the "right" film for the "right" light source? Or how do you compensate so that an indoor film can be used outdoors?

The *Kelvin Color Temperature Scale* is the measurement system used by filmmakers to make sure that an apple will look like an apple and that your favorite movie star will have the "correct" flesh color when he or she appears on screen. The Kelvin Scale measures degrees of color temperature. Sunlight is rated at 5400°K. The 100-watt household bulb is rated at 2860°K. A candle flame is 1850°K. Almost all artificial lighting systems used in moviemaking are manufactured so that their rating will be either 3200°K or 3400°K. Obviously the two ratings are very close. Film stocks designed to be used with artificial lighting are also rated 3200°K or 3400°K.

The quality control of commercially manufactured film stocks and lighting equipment virtually assures that, if you match the Kelvin scales of both film stock and lighting tools, what you see with the naked eye will be what you see when the exposed and processed film is projected on a movie screen. If problems occur it is usually because there are mixed sources of light, say a fluorescent light or ambient sunlight in addition to the proper artificial lighting. In case you ever have a weird shooting setup that keeps giving you problems, you may want to use a special *color temperature light meter.* These specialized devices will let you measure the precise temperature value of any lighting situation. They are expensive, about $600.

Lighting Problems

Metering and Exposure. Many super 8mm cameras have built-in light-metering systems that will automatically set the camera's diaphragm at the proper f-stop opening for the given light intensity and for the particular sensitivity of the film stock being used. As noted earlier, there is a tendency in animated filmmaking for these built-in, automatic meters to overexpose the film's subject when a brightly colored background is being used. For this reason, a manual override capability is strongly recommended.

Or better, the animator should take manual light readings by using a standard photographic light meter (Figure 18.1). Light meters measure *reflected light* (bouncing off the surface) or *incident light* (light that is falling on the surface being filmed.) The utilization and price of meters won't be covered in these pages. Your local camera shop will explain the tool or you can check a volume on the basics of filmmaking. What ought to be noted here, however, is that the animator should always shoot test footage in order to *judge by eye* the proper setting for a specific kind of artwork under a specific lighting setup. The process of testing exposure is called *bracketing,* and it is accomplished by filming the same surface under the same lighting but at aperture variations of ½ an f-stop. By studying the exposed film, the perfect setting can be selected.

When measuring light with either an automatic or a manual metering system, you should place a *gray card* under the camera. A piece of paper or cardboard of grayish hue has a value that is exactly halfway betwen white and black; the card's purpose is to help the meter estimate the f-stop that will yield an exposure that best captures the midrange of color and brightness intensities (Figure 18.2). The gray card will compensate for the tendency of meters to underexpose the film. But if you're unsure about a reading and can't do a test, follow the time-proven rule of still photographers—expose for shadows. When in doubt, underexpose rather than overexpose.

18.2   GRAY CARD: The gray reproduced here is exactly midway between white and black. Hence it is used in establishing a balanced light reading for animation artwork. Eastman Kodak sells gray cards or you can make your own. For a comprehensive camera test, combine a gray scale with a color chart.

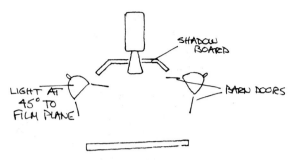

18.3 AVOIDING REFLECTION: The 45-degree angle of the lights should mean that reflections will never bounce back into the camera's lens. That assumes, of course, that the surface being filmed is flat. This is one reason why a glass platen is recommended for most kinds of animation. The shadowboard's black matte finish absorbs light and helps shield the lens from direct flaring from a nearby light source or reflecting surface.

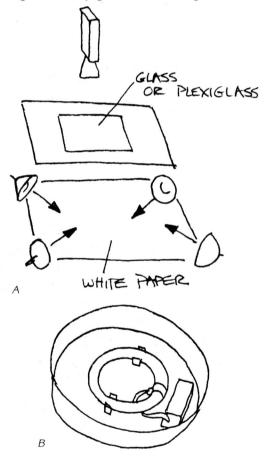

18.4 BACKLIGHTING: Self-rigged backlighting (A) can be done by mounting two or (better) four lights under the compound surface. These must be arranged so that they provide even illumination through the translucent surface that is mounted into the compound. Commercially manufactured backlights must also provide even illumination. A Fax backlight is pictured in B with a fluorescent bulb.

Even Illumination. The use of artificial lights can make it difficult to evenly illuminate the surface underneath the camera. Because the lights are mounted so close to the compound surface, there is a tendency for a *hot spot* to develop. This is an area that is more brightly lighted than the rest of the surface. In order to get a balanced intensity of lighting, animators will usually mount the same size light sources in matching positions on either side of the artwork. Although a light meter can help determine if all areas are evenly illuminated, I think the best way to judge the correct balance is not with a meter but with the naked eye.

Reflection and Glare. Artificial lights tend to reflect off almost any surface, even one that has a matte finish. The woeful result can be glare or flashing in what is otherwise a perfectly exposed animation sequence. To fight this problem, animation stands are designed so that lights are mounted at a 45-degree angle to the plane of the camera (or compound). Theoretically at least, this causes the reflections from the artificial lighting system to bounce past and not into the camera.

The use of a *platen* to hold artwork flat under the camera is also important in defeating reflection and glare. Finally, many stands feature *shadowboards* with hinged wings. These devices are mounted close under the camera, with a hole cut for the lens. The shadowboard also reduces reflections caused by the camera body and the lens itself. Shadowboards can be easily made out of black matte board or similar cardboard material. (Figure 18.3).

Heat. Artificial lights get hot. Just how hot they get will be appreciated the first time you work under them for any length of time. Animators are always trying to escape the heat. This can be accomplished by the use of *low wattage* bulbs and lamps when possible; *barn doors* on the lighting units in order to focus brightness on the table as much as possible; *heat absorbing glass filters* in front of the bulbs; and the use of *fans* to cool the lighting units (or an air-conditioner to cool the camera operator!).

3-D Lighting. As you've observed with clay, puppet, pixilation and a few other techniques, there are times when animation requires the same kind of lighting used in live-action filmmaking. In setting up for these filming techniques the animator must use combinations of lights in order to heighten the three-dimensionality of the scene. Check a filmmaking manual for more information. Lighting for movies is a highly specialized art. Entire catalogues of lighting systems exist and there are volumes about the craft of lighting.

Bottomlighting. A *backlighting* unit is required when filming layers of paper sheets or with techniques such as sand and ink-on-glass animation. Naturally, bottomlighting requires a transparent or translucent surface mounted under the camera. Here are three options, in recommended order: (1) a sheet of white, opal, translucent, and shatterproof Plexiglas (Plexiglas 2447), (2) a sheet of frosted plate glass, or (3) a sheet of clear glass that is covered with a thin piece of tracing paper in order to diffuse the light.

Underlighting devices can be jerry-rigged. Perhaps the best and simplest way to backlight is to remount the standard lamps that are used for toplighting. These lamps are positioned so that they either shine up through the glass window beneath the stand and camera or they bounce light off a white surface below the translucent window on the compound bed. All the factors discussed above apply to bottom-lighting as well as to toplighting: color temperature, metering and exposure control, heat, and balance of illumination.

Professionally manufactured bottomlighting units are recommended (Figure 18.5). Specific models include a 3200°K cathode lamp mounted in a metal tray, produced by Oxberry ($290). This backlight provides even illumination beneath the drawing disc and it can be used under the camera for pencil tests and other shooting. It covers a full #12 field (10½ by 12 inches) and can be mounted under a drawing disc to provide art preparation as well as photographic backlighting.

The Fax Corporation makes a circular metal frame with a circular fluorescent bulb, which can be used under an animation disc, but it is not recommended for under-camera use. It costs $85 and requires a special filter.

Lighting Systems

Although *Movie lights* are often used in amateur live-action filmmaking, they are *not* recommended for animation. Color balanced at 3400°K, they have a very high wattage (650 watts to 1,100 watts) that produces an intense and very, very hot light output, which is uneven and harsh. They are also expensive.

Photoflood bulbs and reflector scoops are one of the least expensive ways to light for animation. The bulbs fit standard sockets and some of them, called EAL bulbs, have a built-in reflector, which eliminates the need for a reflector scoop. Photofloods are available in most camera stores in either 3200°K or 3400°K color temperatures.

Photofloods come in various power ratings, from 150 watts to 1000 watts. Animators generally prefer the lower wattage versions. They are cooler to work near, yet they produce enough brightness for midrange f-stop settings with even the slowest stocks. Photofloods are relatively cheap (60 cents to $1.50), but they don't last a long time. The average life of a photoflood is six hours and the color temperature will shift with age, caused by the carbonization of the bulb. This is not a problem except when one set of aged bulbs is replaced by a set of fresh bulbs. Animators solve this problem by removing all four bulbs when one burns out and replacing them with four fresh bulbs—or with whatever number of bulbs your stand requires. When one of these burns out replace it with one of the used bulbs.

Low Kelvin (2750°K) lamps have a long life—up to 2,000 hours. The unacceptable color can be compensated for with an 82C filter on the camera lens. Ask your local hardware store for 75-watt *reflector floods*. The low wattage is a plus factor in cutting heat on the artwork. Using four bulbs also helps to achieve a more even coverage at #12 field. These lamps fit into any incandescent socket, have built-in reflectors, and cost under $2. They are also called flood lamps.

The *Lowell-Light* is a porcelain socket mounted on a universal swivel base, which can be clamped, taped, nailed, or hooked to almost any surface. Under $15, the socket uses a number of R-40 reflector bulbs with various wattages costing around $5 each.

Quartz lamps, which are specially manufactured for film production, including halogen and iodine cycles, come in a variety of forms rated at 3200°K or 3400°K, with wattages from 250 to 2000.

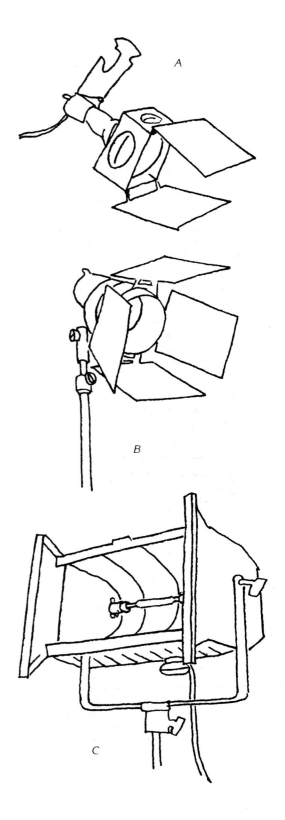

18.5 LIGHTING SYSTEMS. The Lowell-Light with barn doors *(A)*; The Colortran Mini-Pro with barn doors *(B)*; and the Colortran Multi-Broad *(C)*. Both Colortran models use quartz lighting.

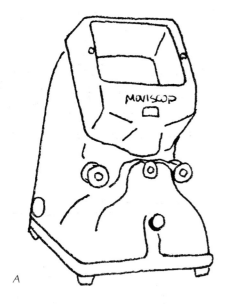

A

B

18.6   VIEWERS: The Zeiss Moviscop is pictured in A. A Bolex super 8mm viewer, with rewinds, is shown in B.

Through the use of quartz, a high temperature glass, these lighting systems are able to maintain the same color temperature their entire lives by eliminating carbonization.

Among many, many styles and designs of quartz lighting systems, here are four possibilities, from lowest in price to highest.

Smith Victor Model 770 Quartz Broad Hi-Fi Studio Light provides an even, broad lighting, which makes it specially suited to animation. Of all-aluminum construction for cooler operation, the light mounts to a standard ⅜-inch stand. Barn doors must be used to hold scrims and various filters. Price: with accessories, about $60; lamps, $15 each (75 hours).

Lowel Tota-Light, an innovatively designed fixture, uses long-lasting bulbs and provides an exceptionally wide and even, bright light pattern when used with a gull-wing reflector. The Tota-Light can accommodate 300-, 500-, 750-, and 1000-watt quartz lamps. There are many accessories for mounting. Price: around $100; 300-watt lamp, $23 (2,000 hours).

Berkey Colortran Mini-Pro Lights have a recessed power receptacle permitting use of a detachable 120-volt or 30-volt power cable. Bulbs are interchangeable. The lamp has a 3:1 variable focus and weighs 30 ounces. Attachments facilitate mounting in almost any situation. Price: a complete unit, about $125; bulbs, under $20.

Colortran 750-Watt Soft-Lite, a relatively small and lightweight studio lamp, provides a smooth, diffuse, shadowless light. Its dimensions are 13½ by 16 by 6½ inches. Price: $210; bulbs, around $20.

Filters

Camera manufacturers and filter supply companies offer filters of all kinds for all cameras. Here is an introductory primer that applies to both 16mm and super 8mm formats. How one actually mounts a filter will vary from camera to camera—check an instruction booklet. Most super 8mm cameras take glass filters, which are screwed into the front of the lens casing. While many 16mm cameras take the same kind of glass, front-mounting lenses, others often use a filter gel, either directly in front of the camera gate or in front of the lens via a matte box or similar mounting device.

Color Correction. The 80A filter corrects daylight-balanced films to 3200°K (tungsten) lighting conditions, while the 80B filter corrects daylight stocks to 3400°K. The 82A filter compensates Type A film (most super 8mm color stocks, which are valued at 3400°K) by cooling the light to match the 3200°K output of most quartz lamps. Filming with a Type A film without this filter will produce a slightly reddish or "warm" tone. The 85 filter, which is built into all super 8mm cameras, converts 5500°K rated daylight film so that it can be shot under tungsten lighting. A FLB filter is designed for use with fluorescent lighting to compensate for the green-blue cast that fluorescent lighting produces on tungsten film. Note that color-correction filters require a slight adjustment in the f-stop exposure. Automatic, through-the-lens metering systems will compensate for this factor by themselves.

A number of other color filters are available but are omitted here because they are seldom used in animation. A lighting manual or production guide will provide information about such filters as the Skylight 1A, 82B, 82C, 85B, CC30R, CC20Y, FLD, and the Decamired Filter series, which provides graduated warming or cooling changes by altering the color temperature of any stock.

Damping Light Intensity. Sometimes during animation filming one discovers that more light is present than can be used. In these situations a *neutral density filter* can be employed to cut down on the amount of light entering the camera. Such filters have no effect on color. Tiffen, a producer of still and motion picture filters, manufactures fifteen different density filters, which are measured according to Light Transmission Percentage and F/Stop Increase. Here are a few samples:

ND 0.1	80%	½ stop
ND 0.3	50%	1 stop
ND 0.6	25%	2 stops
ND 0.9	13%	3 stops

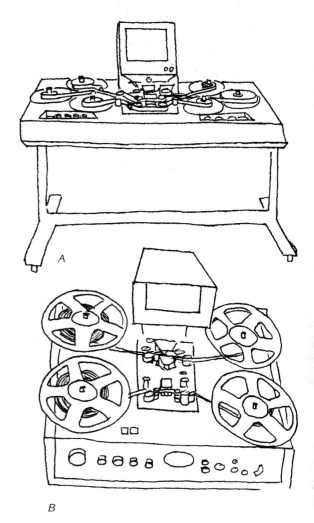

Polarizing Filters. Polarized filters are useful in animation because they help block out and reduce reflections from glass, water, and dust. The use of polarizing filters is quite complicated and you are advised to check a thorough production manual for more detail on how they work and what they will do.

Special Effect Filters. Quick reference here to a number of specialty filters that can provide unique effects. The use of such filters for animators is somewhat limited because the medium itself allows for such complete control, manipulation, and transformation of imagery.

Diffusion filters "soften" the lines of an image. A *fog-effect filter* creates a bluish halo around every object, much as fog does through defraction of water droplets in the air. *Star-effect filters* are engraved with patterned lines that transform highlights into "stars" of light. Different versions provide a different number of facets for the star and changes the character of the defraction. *Multi-image filters* come in many forms: concentric images (three or four) that move when the filter is rotated, six images that "circle" a fixed central image, and many, many more. Check your dealer for literature on these trick filters. Others to check out include Rayburst, Colorflow, Vibracolor, Curvatar, Birdseye, Vignetar, and more. The costs of such filters vary widely.

General Audio Requirements

There is an especially intimate relationship in animation between the sound track and the moving image. Many of the techniques for working creatively with sound have been discussed in Chapter 7. The comments that follow here deal primarily with audio tools. First there's a brief recapitulation of the sound production systems available within today's 16mm and super 8mm technologies. After that you'll find a fast run-through of recording tools and audio editing processes. While brief, this information should at least prepare you to approach audio with the respect it deserves.

Once a film has been completed, it's easy to create a *wild track,* an audio tape recording that provides (and sometimes combines) music, voice, and sound effects. Wild tracks can be created for both super 8mm and 16mm films. The liabilities of such audio accompaniment is that it cannot be matched very accurately to the progression of

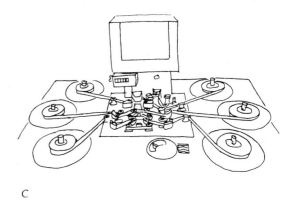

18.7 EDITING CONSOLES: The Movieola 6-plate "flatbed" is illustrated in *A.* A super 8mm editing machine is shown in *B,* the MKM model 824. In illustration *C* the surface of a Steenbeck 6 plate is shown. The top two plates carry the picture (16mm work print) and the bottom two sets of plates carry two different sound tracks (16mm magnetic recording stock).

18.8   SUPER 8 SOUND MOTORIZED EDITING BENCH: The illustration shows, from left to right, a rewind crank (note long shaft), a modified cassette tape recorder, a super 8mm viewer with soundhead mounted directly in front of the viewing gate, a two-gang synchronizer with a motor drive assembly (the rear section), and a forward wind crank that carries two up-reels.

the film. The best system for keeping image and audio more or less together is through a coordinated start-up system. (See Chapter 7.)

A more satisfactory system is made possible by the relatively new super 8mm *sound-on-film* technology (Figure 18.8). After an animated film is shot and edited, the film can be *striped* with a thin surface of audio recording tape that is applied directly to one edge of the film stock. Striped super 8mm raw stock is also available. An audio track can now be recorded directly on the film. This is done with a *super 8mm sound projector.* These projectors are used both to *record* the sound on the film and then to *play back* the sound with the film images during normal projection.

Such a system permits the animator to create a fairly well matched track, for the audio can be recorded and rerecorded on the completed and striped film until it is "just right." Thereafter, the track will be synced properly with the movie's visuals. A similar system exists for striping 16mm film, but it has become so infrequently used that you're advised not to try it.

Sixteen-millimeter film technology permits a more detailed analysis of audio materials. This is accomplished by transferring recorded sound from a reel-to-reel or cassette tape recording to *16mm magnetic recording film,* called *mag stock.* (Again, see Chapter 7 for a more complete description.) Various tools permit frame-by-frame *sound reading* and *track analysis.* The most important tool is a motorized *film editing console* and/or a *gang synchronizer with a soundhead and an amplifier.* These tools permit a very, very precise matching of frames of picture to corresponding frames in the 16mm sound track. In fact, most sophisticated films begin with an analysis of the track. The images are then designed to match the track.

When a 16mm film and a set of 16mm audio tracks are fully edited and synced, the tracks are *mixed* to form a *master track.* This is then taken to a lab and turned into an *optical master,* which is subsequently printed along with the original film on a single strip of 16mm film. Voilá! A completed 16mm *optical print,* which can be distributed and screened wherever there is a standard 16mm sound projector.

Very briefly (indeed), those are the options presently available to independent animators. The process is more fully outlined elsewhere, but for a really complete discussion you must consult one of the excellent live-action filmmaking guides noted in Chapter 20.

Before proceeding to a list of recording tools, I'd like to mention two additional systems for creating the audio component of an animated film.

First, the fast development of super 8 technologies may allow the filmmaker to do a complete frame-by-frame analysis of tracks that have been transferred from ordinary recording tape to a *super 8mm full-coat magnetic recording film.* After the final editing of image and tracks, the super 8mm mag stock is transferred onto a striped duplicate of the original film.

Commercial cel animations have traditionally shot their films in 35mm format. They have also analyzed their sound tracks from a sound recording stock that is also in 35mm format. In making bar sheets for lip synchronization, the 35mm gauge is much easier to work with than the 16mm gauge (since the stock is physically larger, a given sound is spaced over a larger area and is, therefore, easier to identify). Because 16mm and 35mm are projected at a standard speed of 24 frames per second, it is simple to match up track with visuals and to transfer from one gauge to another.

Sound Recording Equipment

Cassette Tape Recorders. There are hundreds and hundreds of cassette recorders. Many come with built-in microphones. Some accept "line" input from other recorders or from phonographs and some take auxiliary mikes. A major drawback to these recorders is that it is almost impossible to do sharp editing with them. The quality of such machines varies hugely, as does their price. Generally, the more one pays, the better the quality and performance of the cassette machine.

Reel-to-Reel Tape Recorders. Because of quality and ease in manual editing, reel-to-reel recorders are generally preferred for filmmaking. Decent monaural recorders begin at about $150 and are manufactured by all major audio firms. Synchronous monaural tape recorders made by Nagra and Stellavox cost at least $3,000. They are *not* required for animation. Stereo reel-to-reel recorders can be useful for the amateur and independent animator. They enable one to record two different tracks—one on each channel—and then to "mix" these down to one track via a "y" cable that transfers the stereo onto a single track machine or onto the edge of the film itself. The mixing of 16mm tracks is usually done at a professional sound studio, which provides more control. The technology at a good sound-mixing studio provides extraordinary control in shaping individual tracks as well as the eventual master track. Stereo tape recorders begin at $150 and just keep going up.

Microphones. You can spend just about anything you want for a mike. The cheapest is about $15; the most expensive, around $1,000. There are totally different mikes that will handle different recording jobs. The list includes omni-directional, cardiloid, and shot-guns. There are condenser mikes, dynamic mikes, and radio mikes. Along with these are mixers and amplifiers and filters and all manner of auxiliary attachments. And a universe of plugs. For further guidance, check Part Four: Resources.

Film Striping and Transfer. Although you can purchase machines to transfer ¼-inch audio tape to super 8mm and 16mm magnetic stocks, most animators have this done at a film laboratory. Similarly, like most people, you will probably send out a super 8mm film to have it striped even though specialized equipment is available to allow you to do it yourself. The cost of such services is given in the next chapter.

Audio Tape Editing

By connecting two audio tape recorders with a patch cord, it is possible to selectively transfer audio material from one machine to a fresh roll of audio tape on the second machine. In this way, a simple editing of sound tracks can be quickly, easily, and inexpensively accomplished.

A more precise way to edit involves actually splicing the recording

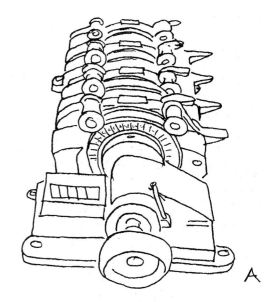

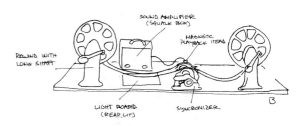

18.9 SYNCHRONIZER: A four-gang synchronizer is pictured in drawing A. The synchronizer's position on an editing bench is indicated in drawing B.

18.10 SPLICERS: The Maier-Hancock portable hot splicer is shown in *A*. Bolex's super 8 Guillotine splicer is shown in *B*. A Rivas 16mm tape splicer is shown in *C* and an inexpensive splicing bar that uses Kodak Press-Tapes is shown in *D*. There are many other brands and styles of cement and tape splicers for both super 8mm and 16mm editing.

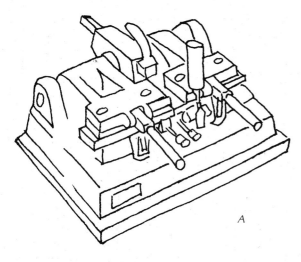

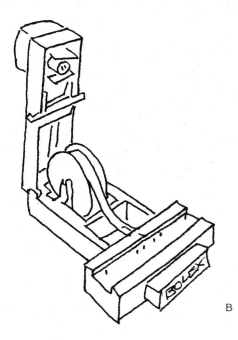

A

B

tape. The tape is run forward and backward past the recording head until the exact point for a cut is selected and identified. A soft-lead pencil is used to mark the spot. When cut diagonally with a razor blade (a grooved metal splicing block is used to position and hold the tape), the end of one segment can be spliced together with the start of another segment. A special audio splicing tape is used. This procedure is fully explained in numerous source volumes or in the directions accompanying an audio splicing kit, which can be purchased for under $10.

Overview: Editing and Splicing

Editing matters *less* in animation.

This is so for a number of reasons: animators preplan their films with greater precision than live-action filmmakers; there is greater control during the shooting process itself; animated films are generally shorter than live-action films; certainly the ratio of shot film to used film is far, far lower in animation than in any other kind of film production.

Depending, of course, on which technique is being used, the animator approaches the task of editing with two objectives. First, there is a need to place the exposed sequences into the proper order—an order that has usually been carefully storyboarded or scripted in advance of the actual production. Second, the animator edits the film so that it conforms to a prerecorded sound track. This involves a series of *fine cuts*—minor alterations in the picture and sound track so that they run together synchronously. If a wild track is being used, the editing process is simplified further.

In contrast, the live-action film editor must constantly make selections between possible "takes" and also determine the precise flow and order of the edited footage (a 15:1 shooting ratio is common). In live-action filmmaking there can be up to three or four different sound tracks that must be interrelated and cut to go with the visuals.

The job of editing is generally broken down into a number of sequential tasks. Each editor will have his or her modifications to the process—each will handle the choice-making process in a different way and a different order. For what it's worth, however, here is my own approach to editing—briefly reviewed.

Processed footage (the *rushes*) is screened again and again until the filmmaker/editor is certain of what footage is to be used and in roughly what order it will appear in the finished movie. No cuts are made in the footage until at least a first *rough-cut* version is determined.

The film is next run through a *viewer* or an *editing console* while the editor marks the film at the precise frame at which cuts will be made. The film is then literally cut, with *scissors,* and hung up in an *editing bin* or improvised system that labels each individual strip of film. This is an important stage. The editor has to be certain that the "head" end of each strip of film can be identified and that it will be possible to quickly locate various strips of film in the order they are required for the *rough-cut* assemblage. Note that no footage is ever thrown away. Those pieces that are not included in the final film are called *outtakes* and they should be carefully saved.

Using *rewinds* and a *splicer* and beginning with a strip of *white leader,* the editor now begins to splice pieces of film together—the "head" of one piece to the "tail" of the preceding piece. Splices in both super 8mm and 16mm formats are made in either of two ways: a *butt-end splice* and an *overlapping cement splice.* (Splicing tools are described later in this chapter.)

The rough-cut is spliced to a piece of tail leader and can now be projected with either an editing console or with a projector. At this stage the animator generally makes refinements, which lead to what is called the *fine-cut.* In 16mm film editing the picture is edited in relationship to the *16mm magnetic stock* that bears the sound track(s). Often, of course, the track will be cut and rearranged so that it fits the film's images. When both sound and picture are set, the completed film can be previewed by projecting in *double-system* with a special kind of film projector or by using a motorized editing console. If all is as the animator wants it, the *camera original film* (a *work print* having been used in editing) is conformed to the fine-cut using a *gang synchronizer,* a tool that advances individual tracks and pictures together. A gang synchronizer can be equipped with a *soundhead and amplifier.* This gives the editor another stage at which to analyze the film to make certain that the picture and sound are aligned as they should be. As noted earlier, the synchronizer is used commonly in animation in order to preanalyze a recorded sound track before the actual filming takes place.

A few paragraphs are not adequate to introduce all the stages, techniques, and tools that are used in film editing. Entire volumes have been written on this topic, and you'll need to consult one if you are beginning to learn editing. But to familiarize you a bit further with the editing and splicing process, and to help you determine what tools you'll need to borrow, rent, or purchase, here is a catalogue of editing and splicing equipment.

Editing Equipment

Viewers. Available in a wide variety of super 8mm and 16mm models, viewers are operated by passing the processed film from left to right through a precision transport mechanism that assures smooth film movement without scratching (Figure 18.6). The viewer has a rotating shutter with a reflecting prism that casts a projected image past polished condenser lenses and onto a ground-glass viewing screen. The sizes of the viewing screens and the intensity of the image vary. Viewers are used in conjunction with hand-operated rewinds. Motorized viewers are available in both 16mm and super 8mm. Sample models and prices: Zeiss Moviscop 16 with 2½- by 3½-inch viewing screen, $300; Movieola 50 16mm table viewer with 4- by 5-inch viewing screen, $295; Minette S-5 super 8mm viewer with 2.8- by 3.8-inch viewing screen, $110; Baia "Brite-View" super 8mm viewer with 18.3-square-inch viewing screen, $35.

Editing Machines. Modern flatbed editing consoles provide speed, accuracy, and convenience through precision engineering (Figure 18.7). These machines are designed in modular units with a large-screen viewing surface, variable speed movement in forward and reverse modes, quality soundhead(s), footage/frame counters, instant start/stop, and other features. *Flatbed* machines hold and transport

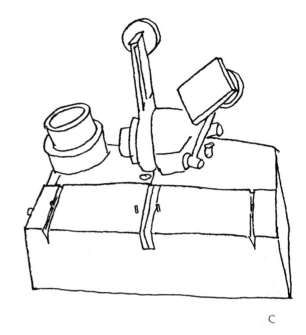

C

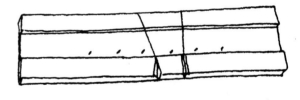

D

18.10

18.11 PROJECTORS: The illustrations show the Kodak S-8 Ektagraphic projector, one of the best ever made *(A)*; the Kodak Instamatic M-100A super 8 projector *(B)*; the Bolex SM80 Electronic super 8 sound projector *(C)*. All the manufacturers of 16mm and super 8mm cameras also produce projectors. Used projectors are a good value.

A

both film and sound in a horizontal position. The capabilities of such machines are measured by the number of *plates,* the loading and tape-up positions that hold *cores* on which film is reeled. A four-plate console has one picture head (for the film and usually designed with a 26-frame advanced optical reader) and one magnetic soundhead (for the mag stock). There are eight and even ten plate models. Though developed for professional 16mm film editing, a number of super 8 models are also marketed: Steenbeck, 6 plate, flatbed, around $14,000; Moviola M-85A-16, 4 plate, almost $6,000; HKM 824 Super 8, 4 plate, $2,000.

Motorized Viewers with synchronizers (see below) constitute an alternative editing-machine system: Moviola M-79 viewer and decoupler, $2,000; Super 8 Sound Editing Bench (two-gang super 8mm synchronizer, 24 fps motor, viewer, single-system mag-head assembly, rewinds, differential assemblies, board), $850. (Figure 18.8.)

Rewinds. Sixteen-millimeter rewinds have gears with a cranking ratio of one handle revolution to four reel revolutions. They are available with friction drags, long shafts, elbow breaks, spacers, tite-winds, and spring clamps. A basic long-arm rewind costs $45. Super 8mm rewinds cost about the same. Note that Super 8 Sound Company manufactures a rewind with a differential adapter that allows rapid transverse of one strand forward or backward at speeds several times sound speed while the other strand is stopped. Many super 8mm viewers have attached plastic rewinds that operate in a one-to-one cranking ratio.

Synchronizers. These essential tools are designed to keep multiple picture and sound tracks locked in absolute mechanical sync. Film and sound sprockets are held by rollers and hinged pressure arms. These roller arms are often drilled to mount a magnetic head, which rests gently on the sound film and is connected by wire to a sound amplifier/speaker called a *squawk box.* The rollers are referred to as *gangs.* Synchronizers are available in one- to six-gang models. All have footage counters. The rollers themselves mark the frame count (Figure 18.9). Moviola SZB two-gang 16mm synchronizer, $140 (four-gang model, $200); magnetic pick-off soundhead, $35; amplifier/speaker, $95; motor-drive attachment for synchronizer, $200; Moviola also manufactures a two-gang and a four-gang super 8mm synchronizer, at $140 and $215, respectively.

Splicers. Cement splicers are preferred (often required) for printing 16mm films. The technique of *wet splicing* involves scraping off the emulsion from one of the ends being joined. These ends are then slightly overlapped and fused together by a *cement* that is specially designed for the purpose and must be fresh or else the splices won't properly bond. An inexpensive 16mm cement splicer such as the Griswold HM6 costs $35; Bolex makes a super 8mm cement splicer at $60.

Hot splicers are the professional standard. They are precision tools with a carbide scraper and a thermostatically heated blade, which makes a quick and perfect weld. Cement is also used. Maier-Hancock Model 816S will take 16mm and super 8mm films. Its cost is $350. Hot splicers can be rented for a few dollars a day.

In what's called *butt-end* splicing, the two ends are cut on the frame line and then taped together without overlapping. *Tape* splicers are preferred in rough editing because they can easily be taken apart without losing even one frame. A tape splice can be done far more quickly than any cement splice. The tape is specially fabricated to withstand the rigors of projection and handling and to remain pliable and colorless.

Guillotine splicers are tape splicers that have machined die-set posts that guide the cutting blade on the frame line. Guillotine splicers also have a diagonal blade for use in editing magnetic stock. When two ends are placed end to end a Mylar splicing tape is stretched across it. With a single stroke of the guillotine handle, the tape is perforated and cut to conform with the film. Guillotine Model M.2-16mm-2T costs $225. A professional super 8mm version (Model S1) costs $276. Guillotine also manufactures a plastic model for super 8mm filmmaking. It's called the Semi-Pro and costs $20. Rivas 16mm tape splicers perform the same function as Guillotine splicers but use a perforated splicing tape. The model is preferred by some editors; costs about $170.

One of the simplest tools in filmmaking is a 16mm *splicing block*. Ediquip's model, which costs $13, is used with a single-edged razor blade and with perforated splicing tape or precut perforated tabs such as Kodak Press-Tapes. The latter, while expensive, are fast and easy ways to make a good butt-end splice with 16mm or super 8mm gauge.

A 50-foot roll of Guillotine optically clear Mylar 16mm splicing tape costs around $3. The super 8mm clear splicing tape costs $3.50 for a box with two rolls. Permacel 16mm single perforated splicing tape costs $8.75 for a 66-foot roll. Kodak Press-Tapes cost 75 cents for a packet of ten 16mm tabs. Super 8 packets cost the same. A ½-ounce bottle of Kodak splicing cement costs $1.

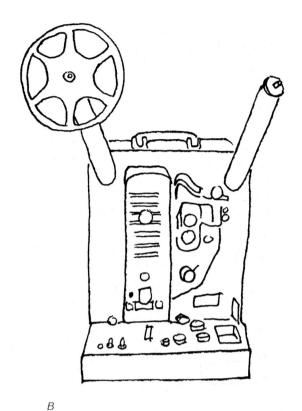

B

Editing Supplies

Here's a shopping list that include editing supplies required in both 16mm and super 8mm production.

trim bins (to hold 16mm film)	$75.00
reels (steel)—400 feet (16mm and super 8mm)	1.00
800 feet (16mm and super 8)	2.75
1,200 feet (16mm and super 8)	3.25
800 feet split reels	17.00
cores (plastic)— 2 inches, 16mm and super 8mm	.10
film leader (available in 1,000-foot rolls only)	
16mm single-perforated positive academy	66.00
16mm single- or double-perforated black (light struck)	15.00
16mm single- or double-perforated clear	7.00
16mm single-perforated white leader	15.00
super 8mm white leader (50-foot rolls)	3.00
grease pencils (white, red, yellow)	.50
Sharpie felt-tip pens	.50
editing gloves (small/large) per dozen	4.50
film-meter stopwatch (plastic housing)	40.00
Lupe magnifier (8x)	2.50

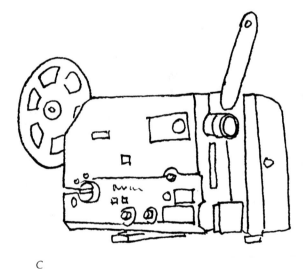

C

18.11

General Projection Requirements

Film projectors are much alike. They project and rewind movie film from metal or plastic reels. Many of them feature *automatic threading* systems. In 16mm sound projectors there is an *excitor lamp* and an *amplification/speaker system.* In super 8 sound projectors there is a *record/playback magnetic head,* plus amplifier, speaker, and input receptacles. (Figure 18.11).

An important feature of any projector is the loving care it provides to film. All projectors claim to be safe, but some aren't—particularly the self-threading mechanism. *Beware the auto-shreds.* Ask around before you purchase a projector.

These four features will generally help you spot and evaluate the differences in various projectors.

Light intensity: Check the wattage of the projector's lamp. If you require a projector for screenings in a large auditorium, check out the specially modified 16mm and super 8mm projectors with Zenon lamps.

Zoom lenses are only occasionally helpful. It's a feature built into many super 8mm projectors. With 16mm projectors you select a specific lens to provide the width of *throw* you'll require.

Variable projection speed is a very, very useful feature for animators. Slower-than-normal speeds allow the study of animated movements in detail, as if the film had been shot at six or seven frames at one time instead of the usual two. Faster-than-normal projection is less useful, but occasionally it helps one to discern qualities within the overall pacing of a sequence. An important feature if you're rotoscoping is a *single-frame* device that allows the projector to hold just a single frame. In order to prevent the hot projection bulb from burning the held frame, a wire screen automatically falls between the film and the lamp when the single-frame device is used. Unfortunately, this screen darkens the image considerably.

Sound: As discussed elsewhere, many of today's super 8 projectors have capabilities of recording and playing back an audio track that is placed on one edge of the super 8 film. Other projectors have outlets that allow them to be synced up with external audio recording and playback devices. There are many, many special features and options and specifications to consider when purchasing a sound projector. Consult a dealer or a technical manual for more discussion and guidance.

19

Art Supplies, Film Stocks, and Lab Services

It's an easy bet that if you've acquired this book you have a special affinity for all those tools and supplies that are involved in making marks and creating art. Browse through the following items to see which art materials you'll need for your own work—and which you'd like to have, well, just to have.

Papers

Animation bond paper— 10¼ by 12½ inches (#12 field size), punched for either Oxberry or Acme pegging: 250 sheets, $12; 5,000 sheets, about $100.

Animation bond paper—10¼ by 25 inches, 250 sheets, $17.

Animation bond paper—10¼ by 12½ inches, unpunched, 250 sheets, $6; 5,000 sheets, $85.

Background paper—2-ply weight, 10¼ by 14 inches, white vellum finished, punched for Oxberry or Acme, 50 cents each.

Background paper—in roll form, from 2-foot to 750-foot lengths, 60 cents per foot.

Tracing vellum—10¼ by 12½ inches, punched for either Oxberry or Acme, 100 sheets, $5.

Standard papers—a wide variety of quality papers, 8½ by 11 inches, which can be easily and effectively used in animation (#10 field), are available. Check your stationery or art supply store for prices of reams of medium quality paper, a finer quality drawing paper, and various gauges of tracing papers.

Flip-books—white pads, 5 by 7 inches, 50 pages. Less than 25 cents each, the cost varies with the number purchased.

Color-Aid papers—These special papers are used because of their adaptability and quality. Each is silk-screened with flat matte color that doesn't bleed. Color-Aid papers come in 210 coordinated colors (24 basic hues with 5 tints and 3 shades each, plus 16 grays and black and white). These papers take pencil, pastel, ink, tempera, and acrylics. The surface is water resistant and heavy enough to withstand handling and erasing. Single sheets, 18 by 24 inches, 50 cents; 24 by 36 inches, $1. Color-Aid Swatch Book (210 colors), 5 by 7 inches, $13. *Note:* Quality colored papers are also manufactured by Color Vu, Pantone, Tru-Tone, etc.

Construction paper—inexpensive, assorted colors, 50-sheet packages; 12 by 18 inches, $2.20; 18 by 24 inches, $4.25.

Day-Glo papers—come in assorted colors and sizes.

Background color cels—#12 field size, punched, pastel colors and black; 50, $7.15.

ELIOT NOYES: Here and on following pages, frames from *Clay: Origins of Species, 41 Barks,* title sequence to PBS's *Visions* series, and *Sandman.*

Cels

Clear acetate animation cels—punched for either Oxberry or Acme, .005-mil thick, 10¼ by 12½ inches (for a #12 field); 100 sheets, $18; 500 sheets, $54. Also 10¼ by 25 inches, 40 cents each; 100 sheets, $30.

Clear acetate animation cels—unpunched, 10¼ by 12½ inches, 200 sheets, $28; 1,000 sheets, $95. Wider sheets are also available.

Clear acetate sheets—for creating your own cels or as overlays and wild cels; thicknesses vary and costs for sheets 24 by 40 inches range from 84 cents to $6.60, depending on thickness.

Frosted and colored cels—available in #12-field dimensions; 20 cents each (frosted), $1.60 (colored).

Implements and Colors

Animation Paints. Professional cel paints are specially fabricated for use on acetate cels, vinyl, foil, glass, illustration board, watercolor paper, and Color-Aid paper. They can be used with an airbrush, are thinned with water and will not chip, crack, or flake. There are approximately 50 standard colors plus 30 shades of gray. All these colors are available with cel-level compensation. Basic colors are rated at #20 and each level of cel requires the next lower number—for example, a green #18 would be two levels below the top level of GR-20. Available in squat glass jars or spout-top squeeze bottles, in sizes of 2 ounces ($2 to $2.50), 4 ounces ($3.20 to $4), pint, quart, and gallon. Sets of colors can be purchased at discount rate from suppliers such as Cartoon Color, Inc. (See Chapter 22).

Black cel ink. This ink is opaque, waterproof, freeflowing, and acetate adhering; 2 ounces, $2, 4 ounces, $3.75.

Inking Pens. Traditional inking pens are comprised of a simple hardwood holder and steel pen points. The holders cost 50 cents each and the pen points (medium, fine, and flexible), 35 cents each. Some animators like to use Rapidograph pens that have interchangeable points. Pens, $11, replacement points, approximately $5 each.

Strip Chart. A set of acetate sheets showing 44 basic colors, 32 grays, and more than 600 compensating tint colors. A strip chart is used in selecting and ordering animation cel paints. Price: $30.

Opaquing Brushes. A crow-quill brush costs 35 cents. Sable watercolor brushes with round points are available in 6 sizes and are priced from $3.50 to $11.

Poster (Tempera) Colors. These opaque paints come in jars, are fully intermixable, and dry to a flat, brilliant surface. They can be used with brush, pen, or airbrush and are available in boxed assortments of colors (six ⅞-ounce jars, $1.80; sixteen ⅞-ounce jars, $4.60) or in individual bottles (2 ounces, $1; and 16 ounces, $3.60).

Watercolor Paints. There are two types of watercolors: transparent and opaque. The latter is generally preferred for use in animation. A large selection of tube colors are available, costing from $1.20 to $2 each. There are also boxed sets; for example, a 24-color Pelikan Opaque Watercolor set costs $11.50.

Acrylic (Polymer Emulsion) Paints. These paints come in tubes, have many of the characteristics of oil paints, yet are water soluble and

dry very quickly. Acrylic paints mix well with watercolors and temperas. A Polymer Gloss Medium mixes with these colors to produce a varnish finish, while a matte medium reduces normal gloss. An introductory set of six 2-ounce tubes, $6.85.

Pastels. Hard or soft pastels in a huge variety of hues, tints, and shades are available. A Grumbacher set of 30 half-length sticks, $5.50. Nupastel Color sticks, which are firmer and stronger than ordinary pastels, are available in 48 hues ($14.40) and 96 hues ($28.80). Cray-Pas, a compound of crayon and pastels, are available in 50 colors ($6.50).

Charcoal Sticks. Hard, soft, regular, and medium textures are available; 24 sticks, $3.

Pencils. Swan All-Stabilo pencils will write on paper, cels, glass, plastic, and metal. They are very smooth and will adhere to cels for a different look. Available in 6 colors at 60 cents each or $6 a dozen.

Markers. For use on paper, there are many, many brand names on today's market. Sets of markers provide more than two dozen different colors. If you want to use markers directly on acetate cels or on strips of 16mm film, you must select a marker that will stick to these plastic surfaces. Be certain to do your own testing—some markers advertised as "writes on anything" simply won't adhere to acetate. Brands that I can recommend are Magic Marker Studio Markers (a set of 12, around $12) and Sanford's Sharpie pens (a set of 8, $3.50).

Miscellaneous Materials

Storyboard Pads. Storyboard layout pads are specially designed as "work-up" aids in visualizing a sequence or entire movie. Each frame (drawn within the format of a television screen) has space beneath it for audio information (dialogue/music/effects) or for script notations. Storyboard layout pads come in a variety of different sizes and sets of frames. Three options: 8- by 18-inch pad with 4 sections per sheet (75 sheets, $3.90); 19- by 21-inch pad with 12 sections per sheet (50 sheets, $7.70); 8½- by 11-inch pad with 21 sections per sheet (50 sheets, $2.70).

Dry Transfer Letters. Dry transfer lettering, an easy and economical way to create professional quality lettering, is available in large plastic sheets bearing multiple individual letter and number forms. The sheet is aligned to the position desired and each form is transferred to the paper beneath the letter sheet by simple burnishing. Dry transfer letters come in all imaginable styles and sizes. Color sheets are also available. The major producers are Chartpak, Letraset, Prestype, Tactype, and Deca-Dry. A single sheet of dry transfer lettering should cost well under $2.

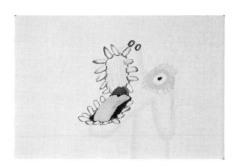

Dimensional Letters. Three-dimensional letter forms, usually ceramic or plastic, which can be used in creating titles that are filmed under an animation camera, are available in various type styles, colors, and sizes. Manufacturers include Craft Industries, Hernard Letters, Mitten Display Letters, and Stickee Pressure Sensitive Letters.

Reinforcements. Double-ply bristol reinforcements are used to strengthen damaged peg holes or to protect heavily used cels, backgrounds, or papers. These are available in strips or in self-sticking single peg-hole reinforcements. The strips cost 8 cents each (a set of

three single reinforcements, 20 cents). (Specify Oxberry or Acme when you order.)

Peg Hole Strips: Bristol paper strips (.009-inch thick), 12½ by 18 inches, are available in Acme and Oxberry punch systems. These are taped onto undersized cels, paper, or background paintings. Also used for changing animation, overlays, or backgrounds and to convert any artwork to standard pegging registration. Price: 100-peg strips, around $3.

Cutout Mattes. Made of heavy black stock, these mattes are used in making "finished" storyboards, which will be formally presented to a client or producer. As with storyboard layout pads, each frame represents a TV screen and beneath it there is space for directions or sound track instructions. Price: one sheet (17 by 22 inches), $1.25.

Cotton Gloves. White cotton gloves are worn in cel animation in order to protect cels from the oil of hands. Ink and paint won't adhere to an oily surface. Price: small and large sizes, 60 cents a pair, $5 a dozen.

A *transparent triangle, French curves,* and *rulers with beveled edges* are all useful tools in preparing artwork for animation. There are also many styles of *lettering templates.*

Additional art materials that are often required for animation include: masking tape, pushpins, scissors, matte knife, single-edged razor blades, rubber cement with applicator and thinner, white-out, white tape, Scotch tape, gaffer's tape, pencils, sharpeners, kneaded and pink-pearl-type erasers, and grease pencils. Experiment with other materials, for through them you can discover a new technique well suited to your drawing style.

Orientation: Film Stocks

Although many, many different film stocks are manufactured for 16mm and super 8mm filmmaking, only a few of these are used regularly for animation. This section introduces them to you. As with everything else in animated filmmaking, there's no end to what you can know about the nature and qualities of different motion picture films— or about the processes of developing and printing.

What goes into the camera is called *raw stock.* There are two basic kinds.

Reversal film is developed so that the *camera original* provides a series of *positive images* that can be projected. All super 8mm film is reversal stock—what goes through the camera is what comes back from the laboratory, ready to be screened. In still photography, a familiar example of reversal film is the ordinary color slide. The film stock that enters the camera unexposed is the same object that is subsequently projected.

Negative film is developed into a negative image in terms of the object that has been photographed—light areas appear darkest on the negative film, etc. When developed, negative film *must be printed* onto another negative film in order to create a projectable series of images. Thus, with negative film the animator always has a "negative"—an unprojectable camera original that has to be reprinted in order to be seen. (Almost all black-and-white still photography involves use of negative stocks that are developed and then printed onto negative papers.)

The overall visual characteristics of reversal films are generally considered to be better than negative films. Prints can be made easily from either kind of camera original. In the printing process, however, negative film yields a greater ability to change the exposure levels. But it is easier to handle and print reversal stocks and, on balance, many animators prefer reversal to negative.

There are, of course, *color* and *black-and-white* stocks. The characteristics of emulsion that differentiate films in either category are classified under these headings:

Contrast refers to the separation of lightness and darkness (called *tones*) in a film or a print. Adjectives like "soft" and "hard" or "flat" and "contrasty" are used to describe variations of contrast. Note that there are special *high-contrast* stocks that polarize the image toward the extremes of black and white in the tonal range. These high-contrast stocks (available in reversal or negative 16mm film) are useful to animators in filming white paper sheets and many bottomlighting techniques.

Speed of a film stock refers to the inherent sensitivity of an emulsion under specified conditions of exposure and development. Film stocks are constantly being developed that have higher speeds— that is, they require less light to achieve a good image. Such stocks, while very important to live-action filmmakers (especially cinéma-vérité documentarists), are relatively unimportant to animators who have great control over lighting conditions. A more significant factor for the animator is the sharpness and granularity that is related to film speed. The slowest color emulsions are the sharpest and have the finest grain.

Graininess or granularity is a quality of the image's physical/chemical structure. An individual frame of film seen via projection or through magnification will possess a grainy structure. The effect of grain—its perceived value—is largely an aesthetic choice. But granularity is directly related to *photographic sharpness*—the ability of an emulsion to record fine detail distinguishably. Most animators prefer a sharp and highly defined or low-grained image.

Exposure Index is a scale that provides a number that is used with photoelectric meters to help determine the correct exposure of a particular stock. Index ratings are given in *ASA numbers* that appear on every film container. There are two ratings for each stock—one for use of the film outdoors (daylight) and one for use under artificial lights (tungsten). Animators prefer a low index number for overall emulsion quality.

Color saturation and spectral sensitivity are terms that refer to color reproduction characteristics. Different stocks will yield slightly different colors—some are "warmer" (emphasize the red/yellow end of the spectrum) and some are "cooler" (blue/green are emphasized). The reason for this is that color dies (cyan, magenta, and yellow), which make up the emulsion, will respond differently to variations of light wavelengths. Also, different manufacturers of film stocks make different judgments as to what constitutes a pure shade of, say, red. Color specification, it turns out, is a highly subjective judgment. And so also are variations of "richness," of reproduced colors vis-à-vis the original colors being photographed. This latter quality is called *saturation*. Underexposure tends to encourage "rich" saturation.

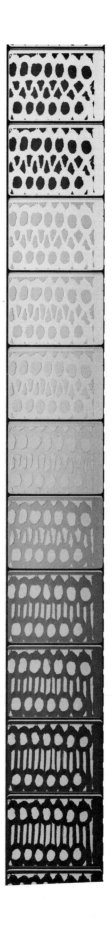

Orientation: The Motion Picture Laboratory

Listen to your mother: Be nice to people who can help you. Don't forget to say thank you. I'm speaking from experience. You never know when you'll need help. Don't worry but be careful. Remember to wear a nice smile. And remember, many a live wire would be a dead end without its connections. Believe me. I'm your mother and I know.

Place the staff of your local film lab at the top of your Maintain Friendly Relations list. The expertise, cooperation, and pride of craft of the film lab combines to form a silent partner for the animator in any creative production.

Although the standard lab services (described below) ought to be enough to convince you that Mother's advice is sound, it is only when you encounter a real problem—a crisis—that you'll appreciate the invaluable counsel and irreplaceable resources that a first-rate lab provides. Next to Direct Relatives, you can count on Lab People.

Along with the "normal" services catalogued here, the lab can deal a bit of wizardry that you should know about. The lab will push or flash your raw stock. It can color-correct. It will blow up, reduce, and otherwise ready a finished film for sale and distribution. The lab can repair damaged footage (the process is called rejuvenation). Labs can help you hide cel scratches, clean dirty film, and in other ways help your movie look as good as possible.

Best of all, the lab's highly trained and thoroughly professional staff can give you the advice, encouragement, and direct support that comes from years of experience with every imaginable film production problem. The lab can troubleshoot for you, direct you to specialists and specialized services, save you time and money and heartache. So, as with a cup of hot chicken soup, equate a good lab with nourishment, friendliness, and survival.

Super 8mm Lab Services

Processing. Although super 8mm animators generally tend to deal with a local camera shop in purchasing and processing super 8mm cartridges, it's important to know that you can go directly to labs that process the film on a same-day and overnight basis (see Chapter 22). Processing of Kodachrome 40 varies in cost from $1.65 per roll to almost a dollar more.

Push Processing. Although available at only a few labs, 1-stop and 2-stop pushed processing can be requested when shooting with very limited light—when the exposed but unprocessed film stock is underexposed. Pushing tends to maximize grain and contrast. These services are not generally needed by animators, but they can be used for creative effect. A minimum billing is usually required. Pushed processing costs about $5 per roll.

Enlargement. Modern lab equipment makes it very possible and usually successful to enlarge super 8mm film to 16mm film. In live-action filmmaking, there is often a problem in that super 8 is shot at a camera speed of 18 frames per second, while 16mm film has a standard of 24 frames per second. This is not, however, a problem with animated films that are shot frame by frame in both formats. If you are planning to enlarge a super 8mm film, you should base your timing of moves and track at the 24 fps speed. Prices for enlargement are always given in cost per 16mm foot. To compute 16mm footage, multiply the super 8mm footage by 1.8. Add 10 feet for lab thread-up. Many labs have a minimum charge for enlargement. Silent enlargement costs from 25 cents to 30 cents per 16mm foot for both color and black and white. Enlargement to 16mm format with optical track costs about 40 cents per 16mm foot.

Reduction. The reduction of 16mm format to super 8mm format may be required in order to include found or original 16mm footage in a super 8mm film. To compute the super 8mm length, divide the given 16mm footage by 1.8. Prices are given in cost per super 8mm foot and there may be a minimum charge required. Add 10 feet for thread-up. Price: silent color or black-and-white super 8mm film, 20 cents per foot; magnetic super 8mm is approximately 30 cents per foot.

Contact Printing. Striking a print from super 8mm film is a relatively infrequent request, and for this reason, you may need to locate a lab that provides this specialized service. There are three kinds of contact prints: work prints, answer prints, and release prints. (see 16mm Lab Services for a description). Price: work prints, about 15 cents per foot; answer prints from A roll or A and B rolls, between 21 cents and 30 cents per foot; release prints, 17 cents to 20 cents per foot.

Opticals. Although one of the features of animated filmmaking is that it affords the filmmaker the control to do in-camera effects, these same optical effects can be done at the lab during contact printing processes. Here is a list of effects and their costs:

Cropping (frame line or image repositioning)	$10 each
Freeze frame	$6 each
Reverse action	$8 each
Matte wipes	$13 each
Lap dissolve	$5 each
Superimposition	depends on length
Step printing	depends on length

Sound Striping. After an edited super 8mm film is completed, it can be sent to a lab for striping—a thin coat of magnetic audio recording tape is attached to one edge. The film's sound track is later recorded onto this magnetic sound striping. If resplicing is necessary the charge is around 20 cents for each splice; there is usually a minimum footage requirement of 50 feet. Price: laminated magnetic striping: from 3 cents to 5 cents per foot; liquid magnetic striping: 8 cents per foot.

Other services for super 8mm include film cleaning, internegatives, prints from internegatives, sound magnetic work prints, answer prints, and release prints. See the discussion of 16mm services for more detail. In general, the trend toward professional super 8mm filmmaking brings to the smaller format all of the specialized lab services that presently exist for 16mm filmmaking.

16mm Lab Services

Developing. The costs vary according to the specific stock that is being developed. (A reminder that costs are always rising and the figures here and elsewhere within these pages are virtually guaranteed to be less than you'll need to spend.)

Forced developing is more common with 16mm labs than it is with super 8mm. Pushing 1 stop costs an additional .02 per foot and pushing 2 stops costs an additional .025 per foot.

Contact printing is commonly used in 16mm animation to produce a *work print* that is used in the editing process. This saves the camera original for use in making "finished" prints of the completed film. In creating what is called a *release print,* the process of 16mm filmmaking calls for the camera original to be laid out in a special way so that, in the printing process, the splices are masked and don't show up in the final film. The special layout is called *A & B rolling.* Consult a live-action manual for further information. At the lab, the A & B rolls are printed along with the optical master of the sound track to produce an *answer print.* If the answer print looks good in terms of printing exposure and color, then an *internegative* is produced. This composite is used to produce multiple *release prints.* Here are some rough costs for these reversal contact printing services:

	per foot
work print (one-light color)	$ .15
answer print (A & B rolls)	.30
internegative (color A & B) from reversal	.35
release prints 1 to 5	.175

Opticals. Fades cost $1.50 each; dissolves, $3 each. As in live-action film production, it is possible to use the lab for other specialized effects including freeze-frames, split screens, mattes, and superimpositions.

Miscellaneous Other Services

Animation Photography. Professional animation camera operators will shoot art materials that you have prepared. Your artwork should use the registration systems of high quality animation stands. *Pencil tests* involve shooting paper cels with a black-and-white reversal stock. Final photography is $8 per foot (without stock or processing). *Final photography of cels* onto color reversal stock costs $9 per foot.

Track Reading Services. The customer provides a ¼-inch magnetic audio tape and the service does the rest. The original tape is transferred to 16mm mag stock and then "read," frame by frame. The reading service completes an exposure sheet and returns this with the original tape and the 16mm mag stock. Track reading costs vary according to the type of reading that is being done: narration, 90 cents per second; lip-synchronization, $1.70 per second; sound effects, $1.20 per second; and music is $1.50 per second.

Sound Transfer. To transfer sound from ¼-inch audio tape to 16mm full-coat magnetic recording stock costs $25 per half hour plus 3 cents per foot for the 16mm mag stock.

PART FOUR: RESOURCES

Photographs from *Animal Locomotion* (1887) by Eadweard Muybridge.

These last four chapters constitute a comprehensive listing of resources for animated filmmaking. In compiling the information that follows, I've been fortunate in being able to pool my research with that of the American Film Institute, an organization dedicated to the preservation and support of motion pictures in this country. Much of the information in Chapters 20, 21, and 22 will appear as an AFI *Factfile,* one of a series of information documents prepared by AFI's National Education Services program. These documents provide basic facts on a variety of topics in film and television. See Chapter 20 for more information on the American Film Institute and its publications.

20
Books, Periodicals, and Organizations

A considerable animation library has developed over the years. In the comprehensive bibliography that follows the material has been organized into three categories: *Books on Making Animated Films; Books on the History of Animation, Studios, Animators;* and *Books on Topics Related to Animation.* The last group is a hodgepodge of titles that, for one reason or another, seem to deserve mention within these pages.

You'll note that a few titles in each list have been given longer annotations than others. In my judgment, these works constitute a "core collection" on animation. I have read each of them carefully and can recommend them all highly. This is not to say that other titles aren't valuable. But I've only skimmed many of the books and a few I've never seen. You will, of course, have to do your own browsing to find works that serve your interests and your needs.

20.1 ANIMATION HISTORY: The history of animation begins with a 1906 film by James S. Blackton entitled *Funny Faces.* Here is a frame from it. *Courtesy John Canemaker.*

Books on Making Animated Films

Andersen, Yvonne. *Make Your Own Animated Movies: Yellow Ball Workshop Film Techniques.* Boston: Little, Brown, 1970. 16mm animation for children. Specific techniques are described for flip cards, clay, drawing on film, cutouts. Filmography.

———. *Teaching Film Animation to Children.* New York: Van Nostrand Reinhold, 1970. The director of the Yellow Ball Workshop describes simplified animation techniques and the equipment needed for animation workshops.

Barton, C. H. *How to Animate Cut-Outs.* New York: Focal Press, 1955. Simplified explanation of animation techniques.

Blair, Preston. *Animation: Learn How to Draw Animated Cartoons.* Laguna Beach, Calif.: Foster, 1949. Part of the "How to Draw" series. Published also as *Advanced Animation.* This large-format publication features Blair's own drawings along with a simplifed methodology of using geometric shapes as structural foundation in designing and drawing your own

animated characters. Although the book doesn't reach beyond the classic American or Disney style of character animation, it covers that art thoroughly and with such abundance of examples that the book is a classic.

———. *Animated Cartoons for Beginners.* Laguna Beach, Calif.: Foster, n. d. A beginning set of approaches for classic cartoon-type characters.

Bourgeois, Jacques. *Animating Films Without a Camera.* New York: Sterling, 1974. Describes the technique of drawing directly on film, information on materials needed and suggestions for projects.

Eastman Kodak Company. *Basic Titling and Animation for Motion Pictures.* 2nd ed., Publication S-21. Rochester, N.Y., 1976. Information designed for the amateur. A concise, clear, and helpful overview in 55 pages.

———. *Editing Single System Sound Super 8 Film.* Publication S-66. Rochester, N.Y., n.d. Equipment, procedures, editing steps, and suppliers of magnetic sound equipment.

_____. *Movies and Slides without a Camera*. Publication S-47. Rochester, N.Y., n.d. Thorough overview with information on Kodak stocks.

_____. *A Simple Wooden Copying Stand for Making Title Slides and Film Strips*. Publication T-43. Rochester, N.Y., n.d. Complete schematics for making a wooden copy stand and light table.

Graham, Donald W. *Composing Pictures*. New York: Van Nostrand Reinhold, 1970. Graham, head of Disney art studio, describes his animation teaching concepts.

Gross, Yoram. *The First Animated Step*. Sydney, Australia: Martin Educational, 1975. An introduction to making animated films within a school setting.

Halas, John, ed. *Computer Animation*. New York: Hastings House, 1974. 25 chapters by different experts in computer filmmaking. Technical information on specific methods. Glossary.

_____. *Film Animation: A Simplified Approach*. New York: UNIPUB, 1977. A 90-page booklet that provides a primer for simple animation techniques.

_____, and Bob Privett. *How to Cartoon for Amateur Films*. London: Focal Press, 1955. Outlines script preparation, use of equipment, cartoon photography, and other technical aspects of animation. Glossary.

_____, and Roger Manvell. *The Technique of Film Animation*. New York: Hastings House, 1968; originally published in 1959. Updated to include information on new animation techniques. A long-standing source book that samples most facets of animation production, aesthetics, and history. The title is somewhat misleading in that the volume is *not* primarily a production manual. While there is some treatment of non-cel forms of animation, the book is heavily biased toward studio production systems and character animation. A generous use of illustrations, sample graphics, and frame enlargements. Resource listings are inadequate. Recommended for a broad orientation to animation.

_____, ed. *Visual Scripting*. New York: Hastings House, 1973. The range of excellent samples that John Halas has built into this volume argues effectively for greater attention to storyboarding. The book begins with a dazzling example of a Sergei Eisenstein storyboard. Animators and film designers from all continents provide samples of their work with discussions of how they approach the basic design of an animated film. A

good book to consult as one is designing and planning a major creative work of his own.

Harryhausen. *Film Fantasy Scrapbook*. New York: Barnes, 1972. Outlines the techniques used in three-dimensional animated filmmaking. Special effects—such as matte process and front projection—are described.

Heath, Bob. *Animation in 12 Hard Lessons*. West Islip, New York: Robert P. Heath Productions, 1972. Step-by-step guidance for the self-taught animator.

Hobson, Andrew, and Mark Hobson. *Film Animation as a Hobby*. New York: Sterling, 1975. Description of basic animation techniques.

Holman, L. Bruce. *Puppet Animation in the Cinema: History and Technique*. New York: Barnes, 1975. Information on specific aspects of equipment, technique, and worldwide use of puppet animation.

Howard, Stan. *Scriptwriting for Animation*. New York: Hastings House, 1978. In press.

Kinsey, Anthony. *How to Make Animated Movies*. New York: Viking Press, 1970. Outlines specific animation processes and describes animation equipment. Brief history of animation. Bibliography.

_____. *Animated Film Making*. London: Studio Vista, 1970. Information for the amateur interested in animation.

Larson, Rodger, Lynne Hofer, and Jaime Barrios. *Young Animators and Their Discoveries*. New York: Praeger, 1973. Interviews with young filmmakers describing their experiences and techniques in making animated films. Glossary. Bibliography.

Levitan, Eli L. *Animation Art in the Commercial Film*. New York: Reinhold, 1960. Techniques used in making one-minute television commercials described. Glossary.

Lutz, Edwin George. *Animated Cartoons: How They Are Made, Their Origin and Development*. New York: Gordon Press, 1976 (originally published in 1920). Describes techniques, tools, and terminology used in animation. Bibliography, filmography, glossary.

Madsen, Roy P. *Animated Film: Concepts, Methods, Uses*. New York: Interland, 1969. This is one of the best volumes on animated filmmaking. Madsen's book is thoughtfully designed and presented. The volume's unique strength is the detail it provides on professional production techniques and tools used in full-cel animation. Additional areas of value include chapters on The Filmograph (Kinestasis), Planning and Drawing Cartoon Animation, Sound Recording and Bar Sheets, and Exposure Techniques. An excellent glossary.

Manvell, Roger. *The Animated Film.* New York: Hastings House, 1955. Information on the history and the craft of animation.

McLaren, Norman. *Cameraless Animation.* National Film Board of Canada, 1958. Available free from NFBC, 1251 Avenue of the Americas, New York, N.Y., 10020

Nelson Roy P. *Cartooning.* Chicago: Henry Regnery, 1975. Overview of the craft and its techniques.

Perisic, Zoran. *The Animation Stand.* New York: Hastings House, 1976. This nifty paperback gives a thorough and clear discussion of all the capabilities of, and the related effects that can be achieved with, the animation stand or, as it's called in Great Britain, the rostrum camera. Through profuse illustration and succinct text, Perisic provides cookbook clarity to the mysteries and high technology of the sophisticated animation stand. Titles of just a few of the 75-odd topics: Split-Scan, Calculating a Motorized Zoom, Travelling Mattes, Bipak Printing Effects, Aereal Image Projection Shooting, Shadow Board Effects, Exposure Aids, and Pantograph Table. Highly recommended.

———. *The Shooting Guide to Shooting Animation.* New York: Hastings House, in press.

Reiniger, Lotte. *Shadow Theatres and Shadow Films.* New York: Watson-Guptill, 1970. Theory and technique for this form of cutout animation.

Salt, Brian G. D. *Basic Animation Stand Techniques.* Elmsford, N.Y.: Pergamon Press, 1977. An introduction to the use of the animation stand.

———. *Movements in Animation.* Elmsford, N.Y.: Pergamon Press, 1976. A guide to technical methods and calculations used by animators.

Trojanski, John, and Louis Rockwood. *Making It Move.* Dayton, Ohio: Pflaum/Standard, 1973. Simplified explanations of animation techniques.

Wentz, Bob. *Paper Movie Machines.* San Francisco: Troubador Press, 1975. Designed for young readers, this book shows one how to make a number of animation toys including a thaumatrope, a phenakistoscope, a zoetrope, and a praxinoscope.

Flip-books

La Cinémathèque Canadienne published twelve flip-

books on the Occasion of the World Retrospective of Animation Cinema, 1967. Available from La Cinémathèque Canadienne, 360 Rue McGill, Montreal, Quebec, Canada, H24 2E9. Titles include: *Baccanal* (Shamus Culhane); *Le Dompteur* (Vladimir Lehnky); *The Room* (Yoji Kuri); *Felix* (Otto Messmer); *Flix* (Robert Breer); *Gaminerie* (Emile Cohl); *Infidélité* (Zdenek Miler); *Man and His World* (Kai Pindal): *Metamor-Flip* (Peter Foldès); *Nudnik* (Gene Deitch); *Le Papillon* (Jan Lenica); and *Premiere Cigarette* (Emile Cohl).

George Griffin publishes a series of flip-books that are available from Printed Matter, Inc., 7 Lispenard St., New York, N.Y. 10013. Titles include: *5 Windows* (from *Head*); *L'Age Door* (from *L'Age Door*); *Untitled;* and *Face Phases* (from *Head*).

Thumbflix International Ltd. publishes two Disney-derived flip-books (one with Mickey Mouse and Pluto, one with Donald Duck and Pluto). For information write 191 King's Cross Road, London WC1, England.

Books on the History of Animation, Studios, Animators

Adamson, Joe. *Tex Avery: King of Cartoons.* New York: Popular Library, 1975. General information on the art of animation and on Avery's contributions to the field.

AFI Report, Vol. 5, No. 2 (Summer 1974). Animation issue. Articles on Hollywood animation, Winsor McCay; interviews with Frank Mouris, Eliot Noyes, Jr., Richard Huemer. Pull-out chart on the history of Hollywood cartoon-producing studios.

Bain, David, and Bruce Harris. *Mickey Mouse: Fifty Happy Years.* New York: Crown, 1977. Picture-book format detailing the films of Mickey Mouse. Filmography, bibliography.

Barrier, Mike. *History of American Animation.* New York: Oxford University Press, 1978.

Bocek, Jaroslav. *Jiří Trnka: Artist and Puppet Master.* Prague; Artia, 1965. Life and work of Trnka, foremost puppet animator.

Cabarga, Leslie. *The Fleischer Story.* New York: Crown Press, 1976. Examines the contributions of animator Max Fleischer. Filmography.

Canemaker, John. *The Animated Raggedy Ann & Andy: The Story Behind the Movie.* New York: Bobbs-Merrill, 1977. This book has value beyond the context of its development, which was the making of Richard

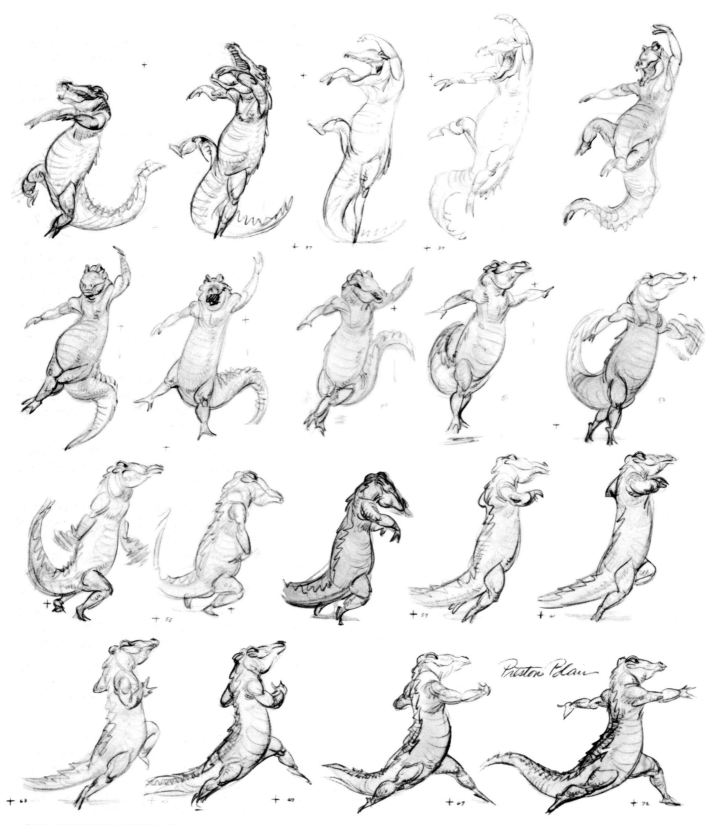

20.2   CARTOON VIRTUOSITY: A master animator's art is not simply to make a series of drawings move, but to make them move with recognizable elements of character, emotion, and life. This series of key drawings is reproduced from *Animation–How to Draw Animated Cartoons* by Preston Blair.

Williams' feature-length animated film *Raggedy Ann & Andy*. Canemaker has collected and presented many pieces of original art and the book provides a valuable case study of the systems (and dangers) of large-scale studio animation. Better, the book portrays fully the techniques used in character animation and it introduces the reader to some of the best animators around. Chapter on history. Beautifully and lavishly designed with many full-color reproductions. Highest recommendations.

Ceram, C. W. *Archaeology of the Cinema*. New York: Harcourt, Brace and World, 1965. A study of early techniques and tools and their developmental process.

Collins, Maynard. *Norman McLaren*. Canadian Film Institute, 1976. A valuable study of McLaren's development as an artist. Discussion of his films.

Edera, Bruno. *Full-Length Animated Feature Films*. New York: Hastings House, 1977. International survey of animated features. History and technique examined. Bibliography.

Field, Robert, D. *The Art of Walt Disney*. New York: Macmillan, 1942. The history, working conditions, and operation of the Disney studios.

Finch, Christopher. *The Art of Walt Disney*. New York: Abrams, 1973. Historical examination of the Walt Disney studio and productions. Information on Disneyworld and Disneyland. Bibliography.

Gelman, Woody. *Little Nemo by Winsor McCay*. New York: Nostalgia Press, 1972. Reprint of the comic strip from 1905-1910, just before it was made into animated cartoons.

Halas, John, *Computer Animation*. New York: Hastings House, 1976. This is a highly technical manual with articles by twenty practitioners within the evolving area of computer animation. Many of the discussions too technical for the beginner, but the photographs of computer-generated imagery lure the reader into the text and a few historical/testimonial passages eloquently forecast new vistas of animation technique and aesthetics.

———, and Walter Herdez. *Film & TV Graphics*. New York: Hastings House, 1967. See following annotation.

———, and Roger Manvell. *Art in Movement: New Directions in Animation*. New York: Hastings House, 1970. Both volumes share the essential service of providing examples of imagery from animated films produced in many countries and for various purposes. The range is terrific. The books become an idea file, a place to cross-reference one's own impulses with graphic styles used by other artists. In both books a spare critical/developmental text is helpful, if limited.

———, and David Rider. *The Great Movie Cartoon Parade*. New York: Bounty Books, 1976. Picture book of major cartoon characters with some historical background. Index to production companies and their animated work.

Heraldson, Donald. *Creators of Life: A History of Animation*. New York: Drake, 1975. Overview of the historical developments in animation, with some information on technique.

Herdeg, Walter. *Film & TV Graphics 2*. New York: Hastings House, 1976. The volume's subtitle is "An International Survey of the Art of Film Animation." It's indeed that. Page after page presents beautifully reproduced frame enlargements for a huge spectrum of recent works, many in full color. Major sections: Entertainment, Television, Commercial Films; Film Titles and Captions; and Experiments.

Holloway, Ronald. *Z Is for Zagreb*. New York: Barnes, 1972. History of the Zagreb (Yugoslavia) Cartoon Studio. Chronological listing of its films. Biographical information on the animators.

Lutz, E. G. *Animated Cartoons—How They Are Made, Their Origin and Development*. New York: Scribner's, 1920. Prehistory of animation.

Maelstaf, R. *The Animated Cartoon Film in Belgium*. Brussels: Ministry of Foreign Affaris, 1970. History of the Belgian animated cartoon from the 1920s to present day. Lists Belgian animation training schools. Filmography.

Maltin, Leonard. *The Disney Films*. New York: Crown, 1973. Information on the Disney feature animated films, live-action films, shorts, and television shows. History of the studio. Credits for the productions.

Manvell, Roger. *The Animated Film*. New York: Hastings House, 1954. Nontechnical information on the history and craft of animation and on the making of *Animal Farm*.

Marek, K. W. *Archaeology of the Cinema*, New York: Harcourt, Brace & World, 1965. Toys and machines that led to development of cinema and animation.

McCay, Winsor. *Little Nemo 1905–1906*. New York: Nostalgia Press, 1976. Reprint of the comic strip before it was made into a film.

Museum of Modern Art Film Library. *A Short History of*

Animation. New York, 1940. International survey of the field.

Russett, Robert, and Cecile Starr, *Experimental Animation: An Illustrated Anthology.* New York: Van Nostrand Reinhold, 1976. I believe this is the first work to deal solely with the films of independent animators who have been and are continuing to chart domains of "experimental" or noncharacter techniques of animated filmmaking. While the artists' own comments and graphic citations are valuable, the volume is somehow disappointing. It seems to canonize without real criticism. Glossary, filmography, bibliography.

20.3 FLIP-BOOKS: A collection of flip-books that have been published by independent animator George Griffin. The photograph also shows a short 16mm film made from one of the books.

Schickel, Richard. *The Disney Version.* New York: Avon, 1968. Observations on the social functions and implications of Disney films.

Singer, Marilyn, ed. *New American Filmmakers.* New York: The American Federation of the Arts, 1976. Lists works shown at the Whitney Museum of American Art Film Program. Also serves as a rental catalogue.

Sitney, P. Adams. *Visionary Films.* New York: Oxford University Press, 1974. A critical study of experimental films, many of which use animated techniques.

Stephenson, Ralph. *The Animated Film.* New York: Barnes, 1973. Information on worldwide animation history and current trends. Bibliography. Filmographies.

_____. *Animation in the Cinema.* New York: Barnes, 1967. History of international animation. Bibliography. Filmography.

Thomas, Bob. *Walt Disney: An American Original.* New York: Simon & Schuster, 1976. Biographical information on Disney and a history of the studio.

_____. *Walt Disney: The Art of Animation.* New York: Simon & Schuster, 1958. Technical aspects of animation as well as filmography and description of Disney animation. Glossary.

White, Michael. *The Drawings of Norman McLaren.* Montreal: Tundra Books, 1975. Collection of McLaren's drawings. Biographical information. Filmography.

Books on Topics Related to Animation

Arnheim, Rudolph, *Art and Visual Perception: A Psychology of the Creative Eye.* Berkeley: University of California Press, 1965. The physiology and psychology of perception. Why we see what we see. Bibliography.

Baird, Bil. *The Art of the Puppet.* New York: Macmillan, 1965. Background and techniques for theatrical puppetry.

Bazelon, Irwin. *Knowing the Score.* New York: Van Nostrand Reinhold, 1976. About film music. This book contains an extensive interview with Gail Kubik, the composer of *Gerald McBoing-Boing.*

Becker, Stephen. *Comic Art in America.* New York: Simon & Schuster, 1959. History and criticism of comics, cartoon strips, and the single panel cartoon.

Bloomer, Carolyn M. *Principles of Visual Perception.* New York: Van Nostrand Reinhold, 1976. The process of visual perception. Chapters on Meaning, Vision, Constancy, The Brain, Space, Depth Distance. Annotated bibliography.

Burder, John. *The Technique of Editing 16mm Films,* rev. ed. New York: Hastings House, 1971. A well-illustrated, step-by-step guide to editing 16mm, including sound.

Churchill, Hugh B. *Film Editing Handbook: Technique of 16mm Film Cutting.* Belmont, Calif.: Wadsworth, 1972. Another good resource for 16mm editing.

Clauss, Hans, and Heinz Meusel. *Filter Practice.* New York: Focal Press, 1965. All you'd ever need to know about photographic filters.

Couperie, Pierre, and Maurice C. Horn. *A History of the Comic Strip.* New York: Crown, 1968. A fully illustrated study of the development of comic art. International perspective.

de Bono, Edward. *Lateral Thinking: Creativity Step by Step.* New York: Harper & Row, 1970. A guide to creative problem solving. Highly recommended.

Faubun, Don. *You and Creativity.* Beverly Hills: Glencoe Press, 1968. A moving and beautifully illustrated treatise on how and why man creates.

Fawcett, Robert. *On the Art of Drawing.* New York: Watson-Guptill, 1958. Considered a classic on its subject.

Fielding, Raymond. *The Technique of Special-Effects Cinematography.* New York: Hastings House, 1969. Comprehensive and fully illustrated resource.

Gillon, Edmund V., ed. *Picture Source Book for Collage & Decoupage.* New York: Dover. A book filled with etchings and other graphic black-and-white materials that can be used in collage films.

Grafton, Carol Belancer. *Optical Designs in Motion with Moire Overlays.* New York: Dover, 1976. Playing with the book relates somehow to the process of animating—not sure how.

Grahm, Donald. *Composing Pictures.* New York: Van Nostrand Reinhold, 1970. Considered a classic in the aesthetics of pictorial arrangement and design.

Hogarth, Burne. *Dynamic Figure Drawing.* New York: Watson-Guptill, 1970. Tips from one of the great masters.

Huntley, John, and Roger Manvell. *The Technique of Film Music.* New York: Hastings House, 1957. Important information and technical backgrounding if you find you want to exploit more fully the relationship between animation and musical sound.

Kuhns, William. *The Moving Picture Book.* Dayton, Ohio: Pflaum/Standard, 1975. A book built on frame enlargements from all kinds of movies. A visual lexicon of value. With a particularly good chapter on animation.

Lawder, Standish. *The Cubist Cinema.* New York: New York University Press, 1975. Backgrounding for appreciation of contemporary independent animators—especially those working in nonnarrative traditions.

Leavitt, Ruth, ed. *Artist and Computer.* New York: Harmony Books, 1976. Backgrounding and techniques for use of computers to generate graphic symbols.

Levitan, Eli L. *An Alphabetical Guide to Motion Picture, Television and Videotape Production.* New York: McGraw-Hill, 1970. An encyclopedia with pictures and descriptions on virtually every aspect of animated production. Good to have around.

Lipton, Lenny. *Independent Filmmaking,* rev. ed. San Francisco: Straight Arrow Books, 1972. Widely considered the best single volume ever produced on the tools and procedures of 16mm film production. I concur. A definitive resource.

————. *The Super 8 Book.* San Francisco: Straight Arrow Books, 1975. A very full and well-researched compendium on the rapidly evolving super 8mm technology. Highly recommended.

Malekiewicz, J. Kris. *Cinematography: A Guide for Filmmakers and Film Teachers.* New York: Van Nostrand Reinhold, 1973. Much like many texts of its kind, only this is particularly intelligent and well designed.

Mascelli, Joseph. *The Five C's of Cinematography.* Hollywood: Cine/Graphic Publications. A standard reference.

McKim, Robert. *Experiences in Visual Thinking.* Monterey, Calif.: Cole/Brooks, 1972. This has been one of the most valuable books that I've ever encountered. It articulates and presents stimulating projects on the process of creativity within the visual realm. Highest possible recommendation.

McLaren, Norman. *The Drawings of Norman McLaren.* Montreal: Tundra Books, 1975. It's nice to spend time with this pioneer's images and his genius.

Megen, Nick. *The Art of Humorous Illustration.* New York: Watson-Guptill. A broad collection of single-panel cartoons. Well selected and well presented.

Mikolas, Mark, and Gunther Hoos. *Handbook of Super 8 Production.* New York: Media Horizons Books, 1976. For my money, this is the best production and resource volume on super 8mm filmmaking. Well illustrated, although some sections are poorly conceived. Excellent overall; high recommendation.

Morrow, Jim, and Murry Suid. *Moviemaking Illustrated: The Comicbook Filmbook.* Rochelle Park, N.J.: Hayden, 1973. Although designed to introduce film language and techniques to young people, this book provides a useful comparison of serial comic art and film form. Valuable to animators.

Muybridge, Eadweard. *Animals in Motion* and *The Human Figure in Motion.* New York: Dover, 1955 and

1956, respectively. The time-motion studies by Muybridge are a continuing source of fascination, appreciation, and instruction to animators. Treat yourself to these volumes.

Prendergast, Roy M. *A Neglected Art.* New York: New York University Press, 1976. Contains an extensive look at music in animated films, focusing on the work of Scott Bradley, a composer, for M-G-M films.

Quigley, Martin *Magic Shadows—The Story of the Origin of Motion Pictures.* New York: Quigley, 1960. Another book on animation prehistory.

Renan, Sheldon. *An Introduction to the American Underground Film.* New York: Dutton, 1967. Although dated now, Renan's book sets an important background to the emergence of today's independent animators.

Rynew, Arden. *Filmmaking for Children.* Dayton, Ohio: Pflaum/Standard, 1971. There are many books that echo the perspective and content of this volume, but none approach its originality or clarity.

Schoenwolf, Herta. *Play with Light and Shadow: The Art & Techniques of Shadow Theater.* New York: Reinhold, 1968. A special sensibility and set of techniques that are useful in direct animation production genres.

Souto, H. Mario Raimondo. *The Technique of the Motion Picture Camera.* New York: Hastings House, 1969. Everything you could possibly want to know about what a camera is and how it works.

Periodicals

The following periodicals often contain information of interest to those making, teaching, and/or studying animation. See also AFI's *Factfile: Film and Television Periodicals in English,* April 1977. Sources of information for current articles on animation can also be found in *The Reader's Guide to Periodical Literature* and film periodical indexes *(Film Literature Index, New Film Index, International Index to Film Periodicals,* and *The Critical Index).*

The American Film. American Film Institute, P.O. Box 1571, Washington, D.C. 20013. Monthly, 10 issues a year, $15. A journal of the film and television arts. Occasional articles on animation.

Cinemagic. Cinemagic Publishing Company, Inc., P.O. Box 125, Perry Hall, MD. 21128. Quarterly, $6. Deals with special effects—particularly puppet animation and stop-motion techniques.

Filmmakers Newsletter. P.O. Box 115, Ward Hill, Mass. 01830. Monthly, $9. Animation column by Howard Beckerman a regular feature; covers festivals.

Media & Methods. North American Building, 401 North Broad St., Philadelphia, Pa. 19108. 9 issues a year, $9. Information on using media in the classroom; guides to teaching film and animation.

Millimeter. 12 East 46th St., New York, N.Y. 10017. Monthly, $10. Animation column by John Canemaker in each issue and annual animation issue; information on new techniques and equipment.

Mindrot. 3112 Holmes Ave., South Minneapolis, Minn. 55408. Published occasionally. 4 issues for $3. Described as a "Fanzine of the Hollywood Animated Cartoon." Has valuable filmographies and serves as a place for dialogue among cartoon fans.

Sightlines. Educational Film Library Association. 43 West 61st St., New York, N.Y. 10023. Quarterly to members of the EFLA. $15 year for personal membership. Reviews and articles on animation.

Super-8 Filmmaker. P.O. Box 10052, Palo Alto, Calif. 94303. 8 issues a year, $9. Regular animation column by Yvonne Andersen. Technical information, new equipment for super 8mm.

Today's Filmmaker. 250 Fulton Ave., Hempstead, N.Y. 11550. Quarterly, $6. Covers technical aspects of filmmaking and equipment.

Zoetrope. Animation Alumni Newsletter. 6737 North Greenview, Chicago, Ill. 60626. Produced by former students of the animation department at the Institute of Design in Chicago. Current information on the animation field, new publications, festivals.

Organizations

The following are national and international organizations that support the art of animation. Some of these are devoted to animated filmmaking and scholarship and some maintain a strong interest in animation within a broader context of support for all forms of the moving image media.

Do not overlook organizations at the local level that can provide important resources for people interested in animation. Schools and colleges with film production programs are usually a center for animation interest. Museums, libraries, and special film screening centers exist in many cities. State arts councils are important supporters of the film arts as well as other art forms, and strong regional film study and film production centers are developing throughout the United States.

American Film Institute (AFI)

The John F. Kennedy Center for the Performing Arts
Washington, D.C. 20566
(202)833-9300
Contact Jane Kearns, Senior Information Associate. AFI is an independent, nonprofit organization established in 1967 by the National Endowment for the Arts. AFI preserves films, operates an advanced conservatory for filmmakers, gives assistance to new American film-makers through grants and internships, provides guidance to film teachers and educators, publishes film books, periodicals and reference works, supports basic research, and operates a national film repertory exhibition program.

International Association of Animated Filmmakers (ASIFA)

ASIFA-International Headquarters
3/7 Kean St.
London W.C.
England

ASIFA-East
Department N, Room 1018
25 West 43rd. St.
New York, N.Y. 10036
(212)354-6410

ASIFA-Hollywood
Suite 210
6087 Sunset Blvd.
Hollywood, Calif. 90028
(213)462-0074

ASIFA is an international animated film association comprised of the leading animation artists from twenty-six countries. The organization sponsors annual festivals of international animation and has participated in the publication of a series of books on animation techniques. The U.S. branches of ASIFA are located in New York City, Hollywood, San Francisco, and Chicago. New branches will be formed in San Diego and Boston. Membership is $15 a year. John Halas is ASIFA president.

International Coordinating Bureau of the Institutes of Animation (BILIFA)

Columbia College
540 North Lake Shore Dr.
Chicago, Ill. 60611
(312)467-0300

Contact Robert J. Edmonds. An organization of U.S. and foreign animation schools. Encourages an exchange of curricula, student films, and general information. High schools, colleges, and universities are eligible for membership.

Center for Cinema Animation

Tully, N.Y. 13159
(607)842-6668
Contact L. Bruce Holman. Animation workshops and publications on a variety of animation topics.

Educational Film Library Association, Inc. (EFLA)

43 West 61st St.
New York, N.Y. 10023
(212)246-4533
Contact Nadine Covert. A membership service that includes individuals and institutions other than libraries. Provides information services, film evaluations, library. Annually coordinates the American Film Festival.

Motion Picture Screen Cartoonists, Local 839

12441 Ventura Blvd.
Studio City, Calif. 91604
(212)766-7151

Motion Picture Screen Cartoonists, Local 841

25 West 43rd St.
New York, N.Y. 10036
(212)354-6410
Locals of IATSE (International Alliance for Theatrical and Screen Employees). Will provide current information on the animation job market and trends in the field.

National Cartoonists Society

9 Ebony Court
Brooklyn, N.Y. 11229
(212)743-6510
Professional society of cartoonists and animators. Conducts placement service for its members, maintains a library of oral histories, and publishes a monthly newsletter.

Screen Cartoonists Guild, Local 986

1616 West Ninth St.
Los Angeles, Calif. 90015
(213)380-9860
A local of the Teamsters Union. Can provide information on animation employment trends.

Walt Disney Archives

500 South Buena Vista St.
Burbank, Calif. 91521
(213)845-3141, ext. 2424
Contact David R. Smith. Open by appointment to students and researchers working on specific projects. The collection includes publicity materials, stills, production files, films, music, and miscellaneous memorabilia of the Disney family, studio, theme parks, and publications.

Gertie the Dinosaur (1914) by one of the greatest early animators, Winsor McCay.

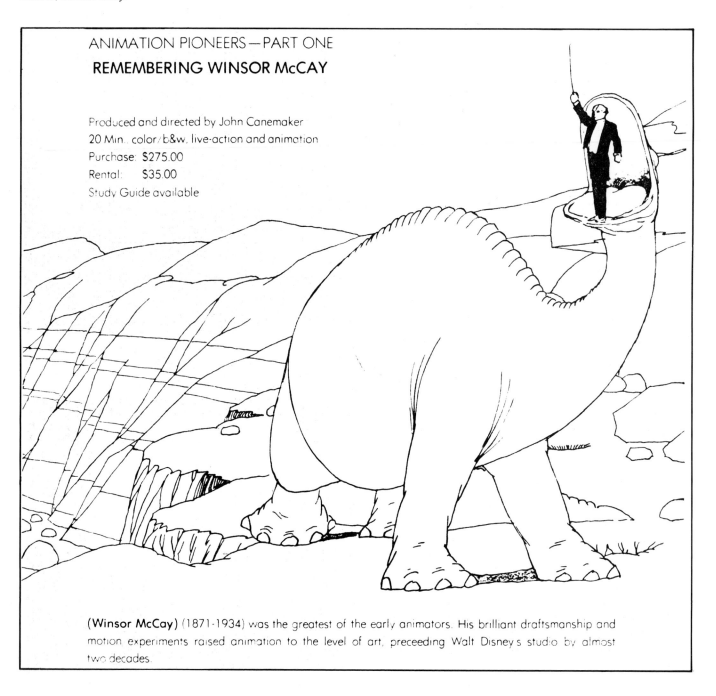

ANIMATION PIONEERS—PART ONE
REMEMBERING WINSOR McCAY

Produced and directed by John Canemaker
20 Min., color/b&w, live-action and animation
Purchase: $275.00
Rental: $35.00
Study Guide available

(Winsor McCay) (1871-1934) was the greatest of the early animators. His brilliant draftsmanship and motion experiments raised animation to the level of art, preceeding Walt Disney's studio by almost two decades.

21
Films, Distributors, Screening Centers, and Festivals

Thousands and thousands of animated films have been made and are presently in distribution. You can acquire 16mm prints of animated feature films as well as many kinds of shorter animated movies— from cartoons to educational films to art films. It's the goal of this chapter to help you see the best of what is available. Toward that end, you'll find titles of outstanding films about animation and also titles of films that have been selected to represent all the techniques covered in this book.

The medium continues to grow, of course. Each year many hundreds of new films are completed. Many of these make their way into distribution and, subsequently, into the collections of film libraries, archives, schools, museums, and private collections.

Unfortunately much of the richest work in today's animation never gets into distribution. It is quite difficult, for example, to rent or purchase prints of animated television spots, animated title sequences from live-action films, animation specials produced for television, or personal films produced by independent film artists. Just about the only place you'll ever have a chance to see such films—or to keep up with current releases—is at a film festival. Hence, you'll find a listing of major festivals at which animated films are regularly screened each year. Finally, the chapter lists 16mm distributors—the primary source of animated movies.

Films About Animation and Animators

Here's a filmography on movies that have been made about animation—its history, its practitioners, its techniques. For more complete descriptions I recommend you write to the appropriate distributor and request either a study-guide to the specific title and/or a copy of the distributor's catalogue.

In the citations that follow, the abbreviations refer to the film's distributor—see the end of the chapter for a key to the abbreviations and for the addresses of the distributors. All films are distributed in 16mm with optical sound tracks.

21.1   ANIMATION PIE: In documenting a workshop for high-school students that he conducted, Robert Bloomberg has created a very compact and stimulating introduction to many different animation techniques. *Courtesy Film Wright.*

ALEXIEFF AT THE PINBOARD. 8 min. (B&W) CS. Demonstration by Alexander Alexieff and Claire Parker of how they animate designs on the pinboard, a technique of their invention.

ANIMATION PIE. 25 min. FW. Film shows junior-high-school kids making a variety of animated films. Their work is sampled. A fine film—best of its kind—by animator Bob Bloomberg.

ANIMATION SAMPLER. 12 min. Distributed by the filmmaker Kit Laybourne, 180 Riverside Dr., New York, N.Y. 10024, and by the New Jersey State Arts Council, 27 West State St., Trenton, N. J. 08625. Collection of films made by high-school students using many different techniques. Documentary footage of workshop program.

ANNECY IMPROMPTU. 52 min. CS. Overview of pinscreen animation techniques and works developed by Alexander Alexieff and Claire Parker. Interviews with critics and animators.

THE ART OF LOTTE REINIGER. 14 min. AB. Demonstration of silhouette techniques pioneered by Ms. Reiniger. Excerpts from her films.

BEHIND THE SCENES AT WALT DISNEY'S STUDIO. 27 min. TF. Humorist Robert Benchley is taken for a tour of the Disney Studios.

COMPUTER GENERATION. 29 min. (B&W) FMC. This 1972 production by CBS-TV shows film artist Stan VanDerBeek making computer films at MIT.

EADWEARD MUYBRIDGE—ZOOPRAXOGRAPHER. 60 min. NYF. A creative biography of Muybridge. His time/motion photographic research is shown and animated.

THE EXPERIMENTAL FILM. 28 min (B&W) McG. A round-table discussion including statements by inde-

21.2 MOVING PICTURES: A frame enlargement from Richard Roger's portrait of animator Jan Lenica. *Courtesy Phoenix Films.*

pendent animators Robert Breer, Jan Lenica, and Norman McLaren. Produced by the National Film Board of Canada.

EXPERIMENTS IN MOTION GRAPHICS. 13 min. PYR. Computer filmmaker John Whitney discusses and samples the processes and aesthetic parameters of the computer animation processes used in his film *Permutations.*

THE EYE HEARS, THE EAR SEES. 58 min. LCA. A full-depth interview with Norman McLaren. He demonstrates his techniques and shows sequences from his work. Produced by the British Broadcasting Corporation.

FRAME-BY-FRAME: THE ART OF ANIMATION. 13 min. PYR. This film was designed to introduce various animation techniques. Features relatively low-technology approaches.

THE GENIUS OF WINSOR McCAY. 40 min. (B&W) CFS. This is a silent compilation of a number of films produced by McCay.

LET'S MAKE A FILM. 20 min. YB. A clear and straightforward study of the techniques developed by Yvonne Andersen in her animation workshops for young people.

THE LIGHT FANTASTIC. 57 min. NFBC. A detailed retrospective describes the development of animation at the NFB. Includes McLaren's hand-drawn and pixilation techniques, Evelyn Lambart's fairy-tale cutouts, Ryan Larkin's work, and more. An excellent resource.

THE MAGIC OF MELIES. 45 min. (B&W) CFS. A compilation of early works by George Melies.

MOVING PICTURES: THE ART OF JAN LENICA. 19 min. PH. Jan Lenica is shown creating a recent animated film *(Landscape)* that uses cutout techniques This documentary portrait was created by Richard Rogers during a year that Lenica spent at Harvard University's Carpenter Center. An excellent film.

OTTO MESSMER AND FELIX THE CAT. 25 min. From filmmaker John Canemaker, 120 West 70th St., New York, N.Y. 10023. Tribute to the man who created Felix, the first cartoon to express an individual personality in drawings that move (1919-1933).

PEN POINT PERCUSSION. 7 min. (B&W) IFB. Norman McLaren explains his techniques for creating an optical track—and film to go with it—by painting on clear 35mm film stock.

PINSCREEN. 40 min. NFBC. Documentary shows Alexander Alexieff and his wife, Claire Parker, working at the pinscreen.

THE PUPPETS OF JIŘÍ TRNKA. 20 min. PH. Valuable insights into the techniques—especially the scale—of Trnka's work. Recommended.

REMEMBERING WINSOR McCAY. 20 min. From filmmaker John Canemaker, 120 West 70th St., New York, N.Y. 10023. McCay was the greatest of the early animators. Film has interview with McCay's assistant, John A. Fitzsimmons. Generous excerpts from *Gertie the Dinosaur* (1914), *The Sinking of the Lusitania* (1918), and a hand-colored version of *Little Nemo* (1911).

THE SHAPE OF FILMS TO COME. 26 min. McG. A CBS-TV documentary provides an introduction to unusual techniques including the computer animation of Stan VanDerBeek and John Witney. Treatment of multiscreen and multi-image work, also. Filmmakers Chris Chapman, Frances Thompson, and Ed Emschwiller interviewed.

A SHORT HISTORY OF ANIMATION: THE CARTOON. 60 min. MOMA.

VANDERBEEKIANA. 29 min. (B&W) FMC. Interview in which Stan VanDerBeek describes and samples his early collage films and discusses the nature of animation.

WINDOW ON CANADA: AN INTERVIEW WITH NORMAN McLAREN. 30 min. (B&W) NFB. McLaren talks about and shows sequences from his work.

Films Representing Different Techniques

In compiling the lists below, I set myself a number of different goals. The most important was to select a very few works that could illustrate the full range of the art form. That alone is a challenging task and it requires some very subjective judgments. The selection process had additional criteria. One was to cite for each technique a group of films that would sample a variety of themes and graphic styles. Another was to include many different animators—with particular emphasis on young independent animators who are working within the kinds of technological parameters that this volume has explored. Finally, the selection process favored those films that are more widely known and which, therefore, are in relatively broad distribution. This will mean that it should be easy for you to rent these films or to find a print of them in a film library in your area.

At best, however, this is a highly arbitrary listing. It makes no pretense of representing a systematic or comprehensive survey of all that is available. It is instead a catalogue of personal favorites. I've tried to follow the criteria discussed above and I've listed only titles that I've seen myself and judge to be interesting examples of the techniques under which they are grouped. No annotations are provided because I find it impossible to represent with just a few words the visual style and meaning of even the shortest and simplest film.

The abbreviation at the end of each entry represents the name of the film's distributor. Often one title will be in distribution by a number of different nontheatrical 16mm distributors. The last section of this chapter lists all the distributors referred to in this and the preceding filmography.

CAMERALESS ANIMATION

Bass, Warren. *Uncle Sugar's Flying Circus*. 2½ min. AB.
Brakhage, Stan. *Mothlight*. 4 min. FMC.
Herbert, Pierre. *Op Hop*. 4 min. NFBC.
Lye, Len. *Colour Box*. 5 min. CFS.
McLaren, Norman. *Begone Dull Care*. 9 min. IFB.
McLaren, Norman. *Blinkety-Blank*. 5 min. IFB.
McLaren, Norman. *Lines Horizontal*. 7 min. CFS.
McLaren, Norman. *Pen Point Percussion*. 9 min. IFB.
Segal, Steven. *Red Ball Express*. 3 min. PER.
Smith, Harry. *Early Abstractions*. 28 min. FMC.

ANIMATING OBJECTS

Codere, Laurent. *Zikkaron*. 5 min. IFB.
Fischinger, Oskar. *Composition in Blue*. 4 min. PYR.
Fischinger, Oskar. *Muratti Cigarette Commercial*. 4 min. PYR.

21.3 WINSOR McCAY: Animator John Canemaker holds an original drawing from McCay's film *Gertie the Dinosaur* (1914). *Courtesy John Canemaker.*

Hoedeman, Co. *Tchou-Tchou.* 14 min. EBC.
McAdow, Ron. *Hank the Cave Peanut.* 14 min. YBF.
Munro, Grant. *Toys.* 8 min. McG.
Patel, Ishu. *Beadgame.* 6 min. NFBC.
Svankmajer, Jan. *Jabberwocky.* 14 min. SIM.
Varsanyi, Ferenc. *Honeymation.* 4 min. PYR.
Wilkosz, Tadeusz. *Bags.* 10 min. PYR.

CUTOUT AND SILHOUETTE ANIMATION

Faccinto, Victor. *The Secret of Life.* 15 min. AFA.
Griffin, George. *The Club.* 4½ min. SBC.
Jodoin, René. *Notes on a Triangle.* 5 min. IFB.
Kraning, Susan Pitt. *Crocus.* 7 min. SBC.
Lambert, Evelyn. *The Story of Christmas.* 8 min. FI.
Lambert, Evelyn. *Fine Feather.* 5 min. BM.
Lambert, Evelyn. *The Lion and the Mouse.* 4 min. BM.
Lenica, Jan. *Labyrinth.* 15 min. CFS.
Lenica, Jan. *Landscape.* 8 min. PH.
McLaren, Norman. *Spheres.* 8 min. IFB.
Munro, Grant, and Gerald Potterson. *My Financial Career.* 7 min. STERL.
Patel, Ishu. *How Death Came to Earth.* 14 min. McG.
Pintoff, Ernest. *The Critic.* 4 min. LCA.
Reiniger, Lotte. *Aucassin and Nicolette.* 15 min. NFBC.
Reiniger, Lotte. *Cinderella.* 10 min. McG.
Reznickova, Pavla. *Cecily.* 7 min. LCA.
Slason, Alan. *Tangram.* 4 min. PYR.
Smith, Lynn. *Shout It Out Alphabet.* 12 min. PH.
Smith, Lynn. *Teacher, Lester Bit Me.* 9 min. EDC.

TIME-LAPSE

Borowczyk, Walerian. *Renaissance.* 10 min. PYR.
D'Avino, Carmen. *Pianissimo.* 8 min. GP.
Feeney, John. *Sky.* 10 min. MCG.
Fischinger, Oskar. *Motion Painting #1.* 12 min. CFS.
Harris, Hillary. *Organism.* 20 min. PH.
Lamb, Derek. *House-Moving.* 8 min. (B&W), PH.
Laughlin, Kathleen. *Opening/Closing.* 5 min. SBC.
Martin, Eric. *USA Film.* 17 min. PH.
Stutz, Roland. *Taxi.* 3 min. NFBC.

PIXILATION

Laughlin, Kathleen. *The Disappearance of Sue.* 2½ min. SBC.
Leduc, André. *Tout Ecartille.* 6 min. NFBC.
Longpre, Bernard, and André Leduc. *Monsieur Pointu.* 12 min. NFBC.

21.4 LYNN SMITH—SHOUT IT OUT ALPHABET FILM: Frame enlargement. *Courtesy Lynn Smith.*

McLaren, Norman. *Neighbors.* 9 min. IFB.
Melville, Chuck, and Len Johnson. *Blaze Glory.* 10 min. PYR.
Severson, Anne, and Shelby Kennedy. *I Change, I Am the Same.* 1 min. SBC.

KINESTASIS

Braverman, Charles. *An American Time Capsule.* 3 min. PYR.
Dees, Sylvia, and Ken Rudolph. *Deep Blue World.* 7 min. PYR.
Hanson, David. *Homage to Eadweard Muybridge.* 3 min. CFS.
Jones, Phillip. *Secrets.* 13 min. PYR.
Koenig, Wolf. *City of Gold.* 23 min. McG.
Marker, Chris. *La Jette.* 20 min. McG.
McLaughlin, Dan. *God Is Dog Spelled Backwards.* 4 min. McG.
Mogubgub, Fred. *Enter Hamlet.* 4 min. PYR.
Straiton, John. *Animals in Motion.* 7 min. SBC.
Szasz, Eva, and Tony Ianzelo. *Cosmic Zoom.* 8 min. McG.

COLLAGE

Breer, Robert. *Blazes.* 3 min. FMC.
Jordan, Larry. *Our Lady of the Spheres.* 10 min. SBC.
Mouris, Frank. *Frank Film.* 9 min. PYR.
VanDerBeek, Stan. *Breathdeath.* 15 min. FMC.
VanDerBeek, Stan. *Nosmo King.* 3 min. (B&W). SBC.

SAND

Leaf, Caroline. *The Owl Who Married the Goose.* 8 min. NFBC.

Leaf, Caroline. *Sand or Peter and the Wolf.* 10 min. PH.
Leaf, Caroline. *Metamorphosis of Mr. Samsa.* Soon to be released by NFB.
Noyes, Eliot, Jr. *Sandman.* 4 min. EC.

PAINT ON GLASS

Leaf, Caroline. *The Street.* 10 min. NFBC.
Leaf, Caroline. *Orfeo.* 3 min. PYR.

CLAY

Borenstein, Joyce. *Traveller's Palm.* 2 min. NFBC.
Noyes, Eliot, Jr. *Clay: Origin of Species.* 8 min. PH.
Noyes, Eliot, Jr. *Fable of He and She.* 10 min. LCA.
Pierson, Arthur. *Whazzat.* 10 min. EBE.
Straiton, John. *Eurynome.* 7 min. SBC.
Vinton, Will. *Closed Mondays.* 8 min. PYR.

PUPPET

Andersen, Yvonne. *Amazing Colossal Man.* 6 min. YB.
Hoedeman, Co. *The Owl and the Lemming.* 6 min. ACI.
Hoedeman, Co. *Sand Castle.* 10 min. NFBC.
Munro, Grant. *Toys.* 8 min. McG.
Pal, George. *Tubby the Tuba.* 10 min. CFS.
Trnka, Jiří. *The Hand.* 19 min. McG.
Trnka, Jiří. *Song of the Prairie.* 18 min. CFS.

LINE ANIMATION (registered paper sheets)

Beams, Mary. *Tub Film.* 2 min. BFA.
Beams, Mary. *Seed Reel.* 4 min. SBC.
Dunbar, Geoff. *Lautrec.* 6 min. Fl.
Dunning, George. *Damon the Mower.* 3 min. AFA.
Geersten, George. *The Men in the Park.* 6 min. (B&W). NFBC.
Goldsholl, Mildred. *Up Is Down.* 6 min. PYR.
Griffin, George. *L'Age Door.* 1 min. SBC.
Griffin, George. *Viewmaster.* 2½ min. SBC.
Jankovics, Marcel. *Sisyphus.* 2½ min. PYR.
Lamb, Derek, and Janet Perlman. *Why Me?* (working title), in production, NFBC.
Larkin, Ryan. *Street Musique.* 9 min. LCA.
Larkin, Ryan. *Walking.* 9 min. LCA.
Munro, Grant, and Ron Tunis. *The Animal Movie.* 10 min. McG.
Perlman, Janet. *Lady Fishbourne's Complete Guide to Better Table Manners.* 6 min. CAR.
Pies, Dennis. *Sonoma.* 8 min. SBC.
Rose, Kathy. *The Doodlers.* 5 min. SBC.

Tunis, Ron. *Wind.* 10 min. LCA.

CEL ANIMATION (acetates)

Avery, Tex. *Miss Glory.* 9 min. UA.
Baker, Suzanne, and Bruce Petty. *Leisure,* 14 min. PYR.
Blechman, R.O. *The Emperor's New Armor.* 6 min. PYR.
Borowczyk, Walerian. *Game of Angles.* 13 min. PYR.
Bosustow, Stephen. *The Legend of John Henry.* 11 min. PYR.
Bozzetto, Bruno. *Opera.* 11 min. Fl.
Bunikovic-Bordo, Borivoj. *Second Class Passenger.* 12 min. McG.
Collins, Vincent. *Euphoria.* 4 min. From filmmaker, 5132A Geary, San Francisco, Calif. 94118
Crukshank, Sally. *Fun on Mars.* 4½ min. SBC.
Crukshank, Sally. *Chow Fun.* 4½ min. SBC.
Disney, Walt. *The Band Concert.* 9 min. WDP.
Driessen, Paul. *Le Bleu Perdu.* 8 min. DM. NFBC.
Driessen, Paul. *An Old Box.* 9 min. NFBC.
Fischinger, Oskar. *Radio Dynamics.* 4 min. PYR.
Fleischer, Max. *Superman.* 11 min. UA.
Grgic, Zlatko. *Hot Stuff.* 9 min. NFBC.
Halas, John, and Joy Batchelor. *Animal Farm.* 73 min. PH., 10 min. McG.
Hubley, John and Faith. *Cockaboody.* 9 min PYR.
_____ *Everyone Rides the Carousel.* 72 min. PYR.
Hubley. John. *Gerald McBoingBoing.* 7 min. CFS.
Hubley, John. *The Hat.* 18 min. CFS.
Hubley, John. *The Hole.* 15 min. Fl.
Jarnow, Al. *Autosong.* 9 min. From filmmaker, 83 Highland Ave., Northport, N.Y. 11768
Jones, Chuck. *Duck Amuck.* 8 min. WB.

21.5 ISHU PATEL—HOW DEATH CAME TO EARTH: In his work at the National Film Board of Canada, Ishu Patel has explored many techniques. Here the animator works on his film *How Death Came to Earth. Courtesy NFBC.*

Lamb, Derek, and Jeffrey Hale. *The Great Toy Robbery.* 7 min. McG.

Lamb, Derek, and Jeffrey Hale. *The Last Cartoon Man.* 5 min. FW.

Lantz, Walter. *Boogie Woogie Bugle Boy.* 1 min. MCA.

Lantz, Walter. *Woody Woodpecker Cartoons.* MCA.

Leach, John. *Evolution.* 7 min. LCA.

Mallette, Yvon. *The Family That Dwelt Apart.* 8 min. LCA.

Miler, Zdenek. *The Mole and the Music.* 6 min. PH.

Mitchell, Robert, and Dale Chase. *The Further Adventures of Uncle Sam.* 13 min. CFS.

Mitchell, Robert, and Robert Swarth. *K9000: A Space Oddity.* 11 min. CFS.

Zamnovic, Ante. *The Wall.* 4 min. McG.

OTHER TECHNIQUES

Alexieff, Alexander. *The Nose.* 16 min. (B&W). McG. (pinscreen)

Beams, Mary. *Paul Revere Is Here.* 7 min. (B&W). SBC. (rotoscoping)

Beckett, Adam. *Evolution of the Red Star.* 8 min. SBC. (optical printing)

Beckett, Adam. *Flesh Flows.* 7 min. SPB. (optical printing)

Belson, Jordan. *Music of the Spheres.* 10 min. PYR. (optical printing)

Drouin, Jacques. *Mindscape.* 8 min. (B&W). PYR. (pinscreen)

Foldes, Peter. *Hunger.* 12 min. LCA. (computer)

Foldes, Peter. *Metadata.* 9 min. Fl. (computer)

Griffin, George. *Head.* 10 min. SBC. (xerography and mattes and others)

Herbert, James. *Glass.* 19 min. From filmmaker, Art Department, University of Georgia, Athens, Ga. 30601. (optical printing)

McLaren, Norman. *Pas De Deux.* 12 minutes. LCA. (optical printing)

Pies, Dennis. *Aura Corona* and *Luma Nocturna.* 4 min. each. SBC. (optical printing)

Rose, Pete. *Analogies: Studies in the Movement of Time.* In progress. From filmmaker at Daedalus Productions, 759 S. 6th St. Philadelphia, Pa. 19147. (optical printing)

Schwartz, Lillian, and Ken Knowlton. *Metamorphosis.* 9 min. LIL. (computer)

Schwartz, Lillian, and Ken Knowlton. *Olympiad.* 4 min. LIL. (computer)

Selwood, Maureen. *Odalisque.* In progress. (rotoscoping)

Smith, Lynn. *Why a Museum?* (working title). In progress. NFBC. (pastel)

VanDerBeek, Stan. *Science Friction.* 9 min. PYR. (computer)

Whitney, John. *Arabesque.* 7 min. PYR. (computer)

Whitney, John. *Permutations.* 7 min. PYR. (computer)

COMBINED TECHNIQUES

Andersen, Yvonne. *I Saw Their Angry Faces.* 12 min. YB. (rotoscoping with cels, cutouts and others)

Andersen, Yvonne. *Trembling Cartoon Band.* 20 min. YB.. (films by children ages 7 to 18, including cutouts, puppet, flip cards, stuffed cloth.)

Beydler, Gary. *Pasadena Freeway Stills.* 6 min. From filmmaker, 3724 Wasatch Ave., Los Angeles, Calif. 90066. (still photography, pixilation)

Breer, Robert. *Rubber Cement.* 10 min. SBC. (rotoscoping, collage, and others)

21.6   RYAN LARKIN—STREET MUSIQUE: These series of frame enlargements suggest the graphic range, fluidity, and transformational qualities of Ryan Larkin's classic film. *Street Musique* was created completely with registered paper sheets. *Courtesy NFBC.*

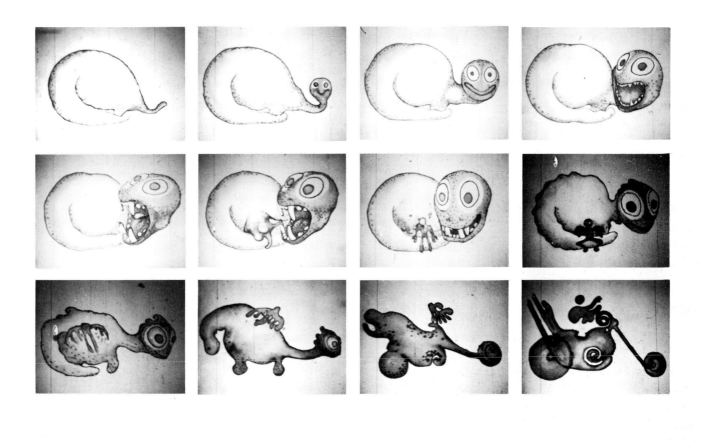

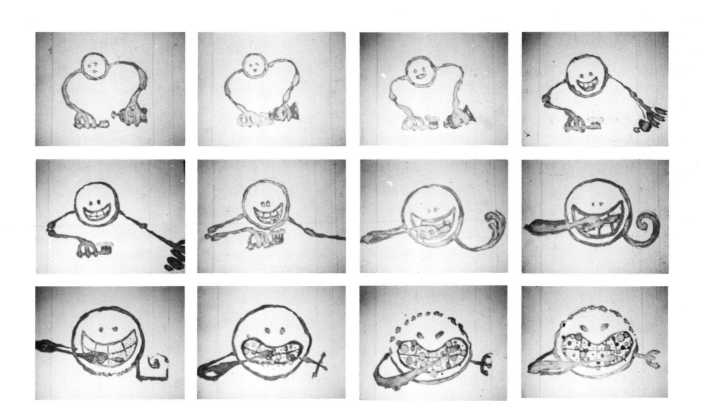

Canemaker, John. *The 40's.* 3 min. From filmmaker at 120 West 70th St., New York, N.Y. 10013. (collage, cutouts, cels)

Carpenter, Jeff. *Rapid Eye Movements.* 13 min. SBC. (rotoscoping, cel)

Griffin, George. *Candy Machine.* 4 min. SBC. (Xerox copies, cutouts, and cel)

Griffin, George. *Thumbnail Sketches.* 3 min. SBC. (flipbooks)

Hoedeman, Co. *The Sandcastle.* 13 min. NFBC. (sand and puppet)

Laughlin, Kathleen. *Madsong.* 5 min. SBC. (optical printing, mattes)

Laybourne, Kit. *Family Spots.* In production. From filmmaker at 132 West 31 St., New York, N.Y. 10001 (Xerox copies, rotoscoping, cel, and others)

Patel, Ishu. *Perspectrum.* 5 min. NFBC. (multiple exposures, cutouts)

Russett, Robert. *Brain Field.* 7 min. From filmmaker, Box 4-1097, Lafayette, La. 70504. (mattes and rear-lit cels)

Somersaulter, J. P. and Lillian. *The Light Fantastic Picture Show.* 7 min. Fl. (cutouts, line, and others)

Swarthe, Robert. *Kick Me.* 8 min. From filmmaker at 602N Canon Dr., Beverly Hills, Calif. 90210 (hand-drawn and optical printing)

Distributors of Animation

The following is a selected list of distributors of animated films. For specific titles and current prices, request the distributor's catalogue.

General guides to film distributors include *Films on 8mm and 16mm,* 5th edition, by James L. Limbacher (R. Bowker, 1977), *Film Programmer's Guide to 16mm Rentals,* 2nd edition, by Kathleen Weaver (Reel Research, 1975), and *Non-Theatrical Film Distributors,* by Carol A. Emmens (Educational Film Library Association, 1974).

AB
Audio Brandon/Macmillan Films
34 MacQuesten Parkway South
Mount Vernon, N.Y. 10550
(914) 666-5091

ACI
ACI Media, Inc.
35 West 45th St.
New York, N.Y. 10036
(212) 582-1918

AEF
American Educational Films
132 Lasky Dr.
Beverly Hills, Calif. 90212
(213) 278-4996

AFA
American Federation of Arts
41 East 65th St.
New York, N.Y. 10021
(212) 988-7700

BFA
BFA Educational Media
2211 Michigan Ave.
Santa Monica, Calif. 90404
(213) 829-2901

BM
Benchmark Films
145 Scarborough Rd.
Briarcliff Manor, N.Y. 10510
(914) 762-3838

BV
Buena Vista Distribution Co.
Walt Disney Productions
500 South Buena Vista St.
Burbank, Calif. 91521
(213) 845-3141, ext. 1726

CAR
Carousel Films, Inc.
1501 Broadway
New York, N.Y. 10036
(212) 524-4126

CCC
Canyon Cinema Cooperative
Industrial Center Building, Room 220
Sausalito, Calif. 94965
(415) 332-1514

CFS
Creative Film Society
7237 Canby Ave.
Reseda, Calif. 91335
(213) 881-3887

CONN
Connecticut Films, Inc.
6 Cobble Hill Rd.
Westport, Conn. 06880
(203) 227-2960

CS
Cecile Starr
50 West 96th St.
New York, N.Y. 10025
(212) 749-1250

DM
Doubleday Multimedia
Box 11607, 1371 Reynolds Ave.
Santa Ana, Calif. 92705
(714) 540-5550

EC
Eccentric Circle, Inc.
P.O. Box 1481
Evanston, Ill. 60624
(312) 864-0020

ECB
Encyclopaedia Britannica Educational Corp.
425 North Michigan Ave.
Chicago, Ill. 60611
(312) 321-6800

EDC
Educational Development Center
39 Chapel Hill
Newton, Mass. 02160
(617) 969-7100

FI
Films Incorporated
1144 Wilmette Ave.
Wilmette, Ill. 60091
(312) 256-4730

FMC
The Film-makers' Cooperative
175 Lexington Ave.
New York, N.Y. 10016
(212) 889-3820

FW
FilmWright
4530 18th St.
San Francisco, Calif. 94114
(415) 863-6100

GP
Grove Press Films
53 East 11th St.
New York, N.Y. 10003
(212) 677-2400

IFB
International Film Bureau
332 South Michigan Ave.
Chicago, Ill. 60604
(312) 427-4545

KP
Kit Parker Films
Carmel Valley
Carmel, Calif. 93924
(408) 659-3474

LCA
Learning Corporation of America
1350 Avenue of the Americas
New York, N.Y. 10019
(212) 397-9330

LIL
Lilyan Productions
524 Ridge Road
Watchung, N.J. 07060
(201) 582-4339

MCA
MCA Television
445 Park Avenue
New York, N.Y. 10022
(212) PL-9-7500

McG
McGraw-Hill/Contemporary Films
Princeton Road
Hightstown, N.J. 08520
(609) 448-1700

MOMA
Museum of Modern Art Film Library
21 West 53rd St.
New York, N.Y. 10019
(212) 956-4205

NFBC
National Film Board of Canada
1251 Avenue of the Americas
New York, N.Y. 10020
(212) 586-2400

NYF
New Yorker Films
43 West 61st St.
New York, N.Y. 10023
(212) 247-6110

PER
Perspective Films
369 W. Erie St.
Chicago, Ill. 60610
(312) 977-4000

PH
Phoenix Films
470 Park Avenue South
New York, N.Y. 10016
(212) 684-5910

PYR
Pyramid Films
P.O. Box 1048
Santa Monica, Calif. 90406
(213) 828-7577

SBC
Serious Business Company
1145 Mandana Blvd.
Oakland, Calif. 94610
(415) 832-5600

SIM
Sim Productions
Weston Woods
Weston, Conn. 06880
(203) 226-3355

STER
Sterling Educational Films
241 East 34th St.
New York, N.Y. 10016
(212) 593-0198

TF
Twymen Films
329 Salem Ave.
Dayton, Ohio 45401
(800) 543-9594

UCEMC
University of California Extension Media Center
Berkeley, Calif. 94720
(415) 642-0460

UN
Universal Education 100 Universal City Plaza
Universal City, Calif. 91608
(213) 985-4321

VNR
Van Nostrand Reinhold Co.
450 West 33rd St.
New York, N.Y. 10001
(212) 594-8660, ext. 409

WB
Warner Brothers, Inc.
Non-Theatrical Division
4000 Warner Blvd.
Burbank, Calif. 91522
(213) 843-6000

WDP
Walt Disney Productions
(see Buena Vista Distribution Co.)

YB
Yellow Ball Workshop
62 Tarbell Ave.
Cambridge, Mass. 02173
(617) 862-4283

YBF
Yellow Bison Films
Box 354
Holliston, Mass. 01746
(416) 429-6116

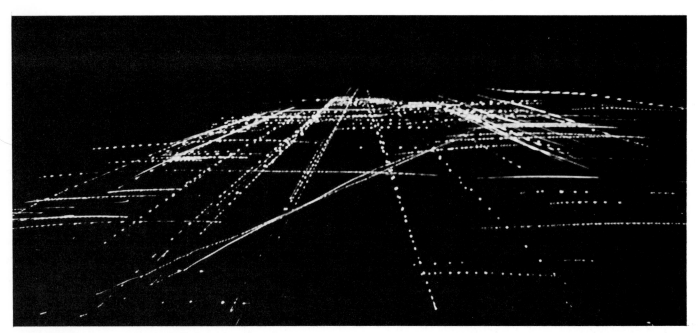

21.7   DENNIS PIES—LUMA NOCTURNA: A frame from the final scene that suggests an airport landing at night. *Courtesy Serious Business Company.*

Screening Centers

The work of independent animators is seldom presented commercially in theaters or on television. Similarly, it's hard to find a place to screen one's own work for an audience that values independent filmmaking.

Each of the screening centers listed below, however, represents an exception to the general rule. It is important to know about them and to support them. The individuals who program such screening centers are always receptive to new works by animators, and most of these centers schedule the screening of animated films on a regular basis.

Anthology Film Archives, 80 Wooster St., New York, N.Y. 10012

Art Institute of Chicago, Film Center, Columbus Dr. & Jackson Blvd., Chicago, Ill. 60603

Carnegie Institute, Film Section, Museum of Art, 4400 Forbes Ave., Pittsburgh, Pa. 15213

Center for Media Study, SUNY Buffalo, Buffalo, N.Y., 14214.

Center Screen, University Film Study Center, Box 275, Cambridge, Mass. 02138

Detroit Institute of Arts, Theater Arts Department, 5200 Woodward Ave., Detroit, Mich. 48202

Film Forum, 15 Vandam St., New York, N.Y. 10013

Indianapolis Museum of Art, 1200 W. 38th St., Indianapolis, Ind. 46208

Museum of Modern Art (MOMA), 21 West 53rd St., New York, N.Y. 10019

Northwest Film Study Center, Portland Art Museum, 1219 S.W. Park, Portland Ore.

Pacific Film Archive, University Art Museum, 2625 Durant Ave., Berkeley, Calif. 94720

Pittsburgh Film-Makers, Inc., P.O. Box 7200, Pittsburgh, Pa. 15213.

Sheldon Film Theater, Sheldon Memorial Art Gallery, University of Nebraska, Lincoln, Neb. 68558

South Carolina Arts Commission, Independent Filmmakers Film Lecture Bureau, 825 Richland St., Columbia, S.C.

Tennessee Performing Arts Center, 4304 Harding Rd., Nashville, Tenn. 37205

Theater Vanguard, 9014 Melrose Ave., Los Angeles, Calif. 90069

Walker Art Center, Vineland Place, Minneapolis, Minn. 55403.

Walnut Street Theater, Film Center, 825 Walnut St., Philadelphia, Pa.

White Ox Films, Inc., 3690 East Ave., Rochester, N.Y. 14618

Whitney Museum of American Art, New American Filmmakers Series, 945 Madison Ave., New York, N.Y. 10021

Film Festivals

The following U.S. and foreign festivals are either entirely devoted to animated films or have special categories for animation. Unless otherwise noted, these are annual events.

American Film Festival
Educational Film Library Association
43 West 61st St.
New York, N.Y. 10023
January deadline; May awards; 36 categories for nontheatrical films and "Film As Art" program.

Annency International Animated Film Festival
21 rue de la Tour d'Auvergne
75009 Paris
France
March deadline; June awards. ASIFA-sponsored festival for short and feature-length animated films, 16mm and 35mm. Biennial (alternating with the animated film festival at Zagreb), next will be 1979.

ASIFA-East Animated Film Awards
ASIFA-East
25 West 43rd St., Room 1018
New York, N.Y. 10036
January deadline; January awards. Animated work in 16mm by independents. Winning films are sent to the International Tournée of Animation for consideration.

Athens International Film Festival
Box 388
Athens, Ohio 45701
April deadline; April awards. Division for animation, features, or shorts. Super 8mm, 8mm, 16mm, and 35mm. Animation workshops and seminars held during the festival.

Avant-Garde International Super-8 Film Festival
Avenue Rio de Janeiro
Lorenzi B., Apt. 52
Chuao, Caracas
Venezuela
June deadline; August awards. Animation category for super 8mm only.

Canadian International Amateur Film Festival
P.O. Box 515
Etobicoke Postal Station
Etobicoke, Ontario M9C 4V5
Canada
May deadline; June awards. Animation category—8mm, super 8mm, or 16mm—for films 30 minutes or less in length.

Cartagena International Film Festival
Apartado Aéreo 1834
Cartagena
Colombia
February deadline; March awards. Animated short film category for 16mm and 35mm.

Chicago International Film Festival
415 North Dearborn
Chicago, Ill. 60610
September deadline; November awards. Animation categories for 16mm and 35mm.

Great Lakes Film Festival
P.O. Box 11579
Milwaukee, Wisc. 53211
October deadline; November awards. Category for animated films by filmmakers from the Midwest.

Golden Knight International Amateur Film Festival
Malta Amateur Cine Circle
P.O. Box 450
Valetta
Malta
September deadline; November awards. Animation category—super 8mm, 8mm, and 16 mm.

International Festival of Documentary and Short Films of Bilbao
Gran Via, 17-30
Bilbao
Spain
October deadline; December awards. Animation category—16mm and 35mm—30 minutes or less in length.

International Tournée of Animation
Diamond Heights Box 31349
San Francisco, Calif. 94131
February deadline; April screenings. Annual touring program of international animated films selected by members of ASIFA. Films 15 minutes or less in length, 16mm or 35mm.

New York Film Festival
Lincoln Center for the Performing Arts
1865 Broadway
New York, N.Y. 10023
October. Noncompetitive event featuring a special animation series.

Ottawa International Animated Film Festival
Canadian Film Institute
75 Albert St., Suite 1105
Ottawa, Ontario K1P
Canada
July deadline; August awards. ASIFA-sponsored all-

animated film competition. Films less than 35 minutes in length, 16mm and 35mm. (irregularly scheduled.)

Tampere International Festival of Short Films
P.O. Box 305
SF-33101
Tampere 10
Finland
December deadline; February awards. Animated category. Films less than 35 minutes in length, 16mm and 35mm.

Tehran International Festival of Films for Children
Takhte-Tavous Avenue
No. 31, Jam St.
Tehran
Iran
September deadline; October awards. Animated films,

short or feature length, 16mm, 35mm, or 70mm, content aimed at children.

Virgin Islands International Film Festival
Festival of the Americas
St. Thomas
U.S. Virgin Islands 00801
September deadline; November awards. Feature- and short-length animated films, any gauge. Animated television commercials category.

World Animated Film Festival
Zagreb Film
Vlaška 70
4100 Zagreb
Yugoslavia
May deadline; June awards. ASIFA-sponsored all-animated film competition. Short and feature length, 16mm and 35mm. Biennial.

21.8 GARY BEYDLER—PASADENA FREEWAY: By holding some 1,200 black and white photos (printed from 16mm negative film) against a glass sheet and shortening the interval between refilming until the camera took one frame for one photo, the picture within the picture comes to life. The film explores the nature of animation. *Courtesy Educational Film Library Association.*

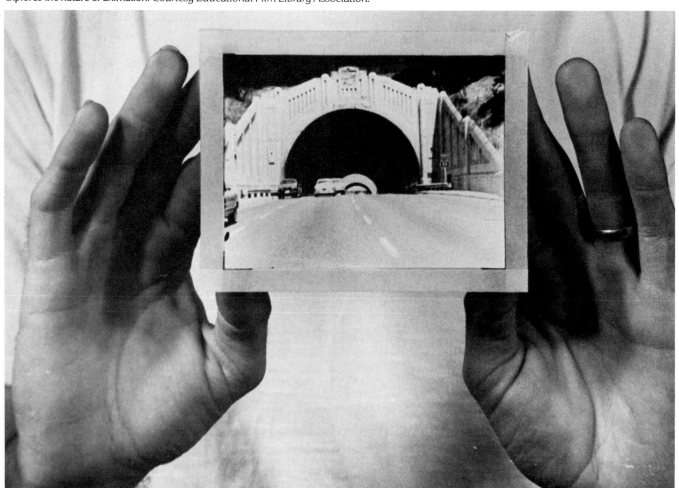

21.9   FILM FESTIVAL LOGOS: A sampling of graphic symbols representing some of the most prestigious animation festivals in recent years. *A*—1975 Annency International Animated Film Festival; *B*—1975 International Animated Film Society (ASIFA—Hollywood); *C*—2nd International Animation Festival, New York City, 1974; *D*—3rd International Animation Festival, New York City, 1975; *E*—1974 Zagreb World Animated Film Festival; *F*—1976 Ottawa International Film Festival.

22
Training Programs, Suppliers, and Laboratories

The information in this chapter is likely to be dated quickly. Programs that teach animation will—and should—be constantly revising their approaches and personnel. Change is also a fact of life among commercial organizations that serve the animator's needs.

But some outdating shouldn't matter if one of these leads can connect you with an institution or organization that can further your work. Even if the notion of buying equipment or enrolling in a special program seems beyond your interest or your means at the present time, skim the listings anyhow. At one time or another these pages can provide very valuable connections.

Animation Courses and Programs

The 1978 edition of the *AFI Guide to College Courses in Film and Television* indexes more than sixty U.S. colleges and universities offering animation courses. The following is a selected listing from that index. For specific course offerings and requirements, contact the department listed below.

California College of Arts and Crafts
Film Arts Department
5212 Broadway
Oakland, Calif. 94618
(415) 653-8118

California Institute of the Arts
School of Film/Video
24700 McBean Parkway
Valencia, Calif. 91355
(805) 255-1050

California State University-Fullerton
Communications Department
Fullerton, Calif. 92634
(714) 870-3517

Columbia College
Film Department
540 North Lake Shore Dr.
Chicago, Ill. 60611
(312) 467-0300

22.1 JULES ENGEL, chairman of the Animation and Film Graphics Department of the California Institute of Arts at Valencia. A founding member of the UPA animation group, Mr. Engel's work is internationally acclaimed and he heads what is widely considered to be the best animation training program among this country's colleges. *Photo courtesy John Canemaker.*

Edinboro State College
The School of Arts & Humanities
Art Department
Edinboro, Pa. 16444
(814) 732-2799

Illinois Institute of Technology
Institute of Design
Animation Department c/o Larry Janiak
655 West Irving Park Rd.
Chicago, Ill. 60613

Long Beach City College
Theatre Arts Department
Film Program
4901 East Carson Street
Long Beach, Calif. 90808
(213) 420-4279

Philadelphia College of Art
Department of Photography & Film
Broad and Spruce Sts.
Philadelphia, Pa. 19102
(215) 893-3140

Pratt Institute
Film Department
215 Ryerson St.
Brooklyn, N.Y. 11205
(212) 636-3766

Rhode Island School of Design
Film Studies Department
2 College St.
Providence, R.I. 02903
(401) 331-3511

San Francisco State University
Film & Creative Arts Interdisciplinary Department
1600 Holloway Ave.
San Francisco, Calif. 94132
(415) 469-1629

University of California-Los Angeles
Theater Arts Department
405 Hilgard Ave.
Los Angeles, Calif. 90024
(213) 825-7891

Wayne State University
Speech Department
Mass Communications Area
Detroit, Mich. 48202
(313) 577-4163

Other Training Programs and Centers

The following organizations may be contacted directly for more specific information on their animation training programs.

Hanna-Barbera Animation College
3400 Cahuenga Blvd.
Hollywood, Calif. 90068
(213) 851-5000
Contact Harry Love. Offers training for artists in all phases of animation. Students for the program are selected from within the studio's apprentice program and the animation industry.

International Alliance for Theatrical and Screen Employees (IATSE)
1515 Broadway
New York, N.Y. 10036
(212) 730-1770
Contact Mr. René Ash for information on any apprentice-

ship programs offered by IATSE's Motion Picture Screen Cartoonists' locals.
IATSE Motion Picture Screen Cartoonists, Local 839
12441 Ventura Blvd.
Studio City, Calif. 91604
IATSE Motion Picture Screen Cartoonists, Local 841
25 West 43rd St.
New York, N.Y. 10036

Sheridan College of Applied Arts & Technology
Trafalgar Rd.
School of Visual Arts
Oakville, Ontario L6H 2L1
Canada
Vocation-oriented three-year course; applicants from all over the world.

Walt Disney Studio
500 South Buena Vista St.
Burbank, Calif. 91521
(213) 845-3141
Contact Don Duckwall. The studio is looking for people who "can really draw." Send sketch pads, portfolios. Training in all aspects of animation techniques.

Yellow Ball Workshop
62 Tarbell Ave.
Lexington, Mass. 02173
(617) 862-4283
Contact Yvonne Andersen. The Workshop offers training in animation techniques to children and adults. Sponsors workshops on the premises and on a traveling basis. Some workshops include Drawing on Film, Short Film Animation, and Extensive Film Animation.

Suppliers

The suppliers of animation tools and supplies listed below can be contacted directly for catalogues and price sheets. I recommend that you specify the items of hardware or software that you are interested in acquiring when you write or telephone any of these organizations.

I also recommend that you check out local suppliers before getting involved in a lot of long-distance shopping and purchasing. The reasons for this are obvious enough. The best is that with local camera stores or equipment rental houses you can find resident expertise that can be helpful as your work continues. So check your local resources.

This is a selected listing of services and organizations useful to animation. More extensive listings may be found in *International Motion Picture Almanac,* an annual publication by Quigley Publishing, and *Motion Picture Market Place 1976-1977* by Tom Costner (Little, Brown, 1976).

Agfa-Gevaert, Inc.
275 North St.
Teterboro, N.J. 07608
—film stocks

Alan Gordon Enterprises, Inc.
1430 N. Cahuenga Blvd.
Hollywood, Calif. 90028
—manufactures animation motors and adapters formerly
produced by National Cine Equipment Co.

Animation Sciences Corp.
144 Miller Pl.
Mt. Vernon, N.Y. 10550
—animation stands and other equipment

Art Color Products
11501 Chandler Blvd.
Hollywood, Calif. 91601
—animation paints and supplies

Arthur Brown & Bros.
2 West 46th St.
New York, N.Y. 10036
—art supplies

Behrend's, Inc.
161 East Grand Ave.
Chicago, Ill. 60611
—animation equipment and supplies

Camera Title Studio
612 Birchlane St.
St. Paul, Minn. 55112
—animation software and title shooting services.

Cartoon Color Co. Inc.
9024 Lindblade St.
Culver City, Calif. 90203
—animation paints and art supplies, registration devices,
books on animation.

Cinebooks
6924 Yonge St.
Toronto, Ont., Canada M4Y 2A6
—mail-order film books

Cinemobilia
10 West 13 St.
New York, N.Y. 10001
—books, posters, and other film memorabilia

Comquip
366 S. Maple Ave.
Glen Rock, N.J. 07013
—special-effects stands and other filmmaking gear

Eastman Kodak
343 State St.
Rochester, N.Y. 14650
—film stocks and technical booklets of all kinds; for index
to Kodak publications, write to Dept. 454.

Fax Co.
374 S. Fair Oaks Ave.
Pasadena, Calif. 01105
—animation stands, cameras, and registration tools

F & B Ceco, Inc.
315 West 43 St.
New York, N.Y. 10036
—animation hardware and software

Fluid Art
8363 Trenton Rd.
Forestville, Calif. 95436
—specialized stand for use of grease pencils on backlighted surface and supplies

Forox Corp.
511 Center Ave.
Mamaroneck, N.Y. 10543
—animation stands, cameras, and registration tools

General Analine and Film Corp. (GAF)
140 West 51 St.
New York, N.Y. 10020
—film stocks

Halmar Enterprises
P.O. Box 7933
Niagara Falls, Ontario, Canada L2E 6V6
—specialized super 8mm gear

Harmony Electronics
4009 N. Nashville Ave.
Chicago, Ill. 60434
—intervalometers for super 8mm equipment

JK Camera Engineering, Inc.
5101 San Leandro St.
Oakland, Calif. 94061
—animation stands, optical benches and accessories,
motors and registration tools.

Larry Edmunds Bookshop, Inc.
6658 Hollywood Blvd.
Hollywood, Calif. 90028
—books, posters, and other film memorabilia

Oxberry
Division of Richmark Camera Service
180 Broad Street
Carlstadt, N.J. 07072
—animation stands, cameras, registration tools, and supplies

Ox Products, Inc.
108 East Prospect Ave.
Mamaroneck, N.Y. 10543
—animation stands and registration tools

Science Dimensions, Inc.
Box 582M
Costa Mesa, Calif. 92627
—intervalometers for super 8mm equipment

Solar Cine Products, Inc.
4247 S. Kedzie Ave.
Chicago, Ill. 60632
—mail order, super 8mm and photography

SOS Photo-Cine-Optics
311 West 43 St.
New York, N.Y. 10036
—animation hardware and software

Spiratone, Inc.
130 West 31 St.
New York, N.Y. 10001
—bellows, lights, filters, and lenses

Stop-Frame Enterprises
3131 Turtle Creek Blvd.
Dallas, Texas 75219
—metal armatures for puppets

Super 8 Sound, Inc.
95 Harvey St.
Cambridge, Mass. 02140
—complete line of super 8mm equipment

Super 8 Studios
220 Pierce St.
San Francisco, Calif. 94117
—complete lab service and 8mm hardware and software

Thomas J. Valentino, Inc.
151 West 46th St.
New York, N.Y. 10036
—recorded sound effects and pre-cleared music for use with films

Victor Duncan, Inc.
200 E. Ontario St.
Chicago, Ill. 60611
—animation hardware and software

Laboratories

The following list includes well-established laboratories that service the needs of super 8mm and 16mm filmmakers. You should check the Yellow Pages in your area to locate other labs.

Check out the labs that you think you might want to use—they should have price lists and other literature that they will send to you. Specify that you want complete information about all the 16mm and super 8mm services that are offered.

Chapter 19 outlines the sort of services you should locate and the appropriate price. (It's only through using labs that you'll finally be able to determine very important assets such as reliability, courtesy, and quality.) A quick review of options would include *developing and duplication* (work prints, internegatives, push processing, flashing, blowups to 16mm and 35mm, reduction prints, release prints, optical tracks, contact prints); *special effects* (fades, dissolves, superimpositions, reframing, traveling mattes, freeze frames, step printing, multi-image printing, A&B rolls, titling); and *other services* (sound-track analysis, magnetic stripping, edge numbering, sound transfer, sound mixing, video transfer, cartridging, and more).

LAB ADDRESSES
East

Bebell, Inc.
Motion Picture Lab
416 West 45th St.
New York, N.Y. 10036

Byron Motion Pictures
65 K Street N.E.
Washington, D.C. 20002

Cine Magnetics
650 Halstead Ave.
Mamaroneck, N.Y. 10543

22.2 COMMERCIAL ANIMATION STANDS: Produced by the Fax Company in Pasadena, California, model *A*—the Fax Jr. Stand—is designed to sell at a relatively low price. Photograph *B* shows the compound of a top-of-the-line animation stand manufactured by the Oxberry Corporation in Carlstadt, New Jersey.

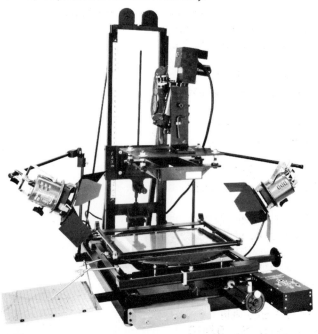

A

B

Cine Service Labs
51 Kondazian St.
Watertown, Mass. 02172

Commercial & Home Movie Service, Inc.
614-616 Washington St.
Allentown, Pa. 18102

Criterion Film Labs
415 W. 55th St.
New York, N.Y. 10019

Film Service Lab
58-62 Berkeley St.
Boston, Mass. 02116

Huemark Films. Inc.
227 E. 44th St.
New York, N.Y. 10017

Kin-O-Lux, Inc.
17 West 45th St.
New York, N.Y. 10036

Marcin-Jeflo Productions
5174 Pennway St.
Philadelphia, Pa. 19124

Slide Strip Lab. Inc.
432 W. 45th St.
New York, N.Y. 10036

Midwest

Calvin Communications
1105 Truman Rd.
Kansas City, Mo. 64106

Colburn Film Lab
164 N. Wacker Dr.
Chicago, Ill. 60606

ESO-S Pictures
47th and Holly
Kansas City, Mo. 64112

Motion Picture Labs
P.O. Box 1758
Memphis, Tenn. 38101

Multi Media Film Lab
15 S. 6th St.
Columbia, Mo. 65201

Omnicom Labs, Inc.
3515 S. Pennsylvania Ave.
Lansing, Mich. 48910

Sly-Fox Films, Inc.
1025 Currie Ave.
Minneapolis, Minn. 55403

Superior Bulk Film
442 N. Wells St.
Chicago, Ill. 60610

West

A.V. Corporation
P.O. Box 66824
Houston, Tex. 77006

Consolidated Film Industry
959 Seward St.
Hollywood, Calif. 90038

DeLuxe Laboratories, Inc.
1546 N. Argyle Ave.
Hollywood, Calif. 90028

Leo Diner Films, Inc.
332-350 Golden Gate Ave.
San Francisco, Calif. 94102

Hollywood Cine Lab
3034 Glendale Blvd.
Los Angeles, Calif. 90039

Newsfilm Laboratory
516 N. Larchmont Blvd.
Hollywood, Calif. 90004

Super-8 Studios
220 Pierce St. #7
San Francisco, Calif. 94117

Supervision
4020 Clayton Ave.
Hollywood, Calif. 90027

W.A. Palmer Films
611 Howard St.
San Francisco, Calif. 94105

Kodak and Fuji

Eastman Kodak processes Kodachrome and Ekta-chrome film; processing services are available at these labs around the country.

Eastman Kodak Company Processing Labs:
1017 N. Las Palmas Ave.
Los Angeles, Calif. 90038

925 Page Mill Rd.
Palo Alto, Calif. 94304

4729 Miller Drive
Atlanta, Ga. 30341

P.O. Box 1260
Honolulu, Hawaii 96807

1712 S. Prairie Ave.
Chicago, Ill. 60616

1 Choke Cherry Rd.
Rockville, Md. 20850

16-31 Route 208
Fair Lawn, N.J. 07410

Building 65, Kodak Park
Rochester, N.Y. 14650

1100 E. Main Cross St.
Findlay, Ohio 45840

3131 Manor Way
Dallas, Tex. 75235

Fuji Film Processing Labs process only single-8 film at the following locations:

Fuji Film Processing Labs:
P.O. Box 300
Harrison, N.J 07029

P.O. Box 1700
Santa Monica, Calif. 90406

P.O. Box 598
Rochester, N.Y. 14603

22.3 EDITING 16MM FILMS: A time-lapse photograph suggests the flurry of activity in preparing 16mm camera original and magnetic recording stock for subsequent printing at a film laboratory. Pictured are a portable hot splicer and a four-gang synchronizer with soundhead. *Photo by Elissa Tenny.*

23
Things to Use

Here are four items that you may want to detach from the binding of this book so that you can use them in your own animated filmmaking.

23.1   REGISTRATION GUIDE FOR DRAWING DIRECTLY ONTO CLEAR LEADER: Two strips of Academy Leader are provided in both 16mm and 35mm formats. By placing clear leader over these full-scale prints, you should be able to locate with precision any point or series of points when drawing onto a succession of single frames. The page also bears clear strips of 16mm and 35mm film that indicate the exact position of frames and of sound-track areas.

23.2   ANIMATION TIMING CHART: It is often helpful to have a chart such as this one pinned up near where you draw, film, or edit your animated films.

23.3   16MM ANIMATION FIELD GUIDE: Reproduced in full scale, this is a portion of the standard field guide. Full-sized guides are printed on thick acetate, cover a 12 field (12 inches wide), and come with professional peg holes cut into them (either Oxberry or Acme registration systems are available). This guide can be modified for your own use if you punch it to fit the pegging system that you use. Note that a test must be done to make certain that the center of the field guide corresponds to the center of the camera's frame.

23.4   EXPOSURE SHEET: This sheet can be duplicated so that you will have enough copies to record every frame in an animated film. Regardless of technique, an exposure sheet should be employed whenever one is working with a prerecorded sound track.

23.1

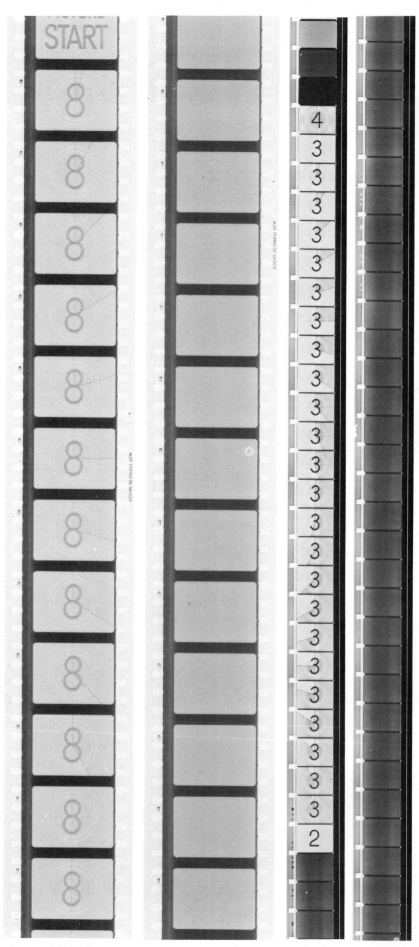

ANIMATION TIMING CHART

FILM FORMAT	SUPER 8MM		16 MM		35 MM	
PROJECTION SPEED (FRAMES PER SEC.)	18		24		24		24	
RUNNING TIME AND FILM LENGTH	FEET+FRAMES		FEET+FRAMES		FEET+FRAMES		FEET+FRAMES	
SECONDS 1	0	18	0	24	0	24	1	8
2	0	36	0	48	1	8	3	0
3	0	54	1	0	1	32	4	8
4	1	0	1	24	2	16	6	0
5	1	18	1	48	3	0	7	8
6	1	36	2	0	3	24	9	0
7	1	54	2	24	4	8	10	8
8	2	0	2	48	4	32	12	0
9	2	18	3	0	5	16	13	8
10	2	36	3	24	6	0	15	0
20	5	0	6	48	12	0	30	0
30	7	36	10	0	18	0	45	0
40	10	0	13	24	24	0	60	0
50	12	36	16	48	30	0	75	0
MINUTES 1	15	0	20	0	36	0	90	0
2	30	0	40	0	72	0	180	0
3	45	0	60	0	108	0	270	0
4	60	0	80	0	144	0	360	0
5	75	0	100	0	180	0	450	0
6	90	0	120	0	216	0	540	0
7	105	0	140	0	252	0	630	0
8	120	0	160	0	288	0	720	0
9	135	0	180	0	324	0	810	0
10	150	0	200	0	360	0	900	0

SUPER 8MM — 72 FRAMES PER FOOT

16 MM — 40 FRAMES PER FOOT

35 MM — 16 FRAMES PER FOOT

23.2

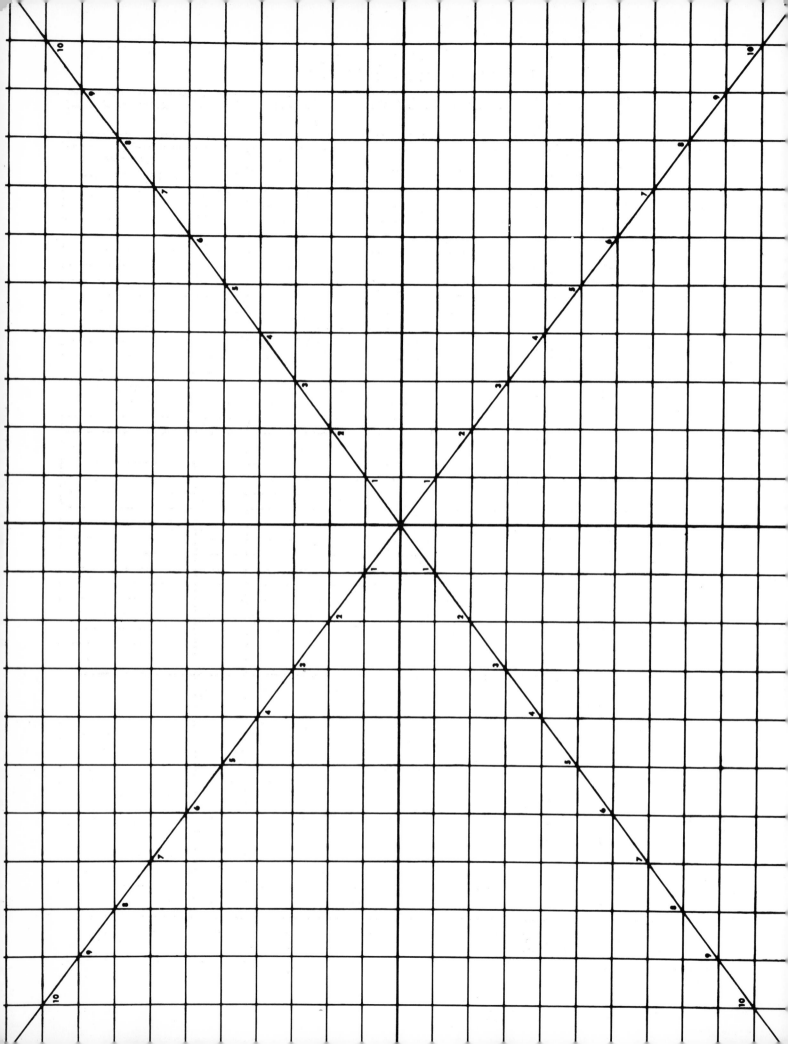

EXPOSURE SHEET

SCENE	TITLE	ANIMATOR	FOOTAGE	SHEET NO.

ACTION	DIAL	4	3	2	1	BKG	DIAL	CAMERA INSTRUCTIONS
	1						1	
	2						2	
	3						3	
	4						4	
	5						5	
	6						6	
	7						7	
	8						8	
	9						9	
	0						0	
	1						1	
	2						2	
	3						3	
	4						4	
	5						5	
	6						6	
	7						7	
	8						8	
	9						9	
	0						0	
	1						1	
	2						2	
	3						3	
	4						4	
	5						5	
	6						6	
	7						7	
	8						8	
	9						9	
	0						0	
	1						1	
	2						2	
	3						3	
	4						4	
	5						5	
	6						6	
	7						7	
	8						8	
	9						9	
	0						0	
	1						1	
	2						2	
	3						3	
	4						4	
	5						5	
	6						6	
	7						7	
	8						8	
	9						9	
	0						0	

23.4

Index

Pages in italic refer to illustrations.
CS refers to color section.